The Japanese Business and Economic System

History and Prospects for the 21st Century

Edited by
Masao Nakamura

palgrave

First published 2000 by
PALGRAVE
Houndmills, Basingstoke, Hampshire RG21 6XS and
175 Fifth Avenue, New York, N.Y. 10010
Companies and representatives throughout the world

PALGRAVE is the new global academic imprint of
St. Martin's Press LLC Scholarly and Reference Division and
Palgrave Publishers Ltd (formerly Macmillan Press Ltd)

ISBN 0–333–94566–2

This book is printed on paper suitable for recycling and
made from fully managed and sustained forest sources.

A catalogue record for this book is available
from the British Library.

Library of Congress Cataloging-in-Publication Data

The Japanese business and economic system : history and prospects for the
21st century / edited by Masao Nakamura.
        p.   cm.
    Includes bibliographical references (p.   ) and index.
    ISBN 0–333–94566–2
    1. Japan—Economic conditions—1945–   2. Economic forecasting—
Japan.   I. Nakamura, Masao.

HC462.9 .J3278   2000
330.952—dc21

                                                        00–062600

10   9   8   7   6   5   4   3   2   1
10   09 08 07 06 05 04 03 02 01

Printed in Great Britain by
Antony Rowe Ltd
Chippenham, Wiltshire

Contents

v

List of Maps

List of Tables

List of Figures

Preface

A number of historically noteworthy events in the last f(
triggered a change in Japanese business and economic policy practices.
For example the first oil crisis, which brought a huge increase in world
oil prices in 1973, provided an important opportunity for Japanese car
manufacturers to expand into North America, where small, fuel-
efficient Japanese cars became an economically sensible alternative to
the traditionally favoured, large North American cars with high petrol
consumption. Toyota, which had completed the implementation of its
revolutionary just-in-time (JIT) manufacturing system by 1973, also
began voluntary dissemination of its JIT manufacturing technologies
not only to domestic rival firms in the car industry but also to firms in
other manufacturing industries in Japan.

Beginning in the late 1970s, Japanese manufacturing firms
equipped with the new JIT manufacturing technologies began to
produce and export high-quality, competitively priced products. Japanese exports became a threat to many US firms, particularly in the
car, electronics and semiconductor industries. Well-established US
firms lost market share to Japanese competitors, and the consequent
industrial rivalry between US and Japanese firms in the global market
resulted in a serious trade dispute between the two countries. While
US–Japan trade disputes had arisen before, the dispute in the 1980s
was quite different as it involved pivotal US industries that had
traditionally defined and controlled the global markets for their products. The Japanese challenge to this US dominance seemed to pose a
threat not only to the survival of US firms in the industries in question
but also to US economic growth, which was thought to depend on the
successful development and commercialization of new technologies by
these industries.

The US–Japan governmental talks on resolving the trade dispute
have continued into the 21st century. These have dealt with a wide
array of practices that the US government views as unfairly impeding
US and other foreign firms' entry into the Japanese market. For
example the US–Japan Structural Impediments Initiative Talks have
included discussions on the regulation of the *keiretsu* business organizations that are prevalent in Japan, and on relaxation of the protection afforded to small stores in Japan (under the Large-Scale Retail
Store Law).

Preface

In order to facilitate the development of new technologies in US industries the US government has enacted a number of laws that emulate Japanese ones. For example the US Cooperative Research Act of 1984 allows competing US firms to form joint research organizations for the development of new technologies. Joint research organizations registered under this law with the Department of Justice are not subject to the standard treble damage loss penalty in the event of antitrust prosecution. Few antitrust cases have been brought against registered joint research organizations so far. This 1984 law and further modifications of the law to include production joint ventures are among a number of US initiatives for promoting the joint development of technology by competitor firms, a practice that is widely engaged in by Japanese firms and the government. Another aspect of the US response to Japan's challenge in technology was the funding in the early 1990s of 12 Japanese technology management programmes at various US universities. This funding was provided by the Air Force Office of Scientific Research. The primary purpose of these programmes was to improve US industrial competitiveness by conducting research on the technology management practices that provide leading Japanese firms with a competitive edge in the global market.

In 1985 the Japanese economy experienced another major shock in the form of a massive appreciation of the Japanese currency (the Plaza Accord). A perhaps inappropriate set of economic policies put in place to deal with the recession after the Plaza Accord led to another major economic event: the formation of a financial bubble in the late 1980s and the bursting of this bubble in 1990. The Japanese economy has been in recession since then and full recovery is not likely until about 2005 at the earliest.

For the last few decades of the 20th century the Japanese business and economic system faced various challenges and often made evolutionary progress in the process of meeting those challenges. Unlike market-driven economies such as those in North America, where competition is primarily price-based and transparent to new entrants to the markets, the Japanese business and economic system places priority on interconnections that bind together Japanese firms, the government, managers, workers and shareholders. Analysis of Japanese business and the economy requires an interdisciplinary approach, taking into account historical impacts on Japanese thinking, economic incentives, political institutions and other factors.

In order to discuss the issues surrounding the contemporary Japanese economy from a historical perspective, the Centre for Japanese

Research of the University of British Columbia held a conference in February 1999 entitled 'The Japanese Business and Economic System: History and Prospects for the 21st Century'. This is a part of an ongoing research project on international business and technology management at the Centre for Japanese Research. Leading researchers from various academic disciplines presented papers and also comments on the papers. These papers and comments constitute most of the chapters and associated comments in this book, discussing topics and providing perspectives that range over space, time and academic disciplines. The approach adopted in this book is essential for the analysis of the Japanese business system, given the important role that history and relationships play in the economy. The topics covered in the book are briefly reviewed below.

THE DYNAMIC NATURE OF THE JAPANESE BUSINESS SYSTEM

The Japanese business and economic system has been subject to continuous and dynamic change. For example in the 1970s the first oil price hike not only accelerated the dissemination of Toyota's JIT manufacturing system but also encouraged the use of energy-saving devices in Japanese industries. It was also in the 1970s that Japanese firms and the government accepted the principle that a clean natural environment must be sustained. This was a major departure from the general practices of the 1960s, when serious physical damage was inflicted on both people and the natural environment. It is of interest to note that by the end of the 1970s Japan was globally ahead not only in JIT technology, but also in the development and use of energy-saving technologies. In the 1990s Japanese firms made considerable progress towards meeting the global challenge of becoming environmentally friendly producers. The Japanese government also introduced laws in 1999 to force firms to comply with global demands in respect of sustaining the environment.

THE TRANSFER OF TECHNOLOGY INTO AND OUT OF JAPAN

Historically viewed, there is considerable evidence of Japanese responsiveness to changes in the technological environment, both at home and abroad. How did Japan take advantage of new technologies when developing its economy in the 19th century? Why did the Japanese economy respond to technological developments in the late 19th and early 20th centuries by shifting industrial investment from Osaka to Tokyo? These historical issues can be compared to the current issues of technology transfer faced by Japanese manufacturers. JIT manufacturing technologies, for example, are an essential source of the competitiveness enjoyed by Japanese manufacturers' overseas operations. Yet JIT embodies many aspects of Japanese practices in management and economic decision making, as well as the Japanese culture. How would JIT manufacturing fit the cultural and management environment in North America and Asia?

US–JAPANESE RELATIONS

Since the Meiji Restoration in 1868, US–Japanese relations have been at the core of Japanese economic policy. The United States has always been an important export market for Japan and a major source of new technologies and management skills. As a result, economic relations with the United States have been an influential determinant of Japan's economic performance. Traditionally Japan has relied on bilateral negotiations with its trading partners, including the United States. However the recent development of multilateral trade arrangements, driven by the World Trade Organization (WTO), has forced Japan (and other countries) to reevaluate its policies towards trade negotiations. The impact of the WTO on Japan, which had never been a member of any multilateral free trade grouping, is likely to be more significant than on other major developed countries.

CORPORATE GOVERNANCE

Japan's corporate governance mechanisms have recently been singled out as a major source of economic inefficiency. Entrenched government–business relationships have caused Japan's heavily regulated industries (including the finance, utility and resource industries) to become seriously inefficient and uncompetitive by global comparison. It is, however, in the sectors where the Japanese economy has been particularly weak that new technological developments based on the internet and other information technologies are enabling spectacular progress in productivity in both North America and Europe. For example, the weak internet infrastructure in Japan has so far prevented it from developing a large consumer market for internet-based financial and other services. Similarly, regulated power utilities continue to provide overpriced electricity to industry, which significantly constrains Japanese manufacturers' competitiveness.

In the past the Japanese economy relied on efficient and highly competitive manufacturing industries to subsidize inefficient industries. But this policy had become impractical by the 1990s because many foreign competitors had significantly improved their cost performance (in part by means of the successful transfer of JIT and other Japanese manufacturing technologies), reducing Japanese manufacturers' profit margins significantly.

This problem was made worse by the fact that Japan's corporate governance structure, based on banks and *keiretsu* firms, was ineffective in the 1990s in restructuring and rescuing manufacturing and other firms in financial distress. This was primarily because the main actors in governance, *keiretsu* firm shareholders, individual shareholders, banks, managers and workers all had different incentives. Aligning their incentives has been very difficult in periods of distress. It is imperative for the factors and regulations that generate disincentives in corporate governance to be removed. The system must also be changed. Business people, firms and government policy makers outside Japan have been awaiting indications of Japan's emergence from the lengthy post-bubble recession.

The reader will find in this book alternative interpretations of Japan's business history and perspectives on the future of the Japanese business system.

MASAO NAKAMURA

Acknowledgement

The editor gratefully acknowledges that production of this volume was in part supported by research grants from the Centre for Japanese Research at the University of British Columbia, Mitsui and Company (Canada), Sumitomo Corporation Canada and the Social Sciences and Humanities Research Council of Canada.

List of Contributors

Werner Antweiler, Assistant Professor of Commerce and Business Administration, University of British Columbia, Vancouver, British Columbia.

Mukesh Eswaran, Professor of Economics, University of British Columbia, Vancouver, British Columbia.

David Flath, Professor of Economics, North Carolina State University, Raleigh, North Carolina.

Murray Frank, Associate Professor of Commerce and Business Administration, University of British Columbia, Vancouver, British Columbia.

Robert Hart, Professor of Economics, University of Stirling, Stirling, Scotland.

Masanori Hashimoto, Professor and Chairperson, Department of Economics, Ohio State University, Columbus, Ohio.

Takabumi Hayashi, Professor of International Business, Rikkyo University, Tokyo.

Keith Head, HSBC Bank of Canada Professor in Asian Commerce, Faculty of Commerce and Business Administration, University of British Columbia, Vancouver, British Columbia.

Susan Helper, Associate Professor of Economics, Case Western Reserve University, Cleveland, Ohio.

Kozo Horiuchi, Professor and Dean, Faculty of Humanity and Environment, Hosei University, Tokyo.

Takao Kato, Professor and Chair, Department of Economics, Colgate University, Hamilton, New York.

xxi

Yukihiko Kiyokawa, Professor, Institute of Economic Research, Hitotsubashi University, Tokyo.

Kaz (Kasuhito) Masui, Professor in Residence, Davis and Company, Vancouver, and Associate Professor, Faculty of Law, Kokushikan University, Tokyo.

Terry McGee, Professor, Department of Geography and former Director, Institute of Asian Research, University of British Columbia, Vancouver, British Columbia.

Randall Morck, Jarislowsky Distinguished Professor of Finance, Faculty of Business, University of Alberta, Edmonton, Alberta.

Carl Mosk, Professor of Economics, University of Victoria, Victoria, British Columbia.

Takanobu Nakajima, Associate Professor of Business and Commerce, Keio University, Tokyo.

Masao Nakamura, Professor, Faculty of Commerce and Business Administration and Faculty of Applied Science, Konwakai Japan Research Chair and Director, Centre for Japanese Research, Institute of Asian Research, University of British Columbia, Vancouver, British Columbia.

John Ries, HSBC Bank of Canada Professor in Asian Business, Faculty of Commerce and Business Administration, University of British Columbia, Vancouver, British Columbia.

Gary Saxonhouse, Professor of Economics, University of Michigan, Ann Arbor, Michigan.

Hiroki Tsurumi, Professor of Economics, Rutgers University, New Brunswick, New Jersey.

Yoshi Tsurumi, Professor of International Business, Baruch College, City University of New York, New York.

Teri Ursacki, Associate Professor of Management, University of Calgary, Calgary, Alberta.

Kanji Yoshioka, Professor and Director, Keio Economic Observatory, Keio University, Tokyo.

1 Introduction

Masao Nakamura

In the 1980s, US academics and business and government decision makers put massive effort into studying Japanese practices and adopting those which appeared to have improved economic performance and could be transplanted to the United States. When looking at Japan's economic achievements, some Japanese interpreted the title of Ezra Vogel's (1980) book, *Japan as Number One*, as meaning 'Japan *is* Number One'.

Those days are long gone. The current prolonged recession has forced many Japanese to reconsider the so-called Japanese way of doing things. For example a Japanese best seller entitled *Those Who Can Become Anglo-Saxon Will Succeed* (Itose, 1998) argues that the United States and Britain currently set the global standard. It therefore encourages Japanese corporations and workers alike to adopt 'Anglo-Saxon' practices in industrial relations and employment behaviour, work practices, corporate control and other business management areas. This US triumph is undoubtedly echoed by many US government officials and business leaders.

It is by no means clear what has caused Japan's current crisis. Suspected causes include macroeconomic policy failure, problems with Japanese business practices and failed institutions, or perhaps a systemic failure involving all of these elements. Many of these suspected causes of Japan's current economic problems are discussed in the chapters of this volume, some of which consider business and economic issues from a historical and institutional perspective. It is our hope that these chapters will provide the reader of this book with new insights and will raise new questions about the future development of the Japanese economic and business system. Earlier versions of many of the chapters included in this book were first presented at the Interdisciplinary Conference on Japanese Business and Economic History and Practices, held at the Centre for Japanese Research, University of British Columbia in February 1999.

The chapters, most of which are accompanied by discussants' comments, with often alternative views, are divided into five broad and non-exclusive topical areas that are thought to be fundamental to understanding Japan's contemporary economic and business system and the evolutionary changes Japan may undergo in the 21st century. They are Japanese industrial and employment relations and their contribution to Japanese economic growth (Part I), issues arising from Japanese technology transfer to overseas (Part II), the historical role of technology in Japan (Part III), Japanese–US relations (Part IV) and Japanese business practices (Part V).

Chapters 2, 3 and 4 (Part II) discuss Japan's economic growth, the labour market and industrial relations practices. Nakajima, Nakamura and Yoshioka (Chapter 2) first discuss the sources of Japanese economic growth from a historical perspective. Their review of Japanese economic growth from the late 1880s to 1990 shows that even though Japan's real gross domestic product (GDP) growth rate during the period was consistently high in comparison with those for the US and European countries, Japan's growth rate fell significantly for the entire period following the first oil shock in the early 1970s. It is shown that a significant structural change involving a significantly reduced rate of technical progress accompanied this decline in GDP growth. They point out that the low rate of technical progress exacerbated the negative impact on the economy of the misplaced investments made during the financial bubble period in the late 1980s. Japan's economic growth during the bubble period was mostly due to increased production inputs such as labour and capital equipment rather than to technical progress. This finding is important since it implies that despite the well-recognized excellence of Japanese production workers in the manufacturing industry, their productivity started to fall in the 1980s before the burst of the financial bubble. The authors provide empirical evidence that, contrary to popular belief, during the bubble period bad investment decisions on output expansion were accompanied by a significant reduction in the productivity of Japanese industrial workers. However the negative impact of this productivity decline on Japan's economic growth was mitigated by the increased productivity of Japanese white-collar workers, including managerial and skilled non-production workers.

The Japanese employment and industrial relations practices that evolved after the Second World War were probably the most important factor in Japan's postwar economic success. Participatory employment practices have been the cornerstone of the employment system for Japanese firms of all sizes. Kato (Chapter 3) discusses Japanese participatory employment practices as they were, and where they are heading. For example the team work and other shop floor practices developed in Japanese factories during the postwar period have had a significant influence on many manufacturing plants not only in Japan but also in North America, Europe and Asia. These practices formed the basis of the celebrated just-in-time manufacturing system and associated high levels of quality control. Will these participatory practices survive the post-bubble economy? If they do, how are they likely to evolve? Kato argues that these practices, which have significantly contributed to the productivity of Japanese firms, will survive in terms of fundamentals, but that there are signs that many of the specifics will change.

One of the consequences of the maturing of the Japanese economy was internationalisation, which was boosted by the rapid appreciation of the yen after the Plaza Accord in 1986. The massive expansion of Japanese firms' foreign direct investment (FDI) began in the early 1970s and continued until the early 1990s. With the continuing post-bubble recession forcing many Japanese firms to restructure their operations, Japan's unemployment rate rose to a historical high, and had exceeded the US rate by the mid 1999s. Japanese government statistics suggest that Japan lost more than two million jobs to overseas operations during that period. This was the hollowing out (*kudoka*) of the Japanese economy. A similar hollowing out has been experienced in the United States in the last few decades, although the implications of this are not well understood. Head and Ries (Chapter 4) examine empirical evidence of the hollowing out effects of Japanese FDI. They argue that there were numerous reasons for the expansion of Japanese firms' FDI and that cheap overseas labour was only one of the reasons. They note that Japanese FDI in North America and Europe during the 1970s and early 1980s was made despite the high wages in those countries compared with Japanese wages, measured by the prevailing yen–dollar exchange rate. Their empirical estimates suggest that the hollowing out was not overwhelming. In fact in some industries FDI may have been an important and necessary step towards freeing Japanese domestic labour from the production of low-value-added products so that it could be used to produce high-value-added products.

Two important geographical areas that have attracted considerable Japanese FDI in manufacturing are Asia and North America. Chapters 5 and 6 (Part II) discuss the transfer of Japanese production technologies to Asia and North America. While many Japanese manufacturers are engaged in FDI in Asia, North America and Europe, it is estimated that only a small number of these operations are profitable. Excellent production technologies are thought to be the reason for the competitiveness of many Japanese firms. Japanese firms that are successful in transfering their production technologies to their FDI operations tend to end up with profitable operations. The recent transfer by Japanese firms of their just-in-time production methods to their North American operations was a significant event in the history of FDI because of the size of the manufacturing operations involved (for example car production). Also, the transfer of production technology from Japan to the West would seem to be much more difficult than between North America and Europe, a more standard routing of large-scale technology transfer. While the cultural barriers for Japanese firms operating in North America and Asia are equal, the types of technology transfer required for these regions are quite different. In addition Japanese multinationals' approaches to the management of their FDI operations in both developing and developed countries are often different from the traditional approaches employed by North American and European multinationals, with their well-established management processes. Typically, Western firms rely more on local employees for the management of their FDI operations than is the case with their Japanese counterparts. Furthermore, recognizing that their competitive advantage comes from the management methods practiced in Japan, Japanese firms have tried very hard to transfer these methods overseas.

Hayashi (Chapter 5) discusses the methods of technology transfer employed by Japanese companies in Asia. Hayashi argues that some Japanese firms have attempted to transfer their production technologies by assigning their foreign workers in Asia to on-the-job training at their mother plants in Japan. Hayashi provides evidence that this mode of technology transfer has been generally successful and has significantly shortened the time lapse between the launch date of a new product in Japan and the successful transfer of the production of that product to Asian manufacturing plants. Helper (Chapter 6) discusses the Japanese car industry in North America, which is one of the most important FDI operations for Japanese companies. Her analysis of Japanese car suppliers in the United States and Canada shows that despite their effort to transfer lean production technologies such as just-in-time manufacturing and participatory industrial relations, Japanese car suppliers have not been as successful as their assembly counterparts (for example Toyota and Honda Motors) in transferring those methods to their US manufacturing plants. She also argues that Japanese car suppliers in North America are not necessarily more efficient than domestic suppliers. Those which have been modestly successful are those which adopted a hybrid strategy whereby Japanese production methods were combined with North American ones. These two chapters also suggest that Japanese firms face significant limitations with the transfer of Japanese manufacturing practices to their FDI operations.

While the key to the success of Japanese FDI is Japanese firms' ability to transfer their production technologies to their FDI operations, the role of technology in Japanese economic history has been equally important, although it is not well understood. Japanese evidence is often not consistent with standard findings on economic development in the West. Understanding the historical situation may help us to understand the mechanisms that underlie the Japan's success in modern manufacturing.

Chapters 7 and 8 (Part IV) deal with the historical diffusion of technology. Many historians agree that the diffusion of evolving technologies among competitors, industries and geographical areas played as important a role in Japan as the creation of new technologies. Kiyokawa (Chapter 7) discusses alternative hypotheses to explain the historical development of the Japanese economy. Kiyokawa first questions the standard hypothesis that attributes Japan's success in economic development primarily to cheap labour. He questions this on the ground that many developing countries with abundant cheap labour have not achieved economic success. He proposes a technological gap hypothesis that explains the speed of adaptation of new technologies in Japan by the size of the gap between the technological levels of Japan and the technology-originating countries. Depending on the size of this gap, the speed at which new foreign technologies were introduced, diffused and adapted in Japan varied systematically among Japanese industries in the late 19th and early 20th centuries. Kiyokawa discusses the implications of this hypothesis for the technology transfer issues facing many developing countries today.

Japan's Pacific coastal region, stretching from Tokyo to Osaka, has always been the most important area for economic development, accounting for a significant proportion of Japanese industrial output and serving as the driving force of commercial and household activities. Mosk (Chapter 8) focuses on the role of technological changes in Japan in the development of the cities of Osaka and Tokyo in the 19th and 20th centuries. He argues that the geographical importance of technologically equipped Osaka and Tokyo, which were also endowed with well-educated and trained workers, cannot be underestimated as an explanation of Japan's development. Historically Osaka, much more than Tokyo, acted as Japan's commercial centre. This situation changed after the Meiji Restoration in 1868. Thereafter Tokyo emerged as Japan's predominant city for the launching of new technologies and business activities. Mosk presents evidence that there are technological and geographical reasons why Tokyo gradually surpassed Osaka in industrial, business and innovative activities in the 20th century. For example water-based transportation, which favoured Osaka until the 19th century, was replaced by powered land transportation from the late 19th century, which favoured Tokyo.

Of all the foreign countries with which Japan interacts, no country has had a more important influence on the Japanese economy than the United States. Since the visit to Japan by Commander Perry in 1853–4, backed by the gunboats of the US Navy, there have been many significant US–Japan interactions that have shaped Japan's policy agenda. Economic and political issues have been intertwined. For this reason it is interesting to study various aspects of US–Japanese relations in conjunction with the development of the Japanese economy. Chapters 9 and 10 (Part V) deal with these topics. Saxonhouse (Chapter 9) discusses the political economy of two specific events in the United States that were caused by Japanese competition: the enactment of the so-called 'Super 301' legislation in 1988 and the adoption of significantly strengthened dispute settlement mechanisms by the World Trade Organization. Saxonhouse empirically evaluates the impact of these events on the stock returns of representative US and Japanese firms. He finds that Super 301 had a negative effect and the settlement mechanisms a positive effect on Japanese stock prices, but neither event had a statistically significant effect on US stock prices. This raises interesting questions. For example did the United States achieve what it had intended to achieve with Super 301? Does the WTO dispute settlement mechanism work favourably for Japan? Is the recent WTO ruling justifying Japan's claim that the US–Canada pact unfairly discriminates against Japanese (and European) car makers consistent with Saxonhouse's empirical evidence?

One notable trade dispute between Japan and the United States is about the closed nature of Japan's markets in the case of foreign products. The US government alleges that this is the result of certain Japanese business practices, particularly the corporate groupings (*keiretsu*). It is often thought that Japanese firms prefer to purchase products from their *keiretsu*-affiliated firms rather than non-*keiretsu* firms, including foreign firms. One type of *keiretsu* is the distribution *keiretsu*, which consists of wholesalers and retailers that primarily or exclusively deal with the products of a specific Japanese manufacturer. In the case of the Japanese market for photographic film and paper, Kodak has long accused Fujifilm and the Japanese Ministry of International Trade and Industry (MITI) of exerting power over film and paper wholesalers and retailers in Japan to exclude the sale of Kodak products. Tsurumi and Tsurumi (Chapter 10) first describe the history and surrounding politics of the Fujifilm–Kodak dispute. They then discuss the ruling in December 1997 by the WTO in favour of Fujifilm. (The US government did not appeal against the WTO's decision.) They explain the underlying production technology, marketing, strategic and other business reasons that led the WTO to settle this dispute in favour of Fujifilm, and present empirical evidence to support their conclusions.

The three main practices that underlie the postwar Japanese economic and business system are the long-term employment and industrial relations practices discussed in Chapter 3, the *keiretsu* (corporate groupings) and the resulting corporate governance practices. Part VI of the book discusses *keiretsu* and corporate governance, followed by a description of the environmental strategies of Japanese firms.

Two major types of *keiretsu* – bank-based financial (horizontal) *keiretsu* and manufacturer-based capital (vertical) *keiretsu* – are going through a major restructuring. Two recent mergers, the Fuji Bank–Daiichi Kangyo Bank–Industrial Bank of Japan merger and the Sumitomo Bank–Sakura Bank (of the Mitsui Group) merger, will certainly reshape the bank-based *keiretsu* groups. Similarly the assembler–supplier relationship that characterizes vertical *keiretsu* groups, such as the Nissan and Mazda groups, appears to be disintegrating. This is believed to be due in part to the foreign controllers (Renault for Nissan and Ford for Mazda) brought in by failing Japanese car makers. Clearly the form of the *keiretsu* is changing, but few believe that Japanese firms' *keiretsu* behaviour will disappear or become unimportant.

Flath (Chapter 11) considers the history and character of various types of *keiretsu*. The persistent tendency of Japanese corporations to group themselves together, often holding each other's shares to strengthen the bond, has attracted the attention of researchers from a diverse range of disciplines, including economics, sociology and anthropology. The US and other foreign governments have accused the *keiretsu* of conspiring to maintain effective, though largely invisible, trade barriers. For example *keiretsu* relationships cause Japanese firms to choose their suppliers based on *keiretsu* membership, Japanese firms use *keiretsu* group wholesalers and retailers to prevent foreign competitors' products from reaching consumers (for example the Fujifilm–Kodak dispute) and cross-held *keiretsu* firms prevent justifiable foreign takeovers (for example the Pickens case). Flath provides economic and historical explanations of various aspects of *keiretsu* practices and their implications for foreign firms.

The prolonged post-bubble recession in Japan has caused analysts to look for the reasons for the bubble's formation and the subsequent failure of the Japanese economy. It is generally agreed that the failure of Japanese macroeconomic policy to deal with the immediate post-bubble situation has caused the recession to last much longer than necessary. Morck and Nakamura (Chapter 12) discuss the macroeconomic implications of Japanese corporate governance for the formation of the bubble and the prolonged recession. In particular they discuss the role of banks in the corporate governance system, the formation of the bubble and the post-bubble recession. The current form of corporate governance in Japan has been hotly debated and various institutional changes have been legislated by the government (for example, legalizing certain types of holding firm). The corporate governance system of a Japanese firm must typically take into account not only the power of the firm's individual shareholders but also other stakeholders in the firm. For example banks are significant creditors of many firms and are also major shareholders. For these and other reasons the Japanese corporate governance system, compared with the Anglo-American system, appears to be complex and less transparent. Morck and Nakamura argue that under Japan's bank-based corporate governance system it is difficult to align firms' investment decisions with the interests of the shareholders. This misalignment of interests among stakeholders may have helped to prolong the post-bubble recession.

One issue that has had a serious impact on the strategies of Japanese manufacturing firms since the mid 1960s is that of the environmental. The recent accelerated trend towards the internationalization of Japanese firms has forced them to become more aware of the strategic importance of environmental management. Horiuchi and Nakamura (Chapter 13) discuss the environmental measures adopted by Japanese manufacturers and the environmental issues facing them. These issues, including the problem of global warming, are international in nature and their solution must be oriented towards the public good (that is, some of the returns from business investments in the environment will necessarily be absorbed by the public, including competing firms). The manner in which Japanese firms and the government react to these environmental issues will be particularly interesting. In the past the government has often been involved in strategically important investment decisions by Japanese firms, particularly when their projects have had some public-goods aspect. For example the development of certain manufacturing technologies that would be useful for all Japanese manufacturers was often undertaken in a cooperative research effort sponsored by MITI (for example fibre optics and semiconductors). Horiuchi and Nakamura also discuss the extent of the Japanese government's involvement in manufacturers' investment in the environment and the associated public policy options.

Reference

Itose, S. (1998) *Those Who Can Become Anglo–Saxon Will Succed*, (in Japanese) (Tokyo: PHP Software Group).

Part I
Economic Growth and Industrial Relations

2 Japan's Economic Growth: Past and Present[1]

Takanobu Nakajima, Masao Nakamura
and Kanji Yoshioka

INTRODUCTION

Since the burst of the economic bubble in 1990, Japanese economic growth has been minimal, with an average GDP growth rate of less than 1 per cent in the 1990s. Japan's recent economic performance contrasts with that achieved in earlier years: in the 1960s the GDP growth rate was around 10 per cent, but it declined to 4 per cent in the 1970s and 1980s, and to 1 per cent in the 1990s. (Figure 2.1).

The two major economic downturns took place in the 1970s and 1990s, with subsequent structural changes. The overall drop of 5.4 percentage points in economic growth from the 1960s to the 1970s is significant and is often attributed to the increase in oil prices during the oil crisis. The oil crisis and the burst of the bubble helped to trigger the economic downturns of the 1970s and 1990s. There is,

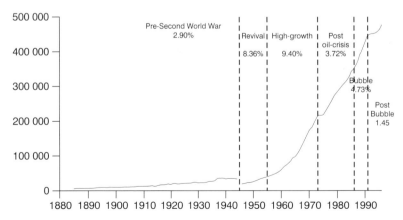

Figure 2.1 Japan's economic growth, 1880–1991 (GDP in billion yen, 1990 value)

Sources: Ohkawa (1974); EPA (1988).

13

Table 2.1 WPI and CPI, Japan, United States and
West Germany, 1973–75 (per cent)

		1973	1974	1975
Japan	WPI	15.8	31.4	3.0
	CPI	11.7	24.5	11.8
United States	WPI	13.1	18.9	9.3
	CPI	6.2	11.1	9.1
West Germany	WPI	6.6	13.4	4.7
	CPI	6.9	7.0	6.0

however, some recognition that the macroeconomic policy failures of the government and the Bank of Japan served to worsen the situation. After years of stable prices, the 1973 oil crisis caused a sharp increase in the price of imported oil, followed by severe inflation. Inflation in Japan was much more severe than that experienced by the United States and West Germany. The Wholesale and Consumers Price Indexes, WPI and CPI, in 1973–75 for these three countries are presented in Table 2.1.

In addition to the oil price increase, the reduction of the official discount rate in June 1972 and the excess money supply policy adopted by the Bank of Japan for the period 1972–73, before the oil crisis, are believed to have contributed to the 1973–74 inflation (Komiya, 1988). With restrictive fiscal and monetary policies causing the official discount rate to rise from 4.25 per cent in early 1973 to 9 per cent by December 1973, self-imposed wage restraint on the part of unions and the efforts of firms to achieve productive efficiency eventually returned inflation to a relatively low level.

The high cost of energy and the consequent massive effort to promote energy efficiency in manufacturing industry resulted in a significant shift in the pattern of growth in the manufacturing sector. For example the general machinery industry, which consumes relatively little energy, emerged as an important growth industry in the late 1970s and 1980s.

The burst of the financial bubble in 1990 produced another major downturn in economic growth. One of the differences between the two triggering events is that the 1973 oil crisis was an exogenous event while the bubble was mostly endogenously generated. The Plaza Accord of 1985 contributed to the severe recession, and subsequent fiscal and monetary policies laid the groundwork for the bubble and led to the radical appreciation of the yen against the US dollar.

There was a major structural change in the economy as a result of the oil crisis in the 1970s, with an emphasis on energy efficiency and lean manufacturing. Further and substantial changes may be introduced by industrial and business organizations when the economy fully recovers from the post-bubble recession. It will be of particular interest to see if the Japanese economy will revert to a long-term growth path.

This chapter will concentrate on the evolution and sources of Japan's economic growth, and how Japan's economic performance compares with that of the United States. The chapter is organized as follows. The next section reviews the long-term growth rates in Japan and several other countries. The third section discusses structural changes that have taken place since the Second World War, while the sources of economic growth in earlier years are reviewed in the fourth section. The final section discusses the post-bubble period.

LONG-TERM GROWTH RATES

The long-term real GDP growth rates for Japan and the United States from the late 1800s to the mid 1980s are shown in Figures 2.2 and 2.3. The US rates were relatively stable, but fell sharply during the Great Depression and after the Second World War. During the war the rates rose to an all-time high. In contrast the Japanese rates were particularly low during and immediately after the war, followed by

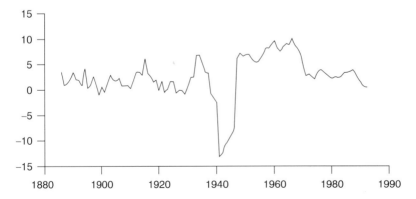

Figure 2.2   Long-term real GDP growth, Japan, 1880–1986 (5-year moving average, per cent)
Sources: Ohkawa (1974); EPA (1998).

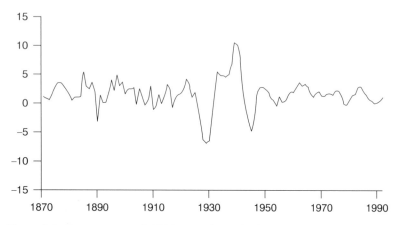

Figure 2.3   Long-term real GDP growth, United States, 1870–1991 (5-year moving average, per cent)
Sources: Maddison (1987); USBEA (1997).

Table 2.2   Long-term per capita GDP growth, Japan and the United States, 1885–1996 (per cent)

	1885–1919	*1920–54*	*1955–73*	*1974–91*	*1992–96*
Japan	1.98	1.17	8.40	3.29	1.47
United States	1.84	1.84	2.23	1.60	1.56

Sources: Maddison (1987); EPA (1998); UBEA (1997).

high rates throughout the 1960s. This can also be seen in Table 2.2, which shows the average growth rates of per capita real GDP for Japan and the United States.

It appears that the growth rate trend for both countries during this period was not necessarily consistent with the predictions of traditional growth models of the Solow type or of convergence theory.[2] It is possible that the observed economic growth may reflect factors such as increasing returns to scale, networking and other external factors associated with technology and the management of production activities. These factors could be treated within the framework of endogenous economic growth models (Romer, 1986, 1990). Theories of endogenous economic growth might also provide a basis for justifying government intervention in the planning and organization of a nation's economy. Such government intervention, however, may not be successful.

Table 2.3   Average per capita GDP growth rates for selected developed economies

	1885	1990	50% of 1990	10% of 1990	Average growth rate (%, before and after WWII)
Japan	16	345	1971	1951, 1925	3.29 (1.78, 5.83)
United States	58	420	1955	Prior to 1870	1.87 (2.09, 1.50)
Germany	23	360	1963	1946, 1911	2.74 (2.02, 3.87)
Sweden	30	330	1960	1892	2.30 (2.11, 2.53)
England	66	310	1957	Prior to 1870	1.48 (1.13, 2.08)

Notes: The figures are in PPP based on 10 000 Japanese yen (1990 values). The postwar figures for Japan and Germany do not include the years immediately after the end of the war.
Sources: Maddison (1987); EPA (1998); UBEA (1997); Ohkawa (1974).

According to Ohkawa (1974), in 1885 Japan's GDP was 60 billion yen (in 1990 yen), which was only 1.4 per cent of the 1990 GDP. Thus GDP grew 71-fold during the 105 years between 1885 and 1990, providing an average annual growth of 4.06 per cent. During the same period the average annual growth rate of US GDP was 3.28 per cent, or a 31-fold increase.

Table 2.3 provides a comparison of per capita GDP growth over the period 1885–1990 for Japan, the United States, Germany, Sweden and Britain. We can see from the table that the per capita GDP growth rates for Japan, and to a lesser extent Germany, for the period after the Second World War were relatively high. Also, in 1885 Japan's per capita GDP was almost 25 per cent of that of Britain, which was the highest income country at that time. On the other hand the real gap in per capita GDP between Japan and Western countries, for example Britain, the United States and some European countries, was extremely large. These Western countries had either long completed or were about to complete their industrial revolution, which had brought with it a significant improvement in living standards.

ECONOMIC GROWTH AND STRUCTURAL CHANGE

A significant amount of structural change accompanied Japan's economic growth. We shall look at the structural changes in the Japanese economy over time; first from the expenditure side and then from the production side.

Private household consumption

Figure 2.4 shows the components of Japan's GDE in nominal terms for the period 1885–1996: final private consumption, final government consumption, capital formation and exports. It is striking that private consumption's share of GDE fell sharply from 70 per cent in the 1930s to 35 per cent in the 1940s. Due to Japan's war efforts, government consumption under went a significant increase, thus reducing the share of private consumption. Excluding the period around the Second World War, the share of final private consumption declined gradually over the sample period. The contribution of private consumption to GDE declined gradually and steadily from 6 per cent in the high-growth period of the 1950s and 1960s to the present 2 per cent level (Table 2.4).[3]

Table 2.5 shows the decomposition of GDP growth for the United States, Britain and West Germany. The contribution of private consumption to GDP growth in these countries stayed around 2 per cent for many years (particularly in the United States) and Table 2.4 suggests that the Japanese economy had reached the same stage by the 1980s.

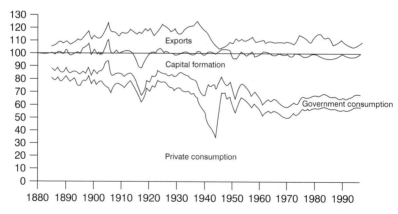

Figure 2.4   Components of Japan's nominal GDE, 1885–1996 (per cent)
Notes: Import share is measured by the distance from the top graph line to the 100 per cent straight line.
Sources: Ohkawa (1974); EPA (1998).

Table 2.4 Decomposition of GDE growth, Japan, 1956–96 (per cent)

	Contribution to GDE growth							GDE growth rate
	Private consumption	Govt consumption	Private housing	Private invest.	Govt capital formation	Inventory investment	Exports	Imports	
1956–61	5.8	0.6	0.5	1.8	0.7	0.3	0.4	−0.8	9.3
1962–67	5.6	0.7	0.9	1.2	1.0	0.0	0.6	−0.7	9.3
1968–73	4.9	0.5	1.0	1.8	1.1	0.1	0.8	−1.1	9.2
1974–79	2.3	0.5	0.0	0.1	0.3	−0.1	0.7	−0.3	3.5
1980–85	1.6	0.3	−0.2	0.8	−0.2	0.0	0.9	0.1	3.3
1986–91	2.4	0.2	0.3	1.6	0.3	0.1	0.3	−0.7	4.5
1992–96	1.2	0.2	0.1	−0.3	0.6	−0.1	0.5	−0.7	1.5

Sources: Ohkawa (1974); EPA (1998).

Table 2.5 Decomposition of GDE growth, United States, Britain and West Germany (per cent)

	Contribution to GDE growth						GDE growth rate
	Private consumption	Govt consumption	Private investment	Inventory investment	Exports	Imports	
United States:							
1951–55	2.1	2.2	0.4	−0.1	0.3	−0.3	4.5
1956–61	1.6	0.7	0.1	−0.1	0.3	−0.3	2.3
1962–67	2.7	1.2	0.8	0.2	0.4	−0.5	4.9
1968–73	2.4	−0.1	0.9	0.1	0.7	−0.8	3.2
1974–79	1.8	0.3	0.4	−0.1	0.6	−0.5	2.6
1980–85	1.8	0.6	0.3	0.0	0.1	−0.6	2.2
1986–91	1.6	0.4	−0.1	−0.1	0.8	−0.4	2.1
1992–96	1.9	−0.1	1.2	0.1	0.9	−1.2	2.8
Britain:							
1956–61	1.6	0.1	1.0	–	0.5	−0.6	2.5
1962–67	1.6	0.6	1.1	–	0.6	−0.8	3.0
1968–73	2.0	0.4	0.9	–	1.6	−1.5	3.3
1974–79	0.7	0.4	0.2	–	1.1	−0.5	1.5
1980–85	1.1	0.2	0.2	0.1	0.5	−0.6	1.4
1986–91	2.1	0.3	0.6	0.2	0.8	−1.2	2.5
1992–96	1.3	0.2	0.2	0.3	1.7	−1.6	2.2
West Germany:							
1969–73	3.0	0.9	1.4	0.0	1.7	−2.1	4.9
1974–79	1.8	0.6	0.1	0.1	1.1	−1.3	2.4
1980–85	0.4	0.3	0.1	0.3	1.6	−0.6	1.3
1986–90	2.1	0.2	1.0	0.1	2.0	−1.8	3.7
1991–94	0.5	0.3	0.7	0.1	1.1	−0.6	0.7

Source: OECD national accounts (1998).

Table 2.6 Decomposition of private consumption growth, Japan, 1956–88 (per cent)

	Consumption expenditure growth by type*								Private consumption growth rate
	Food	Clothing	Housing	Furniture	Medical care	Transportation and communications	Entertainment and education	Other	
1956–61	2.8	0.8	1.3	0.7	0.4	0.5	0.7	1.6	8.8
	(32.2)	(8.6)	(14.6)	(8.1)	(4.4)	(6.1)	(7.8)	(18.2)	(100)
1962–67	2.2	0.9	1.3	0.8	0.8	0.8	0.7	1.4	8.8
	(24.6)	(10.3)	(14.8)	(8.9)	(9.3)	(9.2)	(7.5)	(15.4)	(100)
1968–73	1.6	0.7	1.2	0.6	0.8	1.2	1.1	1.5	8.6
	(18.1)	(8.2)	(14.1)	(7.5)	(9.0)	(13.5)	(12.4)	(17.0)	(100)
1974–79	0.5	0.2	1.4	0.1	0.7	0.6	0.2	0.7	4.3
	(12.0)	(3.7)	(32.2)	(1.3)	(15.4)	(13.9)	(5.2)	(16.3)	(100)
1980–85	0.2	0.0	0.3	0.1	0.4	0.1	0.5	0.7	2.3
	(7.4)	(1.9)	(11.9)	(5.4)	(18.5)	(5.6)	(20.0)	(29.3)	(100)
1986–91	0.2	0.2	0.8	0.2	0.2	0.9	1.0	0.4	4.0
	(5.3)	(4.7)	(21.1)	(5.2)	(6.2)	(22.1)	(24.1)	(11.3)	(100)
1992–96	−0.1	−0.2	0.9	0.1	0.3	0.3	0.4	0.2	2.0
	(−4.5)	(−8.9)	(43.5)	(5.3)	(16.1)	(16.3)	(21.0)	(11.1)	(100)

* The numbers in parentheses are proportions.
Source: EPA (1998).

The contribution of specific consumption items to total private consumption in Japan for the period 1956–96 is shown in Table 2.6. We can see from this table that the only consumption items whose contribution to final consumption remained constant or increased during this period were medical care, transportation and communications, and entertainment and education. The relative shares of housing, food and clothing in total private consumption significantly decreased during this period, as expected.

The significant decline over time of the contribution of private consumption to Japanese economic growth from the first oil crisis to the 1980s partly explains the relatively low but stable growth rate over the same period. The contribution of private consumption to Japanese macroeconomic growth had become very similar to that in the United States, West German and Britain by the 1980s.

By the 1990s, household sector consumption as a percentage of the total economy was approximately the same in Japan as in the Western economies. For example Figure 2.5 shows the components of US GDE for the period 1950–96. Compared with the figures for Japan for the same period, the share of US GDE components remained very stable over time. The US final private consumption share was around 60 per cent – the average for developed countries – although it showed some increase. The share of GDE in private consumption in

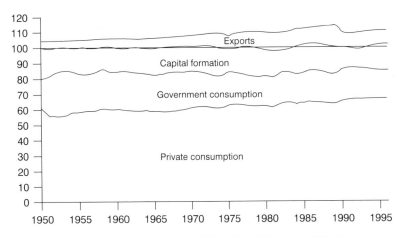

Figure 2.5   Components of nominal GDE, United States, 1950–96
Note: Import share is measured by the distance from the top graph line to the 100 per cent straight line.
Source: USBEA (1997).

Japan had fallen to around 60 per cent by the 1980s from the much higher levels of 70–80 per cent in the pre- and post war years.

These changes in the pattern of private consumption may have affected the Japanese post-bubble economic policies of the 1990s. For example the traditional massive spending on commercial and residential building construction would not have been likely to promote increased private consumption for economic growth, but public spending on infrastructure for the information and health services might.

Engel's law

Figure 2.6 shows various components of private consumption in Japan over the period 1874–1990. As expected, except for some reversal during the Second World War the share of food expenditure (the Engel coefficient) declined consistently. On the other hand the shares of clothing and housing remained fairly stable from the late 1800s to the 1950s. The decline in the share of food expenditure was absorbed by such items as health care, transportation and communications, education and entertainment. The share of these items in final private consumption increased from 20.3 per cent in 1963 to 27.9 per cent in 1996 (household survey, 1996).

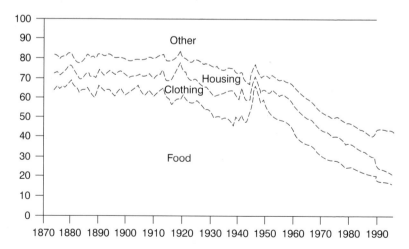

Figure 2.6   Components of private consumption, Japan, 1874–1990
Sources: Ohkawa (1974); EPA (1998).

Industrial structure and gross domestic product

The long-term structural change associated with economic development in Japan is depicted in Figure 2.7 (the proportions accounted for
by primary, secondary and tertiary industries). It can be seen that the
share of primary industries, including agriculture, forestry and fishing,
consistently declined from about 45 per cent in the late 1800s to less
than 3 per cent in the 1990s, although there was a brief rise after the
Second World War when about eight million former soldiers entered
the labour force. The share of secondary industries, including mining,
manufacturing and construction, increased gradually from the late
1800s to the 1940s, followed by another gradual increase after the
Second World War. In the 1990s the share of manufacturing fell to
less than 40 per cent. The aggregate share of tertiary industries,
including services, finance, entertainment and so on, remained at a
relatively constant level until the early 1920s, after which there was a
generally increasing trend, particularly after the Second World War.
Clearly the long-term development of productive activities in Japan
was consistent with that in other developed countries.

As economies develop, changes take place in consumption patterns
and these changes are reflected in structural changes in productive
activities. In fact these changes are merely the two sides of the same
economic coin.[4]

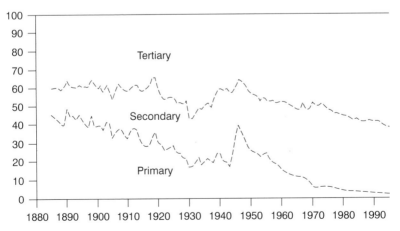

Figure 2.7   Industrial structural change, Japan, 1885–1995
Sources: Ohkawa (1974); EPA (1988).

SOURCES OF ECONOMIC GROWTH: SOME EARLIER ESTIMATES

In his pioneering work on growth accounting, Solow (1957) presented a framework by which the sources of economic growth are estimated. Sources of economic growth include production factors such as labour, capital, technical progress and economies of scale. Assuming the presence of a homogeneous aggregate production of degree one and rational behaviour on the part of producers, Solow concludes that more than 50 per cent of US economic growth in non-agricultural sectors for the period 1909–49 was due to technical progress. In Solow's study and subsequent empirical studies it has been customary to attribute to technical progress the residual portion of economic growth unexplained by growth in production input factors such as labour, capital and raw materials. Much effort in growth accounting since Solow's (1957) work has been devoted to reducing the proportion of growth that cannot be explained.

Because of the many alternative specifications and data sets used in the literature, one way of identifying the sources of long-term economic growth is to compare estimates obtained under different assumptions using different data sets. Table 2.7 provides a decomposition of Japan's GDP growth over the period 1890–1996 in terms of contributions by and changes in the number of workers and labour productivity. It is interesting to note that the contribution of labour input (number of workers) was relatively stable over this period despite significant fluctuations in the labour supply – the average annual increase in workers ranged from 0.36 per cent to 1.89 per cent.

Table 2.7   Decomposition of economic growth, Japan, 1890–1996

	1890–1913	1913–29	1929–40	1947–55	1956–73	1974–85	1986–91	1992–96
Change in number of workers	0.90	0.71	1.03	1.89	1.36	0.98	1.54	0.36
Contribution[1]	26	20	32	22	14	23	35	26
Change in labour productivity[2]	1.57	2.93	2.23	6.59	8.16	3.32	2.85	1.00
Contribution[1]	74	80	68	78	86	77	65	73

Notes:
1. Figures add upto 100 per cent.
2. Annual average (%).
Sources: EPA (1998); MCAJ (1998a).

It is also evident that a substantial increase in labour productivity took place after The Second World War, when the increase in the number of workers was much higher than in the previous 50 years. Since this model does not consider contributions other than labour input and labour productivity, the estimated contributions of labour productivity include the contribution of all other sources of GDP growth, such as capital input and technical progress. We now turn our attention to estimating the effects of these omitted sources of growth for the postwar period, for which more data is available.

Postwar sources of economic growth

A considerable body of literature exists on Japanese economic growth. It is generally believed that the Japanese economy had recovered to its prewar level by the mid 1950s (Sato, 1971; Ohkawa, and Rosovsky 1973). This was followed by extraordinary growth in the 1960s. Despite differences in the estimation methods and data sets used,

Table 2.8   Sources of post war economic growth: estimates for the 1950s to the late 1960s (per cent)

	Labour input	Capital input	TFP	Period and comments
Watanable and Ekaizu (1965)	13	–	70	1950–60
Sato (1971)	19	–	30–50	1930–67
Ohkawa and Rosovsky (1973)	–	–	30–40	1955–63
Kanamori (1972)	–	–	60	1955–67
Yoshihara and Ratcliffe (1972)	–	–	27	1952–65
Denison and Chung (1976)	21	24	22	National income, 1953–71; economies of scale and other factors account for 33 per cent
Ezaki (1977)	–	–	37	1952–71
Jorgenson and Nishimizu (1978)	–	–	44	1952–73
Kosai and Toshida (1981)	15	45	35	1955–80
Kuroda *et al.* (1987)	16	45	34	GDE growth, 1960–73; sources outside the household sector account for 5 per cent

there seems to be a general consensus on the sources of economic growth from the 1950s to the 1960s. Table 2.8 shows various estimates presented in the literature. The estimates for the contribution of growth in labour input to economic growth range between 13 per cent to 21 per cent. This lays the basis for the consensus view that labour input expansion played a relatively minor role in postwar economic growth. Hence technical progress and the associated expansion of capital input together with factors such as economies of scale must have played a significant role in economic growth from the mid 1950s to the late 1960s.

Identifying and separating these non-labour effects is more difficult. This is reflected in the wide-ranging estimates for technical progress and capital input in Table 2.8. It is however the case that, by definition, estimated residual effects (TFP) are lessened as more significant input factors are introduced into the growth accounting equation. For example Denison and Chung (1976) include scale economy in their estimation, which reduces their estimates for TFP significantly. Nevertheless the effects of economies of scale appear to be mostly prevalent and significant for cross-sectional samples. Estimation based on pooled time series of cross-sections indicates that cross-sectional economies of scale mostly disappear when aggregate industry TFP is estimated. In fact most of the aggregate TFP for 1960–88 at the industry level in Japan is explained by technical progress (Nakajima *et al.*, 1998). Table 2.8 suggests that the annual contribution of technical progress, represented by TFP gains, to economic growth was around 30–40 per cent or less from the 1950s to the late 1960s.

Comparison between Japan and the United States

The relative importance of input factors in explaining economic growth varies considerably depending on the degree of economic development. Table 2.9 shows sources of GDE growth estimated using a similar framework and method for Japan and the United States (Jorgenson and Kuroda, forthcoming). The contribution of capital input growth was about the same in both Japan and the United States for the period 1960–80. On the other hand the contribution of labour input growth was significantly less in Japan than in the United States. The growth rates for each factor were larger in Japan than in the United States. It is possible that the US economy was more driven by labour intensive advanced manufacturing

Table 2.9 Sources of economic growth, Japan (1960–92) and the United States (1960–79) (per cent)

	Japan				United States			
	GDE growth per year	Labour	Capital	TFP	GDE growth per year	Labour	Capital	TFP
1960–65	10.1 (100)	1.8 (18.0)	2.9 (28.7)	5.4 (53.3)	4.5 (100)	1.1 (25.4)	1.5 (32.9)	1.9 (41.7)
1965–70	11.7 (100)	1.9 (16.6)	3.6 (30.6)	6.2 (52.8)	3.1 (100)	1.2 (39.2)	2.0 (64.0)	−0.1 (−3.2)
1970–75	5.0 (100)	0.7 (13.7)	4.4 (88.0)	−0.1 (−1.7)	1.7 (100)	0.5 (32.3)	1.6 (95.5)	−0.4 (−27.8)
1975–80*	4.2 (100)	1.7 (41.6)	1.6 (37.5)	0.9 (20.9)	3.8 (100)	2.2 (57.4)	1.2 (30.3)	0.4 (12.3)
1980–85	3.7 (100)	1.1 (29.8)	1.6 (42.0)	1.0 (28.2)	–	–	–	–
1985–90	4.6 (100)	1.3 (28.3)	2.0 (43.5)	1.3 (28.2)	–	–	–	–
1990–92	2.3 (100)	−0.3 (−13.9)	2.1 (90.6)	0.5 (23.3)	–	–	–	–
1960–72	10.4 (100)	1.8 (17.4)	3.6 (34.3)	5.0 (48.3)	3.8 (100)	1.2 (31.5)	1.7 (44.4)	0.9 (24.1)
1972–92	3.8 (100)	1.0 (27.0)	2.1 (54.0)	0.7 (19.0)	–	–	–	–
1960–92	6.2 (100)	1.3 (21.1)	2.6 (41.9)	2.3 (37.1)	–	–	–	–

*The US figures in this row are for 1975–79.
Sources: Nakajima, Nakamura and Yoshioka (1998).

Table 2.10 Structural change in production inputs, Japan, 1960–92 (per cent)

	Labour input contribution					Capital input contribution				
	Growth per year	Total	Simple aggr.*	Quality change	Structural change	Growth per year	Total	Simple aggr.*	Quality change	Structural change
1960–65	3.3	18.0	9.5	1.5	7.0	6.4	28.7	17.4	11.9	−0.6
1965–70	3.6	16.6	11.8	4.1	0.7	7.6	30.6	22.4	4.7	3.5
1970–75	1.3	13.8	−4.5	12.4	5.9	9.9	88.0	71.0	15.9	1.1
1975–80	2.8	41.6	24.8	11.7	5.1	4.1	37.4	39.0	−0.9	−0.7
1980–85	1.8	29.8	8.2	17.0	4.6	4.0	42.0	40.0	2.5	−0.5
1985–90	2.2	28.3	20.3	5.9	2.1	4.8	43.5	45.7	2.1	−4.3
1990–92	−0.5	−13.9	−31.3	16.2	1.2	5.1	90.6	103.1	2.8	−15.5
1960–72	3.3	17.4	10.1	3.7	3.6	7.6	34.3	23.9	8.4	2.0
1972–92	1.7	27.1	10.1	12.4	4.6	5.1	54.0	53.0	4.0	−3.1
1960–92	2.3	21.1	10.2	6.9	4.0	6.1	41.9	35.5	6.5	−0.1

* The numbers in these columns were calculated by adding up hours of work and real capital stock, respectively.
Sources: Nakajima, Nakamura and Yoshioka (1998).

industries and service industries during the sample period. This may explain the significantly more important role played by labour input in US output growth relative to Japan. In Japan, labour input growth was greater for secondary industries than for tertiary industries until the early 1970s, but this situation reversed after the first oil crisis in 1973.

The oil crisis triggered considerable changes in both labour and capital inputs. Ohkawa and Rosovsky (1973) emphasize the importance of structural change in the allocation of labour across different sectors in Japanese economic growth. Table 2.10 shows that such structural change was important in the early 1960s, accounting for 7 per cent of the 18 per cent contribution made by labour input growth to economic growth. The quality of labour input, however, gradually became more important than structural change in the late 1960s and early 1970s, and became the most important factor in labour input growth (12 per cent out of 27 per cent) during the period 1973–92. Essentially the same phenomenon is observed for capital input growth, for which structural change gradually became less important and the quality of capital input, which was important in the early 1960s, became important again during the oil crisis period in the 1970s. It is also interesting to note that labour input growth was quite low during the oil crisis period (1.3 per cent in 1970–75), while capital input growth rose to a high of 9.9 per cent compared with the long-term average of 6.1 per cent per year.

One of the main policy issues after the oil crisis was whether the Japanese economy would be able to achieve high growth again. We have seen in Tables 2.9 and 2.10 that the fall in growth after the oil crisis in 1973 was mainly caused by a slowing of technical progress. There is considerable empirical evidence to support the observed decline in technical progress from the late 1970s. These supply side factors were mirrored by a demand side factor: a significant decline in the growth of private consumption.

It is likely that the decline in technical progress after the oil crisis resulted from a shift in the types of R&D investment firms chose to adopt. While Japanese manufacturers continued to invest heavily in R&D, factors such as increases in the price of oil and other energy sources, greater public awareness of pollution problems and Western-style consumption patterns probably caused firms to shift the emphasis of their R&D investment away from mass-production-based research and towards cleaner, more energy-efficient equipment, new product development and efficient manufacturing.

SOURCES OF ECONOMIC GROWTH SINCE THE BUBBLE PERIOD

Given the prolonged recession in Japan, it is interesting to investigate the trend in productivity gains in the manufacturing sector since the 1980s. For convenience we shall define the following periods as characterizing the Japanese macroeconomy: the high yen recession period (1985–88), the bubble period (1988–91), and the post-bubble recession period (1991 onwards). In particular we wish to ascertain empirically whether or not Japanese manufacturers mainly expanded their output by increasing their inputs: purchasing more raw materials, hiring more workers and investing in more capital equipment. If this was indeed the case it would be consistent with one of the major implications of a financial bubble – that a bubble significantly distorts economic decision making. In Japan's case, firms under the influence

Table 2.11   The cost shares of production sectors: Japanese electrical machinery firms, 1985–93 (per cent)

	All firms	HEE	ECE	OLEE	Big Six	Other 49
1985	68	67	69	62	67	69
1986	68	65	68	62	67	69
1987	66	66	67	58	66	69
1988	66	67	67	57	65	69
1989	66	66	67	56	65	69
1990	66	66	67	55	65	69
1991	66	67	67	55	65	69
1992	65	64	66	54	64	67
1993	64	64	65	53	63	67

Notes: The sample consists of 54 listed firms in the Japanese electrical machinery industry. The firms in each group are as follows. (the Big 6 firms are marked with asterisks). Heavy electrical equipment (HEE): Shinko Elec., Nisshin Elec., Yasukawa Elec., Meidensha, Origin Elec., Shibaura Elec., Takaoka, Nippon Denki Seiiki, Fuji Elec., Koa, Omron and Hokuriku Denki. Electronics and communications equipment (ECE): Toshiba,* Mitsubishi Elec.,* Hitachi Ltd.,* Horiba, Advantest, Chino, Yokogawa Elec., Nichikon, Fujitsu,* Oki Elec., NEC,* Fanuc, Nitsuko, Toyo Tsushinki, Anritsu, Tamura Denki, Hitachi Denshi, Iwasaki Elec., Kokusai Denki, Nihon Radio, Nobi Bosai, Sanken Elec., Rohm, Tokin, Kinseki, Nihon Kemikon, Teikoku Tsushin, Nihon Koku Denshi, Nihon Denshi, Tamura Seisakusho, Fuji Denki Kagaku, Alps Elec., Sumitomo Tokushu Kinzoku, Nitto Denko, Hoshiden and Kyocera. Other light electrical equipment (OLEE): Sharp,* Shinko Denki, Hitaci Maxcel, Shinkobe Elec., Ushio Elec. and Furukawa Elec.

of the bubble may have invested heavily in non-profitable projects by overestimating the expected returns from their investments. One of the consequences of such behaviour is overcapacity of production equipment and a resulting rapid decline in the productivity of the sector in question.

Given the fixed nature of investment in plant and equipment and the quasi-fixed nature of hiring new workers in Japan, the excess capacity Japanese manufacturers may have ended up with before and after the bubble would have been a very serious management problem. In order to assess managerial responses to the possible overcapacity problem, we shall decompose manufacturers' productivity gains into those due to production operations (blue-collar productivity) and those due to managerial operations (white-collar productivity). The non-production staff of manufacturing firms, who include managerial, engineering, R&D and other professional staff, are becoming increasingly more important. Table 2.11 shows a decreasing (increasing) trend for the cost share of the production sector (non-production sector) activities in Japanese electrical machinery firms. These trends are also observed for firms in all other manufacturing industries.

In order to estimate TFP growth for the blue-collar (production) and white collar (non-production) sectors of electrical machinery firms for the sample period 1985–93, we assume that firm output Y is given by the following Cobb–Douglas aggregate function:[5]

$$Y = AU^{\alpha}V^{1-\alpha} \qquad (2.1)$$

where U and V are the output by the blue-collar and white-collar sectors respectively. U and V are themselves production functions with their respective input vectors X_p and X_n as follows:

$$U = F_p(X_p) \qquad (2.2a)$$

and

$$V = F_n(X_n) \qquad (2.2b)$$

If we denote the quantity indexes for the input vectors X_p and X_n by Q_p and Q_n and denote the productivity of the firm, its blue-collar sector and its white-collar sector by T_f, T_p and T_n, respectively, we can rewrite Equation 2.1 as follows:

$$\frac{d\ln Y}{dt} = \alpha \frac{d\ln Q_p}{dt} + \alpha \frac{d\ln T_p}{dt} + (1-\alpha)\frac{d\ln Q_n}{dt} + (1-\alpha)\frac{d\ln T_n}{dt}$$

$$(2.3)$$

We then obtain

$$\frac{d\ln T_f}{dt} = \alpha \frac{d\ln T_p}{dt} + (1 - \alpha)\frac{d\ln T_n}{dt} \qquad (2.4)$$

Given that data are available on firms' total operations and production sector operations but not on their non-production sectors, our strategy is to estimate Equation 2.4 in two stages. We first estimate $(d\ln T_f/dt)$ using firm data and estimate $(d\ln T_f/dt)$ using data on the firms' production units. Then, using estimated α and Equation 2.4, we estimate $(d\ln T_n/dt)$. Since total firm input vector X_f is given by

$$X_f = X_p + X_n \qquad (2.5)$$

time change for the quantity index Q_f for the entire firm is given by

$$\frac{d\ln Q_f}{dt} = \sum_i S_{fi} \frac{d\ln X_{fi}}{dt}$$

$$= \sum_i (S_{pi}W_p + S_{ni}W_n)\left(W_{pi}\frac{d\ln X_{pi}}{dt} + W_{ni}\frac{d\ln X_{ni}}{dt} \right) \qquad (2.6)$$

where i denotes the ith element of the production input vector. The cost shares are defined as follows:

$$S_{pi} = \frac{P_{pi}X_{pi}}{C_p}, \quad C_p = \sum_i P_{pi}X_{pi}$$

$$S_{ni} = \frac{P_{ni}X_{ni}}{C_n}, \quad C_n = \sum_i P_{ni}X_{ni}$$

$$W_{pi} = \frac{P_{pi}X_{pi}}{P_{pi}X_{pi} + P_{ni}X_{ni}}, \quad W_p = \frac{C_p}{C_p + C_n}$$

$$W_{ni} = \frac{P_{ni}X_{ni}}{P_{ni}X_{pi} + P_{ni}X_{ni}}, \quad W_n = \frac{C_n}{C_p + C_n}$$

On the other hand Equations 2.3 and 2.4 imply that the time change for the quantity index for the whole firm is given by the following:

$$\alpha\frac{d\ln Q_p}{dt} + (1 - \alpha)\frac{d\ln Q_n}{dt} = \sum_i \left(\alpha S_{pi}\frac{d\ln X_{pi}}{dt} + (1 - \alpha)S_{ni}\frac{d\ln X_{ni}}{dt} \right)$$

$$(2.7)$$

In order to utilize Equation 2.4 in our estimation strategy we need to establish that Equation 2.6 and 2.7 are equal to each other. It has been shown (Nakajima, Maeda and Kiyota 1998) that if the production functions for the blue-collar and white-collar sectors are homogeneous functions of degree η, then cost minimization implies that Equation 2.6 equals Equation 2.7 and $W_p = \alpha$.

Thus under the assumption of cost minimization and homogeneous production functions, it is possible to estimate TFP growth for the white-collar sector as the difference between the TFP growth for the entire firm and the TFP growth for the blue-collar sector. Note also that firms' observed cost shares for the blue-collar sector gives an estimate for α. The estimated values of $\alpha(=W_p)$ are shown in Table 2.11.

Empirical results

Filed financial statements (*Yuka shoken hokokusho*) provide relevant firm data for the sample of 54 electrical machinery firms listed under Table 2.11. Only firms with fiscal years ending in March for the sample period 1985–93 were included to minimize errors resulting from differing measurement periods (calendar year). Using this information, each firm's establishments were identified in terms of their main products, number of employees and capital stock. The financial statements, however, do not provide information on output by establishment, but the Ministry of International Trade and Industry (MITI) annually publishes data on these establishments for 4-digit-level industry classification, in group average form. Each cell contains the averages for such variables as number of employees, capital stock, raw materials and the sales revenues for establishments falling into a particular group. The number of employees at each establishment defines the groups as follows: 30–49, 50–99, 100–199, 200–299, 300–499, 500–999 and 1000+. Each of the sample firms' establishments was assigned data for the establishment group that was pertinent in terms of the industry and establishment size (number of employees). For example if Toshiba's semiconductor factory has 3000 employees and Mitsubishi Electric's semiconductor factory 2500 employees in a certain year, these establishments have the same assigned establishment data for that year.[6]

The three capital stock variables used are structures, machinery and land. Perpetual inventory methods were used to calculate the stocks of structures, machinery and land, assuming depreciation rates of

5 per cent, 15 per cent and 0 per cent, respectively. The number of workers employed by the firm or establishment measures the labour input. Because of the lack of data on hours worked, fluctuations in hours are ignored. The input price indexes used were as follows: sector-specific input and output price indexes (published by the Bank of Japan); price deflators for structures and machinery (published by the Economic Planning Agency); and land price indexes (based on the National Land Agency's published land prices). The prices (interest rates) of the capital used are the Bank of Japan's five-year public and corporate bond interest rates, benefits and wages per worker were obtained by dividing the firms' total wage bills, including fringe benefits and other labour costs (total cash wage payments) by the number of workers.[7]

Table 2.12 shows a representative sample firm's output growth and its decomposition into production and non-production sector growth. At both firm and sector levels output growth was positive and high in 1985–91 but dropped to a large negative number in the post-bubble period (1991–93).

Table 2.13 and Figure 2.8 show TFP growth for firm and sector levels. TFP growth was negative not only for the post-bubble period (1991–93) but also for the pre-bubble period for the entire sample.

Table 2.12   Decomposition of a representative firm's output growth

		All firms	HEE	ECE	OLEE	Big Six
Firm output growth:	1985–88	7.16	7.18	7.76	3.38	8.73
	1988–91	5.84	7.60	5.35	5.39	6.87
	1991–93	−3.35	−3.92	−3.16	−3.41	−1.34
	1985–93	4.04	4.56	4.13	2.44	5.51
Production sector output growth:	1985–88	3.11	0.02	4.40	1.40	6.13
	1988–91	3.85	4.50	3.39	4.76	4.06
	1991–93 ·	−3.95	−0.28	−5.90	0.22	−4.18
	1985–93	1.62	1.62	1.45	2.36	2.78
Non-production sector output growth:						
	1985–88	4.04	7.16	3.36	1.98	2.60
	1988–91	2.00	3.10	1.96	0.63	2.81
	1991–93	0.60	−3.64	2.75	−3.63	2.84
	1985–93	2.41	3.85	2.22	0.07	2.73

Notes: HEE = Heavy electrical equipment; ECE = electronics and communications equipment; OLEE = other light electrical equipment.

Table 2.13 Decomposition of a representative firm's TFP growth (per cent)

		All firms	*HEE*	*ECE*	*OLEE*	*Big Six*
Firm TFP growth:	1985–88	−1.89	−0.81	−2.01	−3.75	0.94
	1988–91	1.20	1.30	1.08	2.68	1.60
	1991–93	−1.75	−3.77	−1.07	−4.36	−1.51
	1985–93	−0.70	−0.76	−0.62	−1.49	0.57
Production sector TFP growth:	1985–88	−2.09	−1.75	−2.17	−2.23	−1.37
	1988–91	−0.41	0.39	−0.81	0.51	−0.15
	1991–93	−3.65	−2.81	−4.20	−2.04	−4.59
	1985–93	−1.85	−1.21	−2.17	−1.16	−1.71
Non-production sector TFP growth:	1985–88	0.21	0.94	0.16	−1.52	2.30
	1988–91	1.61	0.91	1.89	2.17	1.74
	1991–93	1.90	−0.96	3.13	−2.33	3.09
	1985–93	1.16	0.45	1.55	−0.34	2.29

Notes: HEE = heavy electrical equipment; ECE = electronics and communications equipment; OLEE = other light electrical equipment.

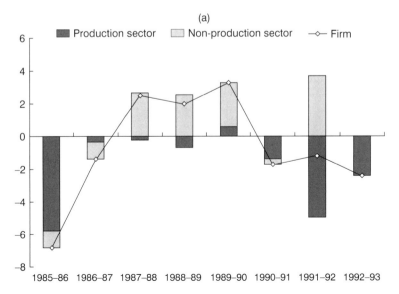

Figure 2.8 *continued overleaf*

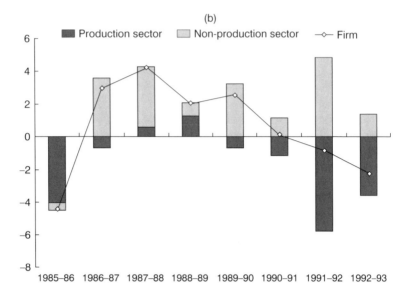

Figure 2.8   Decomposition of a representative firm's TFP growth: (a) all firms; (b) Big six (per cent)

This is particularly noticeable for production sector TFP growth, which is consistent with our earlier finding that these manufacturers' massive production output increases prior to the bubble period were achieved mainly by expanding their inputs. Their TFP growth in the post-bubble period became very negative. Our estimates also suggest that TFP growth in the non-production sectors of these firms was generally positive, counterbalancing the negative TFP growth in the production sectors. We conclude that even the electrical machinery firms, which were thought to be among the best-performing firms in the Japanese economy, made serious investment decision errors during the bubble period, and their performance after the bubble was adversely affected as a result. We also find that the white-collar (non-production) sector of these firms had positive TFP growth, compensating for the loss of productivity in the blue-collar (production) sector.[8]

CONCLUDING REMARKS

We must view Japan's economic growth from a historical point of view. More than half a century has passed since the end of the Second

World War and more than 65 per cent of the Japanese population has been born since then. Today's college students experienced neither Japan's high-growth period nor the oil crisis in 1973.

In this chapter we have reviewed Japan's postwar economic growth using empirical studies based on growth accounting. As mentioned in the introduction, the postwar Japanese economy experienced two turning points. The first was the first oil crisis, which limited the growth of energy-intensive heavy industries. Because the oil crisis resulted in higher energy prices the Japanese economy, as predicted by neoclassical economic theory, smoothly adjusted itself to an energy-saving mode, although it paid a painful price in terms of inflation. The second turning point was the bursting of the bubble in 1991.

The bubble economy, viewed dispassionately, can be defined as an unfinished attempt to recapture the high growth of the postwar period. In the midst of that period, one of the authors was temporarily engaged in a research project at the MITI Research Institute. The entire office was preoccupied with bullish predictions about the future of Japanese business. The research subject was 'Is a high growth period coming again?' Everyone believed that a big surge in demand was imminent. Even the electrical machinery industry, one of the stars of the postwar growth period, raised its production capacity by pouring more resources into factories, as we saw in Table 2.12. Although the situation looked similar to that in the high-growth period in the 1960s, the growth experienced during the bubble economy was neither accompanied nor followed by TFP growth. According to Nakajima, Nakamura and Yoshioka (1998), more than 10 per cent of annual output growth in the 1960s was realized with an annual TFP growth of no less than 5 per cent. The rapid decline in the demand for manufactures after the burst of the bubble led to decreased utilization of fixed inputs and significantly reduced the production sector TFP.

What will the post-bubble economy be like? It is possible that an era of knowledge-based economy is developing. *The Survey of Research and Development* (Management and Coordination Agency of Japan, 1998b) shows that $120 billion, corresponding to more than 3 per cent of GDP or 10 per cent of gross domestic capital formation, is being spent on R&D investment. On the other hand the Japanese Patent Office reports that about 400 000 patents are lying dormant. Does this mean that Japanese R&D investment has been wasted?

Nakajima and Hamada (1997) argue that Japanese intellectual property law emphasizes the practical use of knowledge rather than the protection of intellectual property rights. This may partly explain the low productivity of Japanese R&D. In addition the Japanese education system has supplied homogeneous workers whose abilities are mostly evaluated by one criterion: from which college they have graduated. This has certainly contributed to a rising yield at factories and an improvement in the quality of existing products. But Japanese creativity in R&D may have suffered as a result, since the production of intellectual goods requires a multidimensional evaluation system.

The current economic turmoil in Japan shows that future growth cannot be accomplished by returning to policies of the high-growth period, which emphasized production sector growth. Rather, what seems to be needed now is the development of new value systems and standards, whereby creativity is properly appreciated and efficiently utilized.

Notes

1. An earlier version of this chapter was prepared for the UBC Interdisciplinary Research Conference on Japanese Business and Economic System: History and Prospects for the 21st Century at the University of British Columbia, 12–13 February 1999. The Research was supported in part by the Social Sciences and Humanities Research Council of Canada.

2. Traditional neoclassical growth models based on decreasing-returns-to-scale production functions typically predict that labour productivity (the ratio between output and labour) increases only when an increase in capital input exceeds an increase in labour input. That is, in the process of economic growth for a nation experiencing population growth and accompanying growth in its capital stock, the capital–labour ratio will eventually become constant due to the model's decreasing-returns-to-scale property and a steady state with no per capita GDP growth will be achieved. The convergence theory predicts that, other things being equal, developing economies will exhibit high economic growth while highly developed economies will grow slowly (Baumol, 1986). Abramovitz (1986) and Williamson (1991) discuss the applicability of the convergence theory.

3. There are additional significant differences in the share of various components of the national economy between Japan and other countries. For example, the share of final government expenditure in Japan is about 10 per cent below that in the United States (which is the OECD average), and the share of capital formation is almost twice that in the United States and other OECD countries.

4. It should also be pointed out that when we observe changes in certain economic behaviour, for example consumption patterns or firm behaviour in a developing economy, it is often difficult to distinguish between the effects of development and the effects of other factors on economic behaviour.
5. In the empirical study below we use the trans-log form (Theil–Törnqvist index formula).
6. Some of the sample firms had establishments with fewer than 30 employees. Establishment data for firm size 30–49 was assigned for such establishments.
7. The MITI establishment data lost its definitional consistency over time in 1994 in part because of the physical loss of some establishment survey questionnaires due to the Kobe earthquake and in part because of revised industry classifications. (Variable definitions and sample coverage are not the same before and after 1994.) Further details on the data and estimation methods are provided in Nakajima, Maeda and Kiyota (1998).
8. Many articles have appeared in the Japanese business press lamenting the low productivity of Japanese white-collar workers (see for example Japan Productivity Center, 1994, 1995). These publications are sometimes based on workplace surveys. There seems to be, however, no serious empirical evidence to support their argument.

References

Abramovitz, M. (1986) 'Catching up, forging ahead, and falling behind', *Journal of Economic History*, vol. 46, no. 2, pp. 385–406.

Baumol, W. J. (1986) 'Productivity growth, convergence, and welfare: What the long-term data shows', *American Economic Review*, vol. 76, no. 5, pp. 1072–85.

Denison, E. F. and W. K. Chung (1976) 'Economic Growth and the Source', in H. Patrick and H. Rosovsky (ed), *Asia's New Giant* (Washington, DC: The Brookings Institution).

Economic Planning Agency (EPA) (1998) *System of National Account* (Tokyo: EPA).

Ezaki, M. (1977) *Models of the Japanese Economy: A System of National Accounts Approach* (in Japanese), (Tokyo: Sobunsha).

Japan Productivity Center (1994) *A Survey of White-Collar Productivity* (in Japanese) (Tokyo: Japan Productivity Centre).

Japan Productivity Center (1995) *Towards Enhancing White-Collar Productivity* (in Japanese) (Tokyo: Japan Productivity Center).

Jorgenson, D. W. and M. Kuroda (forthcoming) *International Comparison of Economic Growth: the United States and Japan* (Cambridge, Mass.: MIT Press).

Jorgenson, D. W. and M. Nishimizu (1978) 'U.S. and Japanese Economic Growth, 1952–1974: An International Comparison', *Economic Journal*, vol. 88, no. 352, pp. 707–26.

Kanamori, H. (1972) 'What Accounts for Japan's High Rate of Growth?', *Review of Income and Wealth*, vol. 18, no. 2, pp. 155–71.

Kosai, Y. and S. Toshida (1981) *Economic Growth* (in Japanese) (Tokyo: Nihon-Keizai-Shimbun).

Komiya, R. (1988) *Modern Japanese Economy* (in Japanese) (Tokyo: University of Tokyo Press).

Kuroda, M., K. Yoshioka and M. Shimizu (1987) 'Inter-industry Effect of Productivity Growth', in M. Kuroda, A. Horiuchi and K. Hamada (eds), *Macroeconomic Analysis of the Japanese Economy* (in Japanese) (Tokyo: Tokyo University Press).

Maddison, A. (1987) 'Growth and Slowdown in Advanced Capitalist Economies: Techniques of Quantitative Assessment', *Journal of Economic Literature*, vol. 25, no. 2, pp. 649–698.

Management and Coordination Agency of Japan (MCAJ) (1998a) *Labor Force Survey* (Tokyo: Statistics Bureau).

Management and Coordination Agency of Japan (MCAJ) (1998b) *Survey of Research and Development* (Tokyo: Statistics Bureau).

Nakajima, T. (1992) *Growth Factors of the Japanese Economy* (in Japanese), Ministry of International Trade and Industry Research Institute, Research Series no. 12 (Tokyo: MITI).

Nakajima, T. and K. Hamada (1997) 'Issues on Japan's Intellectual Product' *Managerial and Decision Economics*, vol. 18, pp. 141–52.

Nakajima, T., Y. Maeda and K. Kiyota (1998) 'Is White-collar Productivity Low in Japan? Evidence from the Electrical Machinery Industry', Discussion Paper no. 98-DOF-30 (Research Institute of International Trade and Industry).

Nakajima, T., M. Nakamura and K. Yoshioka (1998) 'A Method for Estimating Scale Economies and Technical Progress: Sources of Total Factor Productivity for Japanese Manufacturing 1964–1988', *Japanese Economic Review*, vol. 49, pp. 310–34.

Ohkawa, K. (1974) *Long-term Economic Statistics Estimation and Analysis* (Tokyo: Toyo-Keizai-Shimposha).

Ohkawa, K. and H. Rosovsky (1973) *Japanese Economic Growth* (Stanford, CA: Stanford University Press).

Romer, P. M. (1986) 'Increasing Returns and Long-run Growth', *Journal of Political Economy*, vol. 94, no. 5, pp. 1002–37.

Romer, P. M. (1990) 'Endogenous Technological Change', *Journal of Political Economy*, vol. 98, no. 5, part 2, pp. S71–102.

Sato, K. (1971) 'Growth and technical change in Japanese non-primary sectors: 1930–1967', *Economic Studies Quarterly*, vol. 22, no. 1.

Solow, R. M. (1957) 'Technical Change and the Aggregate Production Function', *Review of Economics and Statistics*, vol. 39, pp. 312–20.

US Bureau of Economic Analysis (UBEA) (1997) *Survey of Current Business* (Washington, D.C.: US Bureau of Economic Analysis).

Watanabe, T. and N. Ekaizu (1965) 'Labor Quality and Economic Growth', *Economic Studies Quarterly*, vol. 19, no. 1.

Williamson, J. G. (1991) 'Productivity and American Leadership: A Review Article', *Journal of Economic Literature*, vol. 29, no. 1, pp. 51–68.

Yoshihara, K. and T. Ratcliffe (1972) 'Productivity Change in the Japanese Economy: 1905–1965', *Economic Studies Quarterly*, vol. 22.

Yoshioka, K., T. Nakajima and M. Nakamura (1994) *Sources of Total Factor Productivity for Japanese Manufacturing Industries, 1964–1988: Issues in Scale Economies, Technical Progress, Industrial Policies and Measurement Methodologies*, Keio Economic Observatory Research Monograph Series (Keio University Press).

Comments on Chapter 2

Werner Antweiler

Japan's growth in productivity has often been looked at with fascination and envy by other countries. Unsurprisingly the question of what has driven this growth has received much attention and empirical scrutiny. What can other countries learn from the Japanese experience, how does it compare with their own performance, and which strategies can be emulated at home? In Chapter 2, Nakajima, Nakamura and Yoshioka take a fresh look at the data, using a conventional total factor productivity (TFP) approach for the entire sample period, and a novel TFP approach for a smaller data set that covers the electrical machinery industry in the 1985–93 period.

One of the startling facts about economic growth in Japan is the apparent decline in the contribution of private consumption to economic growth. A key finding of the chapter was the identification of three distinct phases of economic growth in Japan:

- In phase 1, during the 1950s and 1960s, growth was mostly attributable to technological progress and capital input expansion.
- Phase 2 was triggered by the oil price shock of 1973, leading to a reallocation of labour across industries. In turn there was a decline in technical progress in the late 1970s.
- Phase 3, during the 1980s was characterized by the onset of recession, the bubble economy and the painful economic adjustments of the post-bubble period. The output increases in the bubble period were mostly fuelled by an expansion of inputs and little or no advances in productivity. TFP growth in the post-bubble period became negative.

The authors' analysis of the third phase is especially compelling. Their results appear to confirm that bubbles distort economic decision making, leading to a misallocation of resources. The data set is too short term, however, to answer the interesting question of whether these adverse effects will outlast the asset price bubble due to lock-in and persistence.

The strength of this chapter is in looking at the post-bubble period through the lens of a refined TFP measurement methodology. This novel approach entails the decomposition of productivity gains into production-related (blue collar) operations and non-production-related (white collar) activities such as management and R&D. The latter types of activity are difficult to measure, and thus the authors obtain measures for the white-collar TFP gains $\hat{T}_n$ as the difference in overall TFP gains $\hat{T}_f$ minus the blue-collar TFP gains $\hat{T}_p$, i.e., $\hat{T}_n = (\hat{T}_f - \alpha\hat{T}_p)/(1 - \alpha)$, where α equals the ratio of the value of blue-collar activities to the value of all activities. On the theoretical level this requires imposing an identifying restriction (homogeneity of degree γ) on the production functions for the different types of workers in a firm. At the empirical level they accomplish their objective by utilizing both firm-level data for estimating TFP growth at the firm level, and plant-level data for estimating the TFP growth of blue-collar activities.

There are a few points of concern about the general validity of TFP studies. What key assumptions are adopted to make them work? For one, we need to assume that goods and factor markets are competitive. Secondly, levels of inputs must be costlessly adjustable. When both conditions hold, inputs are paid their marginal product and thus input shares are the usual $\theta_K \equiv (\partial Q/\partial K)(K/Q)$ and so on. In reality, however, neither condition is likely to be met completely, casting a shadow on the empirical work. Nelson (1981) and Leamer (1994) refer to several points of concern:

- Are inputs being paid their marginal product? What if compensation and marginal products are not 'synchronized' over short periods of time?
- Growth accounting using TFP measures may be conceptually incorrect: technological improvement is a consequence of investment rather than a residual factor.
- Rapid developments in an economy can cause substantial changes in input shares: these coefficients may not be fixed as in simple Cobb–Douglas production functions.

The authors hint at the importance of private consumption versus government consumption in the post-bubble period of the 1990s. They claim that 'the traditional massive spending on commercial and residential construction would not have been likely to promote increased private consumption for economic growth, but public spending on infrastructure for the information and health services might.' While I agree with this conclusion it is difficult to see how it can be derived from the results of a cursory look at macroeconomic data.

Regretfully the chapter does not provide tables showing the TFP regression results. Without seeing the standard errors on these estimates it is difficult to tell what level of confidence one can have in them, especially with respect to the stability of the parameter estimates over the various time periods. It would be particularly useful to see how well the production function works in order to understand what is picked up by the residual. As TFP measures are simply a residual, they may account for other things than technological productivity growth, for example omitted input factors or economies of scale. A disaggregation of TFP growth into scale effects and technical change could have yielded some interesting insights about the prevalence of scale effects in the Japanese electronics industry. A more detailed discussion of the regressions would have benefited the exposition, along with a clearer distinction between the parts that are simply accounting and those that involve regressions.

Table 2.11 points to a steady decline in the input share of the production sector. This appears to be an important result as it indicates a structural shift towards white-collar activities in Japanese businesses, at least in this particular industry. Explaining this shift remains a challenge. One hypothesis would point to greater importance of R&D. It would be beneficial to compare the input shares with the R&D expenditures of these firms.

In their concluding remarks the authors reflect on the growth decomposition depicted in Figure 2.8 and argue that Japanese R&D productivity has been too low in the post-bubble period. While there is certainly some indication of this, the various drawbacks of TFP measures may call into question the robustness of these findings. At any rate I agree with the authors that the question of R&D productivity remains important for policy makers and businesses.

Perhaps the most interesting observation about the current state of the Japanese economy is the fundamental change in Japan's labour market, as made evident by the recent unprecedented increase in unemployment. Perhaps Japan is indeed entering a new phase. It will be interesting to see a continuation of the work of Nakajima, Nakamura and Yoshioka on productivity growth in light of these developments.

References

Edward E. Leamer (1994) 'Testing Trade Theory', in: D. Greenaway and L. Winters (eds), *Surveys in International Trade* (Oxford: Blackwell).

R. Nelson (1981) 'Research on Productivity Growth and Differences', *Journal of Economic Literature*, vol. XIX, pp. 1029–64.

3 Participatory Employment Practices in Japan

Takao Kato

INTRODUCTION

In many countries around the world, management systems are moving away from the traditional employment practices, which are often characterized by adversarial collective bargaining and a fixed-wage contractual payment. Prominent among the changes involved is the widespread adoption of participatory employment practices, or human resource management practices (HRMPs).[1] This chapter provides an overview of important aspects of the postwar Japanese experience with HRMPs. The discussion is in three main parts. The first reviews the scope and nature of Japanese HRMPs and their diffusion among Japanese firms over time. The second looks at the effect of such practices on company performance. The third presents some preliminary findings from our most recent research on the response of participatory employment practices to the economic slowdown of the 1990s and speculates on the future of participatory employment practices in Japan.

The postwar Japanese experience of employee participation and labour–management cooperation in the 1960s, 1970s and 1980s, and their effect on workplace productivity (and thus competitiveness), appears to be of particular public policy interest to those countries which are considering participatory employment practices in order to boost their productivity and competitiveness.

First, as Levine and Tyson (1990) suggest, the relatively higher job security (often ensured by intrafirm transfers or transfers to related firms) and strong group cohesiveness (supported by the compression of wage and status differentials) of Japanese workers in large manufacturing firms in the postwar period was favourable to successful employee participation, as was the relatively rapid and stable growth over the sample period, lower unemployment and stable financial corporate groupings (banks and institutional shareholders as long-term suppliers of capital).

Probably as a result of this favourable environment in the postwar period, particularly in manufacturing, participatory employment practices spread widely and became firmly established, as documented below. Indeed these practices became the hallmark of 'Japanese management', which has since inspired (or necessitated in some instances) many corporations in the world to experiment with employee involvement and labour–management cooperation (see for instance Levine, 1995, p. 5). In short, postwar Japan (particularly in the case of manufacturing) clearly provides one of the most important examples of experimentation with HRMPs.

The economic slowdown in the 1990s, the recent banking crisis and the rapidly aging workforce have allegedly eroded that favourable environment. Did the participatory employment practices that were so successful from the 1960s to the 1980s survive into the 1990s? If so, how did they evolve to cope with the new environment? Were there any differences between sectors in the survival of participatory employment practices? A closer look at the recent Japanese experience will help us to understand better two key questions on participation: (1) what are the conditions under which participatory employment practices are best introduced and sustained; and (2) in what way do such practices need to evolve when the external environment changes? To address these questions we have analyzed recent data on some of these practices.

The chapter is organized as follows. The next section discusses the scope and nature of participatory employment practices in postwar Japan and their diffusion over time. The third section summarizes theoretical arguments about the effects of these practices on company performance, in particular labour productivity, and reviews the evidence on such effects. The fourth section presents our findings on the response of participatory employment practices to the economic slowdown of the 1990s.

THE SCOPE, NATURE AND DIFFUSION OF PARTICIPATORY EMPLOYMENT PRACTICES IN JAPAN

Joint labour–management committees: information sharing at the top

One of the core mechanisms in labour–management relations in large Japanese firms is the joint labour–management committee (JLMC).

Established at the top level (corporate and/or establishment) and involving both management and union representatives, JLMCs serve as a mechanism for information sharing on a large variety of issues, ranging from basic business policies to working conditions. Unlike German works councils, the establishment of JLMCs is voluntary rather than obligatory under Japanese law. In companies where unions exist the labour representatives are almost always union members, and in the absence of unions the majority of labour representatives are elected by employee vote (about 70 per cent, Koike, 1978). Thus labour JLMC members usually legitimately represent the interests of the firm's workforce.

According to Shimada (1992), JLMCs were one of the many labour–management institutions proposed at the beginning of 1950s by the Japan Productivity Center. After a decade of tumultuous labour–management relations between 1945 and 1955, Japanese unions and management, with the endorsement of the central government, began to introduce a number of well-known human resource management techniques, including JLMCs and biannual bonus payments to all employees. According to Kato and Morishima (1999), in 1950 about 20 per cent of all manufacturing and non-manufacturing firms had functioning JLMCs, and by 1970 the figure had risen to nearly 60 per cent. Over the next two decades the institution continued to grow steadily, and as of 1993 80 per cent of all firms had a JLMC.

Many observers attribute the peaceful labour relations that can be observed in Japanese firms to the establishment of JLMCs (Shimada, 1992; Inagami, 1988), which meet about once a month to discuss a number of issues, ranging from basic business policies to social and athletic activities sponsored by the firm (see Kato and Morishima, 1999). According to a survey conducted by the Ministry of Labour in 1985 (reported in Inagami, 1988), firms use JLMCs for information sharing on a wide variety of issues. In particular, more than 60 per cent of firms use them to pass on basic management decisions such as business strategies and production and sales plans. However in many cases the degree of employee influence over these issues is small: almost 79 per cent of firms share information but do not go any further. Conversely, for issues relating to employment conditions (such as working hours, holidays, wages, bonuses, redundancies and employment adjustments) a large proportion of firms allow employee representatives to participate in joint decision making. For example, among those firms that discuss wage and employment security issues in the JLMC arena, more than 87 per cent consult the labour representatives prior to finalising their plans. Thus for direct labour issues, JLMCs appear to go beyond simple information sharing and serve a labour–management consultation function and occasionally even involve joint decision making.

Shop-floor committees: information sharing at the grass roots

As well as JLMCs and formal trade unions, many Japanese corporations have shop-floor committees (SFCs), in which supervisors and employees on the shop floor discuss issues such as their department's operations and environment. Although some have stressed the potentially important role of SFCs in the Japanese industrial relations system (see for instance Koike, 1978), the nature and scope of SFCs have not been studied extensively, largely due to the absence of reliable data. A recent survey conducted by Kato and Morishima (1999) reveals that the average SFC meets about nine times a year (slightly less frequently than JLMCs), and that the topics discussed during SFC meetings tend to go beyond standard shop-floor issues such as safety and health, grievance resolution, fringe benefits, training and development to include business and strategic plans. As such, SFCs are aimed at information sharing at the grass roots level.

Kato and Morishima (ibid.) have also studied the diffusion of SFCs among Japanese firms in the postwar era. In 1950 only 7 per cent of manufacturing and non-manufacturing firms had a standing SFC. This figure grew slowly to 11 per cent by the end of the decade. However in 1993 more than 40 per cent of firms claimed to have standing SFCs (in the case of manufacturing firms, more than 50 per cent).

Small group activities: teamwork

Small group activities (SGAs) include quality control (QC) circles and 'zero defects', in which small groups of volunteers at the workplace level set operational plans and goals and work together to ensure their realization. Although SGAs are now widespread (see for instance Cole, 1989), in 1950 they had been set up in only 3 per cent of firms, rising to 6 per cent in 1960. The rapid diffusion of the institution began in the 1960s, reaching 44 per cent by 1980. Since then the institution has continued to grow steadily: in 1993, 70 per cent of firms claimed to have SGAs (Kato, 1995).

SGAs are clearly more popular among larger firms (80 per cent of firms with 5000 or more employees as opposed to 43 per cent of firms with 299 or fewer) and are more wide-spread in the unionized sector (ibid.).

Employee stock ownership plans: financial participation via stock

Japanese employee stock ownership plans (ESOPs) can perhaps be best understood by comparing their main features with the better known US ESOPs. Unlike in the United States, Japanese corporations that establish an ESOP (called *mochikabukai*) do not receive any tax incentive to do so. To induce individual employees to participate in the scheme, companies offer subsidies – typically the firm provides 5–10 per cent of each employee's contribution as well as bearing the administrative costs. Whereas ESOPs elsewhere are frequently structured to encourage strong participation by top management, Japanese executives (as well as part-time and temporary employees) are normally ineligible for membership. As is the norm elsewhere, individual participants' shares in and dividends from the ESOP are held in trust. Unusually, however, participants have the right to withdraw their shares, and share withdrawals are privately owned. Permission to withdraw is normally subject to the following requirements: (1) the employee must keep at least 1000 shares in the trust; and (2) withdrawals are permitted only in blocks of 1000 shares. It takes more than 20 years for the average participant to accumulate the 2000 shares required to withdraw the designated 1000. While members are free to exit completely from the ESOP, reentry is restricted. Exiting employees receive their shares in blocks of 1000 and must sell the remaining shares to the trust at the prevailing market price. Upon retirement, the rules governing most ESOPs require the retiree to exit completely from the ESOP. Finally, a general director (*rijicho*) is appointed to represent the stockholders. The general director is elected by the other participants on a one-person, one-vote basis. At the general meeting of shareholders, the general director votes on behalf of the shares held by the plan, deciding independently, and hence does not necessarily represent the majority opinion of the employee participants. The general director must be a participant in the ESOP and hence is not a company executive (Jones and Kato, 1995).

ESOPs are relatively new; moreover, they are the most rapidly diffused innovation among the various Japanese HRMPs (Kato and

Morishima, 1999). In 1960 the proportion of firms offering an ESOP was only 4 per cent, but this had reached 26 per cent by 1970. In 1967 a special government committee on foreign capital advocated employee ownership as a way of helping to prevent foreign takeovers of domestic firms and firms were duly encouraged to set up ESOP trusts. While the fear of foreign takeovers diminished in the 1970s, the idea of employee ownership had taken root. Perhaps partly due to this government initiative, the 1970s were characterized by an astonishingly rapid diffusion of the scheme, and by 1980 over two thirds of firms offered ESOPs. By 1993 it had become an almost universal phenomenon – 97 per cent of firms reported having an ESOP, and there was no significant difference between manufacturing and non-manufacturing firms.

In 1993 almost 50 per cent of the labour force in firms with ESOPs were participating in the scheme (ibid.). Jones and Kato (1995) report that in 1988 the combined ESOP stock was worth 4.1 trillion yen (about $32 billion), or 1.7 million yen (about $14000) per participant. However according to Jones and Kato the schemes do not involve a large proportion of company stock. For listed companies the average percentage of stock owned by ESOPs varied between 0.66 per cent and 1.42 per cent in the period 1973–88. In 1988 the average was lower than 1 per cent and holdings over 5 per cent were rare.

Profit sharing plans: financial participation via bonuses

Profit sharing plans (PSPs) are a bonus payment system in which the total amount of bonuses are linked to a measure of firm performance, such as profit. The Japanese bonus payment system has attracted considerable attention and controversy (see Freeman and Weitzman, 1987; Hart and Kawasaki, 1995; Hashimoto, 1990; Nakamura and Nakamura, 1989). In light of the ongoing debate between those who stress the profit sharing aspect of the Japanese bonus system (for example Freeman and Weitzman, 1987) and those who downplay it (for example Brunello, 1991; Ohashi, 1989), we shall consider only the least controversial system, that is, a bonus payment system backed by a formal contract stipulating the existence of a profit-sharing plan.

According to Kato and Morishima (1999), one in four firms had a PSP in 1993 (there was no appreciable difference between manufacturing and non-manufacturing firms). The proportion of firms with a PSP was only 5 per cent in 1960, but it grew steadily and had reached 14 per cent by 1980. Significant growth occurred during the

1980s, with the proportion of firms with PSPs growing to over 20 per cent by 1990.

PSPs are more prevalent in smaller firms. For instance only 11 per cent of firms with 5000 or more employees had a PSP. The large majority (70 per cent) of firms with a PSP reported separate profit-sharing plans for company officers which are different from plans for non-officer employees. However Japanese PSPs do not normally distinguish between union and non-union members (only one third of firms with PSPs had separate PSPs for union and non-union members). PSPs are mostly company-wide and only 12 per cent of firms with PSPs have separate plans for different divisions and occupations. Moreover, nearly all Japanese PSPs are cash plans (98 per cent), which is in sharp contrast to the United States, where deferred plans are more popular (see Kruse 1993, pp. 16–17). Being cash plans, these PSPs have no tax advantage.

The majority of Japanese PSPs (55 per cent) do not have a set formula (or are fully discretionary) for how the contribution should be tied to profits, which is also in contrast to PSPs in the United States, where only 22 per cent are fully discretionary (ibid., p. 75).

THE EFFECTS OF PARTICIPATORY EMPLOYMENT PRACTICES

In general, formal economic theory is ambiguous as to the expected effect of participatory employment practices on productivity and firm performance (for a review, see the essays in Blinder, 1990). Focusing on individual motivation and performance, however, several hypotheses predict positive effects, of which goal alignment effects and human capital effects are perhaps the most important. In addition, there are a few hypotheses concerning the complementarities among HRMPs.

The goal alignment effects of HRMPs

We shall first consider financial participation plans as they are the easiest example with which to show how the goal alignment effects arise. PSPs help align the interests of the firm with the interests of its employees by linking employees' pay to firm performance. Likewise the most direct positive effects of ESOPs result from the firm's success being reflected in a higher price for its equity, and thus higher rewards for its employees. In such cases the interests of the firm are closely aligned with the interests of its employees.

These interest alignment effects of financial participation can be expected to be more significant in Japan than in the United States. First, Japanese firms do not receive a tax incentive to establish PSPs or ESOPs. In this sense, Japanese firms' intentions when introducing financial participation can be interpreted by their employees as more 'genuinely participatory' than in the United States. Second, concerning ESOPs, Japanese executives are normally ineligible for ESOPs whereas ESOPs in the United States are often structured to encourage strong participation by top management (Jones and Kato, 1995). Furthermore US ESOPs are frequently designed to prevent participation by groups of non-executive employees, especially union members (Blasi, 1988). But in Japan typically all full-time non-executive employees are eligible for membership and, based on our interviews with the managers of several Japanese manufacturing corporations, it appears that blue-collar workers actively participate in ESOPs. Third, with regard to PSPs, as Kruse (1993) shows, cash plans tend to have a greater productivity effect than deferred plans, and plans without set formula (and therefore based on trust) tend to do better than other plans. As discussed above, almost all Japanese PSPs are cash plans and a substantially higher proportion of Japanese PSPs than US PSPs lack a set formula. Lastly, the average ESOP participant owns a substantial amount of stock, worth $14 000 dollars on average.

The goal alignment effects of information sharing and employee involvement via JLMCs, SFCs and SGAs are more subtle, but not necessarily weaker. First, information sharing and employee involvement are expected to reduce information asymmetry between labour and management and thus avoid the development of adversarial labour–management relations. In labour–management relations in general, employers have more information about the status of the firm and business strategies. Workers, under the usual collective bargaining arrangements, have no means of obtaining such information except by resorting to hard bargaining, often coupled with the threat of strikes (Tracy, 1986). Such behaviour on the part of unions and employees may lead to adversarial labour relations, which in turn, may have a negative effect on productivity. Voluntary information sharing by management via such mechanism as JLMCs and SFCs is likely to reduce the cost of information asymmetry and have a positive effect on productivity.

Second, employers may voluntarily share information to enhance worker loyalty (Kleiner and Bouillon, 1991) and cooperation.

Enhanced worker loyalty and cooperative behaviour are predicted to have a positive effect on productivity. In economic terms, sharing information that hitherto has been restricted to owners and top management is likely to lead to goal alignment and trust between labour and management. Better informed workers, via JLMCs and SFCs, while still striving for their own goals, are more likely to be convinced that it is in their interest to cooperate with management and improve productivity and firm performance. They may see more clearly the connection between their own behavior and the improvement of benefits through firm prosperity.

Also, information sharing is likely to curtail opportunistic behaviour on the part of management and increase the labour force's trust in management. Where the interdependence between labour and management is likely to continue into the future, the provision of business information is likely to enable labour to detect managerial deception and curtail opportunistic behaviour. All this is likely to have a favourable effect on productivity.

The human capital effects of HRMPs

JLMCs, SFCs and SGAs play the important role of providing employees with a voice in the firm, thus reducing the exit rate and retaining human capital.[2] In the absence of unions, these arrangements may be the sole means by which employees are given a voice, while in the presence of unions they may act as a supplementary mechanism. Also, in order to own shares the average participant in a Japanese ESOP must stay with the firm for a significant number of years (Jones and Kato, 1995). This can be expected to discourage employee turnover and promote the formation of more firm-specific human capital.

The complementary effects of HRMPs

Information sharing and financial participation are likely to have a positive effect on productivity through goal alignment, with financial participation directly aligning employees' and management's goals, and information sharing indirectly aligning the two parties' goals by modifying employee perceptions and expectations about management behaviour. Three specific mechanisms have been proposed. First, as Levine and Tyson (1990, p. 209) argue, financial participation schemes must provide financial rewards for employees' continued participation in information sharing. Information sharing to induce employee cooperation is not likely to be effective in the long term in the absence of tangible rewards, since employees may lose interest in being cooperative and become less loyal.

Second, an important precondition for a successful financial participation scheme is that employees trust the management to be honest when reporting the status of the firm to both employees and outside markets. For its part the management, by voluntarily sharing financial and other business information, knows that such information may be used to discipline its own behaviour and is therefore less likely to engage in deceptive and opportunistic behaviour in respect of the financial participation scheme.

Third, Weitzman and Kruse (1990, p. 100) argue that profit sharing can only work in the absence of the free rider problem. Arguably the free rider problem is alleviated when workers develop a strong long-term commitment to the company and engage in active peer monitoring. As discussed above, information sharing can be thought of a mechanism to facilitate the development of a long-term commitment to the firm.

Discussions on the complementarities between HRMPs often neglect potentially important complementarities between participation at the top level and participation at the grass roots level. It is quite possible that information sharing at the former level without information sharing at the latter will result in a significant gap between labour representatives (often union officials) and the rank and file in terms of their sense of goal alignment with management. This gap may not only reduce the overall goal alignment between labour and management but also create a complex coordination problem between management, labour leaders and the rank and file. Apathy, a sense of alienation and reduced morale among the rank and file may result.

In addition, as Koike (1978, p. 196) suggests, information sharing at the grass roots level may complement information sharing at the top-level by providing a forum for top-level information to be disseminated to the rank and file. For instance, as discussed above, SFCs facilitate the sharing of information not only on standard shop-floor issues but also on the business and corporate strategic plans discussed during JLMC meetings.

The evidence

In spite of the importance of the postwar Japanese experience with HRMPs there has been little systematic investigation of their economic effects.[3] With regard to financial participation, the Japanese bonus payment system has attracted considerable attention and controversy, in particular the claim that it is a form of PSP. Earlier studies focused on the effects on employment of the bonus payment system. Freeman and Weitzman (1987) used industry-level aggregate data to reveal statistically significant positive correlations between bonuses and employment level. However Brunello (1991) used firm-level micro data and found no statistically significant positive correlations between bonuses and employment level for the electrical machinery, car and steel industries.[4] More recent studies turned to the issue of the productivity effects of the bonus payment system. Jones and Kato (1995) used firm-level panel data and found that there is a modest productivity gain from the bonus system. Ohkusa and Ohtake (1997) found that firms with a statistically significant positive correlation between wages and per capita profit are 9 per cent more productive than firms without such a correlation. For ESOPs, Jones and Kato (1995) used firm-level panel data and found that the introduction of an ESOP leads to a 4–5 per cent increase in productivity but that this productivity pay-off does not appear immediately.

For the economic effects of information sharing at the top level, Morishima (1991a, 1991b) used firm-level micro data and found statistically significant positive correlations between the extent of information sharing through JLMCs and productivity, and statistically significant correlations between stronger JLMCs and shorter and smoother wage negotiations. More recently Tsuru and Morishima (1999) used two unique data sets, one from a survey of firms and the other from a survey of employees, and found positive correlations between the presence of JLMCs and the strength of 'employee voice.'

Unfortunately there is no micro data on Japanese firms, especially panel data providing information on *groups* of HRMPs such as JLMCs, SFCs, SGAs, ESOPs and PSPs. The lack of such data has severely limited the ability to study the effects of financial participation schemes and information sharing practices of Japanese firms simultaneously.[5] This weakness in the available empirical evidence is especially troublesome since several authors have recently developed and investigated the hypothesis that some HRMPs may be more effective when used in combination with other HRMPs.[6] Furthermore no study has been able to distinguish information sharing at the grass roots level (SFCs) from information sharing at the top level (JLMCs).

It is against this backdrop of limited data that we conceived the idea of a survey of Japanese firms (the HRM Survey of Japanese Firms), from which such panel data could be assembled. The survey was undertaken in collaboration with Professor Morishima at Keio University's Economic Observatory during the summer of 1993. The sample was obtained from Toyo Keizai (1993), which provides a list of all firms listed in Japan's three major stock exchanges: Tokyo, Osaka and Nagoya. In 1993 there were 2127 firms listed in those three exchanges.[7]

The survey was preceded by a pilot phase in which an earlier version of the instrument was tested on the human resource managers of several firms as well as on researchers from the Japan Institute of Labor, the Japan Productivity Center and the Japan Securities Research Institute, each of which had conducted similar but smaller surveys in the past. On the basis of what we learned from this, the questionnaire was revised. The final version of the questionnaire was mailed to the director of HR/personnel (*Jinji Bucho*) of all 2127 firms using the addresses listed in the Toyo Keizai in August 1993.

We received usable responses from 371 firms (a response rate of 17 per cent), of which 226 were manufacturing firms (a response rate of 20 per cent for manufacturing alone). The 17 per cent response rate was comparable to most prior surveys of a similar nature in Japan.[8] We did attempt to prompt the non-respondents by phone but our efforts were largely unsuccessful.

To study the representativeness of our sample we compared the proportion of firms with HRMPs in our sample with the proportion in the general population. Such comparisons are usually not feasible due to the absence of data on the population as a whole. Fortunately, however, insofar as ESOPs are concerned all the firms listed on Japan's stock exchanges respond to the Survey of Stock Distribution, which has been conducted annually since 1973 by the National Conference Board of Securities Exchanges. Using the Survey of Stock Distribution we calculated that 95 per cent of all listed firms had ESOPs in 1993. Reassuringly the corresponding figure for our sample was 97 per cent. Moreover we also found that the rate of participation of employees in ESOPs in 1993 was about 50 per cent both in our sample and in the general population.

With regard to JLMCs, SFCs and PSPs, pertinent information on the general population was not available, and thus a strict comparison between our sample and the population was not possible. Nevertheless we did find that close to 20 per cent of the firms in our sample had a PSP in 1985 and that this figure was comparable to that reported by a large governmental survey (the General Survey of Wages and Hours Worked System) in the same year. Finally, about 77 per cent of the firms in our sample had a functioning JLMC in 1988, a figure quite similar to that reported in a large governmental survey by the Ministry of Labour (the Survey of Labour–Management Communications in the same year.[9]

Kato and Morishima (1999) merged data from this new survey with corporate proxy statement data to create for the first time a panel data set for Japanese manufacturing firms that would provide information on JLMCs, SFCs, ESOPs and PSPs. The data were then used to estimate production functions augmented by variables to capture the effects of these HRMPs.[10]

Kato and Morishima found evidence of the importance of introducing groups of HRMPs in the following three areas: (1) information sharing at the top level; (2) information sharing at the grass roots level; and (3) financial participation. Specifically, moving from the traditional system of no HRMPs to a highly participatory system with HRMPs in all three areas leads to a significant 8–9 per cent increase in productivity.[11] The full productivity effect is, however, felt only after a fairly long developmental phase (seven years). However they could find no evidence of significant productivity gains being achieved by changing from the traditional system to any intermediate system that lacks HRMPs in any one of the three key areas.

Their findings suggest that the goal alignment process needs to be supported by both direct methods (financial participation) and indirect ones (information sharing). Furthermore, information sharing needs to take place not only at the top level but also at the grass roots level. In other words the goal alignment process works best when the interests of the two parties are aligned through financial participation and when this interest alignment is facilitated by mechanisms at both the top level and the grass roots level; this curtails opportunistic behaviour.

Kato and Morishima's (1999) findings also point to the importance of a long-term perspective in evaluating the success of HRMPs. First, it does take time for the goal alignment process to take root. It is highly unlikely that instituting a HRMP will instantly lead to the alignment of interests among groups of employees within the firm.[12] Furthermore there is substantial 'learning by doing' in the evolution of HRMPs. HRMPs 'mature' over time, and only matured HRMPs tend to yield significant productivity gains.

EVOLVING PRACTICES IN THE 1990s

The economic slowdown in the 1990s (in particular the financial crisis) and the rapidly aging workforce have allegedly eroded Japan's participation-friendly employment environment. Did the participatory employment practices that were so successful in the 1960s to 1980s survive into the 1990s? If so, how have they been evolving to deal with the new environment? Have there been any differences between sectors in the survival of participatory employment practices? An examination of the recent Japanese experience with these practices will help us to gain a better understanding of two important questions about participation: (1) under which conditions are participatory employment practices best introduced and sustained; and (2) in what way do participatory employment practices need to evolve when the external environment changes? To address these questions we have analyzed more recent data on participatory employment practices in Japan, and in this section we shall report some of our first findings on the evolving practices of ESOPs and JLMCs in the 1990s.

ESOPs

As noted above, the National Conference Board of Securities Exchanges conducts annual surveys of stock distribution, to which all firms listed on Japan's stock exchanges respond. The National Conference Board has recently released summary tables from its 1997 survey. Using these and earlier tables we created Figures 3.1–3.3.[13] Figure 3.1 shows the evolution of ESOPs in Japan between 1979 and 1997.

In the 1980s the share prices of most large corporations in Japan rose steadily. It is not too surprising under such a steady growth of corporate profitability that ESOPs gained increasing popularity in Japan. Thus, as shown in Figure 3.1, both the proportion of firms with ESOPs and the ESOP participation rate (the proportion of employees who participate in ESOPs) grew steadily in the 1980s. Moreover the real market value of the shares owned by ESOPs more than quadrupled and the real market value of shares per participant (the real value of the average stake) more than doubled. According to the National Conference Board the average price of shares owned by ESOPs (the total market value of the shares owned by ESOPs divided by the total number of these shares) tripled in the 1980s.

60

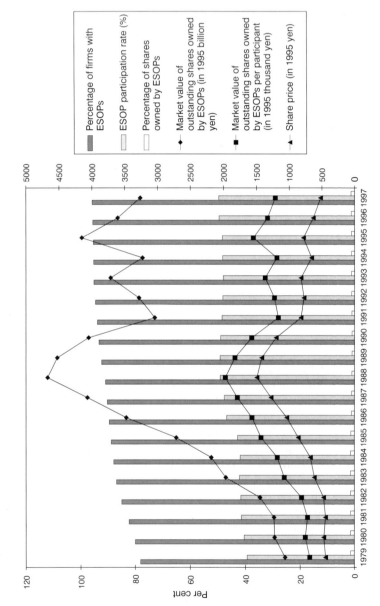

Figure 3.1 ESOPs in Japan, 1979–97

The steady growth of share prices ended rather abruptly at the end of the 1980s, and in the early 1990s the average firm listed in the Tokyo Stock Exchange lost more than half its value (Kang and Stulz, 1998). Accordingly the real market value of the shares owned by ESOPs, the real value of the average stake and the real value of the average price of the shares also fell sharply. As shown in Figure 3.1, recovery from this sharp drop has been slow.

The natural question to ask at this point is whether this powerful adverse shock discouraged employees from participating in ESOPs. Figure 3.1 reveals a surprisingly calm response on the part of the participants – the participation rate did not fall significantly in the 1990s, although the steady increase of the 1980s did level out in the 1990s at 49 per cent. It is not clear, however, whether this was caused by the adverse financial shocks. At any rate there was no sign of a frenzied exit of participants in response to these shocks.

Consistent with this relatively calm response by employees, very few employers terminated their ESOPs. Thus, as shown in Figure 3.1, the proportion of firms with ESOPs did not fall in the 1990s and ESOPs have continued to be a nearly universal phenomenon among publicly traded firms in Japan (95 per cent of all publicly traded firms have ESOPs).

In addition to the summary tables for all publicly traded firms, the National Conference Board also publishes summary tables for two-digit industries. Conceivably the adverse shock might have hit certain industries particularly hard, and in these cases ESOPs might have been terminated and the ESOP participation rate might have fallen significantly. However, as shown in Figure 3.2, there is no evidence of this happening in terms of the termination of ESOPs, although the participation rate (Figure 3.3) fell a small extent between 1988 and 1995 in mining, textiles, steel, primary metals, transportation equipment, communications, wholesale and retail trade, finance and insurance, real estate and services. Somewhat surprisingly the ESOP participation rate actually rose substantially over the same time period in a few industries, in particular oil and coal, land transportation, water transportation and transportation by air.

JLMCs

Figures 3.4–3.11 employ data from the 1995 and 1988 Survey of Labour–Management Communications, conducted by the Ministry of Labour.[14] Figure 3.4 shows how the proportion of establishments

62

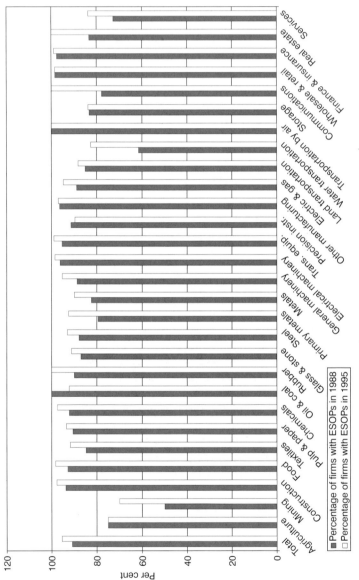

Figure 3.2 Changes in the proportion of firms with ESOPs, by industry, 1988–95

63

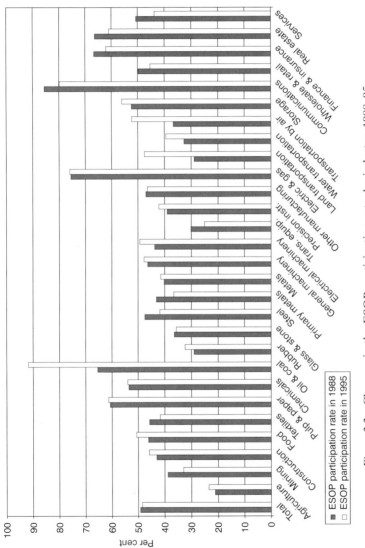

Figure 3.3 Changes in the ESOP participation rate, by industry, 1988–95

with JLMCs changed between 1988 and 1995. Overall, as in the case of ESOPs, the proportion of establishments with JLMCs did not fall significantly during this period. In other words the economic slow-down in general and the banking crisis in particular did not cause a significant dismantling of JLMCs.

Again, conceivably the adverse shock might have hit certain sectors particularly hard and prompted the dismantling of JLMCs. To see if this is was the case, we repeated the same analysis for establishments in different industries, firms of differing size, and firms with and without a union. As shown in Figure 3.4, the proportion of establishments with JLMCs declined noticeably in mining, services, transportation and communications, as well as in non-unionized sectors, although it would be premature to view this an early sign of the crumbling of JLMCs in these sectors.

The absence of evidence of the formal dissolution of JLMCs is probably not too surprising as Japanese firms are more likely to make them dormant by changing their characteristics (for example drastically reducing the frequency of meetings and trivializing the content of information shared) than to dissolve them. Figure 3.5 shows the average number of JLMC meetings per year in 1988 and 1995. The total frequency of JLMC meetings fell substantially from 14 times a year to nine times a year during the period in question. It appears that when news is consistently bad, JLMCs meet much less frequently. The figure also shows a considerable difference between sectors. For example JLMCs in transportation and communications held JLMC meetings 25 times a year in 1988 but only 11 times a year in 1995. The decrease in finance, insurance and real estate was from 11 times a year in 1988 to six times a year in 1995. JLMCs in larger and unionized firms also experienced a sharp drop in the frequency of meetings between 1988 and 1995.

Case histories of Japanese JLMCs suggest that they tend to function well if there are a number of specialized subcommittees, such as those dealing with productivity on health and safety (Japan Productivity Center, 1990). As Figure 3.6 shows, the total average number of special subcommittees declined from 3.3 in 1988 to 2.8 in 1995. There were some differences between sectors, for example sharp drops occurred in manufacturing and services, and in non-unionized sectors.

A possible way of weakening information sharing is to undermine the democratic process of selecting employee representatives. In unionized establishments the democratic selection of employee represent-atives is typically ensured by union representatives participating

65

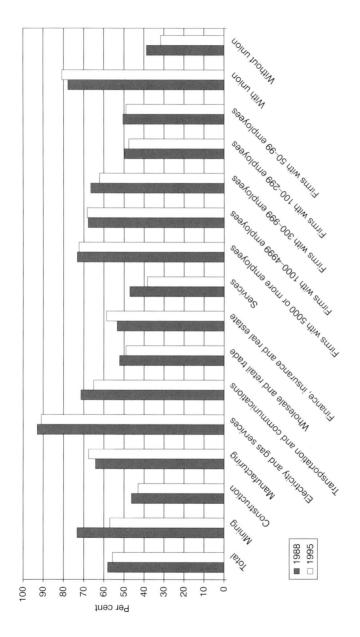

Figure 3.4 Proportion of establishments with JLMCs, 1988 and 1995

66

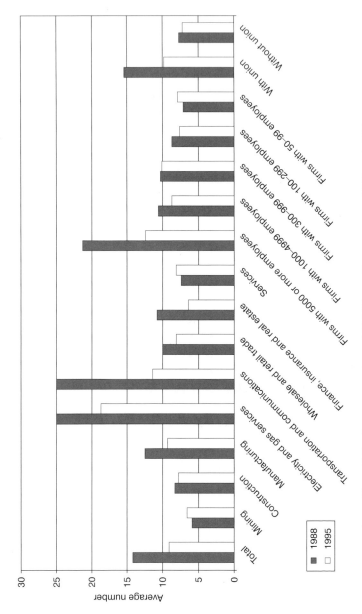

Figure 3.5 Average number of JLMC meetings per year, 1988 and 1995

67

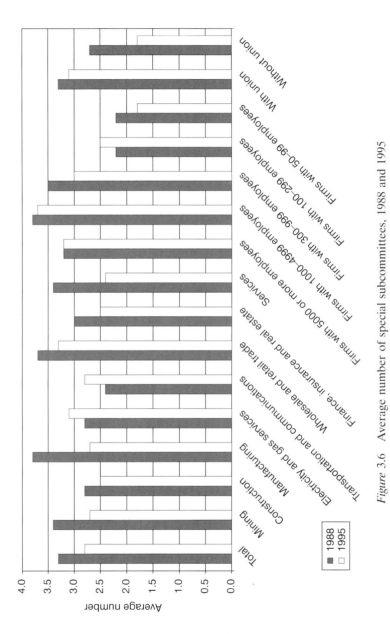

Figure 3.6 Average number of special subcommittees, 1988 and 1995

Average number

- 1988
- 1995

Total
Mining
Construction
Manufacturing
Electricity and gas services
Transportation and communications
Wholesale and retail trade
Finance, insurance and real estate
Services
Firms with 5000 or more employees
Firms with 1000–4999 employees
Firms with 300–999 employees
Firms with 100–299 employees
Firms with 50–99 employees
With union
Without union

in JLMCs as employee representatives. In non-union establishments it is normally ensured through employee elections. Figure 3.7 shows the proportion of unionized establishments in which union representatives participated in JLMCs as employee representatives in 1988 and 1995, and the proportion of non-union establishments with JLMCs in which employee representatives were elected by employees. There is no sign of erosion of the democratic selection of employee representatives over this period.

The nature of information sharing varies considerably, depending on (1) the type of information shared (for example information on business and strategic plans, such as sales and production plans and the introduction of new technology/equipment, as compared with labour issues such as layoffs, working hours, wages and bonuses, fringe benefits and cultural activities/sports), and (2) the nature of the consultation process (for instance whether labour representatives are merely informed or are asked for their prior consent). The Survey of Labour–Management Communication selects certain issues, such as basic business strategies, corporate restructuring, layoffs and mandatory retirement, and asks each establishment with JLMCs whether it discusses these issues during its JLMC meetings, and if so, whether the management asks the employee representatives for their prior consent.

We selected six issues that are of particular relevance to the economic slowdown in the 1990s, and especially the financial crisis. Figure 3.8 shows the proportion of unionized establishments with JLMCs that discussed each of these six issues (corporate restructuring, hiring and staffing, transfer of employees, layoffs, mandatory retirement and severance pay/pension) in 1988 and 1995. Figure 3.9 shows the same figures for non-unionized establishments, and Figures 3.10 and 3.11 show the proportion of union and non-union establishments with JLMCs that discussed each of these six issues and asked employee representatives for their prior consent in 1988 and 1995.

For both unionized and non-unionized establishments, as shown in Figures 3.8 and 3.9, JLMCs were slightly more likely to discuss the transfer of employees and layoffs in 1995 than they were in 1988. For unionized establishments, JLMCs were slightly more likely to discuss mandatory retirement and severance pay/pension in 1995 than they were in 1988, and slightly less likely to discuss corporate restructuring and hiring and staffing in 1995 than in 1988. The opposite took place in non-unionized establishments. Overall it is unclear whether JLMCs

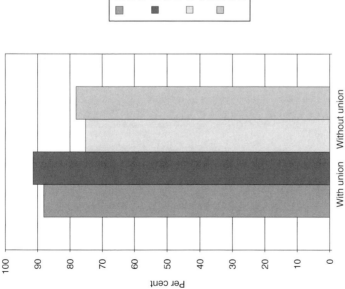

Figure 3.7 Employee representatives in firms with and without unions, 1988 and 1995

70

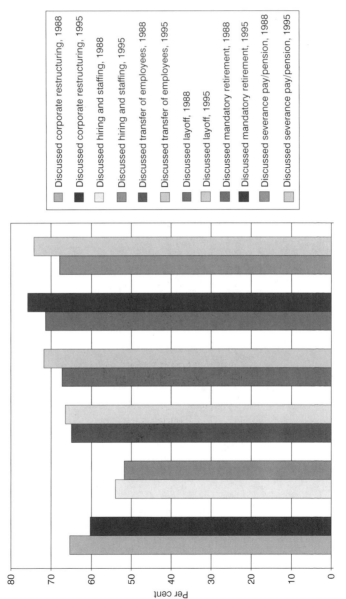

Legend:
- Discussed corporate restructuring, 1988
- Discussed corporate restructuring, 1995
- Discussed hiring and staffing, 1988
- Discussed hiring and staffing, 1995
- Discussed transfer of employees, 1988
- Discussed transfer of employees, 1995
- Discussed layoff, 1988
- Discussed layoff, 1995
- Discussed mandatory retirement, 1988
- Discussed mandatory retirement, 1995
- Discussed severance pay/pension, 1988
- Discussed severance pay/pension, 1995

Per cent

Figure 3.8 Proportion of unionized establishments with JLMCs that discussed restructuring and other relevant issues, 1988 and 1995

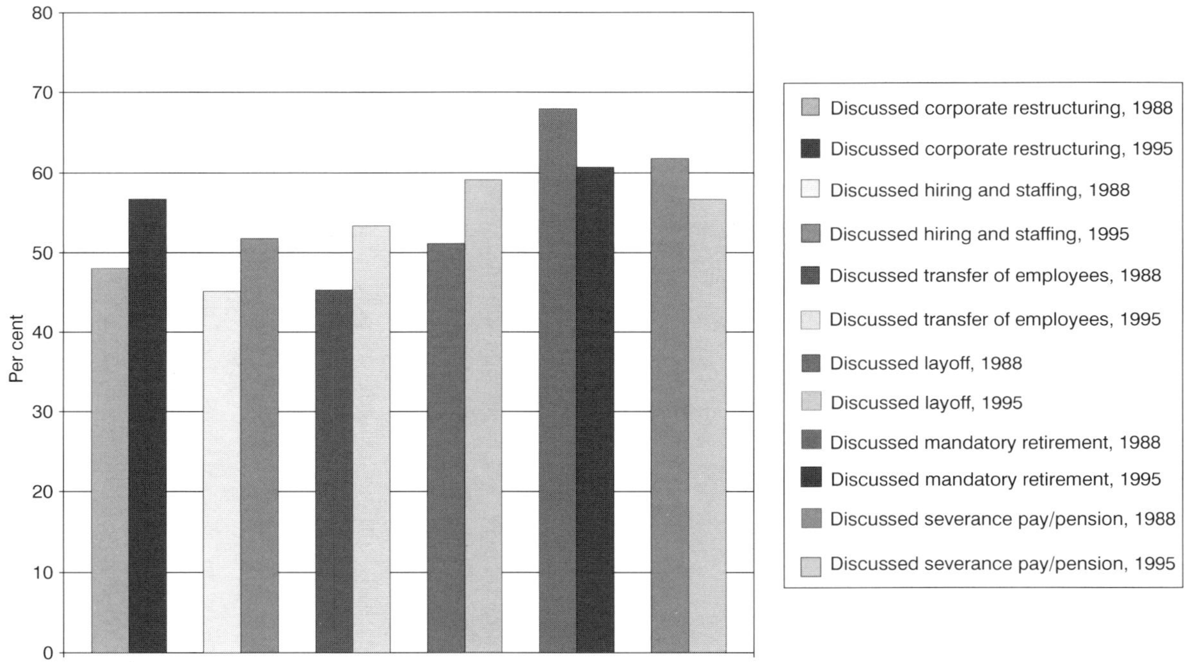
80
70
60
50
40
30
20
10
0
Per cent
Discussed corporate restructuring, 1988
Discussed corporate restructuring, 1995
Discussed hiring and staffing, 1988
Discussed hiring and staffing, 1995
Discussed transfer of employees, 1988
Discussed transfer of employees, 1995
Discussed layoff, 1988
Discussed layoff, 1995
Discussed mandatory retirement, 1988
Discussed mandatory retirement, 1995
Discussed severance pay/pension, 1988
Discussed severance pay/pension, 1995

Figure 3.9 Proportion of non-unionized establishments with JLMCs that discussed restructuring and other relevant issues, 1988 and 1995

were more or less likely to discuss issues of topical relevance in 1995 than in 1988.

Nevertheless, when one takes a closer look at the nature of consultations on each of these six issues, a noteworthy difference between unionized and non-unionized establishments is revealed. As shown in Figure 3.10, JLMCs in unionized establishments that discussed the transfer of employees, layoffs, mandatory retirement and severance pay/pension were more likely to ask employee representatives for their prior consent in 1995 than they were in 1988. In stark contrast, as shown in Figure 3.11, JLMCs in non-unionized establishments that discussed these issues were much less likely to ask employee representatives for their prior consent in 1995 than they were in 1988. This contrast between unionized and non-unionized establishments may indicate that unions effectively prevent JLMCs from becoming dormant by striving to maintain the strong consultative role of JLMCs. As such, unions and JLMCs may be complements rather than substitutes.

CONCLUSIONS

In this chapter we have shown that participatory employment practices were diffused widely and established firmly as a result of the favourable environment in the postwar Japanese economy, particularly in manufacturing. They have been shown to have a positive effect on company performance, although the full effects are felt only after a long developmental phase. Furthermore there exist complementarities among them, and they appear to have survived the economic slowdown of the 1990s, although subtle yet potentially important changes in their characteristics took place.

The complementarity between these participatory employment practices suggest that terminating a single practice will not only eliminate its own positive effect but also reduce the positive effects of other practices. In the extreme case, the termination of a single practice may cause the whole system of employee participation and labour–management cooperation to grind to a halt. For example it was found that the goal alignment process needs to be supported by both direct methods (financial participation) and indirect ones (information sharing). Removing financial participation will cause information sharing to be ineffective, and vice versa. Furthermore, it is necessary for information sharing to take place not only at the top level but also at the grass roots level. Discontinuing information sharing

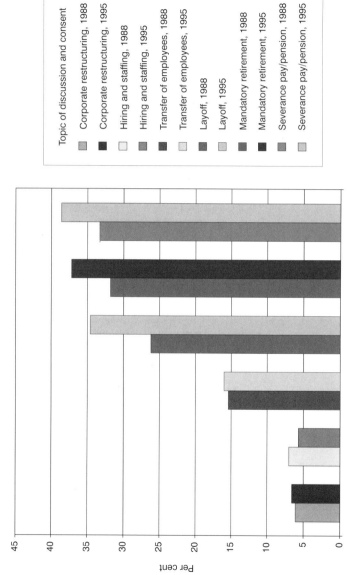

Figure 3.10 Proportion of unionized establishments with JLMCs that discussed restructuring and other relevant issues and asked employee representatives for prior consent, 1988 and 1995

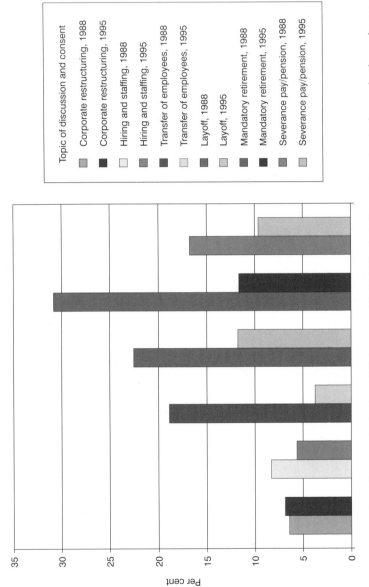

Key (top to bottom):
Topic of discussion and consent
Corporate restructuring, 1988
Corporate restructuring, 1995
Hiring and staffing, 1988
Hiring and staffing, 1995
Transfer of employees, 1988
Transfer of employees, 1995
Layoff, 1988
Layoff, 1995
Mandatory retirement, 1988
Mandatory retirement, 1995
Severance pay/pension, 1988
Severance pay/pension, 1995

Figure 3.11 Proportion of non-unionized establishments with JLMCs that discussed restructuring and other relevant issues and asked employee representatives for prior consent, 1988 and 1995

at the grass roots level will cause information sharing at the top level to be ineffective, and vice versa.

Moreover research points to the importance of a long-term perspective in evaluating the success of participatory employment practices. Coupled with this the complementarity between these practices probably means that individual Japanese employment practices are more enduring than the popular cry of 'the end of Japanese employment practices' suggests. In essence, Japanese firms appear to have responded to the economic slowdown and the financial crisis by fine-tuning the existing practices, not by dismantling them.

Notes

1. See, for instance, Commission on the Future of Worker–Management Relations (1994) and Levine (1995).
2. In the context of trade unions, this argument was first developed by Freeman (1976).
3. In the case of US corporations, however, there is a growing body of evidence. See for example Ichniowski *et al.* (1997), Freeman *et al.* (1997), Black and Lynch (1997), Freeman and Kleiner (1998), Susan Helper (1998) and the articles in a special issue of *Industrial Relations* (vol. 35, July 1996). Many of these recent studies use plant-level panel data within a narrowly defined industry. The benefits of using such data are probably less dramatic for Japan than for the United States since Japanese firms are generally substantially smaller (see for instance Kato and Rockel 1992 comparative study of the 1000 most valuable corporations in the two nations), and their management appears to be less decentralised than in US firms. Based on our interviews with human resource managers at the corporate level and top managers in marketing/sales and accounting/finance at the business unit level of Japanese and US corporations, the power of human resource department at the corporate level relative to top management at the business unit level appears to be much stronger in Japan than in the United States. In addition, as Jones and Kato (1995) and Kato and Morishima (1999) show, there are substantial lags (up to seven years) in the productivity effects of HRMPs in Japan. Plant-level data seldom provide long longitudinal data and thus may not be as useful in the context of the postwar Japanese experience as in the context of the current US experience.
4. He does find, however, a statistically significant positive correlation between bonuses and employment level for the textiles industry.
5. The lack of such data resulted in some researchers resorting to an indirect approach to identify the presence of information sharing by estimating for each firm the correlations between the profit level and the bargaining period. Thus in addition to their convincing and highly

valuable analysis of profit sharing, Ohkusa and Ohtake (1997) assume that the absence of a statistically significant correlation between profit level and bargaining period could be an indication of the presence of information sharing, and proceeded to estimate the productivity differences between firms with and without such correlations. Unfortunately the indirect nature of their approach to identifying the presence of information sharing sometimes makes it difficult to interpret their findings (for example, the productivity of firms with both information sharing and financial participation was estimated to be nearly 50 per cent higher than in other firms). Moreover their indirect approach required them to assume that the presence of profit sharing and information sharing are time-invariant, and this prevented them from using standard fixed effects models to account for the well-known problem of firm heterogeneity. The collection of new panel data that contains information on the presence of information-sharing mechanisms and financial participation schemes allows researchers to measure their presence directly and use standard fixed effects model to account for the issue of firm heterogeneity. Such data also allow researchers to differentiate between information sharing at the top level and at the grass-roots level, which has proved to be important.

6. See for instance Fitzroy and Kraft (1987), Weitzman and Kruse (1990), Levine and Tyson (1990), Jones and Pliskin (1991), Ben–Ner and Jones (1995), Kandel and Lazear (1992), Kruse (1993), Holmstrom and Milgrom (1994), Baker *et al.* (1994), Milgrom and Roberts (1995), Ichniowski *et al.* (1997), Black and Lynch (1997), Helper (1998) and articles featured in a special issue of *Industrial Relations* (vol. 35, July 1996).

7. Our sample included virtually all listed firms in Japan. The only listed firms not included in the sample were the very small number of firms listed only in other local stock exchanges (about three dozen).

8. For instance in June of 1991 the Rengo Research Institute of General Life Development mailed a questionnaire on labour conditions and information sharing to 6800 firms (both public and private) and received usable responses from 689 firms, a response rate of 10 per cent. In June 1989 the Japan Productivity Center mailed a questionnaire on HRMPs to 1030 firms in Japan and received usable responses from 203 firms, a response rate of 19.7 per cent.

9. Since the Ministry of Labour Survey is an establishment-level survey and includes many small private firms that were not included in our sample, the results are not strictly comparable to our survey results. However the survey reports the proportion of unionized establishments with JLMCs, which are probably closest to our sample. The ministry survey reported that the figure for those establishments was 77.8 per cent.

10. The survey included questions on SGAs, but unfortunately including them in the regression analysis resulted in a substantial loss of observations.

11. Although Kato and Morishima (1999) controlled for all unobserved time-invariant firm characteristics by using fixed effects, it is still pos-

sible that the estimated 8–9 per cent productivity gain might include the positive productivity effects of other employment practices that are time-variant. These practices might include small group activities such as QC circles and suggestion boxes. The omission of QC circles may not be too serious since prior evidence on the effects of QC circles in Japan seems to be at best mixed. For example Lincoln and Kalleberg (1996) used a rich and unique comparative data set for Japanese and US manufacturing plants and could find no evidence of positive effects on the commitment of employees who participate in QC circles in Japanese plants (however they did find some evidence of such effects in US plants).

12. For similar arguments see Ichniowski and Shaw (1995) and Pil and MacDuffie (1996).
13. Although the survey began in 1973, data on the market value of shares owned by ESOPs became available only in 1979. Thus our complete data on the evolution of ESOPs began with 1979.
14. Of the establishments in Japan that employ 50 or more employees, the Ministry of Labour selects 4000 and sends a researcher to each one to complete the questionnaire.

References

Baker, George, Robert Gibbons and Kevin J. Murphy (1994) 'Subjective Performance Measures in Optimal Incentive Contracts', *Quarterly Journal of Economics*, vol. 108, no. 8, pp. 1125–56.
Ben–Ner, Avner and Derek C. Jones (1995) 'Employee Participation, Ownership, and Productivity: A Theoretical Framework', *Industrial Relations*, vol. 34, no. 4, pp. 532–54.
Black, Sandra E. and Lisa M. Lynch (1997) 'How to Compete: The Impact of Workplace Practices and Information Technology on Productivity', NBER Working Paper no. 6120 (Cambridge, Mass.: NBER, August).
Blasi, Joseph R. (1988) *Employee Ownership: Revolution or Ripoff?* (Cambridge: Balinger).
Blinder, Alan S. (ed.) (1990) *Paying For Productivity* (Washington, DC: Brookings Institution).
Brunello, Giorgio (1991) 'Bonuses, Wages and Performances in Japan: Evidence from Micro Data', *Ricerche Economiche*, vol. 45, nos. 2–3, pp. 377–96.
Cole, Robert E. (1989) *Strategies for Learning: Small-Group Activities in American, Japanese, and Swedish Industry* (Berkeley, CA: University of California Press).
Commission on the Future of Worker-Management Relations (1994) *Fact Finding Report* (Washington, DC: Department of Labour).
Conte, Michael A. and Jan Svejnar (1990) 'The Performance Effects of Employee Ownership Plans', in Alan S. Blinder (ed.), *Paying For Productivity* (Washington, DC: Brookings Institution), pp. 143–72.
Fitzroy, Felix R. and Kornelius Kraft (1987) 'Cooperation, Productivity and Profit Sharing', *Quarterly Journal of Economics*, vol. 102, no. 1, pp. 23–35.

Freeman, Richard B. (1976) 'Individual Mobility and Union Voice in the Labour Market', *American Economic Review*, vol. 66, no. 2, pp. 361–8.

Freeman, Richard B. and Morris M. Kleiner (1998) 'From Piece Rates to Time Rates: Surviving Global Competition', paper presented at the Industrial Relations Research Association Meetings in Chicago, January.

Freeman, Richard B., Morris M. Kleiner and Cheri Ostroff (1997) 'The Anatomy and Effects of Employee Involvement', paper presented at the American Economic Association Meetings in New Orleans, January.

Freeman, Richard B. and Martin L. Weitzman (1987) 'Bonuses and Employment in Japan', *Journal of the Japanese and International Economies*, vol. 1, no. 2, pp. 168–94.

Hart, Robert A. and Seiichi Kawasaki (1995) 'The Japanese Bonus System and Human Capital', *Journal of the Japanese and International Economies*, vol. 9, no. 3, pp. 225–44.

Hashimoto, Masanori (1990) *The Japanese Labour Market in a Comparative Perspective with the United States* (Kalamazoo, Michigan: Upjohn Institute for Employment Research).

Helper, Susan (1998) 'Complementarity and Cost Reduction: Evidence from the Auto Supply Industry', Revised version of NBER working paper no. 6033 (Cambridge, Mass.: NBER, April).

Holmstrom, Bengt and Paul Milgrom (1994) 'The Firm as an Incentive System', *American Economic Review*, vol. 84, no. 4, pp. 972–91.

Ichniowski, Casey and Kathryn Shaw (1995) 'Old Dogs and New Tricks: Determinants of the Adoption of Productivity-Enhancing Work Practices', *Brookings Papers on Economic Activity* (Washington, DC: Brookings Institution), pp. 1–55.

Ichniowski, Casey, Kathryn Shaw and Prennushi Giovanna (1997) 'The Effects of Human Resource Management Practices on Productivity: A Study of Steel Finishing Lines', *American Economic Review*, vol. 87, no. 3, pp. 291–313.

Inagami, Takeshi (1988) *Japanese Workplace Industrial Relations*, Industrial Relations Series no. 14 (Tokyo: The Japan Institute of Labour).

Japan Productivity Center (1990) *To Improve Joint Labour Management Committees* (Roshikyogisei no Jujitsu o Motomete) (Tokyo: Japan Productivity Center).

Jones, Derek C. and Takao Kato (1993) 'On the Scope, Nature and Effects of Employee Stock Ownership Plans in Japan', *Industrial and Labour Relations Review*, vol. 46, no. 2, pp. 352–67.

Jones, Derek and Takao Kato (1995) 'The Productivity Effects of Employee Stock Ownership Plans and Bonuses: Evidence from Japanese Panel Data', *American Economic Review*, vol. 85, no. 3, pp. 391–414.

Jones, Derek C. and Jeffrey Pliskin (1991) 'The Effects of Worker Participation, Employee Ownership and Profit Sharing on Economic Performance: A Partial Review', in Raymond Russell and Veljko Rus (eds), *Ownership and Participation: International Handbook of Participation in Organizations*, vol. 2 (Oxford: Oxford University Press), pp. 43–63.

Kandel, Eugene and Edward Lazear (1992) 'Peer Pressure and Partnerships', *Journal of Political Economy*, vol. 100, no. 4, pp. 801–17.

Kang, Jun-Koo and Rene M. Stulz (1998) 'Is Bank-centered Corporate Governance Worth It? A Cross-sectional Analysis of the Performance of

Japanese Firms During the Asset Price Deflation', paper presented at the NBER Japan Project Meeting, Cambridge, Mass., 18 April.

Kato, Takao (1995) 'Cooperate to Compete. Employee Participation and Productivity: Evidence from a New Survey of Japanese Firms', Public Policy Brief, no. 19 (Annadale-on-Hudson, NY: The Jerome Levy Economics Institute, Bard College).

Kato, Takao and Motohiro Morishima (1999) 'The Productivity Effects of Participatory Employment Practices: Evidence From New Japanese Panel Data', mimeo (Colgate, NY: Department of Economics, Colgate University, May).

Kleiner, Morris M. and Bouillon L. Marvin (1991) 'Information Sharing of Sensitive Business Data with Employees', *Industrial Relations*, vol. 30, no. 3, pp. 480–91.

Koike, Kazuo (1978) *Worker Participation* (Rodosha no Keiei Sanka), (Tokyo: Nihon Hyoron Sha).

Kruse, Douglas L. (1993) *Profit Sharing: Does It Make a Difference?* (Kalamazoo, Mich.: W. E. Upjohn Institute for Employment Research).

Levine, David I. (1995) *Reinventing the Workplace* (Washington, DC: Brookings Institution).

Levine, David I. and Laura D'Andrea Tyson (1990) 'Participation, Productivity and the Firm's Environment', in Alan S. Blinder (ed.), *Paying For Productivity*, (Washington, DC: Brookings Institution), pp. 183–236.

Lincoln, James R. and Arne L. Kalleberg (1996) 'Commitment, Quits, and Work Organization in Japanese and U.S. Plants', *Industrial and Labor Relations Review*, vol. 50, no. 1, pp. 39–59.

Milgrom, Paul and John Roberts (1995) 'Complementarities and Fit: Strategy, Structure, and Organizational Change in Manufacturing', *Journal of Accounting and Economics*, vol. 19, nos. 2–3, pp. 179–208.

Morishima, Motohiro (1991a) 'Information Sharing and Firm Performance in Japan: Do Joint Consultation Committees Help?', *Industrial Relations*, vol. 30, no. 1, pp. 37–61.

Morishima, Motohiro (1991b) 'Information Sharing and Collective Bargaining in Japan: Effects on Wage Negotiations', *Industrial and Labor Relations Review*, vol. 44, no. 3, pp. 469–85.

Morishima, Motohiro (1992) 'Use of Joint Consultation Committees by Large Japanese Firms', *British Journal of Industrial Relations*, vol. 30 (September), pp. 405–23.

Nakamura, Masao and Alice Nakamura (1989) 'Risk Behavior and the Determinants of Bonus Versus Regular Pay in Japan', *Journal of the Japanese and International Economies*, vol. 3, no. 3, pp. 270–91.

Ohashi, Isao (1989) 'On the Determinants of Bonuses and Basic Wages in Large Japanese Firms', *Journal of the Japanese and International Economies*, vol. 3, no. 4, pp. 451–79.

Ohkusa, Yasushi and Fumio Ohtake (1997) 'The Productivity Effects of Information Sharing, Profit-Sharing and ESOPs', mimeo (forthcoming in *Journal of the Japanese and International Economies*).

Pil, Frits K. and John Paul MacDuffie (1996) 'The Adoption of High-Involvement Work Practices', *Industrial Relations*, vol. 35, no. 3, pp. 423–55.

Shimada, Haruo (1992) 'Japan's Industrial Culture and Labor–Management Relations', in Shumpei Kumon and Henry Rosovsky (eds), *The Political*

Economy of Japan, Volume 3: Cultural and Social Dynamics (Stanford, CA: Stanford University Press), pp. 267–91.

Toyo Keizai, (1993) *Company Data Handbook* (Kaisha Shiki Ho), (Tokyo: Toyo Keizai Shimposha).

Tracy, Joseph S. (1986) 'An Investigation into the Determinants of U.S. Strike Activity', *American Economic Review*, vol. 76, no. 3, pp. 423–36.

Tsuru, Tsuyoshi and Motohiro Morishima (1999) 'Nonunion Employee Representation in Japan', *Journal of Labor Research*, vol. 20, no. 1, pp. 93–110.

Weitzman, Martin, L. and Douglas L. Kruse (1990) 'Profit Sharing and Productivity', in Alan Blinder (ed.), *Paying For Productivity* (Washington, DC: Brookings Institution), pp. 95–140.

Comments on Chapter 3
Robert Hart

Studying the implementation of practices designed to improve information sharing among a firm's employees and to provide direct financial incentives that help achieve shared productive goals is clearly of utmost importance in the area of human resources management (HRM). Takeo Kato provides a stimulating discussion on such initiatives in Japan, where they appear to have received a somewhat higher priority than in many competing economies. In the 1970s and 1980s the growth in employee stock holding and profit sharing schemes in Japan contrasted markedly with the European experience, where progress was uneven and, in several countries, very limited (Commission of the European Communities, 1991).

Kato provides a very useful overview of the growth of Japanese participatory employment practices in the postwar expansion years and their apparent robustness during the more turbulent 1990s, as well as a summary of some related theory and empirics. A particular strength of the adopted approach is the emphasis on the potential complementarities among the various participatory systems. For example it is certainly plausible, *a priori*, that free-rider problems attached to group-based financial incentives may be mitigated by formalised small group and shop-floor activities that promote strong inter- and intragroup communications.

The virtues of participatory practices seem to be so self-evident that it may appear churlish to raise doubts about their benefits to firm performance. However a number of points are worth raising, if only to act out the devil's advocate role often expected of the discussant.

CAUSATION

The interesting discussion of postwar Japanese trends in employee stock ownership plans (ESOPs) and profit sharing plans (PSPs) unequivocally underlines their growth in importance. But have they served to enhance firm-level productivity? Jones and Kato (1995) have found that, after a 3–4 year adjustment lag, ESOPs can be

81

associated with a 4–5 per cent increase in productivity. The rules governing ESOPs in Japan suggest considerable elements of deferred entitlement. In the light of this, it is not difficult to understand that firms – faced with rapid growth, skill and organisational investments and tight labour markets – would be willing to subsidise and incur the administrative costs of ESOPs for the return of longer expected worker tenure. Nor is it difficult, against the background of such favourable growth performance, to understand workers' willingness to accept the subsidies and direct a part of their total remuneration towards stock ownership. Moreover investing in their own stock may not only represent some degree of company loyalty and solidarity but also the fact that most individuals are not sophisticated in selecting from wider investment portfolios.

But does this mean that ESOPs lead directly to productivity improvements in their own right? The ESOP–productivity connection may follow a more circuitous route. For given worker–management communication channels, companies with better performance prospects will have greater success in persuading their employees to hold company stock. Information sharing and financial participation may have complementary effects in the following manner. Wide-ranging and accurate information transfer will serve to inform the parties of planned future developments that are likely to enhance the company's productive performance. Proposed developments in organisational structure, technological and process innovations, training and retraining provisions, private employee welfare schemes (health, recreation, other private fringes) may serve as a signal to employees of higher productivity growth. This follows because employees perceive that these and other factors will impinge directly on the firm's performance, including productivity growth. Furthermore, such productivity improvement may well be viewed as arising independently of increased effort. To the extent that this holds, ESOPs may not have a direct bearing, *per se*, on productivity profiles; rather they might signal successful communication between the parties of the details of other factors that lead to productivity increases. To the extent that this is so, then ESOPs might be acting as proxies for these 'missing' influences, many of which are difficult to measure and to represent in production analysis.

It should be noted that Jones and Kato (1995) tested for (reverse) direction of causality by adding a one year lead variable ESOP dummy to their output equation. Surprisingly perhaps, this turned out to be negative and not precisely estimated, leading the authors to play down the role of reverse causality. Question marks over the precise functional links between ESOPs and productivity remain, however, and this area perhaps deserves deeper investigation.

BONUSES AND ESOPs

If anything, work on the effects of participatory employment practices serves to increase the need to determine more precisely the role of bonus payments in the Japanese firm. Bonus payments comprise over 20 per cent of total labour costs in the main two-digit Japanese industries, the proportion varying directly with firm size. As noted by Kato, the bonus may not fit neatly as an example of a participatory employment device since its profit sharing interpretation has received, at best, only limited empirical support. The bonus system almost certainly does contain elements that serve to enhance company productivity along the lines claimed for ESOPs and other participatory practices. Certainly it appears to exhibit some, albeit modest, influence on productivity (Jones and Kato, 1995). But it also serves other purposes. For example, following the seminal paper by Hashimoto (1979), there is convincing evidence of a link with human capital investment, as displayed most recently by Nakamura and Hübler (1998) for Japan, Germany and the United States. Of course returns to human capital investments are also related to labour productivity, but the form of the relationship – for instance the nature and length of its lag structure – may be considerably different from that expected from a pure profit sharing connection.

In chapter 3 Kato recognises the ongoing controversy over the interpretation of the bonus and deals only with explicit profit sharing plans (PSPs). But even here the joint provision of PSPs and ESOPs may serve to give mixed signals. The rules governing ESOPs in Japan appear to be designed to encourage long-term commitment to firm performance, while PSPs by their nature may well be perceived as representing shorter-term horizons. It is not at all clear that there would be a strong match between those employees primarily interested in receiving profit shares and those holding long-term stock.

On this last point, it is interesting to note the findings of a British study on the effects of employee participation schemes, including financial participation, on the financial performance of 657 establishments in 1990 (McNabb and Whitfield, 1998). This work indicates that establishments with both stock ownership and profit sharing schemes tend to have a *worse* financial performance than those with just one of these. It also suggests that profit sharing schemes have a strong positive impact on financial performance, but that stock ownership schemes have a positive impact (and then not strong) only where there is a downward communication scheme (between managers/supervisors and the workers for whom they are responsible) and/or no profit sharing scheme. In fact, in establishments without downward communication schemes, stock ownership schemes are negatively associated with financial performance. It seems that a key influence on these relationships is the existence of direct communication schemes (for example briefing groups, systematic use of the management chain for communication). McNabb and Whitfield's work suggests that an important influence on improved financial performance is a strengthening of the command chain, and it seems that this works best where there is an associated financial reward mechanism. The presence of upward problem solving mechanisms (for example quality circles) appears in fact to be negatively associated with financial performance. In short, this points to a rather narrow and instrumental set of linkages between employee interactions and financial performance, more akin to the discipline based efficiency wage models than the high-involvement HRM models.

ESOPs IN THE 1990s

The typical worker cannot diversify risk by providing labour services to different sectors and work organisations within the economy. For this reason ESOPs expose workers to an additional income risk (Meade, 1972). In the 1990s this risk was exposed dramatically in Japan. It is hard to know what to make of Kato's findings that ESOP participation was generally not discouraged during this period. One reason may be that, unlike normal stock transactions, exit is free but reentry is restricted. The key point, however, is that insofar as ESOPs encouraged productivity in the booming 1980s it is surely credible to suppose that they had the opposite effect, at least on some employees, in the bubble-bursting 1990s. It is not difficult to imagine that employee financial participation in a company that is performing well may lead to a greater cooperative effort. But since firms overtly induced employees to join ESOPs in the growth years, it seems almost certain that the morale and cooperative zeal of some employees will have been dampened when things started to go wrong.

It will be interesting to see how robust are the productivity effects obtained in earlier empirical studies when a reestimation is carried out on 1990s data.

PRODUCTIVITY AND MOBILITY

Estimated company-level productivity gains due to participatory employment practices may overestimate the 'true' macro-economic productivity effects. Such practices contribute to enhanced voice and reduced exit. The downside is that employees are encouraged to stay in company x instead of moving to company y, where their marginal revenue product might have been higher. Individual firms gain by ensuring that the most productive employees remain in their employment. However society gains if its best workers migrate to those industrial and commercial sectors with maximum growth and value added potential. Obviously these micro and macro goals are not always mutually consistent. Of course this type of argument stops well short of extolling the virtues of fixed wage contracts and adversarial collective bargaining as a means of stimulating a climate of efficiency-enhancing labour mobility. But it certainly points to the fact that studying productivity gains at the micro level stops short of capturing the total net macro effects.

References

Commission of the European Communities (1991) *Social Europe* (The Pepper Report: promotion of employee participation in profits and enterprise results) (Brussels: Directorate General for Social Affairs).

Hashimoto, M. (1979) 'Bonus payments, on-the-job training and lifetime employment in Japan', *Journal of Political Economy*, vol. 87, pp. 1086–104.

Jones, D. and T. Kato (1995) 'The productivity effects of employee stock ownership plans and bonuses: evidence from Japanese panel data', *American Economic Review*, vol. 85, pp. 391–414.

McNabb, R. and K. Whitfield (1998) 'The impact of financial participation and employee involvement on financial performance', *Scottish Journal of Political Economy*, vol. 45, pp. 171–87.

Meade, J. E. (1972) 'The theory of labour managed firms and profit sharing', *Economic Journal*, vol. 82, pp. 402–28.

Nakamura, M. and O. Hübler (1998) 'The bonus share of flexible pay in Germany, Japan and the US: some empirical regularities', *Japan and the World Economy*, vol. 10, pp. 221–32.

4 *Kudoka* and the Japanese Worker

Keith Head and John Ries

INTRODUCTION

Japanese multinational enterprises (MNEs) have rapidly increased their overseas production since the late 1980s. Well-known manufacturers such as Sony and Toyota now employ tens of thousands of local workers in their overseas manufacturing plants, and Matsushita has as many foreign employees as domestic employees. Outflows of direct investment from Japan was not unique to a few large firms: Japanese direct investment reached $67 billion in 1989 and accounted for roughly one-quarter of the world's foreign direct investment in the 1980s. There has been a longstanding concern that overseas investment harms domestic workers. When a firm chooses to produce goods abroad there may be a dislocation of domestic workers, leading to short-term unemployment and long-term downward pressure on wages. The phenomenon of moving manufacturing overseas has been dubbed 'hollowing out' in North America, a term translated into Japanese as *kudoka*. There are theoretical reasons, however, to question the simple logic that overseas production has adverse domestic market consequences. Indeed FDI may increase the demand for certain types of worker or even all workers.

This chapter provides evidence on the effect that outward Japanese FDI has had on wages, employment and skill upgrading in Japan. We summarize the findings of Head and Ries (1994) on whether industries with the highest levels of FDI have suffered a decline in relative employment and wages. We also report the results obtained by Head and Ries (1999), who link firm-level FDI to the use of skilled workers relative to unskilled workers in the firm. We show that there is no evidence that large-scale investment abroad in the electrical equipment and transportation equipment industries resulted in less employment and lower wages in these industries at home. In the textiles industry, however, outflows of FDI did coincide with reduced employment in Japan. Across our sample of 1070 firms, workers in firms with manufacturing investments abroad fared better in terms of employment and wages than workers in firms with no manufacturing FDI activity. Our study of skill upgrading in Japan shows that FDI, especially FDI in low-income countries, is associated with the greater use of skilled workers in Japan. FDI outflows, however, can only account for 8 per cent of the 10 percentage point increase in the skilled worker share of the wage bill in 1966–89.

The theoretical works by Jones and Kierzkowski (1997), Arndt (1997) and Feenstra and Hanson (1996a) consider FDI as part of a process where multinational enterprises (MNEs) fragment the production process into stages according to factor intensity. Once the production process is fragmented, MNEs choose the optimal location of each stage based on comparative advantage. Advances in transportation and information technologies facilitate the fragmentation. Here we shall confine the discussion to two factors – skilled and unskilled labour. Fragmentation creates production stages that are (1) intensive in skilled labour and (2) intensive in unskilled labour. Assume for the moment that an MNE sends the unskilled labour-intensive stages overseas. The key insight of Jones and Kierzkowski (1997) and Arndt (1997) is that even unskilled workers might gain through this process because the division of production into two stages generates productivity gains. The lower costs associated with higher productivity will increase the demand for the MNE's products. If sales increase sufficiently there may be an overall increase in demand for the unskilled workers used in the production stage remaining at home. Consequently the employment and wages of both types of worker may rise.

A third study of ours (Head and Ries, forthcoming) provides evidence that investment in manufacturing facilities abroad stimulates exports from home. This study relates the exports of Japanese firms both to distribution and to manufacturing investments after controlling for measured characteristics of firms such as productivity and capital intensity as well as firm-fixed effects and year effects. For our sample of 1070 Japanese manufacturing firms as a whole, increases in both distribution and manufacturing investment are associated with increases in exports. This result, however, does not hold across all subsamples. For the leaders of vertical *keiretsu* such as Toyota and Matsushita, additional manufacturing investment corresponds to fewer exports. The explanation for this is that these firms are primarily assemblers and rely on subcontractors for parts. For these firms there are no stages left at home to benefit from overseas investment. Thus it remains an open question whether the sales expansion effect of FDI is adequate to generate an overall rise in the demand for labour in Japan and to raise employment and wage levels.

Clearly the process of moving production stages offshore will affect the skill composition of the MNE's workforce. Whether FDI raises or lowers the skill intensity of the domestic workforce depends on what stages are sent overseas. We expect overseas plants in low-income countries to employ mainly unskilled workers. Hence this investment will shift the skill composition of the workforce towards skilled workers as firms replace domestic unskilled workers with overseas workers. However investment in high-income countries may displace highly skilled workers in Japan, resulting in a decline in the skill intensity of production in Japan.

The following section shows trends in FDI levels over time and the industry composition of investment. We also identify the firms that employ the most overseas workers. The third section reports the results obtained by Head and Ries (1994) on the relative changes in wages and employment in Japan for the three industries – electrical machinery, transportation equipment and textiles – that account for much of Japanese FDI. The fourth section presents the results obtained by Head and Ries (1999) when relating firm-level FDI to changes in domestic worker skill composition. This analysis examines whether FDI in high-income coountries has a different effect on the skill intensity of the domestic workforce than does investment in low-income countries. The conclusion considers the results of the two works examined to evaluate whether labour should welcome or resist outward foreign investment.

OVERVIEW OF JAPANESE FDI

The primary source of our data is *Japanese Overseas Investment 1992/93* (Toyo Kezai Inc., 1992). This is a comprehensive listing of the foreign affiliates of Japanese companies. The publication lists the location, establishment date, activity and employment of each affiliate and the equity share held by the parent company. We shall confine our analysis to the manufacturing affiliates of publicly listed companies in Japan. The affiliate data pertains to the date of the survey, which was December 1991 for this edition of the publication. Thus equity shares and employment levels may not match the levels existing at the time of establishment. For a minority of affiliates (less than 20 per cent) the employment data is not recorded. In these cases we assume that employment is equal to the average level of employment for the other foreign affiliates of the parent company. We multiply the parent equity share by the employment level to estimate the number of foreign employees of the parent of the affiliate. Thus for an affiliate that is a 50–50 joint venture by two Japanese parents, half of its employees are deemed to be foreign employees of one parent and the other half are foreign employees of the other parent.

We divide host countries into two goups: high-income countries (HICs) and low-income countries (LICs). Low-income countries are those with less than one-half of Japanese per capita GNP at a given point in time. High-income countries comprise all other countries. Based on the establishment date, we calculate the cumulative level of foreign employment of Japanese companies in HICs and LICs. Figure 4.1 shows the trend in these levels over time. It reveals that until 1980 the majority of foreign employees were in LICs. After 1980 investment in HICs grew rapidly. By the end of 1990 our sample of firms had about 300 000 employees in LICs and 400 000 employees in HICs.

The financial statements of our sample of publicly listed companies are our second source of data. We have data for 1070 such companies,

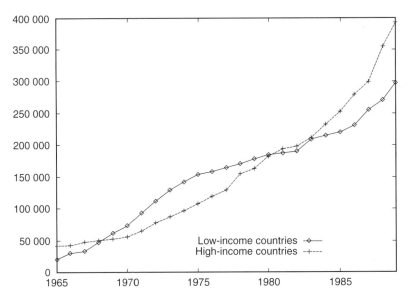

Figure 4.1 Affiliate employment in low-income and high-income nations, 1965–89

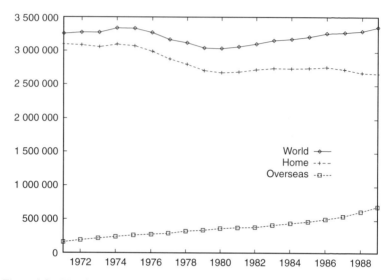

Figure 4.2   Employment at home and at overseas affiliates for 1052 Japanese
manufacturers, 1970–89

of which 448 (42 per cent) had a manufacturing affiliate abroad by
1989. These data enable us to compare overseas activities with domestic activities as well as the performance of MNEs and non-MNEs.
Figure 4.2 shows the levels of overseas and domestic employment of
the 1052 firms for which we have complete data for the 1970–89 period. For this set of firms as a whole, overseas employment grew steadily
while domestic employment contracted, attaining a level of 2.7 million
in 1989. The top line of the figure shows the sum of overseas and
domestic employment, which remained fairly constant. Hence this
figure seems to suggest that foreign employment displaced domestic
employment.

Table 4.1 breaks down overseas investment in 1990 according to the
industry of the parent. The first numerical column lists the number of
parent firms in the industry and the following two columns show
overseas and home employees for the industry. The last column lists
the foreign emplyee share of total employees. The table reveals the
dominance of the electronics industry as an employer of foreign
labour. It accounted for 307 000 of the 697 000 foreign employees in
our sample of firms. The car industry was second. In terms of the
overseas share the rubber industry was highest at 42 per cent,
followed by machinery and textiles with a 25 per cent and 24 per cent
overseas share respectively. Rubber's high overseas share is explained
by Bridgestone acquiring the foreign employees of Firestone.[2]

Table 4.2 lists the 25 largest Japanese investors abroad in terms of employment in 1990. This table also reveals the dominance of the electronics industry, which accounted for four of the top five firms. Matsushita topped the list with almost 50 000 foreign employees and an overseas share of 54 per cent. Sanyo Electric, Sony and NEC were

Table 4.1   World employment by industry: 1990

	Firms	Overseas	Home	Overseas share %
Electronics	154	307 253	733 868	30
Cars	53	91 602	364 114	20
Machinery	158	46 850	210 772	18
Chemicals	133	44 887	214 639	17
Textiles	80	41 052	128 827	24
Rubber	20	34 786	49 021	42
Precision machinery	30	26 538	79 487	25
Non-ferrous metals	90	24 198	128 059	16
Iron and steel	59	17 743	216 001	8
Foods	93	17 726	150 330	11
Glass and cement	57	16 178	78 986	17
Shipbuilding	10	10 757	90 480	11
Other manufacturing	40	9 107	73 792	11
Pharmaceuticals	34	6 390	84 367	7
Pulp and paper	31	2 447	50 910	5
Other transportation	18	1 494	20 158	7
Petroleum	10	109	15 337	1

Table 4.2   The top 25 overseas employers: 1990

		Overseas		Home empl.	Overseas share %
	Industry	Plants	Empl.		
Matsushita Electric	Electronics	84	48 178	41 409	54
Sanyo Electric	Electronics	62	29 719	34 405	46
Sony	Electronics	22	28 866	16 278	64
Honda Motor	Cars	71	23 759	30 022	44
NEC	Electronics	28	22 639	37 721	38
Bridgestone	Rubber	12	22 137	15 791	58
Nissan Motor	Cars	14	21 766	52 808	29
Toshiba	Electronics	29	18 015	69 201	21
Minebea	Machinery	16	17 369	3 646	83
Hitachi	Electronics	29	16 966	76 479	18
Dainippon Ink & Chem.	Chemicals	22	15 586	6 626	70

Table 4.2   *continued overleaf*

Table 4.2   (*continued*)

Toray Industries	Textiles	36	13 249	9 602	58
Toyoto Motor	Cars	27	12 654	67 814	16
Sharp	Electronics	17	12 290	18 282	40
Mitsubishi Electric	Electronics	28	11 732	47 693	20
Mitsumi Electric	Electronics	12	9 493	1 936	83
Sumitomo Rubber	Rubber	7	9 418	4 856	66
Hitachi Koki	Electronics	3	8 680	2 583	77
Asahi Glass	Glass and cement	21	8 269	9 295	47
Suzuki Motor	Cars	23	7 195	12 616	36
TDK	Electronics	17	6 876	7 797	47
Toko	Electronics	5	6 841	1 014	87
Alps Electric	Electronics	12	6 793	6 502	51
Kawasaki Steel	Iron and steel	19	6 660	18 562	26
Ricoh	Precision machinery	6	6 472	10 817	37

the other electronics companies in the top five. The car industry also had a strong presence, with Honda and Nissan the fourth and seventh largest employers of foreign labour respectively.

This section has portrayed the rapid rise of Japanese overseas employment. By 1989, one in five employees of Japanese manufacturing companies was a foreign worker. For the largest MNEs this ratio was closer to one in two. The electronics and car industries account for most foreign employment. The subsequent sections will present the results of our examination of the effect this foreign employment has had on the domestic labour market.

WAGES, EMPLOYMENT AND OVERSEAS INVESTMENT

The previous section indicated that particular industrial sectors and firms are more heavily involved than others in overseas investment. If overseas investment influences the domestic labour market, we should find the strongest effects for the industries and firms that create the most overseas jobs or are the most foreign oriented. This is the logic of the study by Head and Ries (1994), which focuses on three sectors: electrical equipment, transportation equipment and textiles. The first two industries created the most overseas jobs whereas foreign workers accounted for a large share of total parent employment (24 per cent) in the textiles industry.

Figure 4.2 suggests that overseas employment began to take over from domestic employment in the 1970–89 period, with the overall

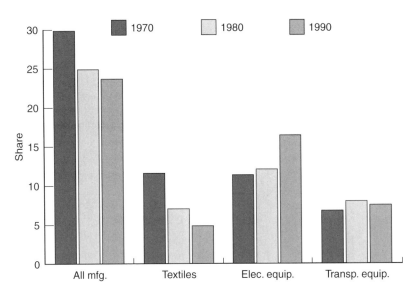

Figure 4.3   Distribution of Japanese workforce, by industry

level of employment remaining roughly constant for our sample of 1052 firms. Slightly more than half this sample were firms that had no overseas manufacturing investments by 1989. How did the non-MNEs fare relative to the MNEs in terms of employment and wages? Our data shows that domestic employment fell for both groups but that the percentage decline between 1970 and 1990 was much higher for non-MNEs – 27 per cent versus 11 per cent. Moreover, average wages in MNEs relative to those in non-MNEs increased slightly over this period. Thus MNE activities are associated with relatively favourable outcomes for domestic employees.

Head and Ries (1994) examined industry-level data to investigate the employment and wages of workers in textiles, electrical machinery and transportation equipment relative to overall manufacturing. The virtue of industry-level data, drawn from population surveys, is that they provide full coverage of workers as opposed to only the publicly listed firms in our sample. Figure 4.3 lists the shares of the total Japanese workforce for total manufacturing as well as our three industries for the years 1970, 1980 and 1990. The total manufacturing share fell from 29.9 per cent in 1970 to 24.9 per cent in 1980 and 23.6 per cent in 1990. Thus Japanese manufacturing employment, like manufactucturing in other industrialized countries, experienced a

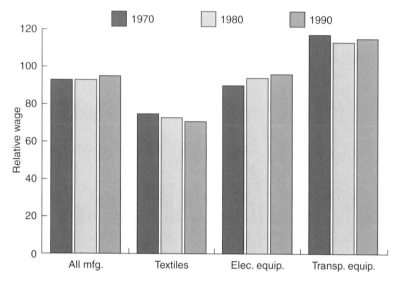

Figure 4.4   Wages relative to average wage of all workers = 100

decline in its share of employment. The figure shows that textiles suffered a more pronounced decline, with its share of employment falling from 11.5 per cent in 1970 to 4.9 per cent in 1990. In contrast the shares of electrical equipment and transportation equipment rose over this period – Electrical equipment from 11.3 per cent in 1970 to 16.4 per cent in 1990, and transportation equipment from 6.8 per cent in 1970 to 7.6 per cent in 1990.

Figure 4.4 shows the trends in relative wages for the years 1970, 1980 and 1990. The manufacturing wage relative to the overall wage in Japan rose slightly from 93.4 to 95.1 over the period. Textile workers fared relatively poorly. Their wages were low to begin with – 74.7 per cent of the average wage in Japan in 1970 – and declined further to 71 per cent in 1990. Workers in transportation equipment, whose wages exceeded the Japanese average, saw a slight decline in their relative wage from a level of 116.9 in 1970 to 115.6 in 1990. On the other hand, workers in the electrical equipment industry did relatively well, with their relative wages rising from 90.1 in 1970 to 96.0 in 1990.

Overall these data provide little evidence that FDI has had a detrimental effect on the labour market in Japan. Instead the favourable performance of employment and wages in MNEs relative to non-MNEs is consistent with fragmentation leading to increased productivity and the maintainance of competitiveness in some Japanese

firms. Of the three industries focused on here, only textiles has
experienced a relatively bad outcome for domestic workers as a result
of the strong orientation towards foreign production. In contrast,
workers in electrical machinery and transportation equipment have
done well relative to overall manufacturing.

FDI AND SKILL UPGRADING

The previous section indicated that FDI has not caused a reduction in
the demand for labour in Japan. FDI does not seem to be associated
with bad outcomes in terms of employment and wages for workers in
firms and industries with substantial offshore production. There may
be, however, differential effects for different types of worker in Japan.
This section reports the results obtained by Head and Ries (1999),
who investigated the effect of FDI on the skill composition of the
manufacturing workforce in Japan.

The top line of Figure 4.5 plots the median for the selling, general
and administration (SGA) worker share of the total wage bill for each
year in our sample of firms. This share rose from 0.21 in 1966 to 0.31 in
1989. SGA workers are those employed in non-production activities.

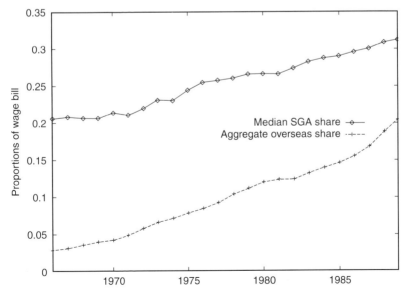

Figure 4.5   Trends in skill intensity and overseas employment, 1966–89

Most scholars consider these workers to be more highly skilled than production workers and the rise in the SGA share reflects a steady skill upgrading in Japanese firms.[3] The lower line shows the aggregate share of overseas employees for our sample of firms. The figure indicates that skill intensity and the overseas worker share both rose over time. Head and Ries (1999) provide theoretical reasons why skill upgrading may have been caused by overseas investment and use regression analysis to test the relationship.

Head and Ries posit three canonical processes associated with MNEs:

- *Replication*: each affiliate is an independent unit, with its own production and knowledge-based activities.
- *Branching*: overseas affliates concentrate on production acitivities. The headquarters provides knowledge services to each foreign production site.
- *Fragmentation*: the MNE subdivides production into separate stages with different factor intensities. It then locates each stage in the country that is relatively abundant in the factors used intensively during that stage.

Under the replication process, the MNE's overseas activities are independent of its home operations. When the MNE invests abroad, in essence it is replicating itself. The branching process is based on the idea that a fixed number of headquarter workers can provide services to any number of production 'branches'. Foreign affiliates therefore use heaquarter services produced in Japan to manufacture goods for new foreign markets. As discussed in the introduction, fragmentation is the process of dividing production into stages according to factor intensity. A MNE might require different combinations of skilled and unskilled labour at different stages of production. For example assembly might require mostly unskilled workers whereas the production of sopphisticated components primarily requires skilled workers. The MNE locates each stage according to comparative advantage.

We hypothesize that skill intensity will be influenced by the firm's scale of operations as well the configuration of production activities across locations (Head and Ries, 1999). We measure scale by total employment, that is, the sum of the Japanese firm's employment at home and abroad. We also calculate the HIC share as the share in total employment of affiliate employment in high-income countries. Correspondingly, the LIC share is the share of low-income country affiliate

Table 4.3   Modes of multinational expansion

MNE form	LIC share	HIC share	Scale
Replication	0	0	0
Branching	+	+	−
Fragmentation	+	−	0

employment. We argue that the different canonical processes we consider can be distinguished by the relationship of these variables to skill intensity.

Table 4.3 shows the predicted relationships. Under replication, by construction foreign activity is independent of home activity and there should be no relationship. Under branching, as the scale expands the number of highly skilled headquarter workers remains constant, causing a lower SGA labour share in the firm. Thus the scale effect is negative under this process. For a given scale of operation of the branching MNE, we expect that a greater share of production in either HICs or LICs would correspond to greater skill intensity at home. Scale will not effect skill intensity under fragmentation as sales expansion involves increasing all stages of production. The effect of fragmentation FDI on skill intensity, however, may depend on where the affiliates are located. We presume that MNEs will shift unskilled intensive activities to low-income countries, hence greater orientation towards LICs will imply skill upgrading in Japanese firms. However investment in HICs might displace highly skilled workers in Japan, causing skill intensity to fall.

To derive an initial regression specification we consider a production process that can be divided into a large number of tasks, each of which is completed by a single worker. A firm allocates each task either to a highly skilled domestic worker, to a highly skilled foreign worker, to a low-skilled domestic worker or to a low-skilled foreign worker. The decision depends on the wages and suitability of each worker for the task. Under a specific formulation of the heterogeneity term in this model, namely that it follows an i.i.d. type-I extreme value distribution, this model gives rise to a specification for the log of the ratio of domestic non-production (highly skilled) workers to domestic production (low-skilled) workers as a function of wages and capital per worker:

$$\ln E_H/E_L = \psi_H \ln k(H) - \psi_L \ln k(L) + \theta_L \ln \omega_L - \theta_H \ln \omega_H \quad (4.1)$$

where E_H and E_L are the respective numbers of highly skilled and low-skilled domestic workers employed by the firm, $k(H)$ and $k(L)$ are the amounts of capital employed with H and L workers, and ω_H and ω_L are the respective wages of highly skilled and low-skilled domestic workers.

The dependent variable – the ratio of skilled to unskilled workers at home – is a measure of skill intensity. Assuming that capital per worker is the same for all types of worker, rearranging generates a specification that we are able to estimate using our data:

$$\ln \frac{\omega_H E_H}{\omega_L E_L} = (\psi_H - \psi_L) \ln k + (\theta_L - 1) \ln \omega_L - (\theta_H - 1) \ln \omega_H$$

$$(4.2)$$

Here the dependent variable is the log of the ratio of the SGA worker payroll to the production worker payroll. We assume that wages are set nationally and capture variations in wages with year dummies. Implicit in the assumption about the error term is that $\ln E_H/E_L$ is

Table 4.4   Log SGA–production ratio regressions

	Dependent variable: $\ln P(H)/P(L)$					
	(1)	*(2)*	*(3)*	*(4)*	*(5)*	*(6)*
Log assets per employee	0.012 (0.007)	−0.003 (0.007)	−0.004 (0.007)	−0.008 (0.009)	−0.070[a] (0.009)	0.069[a] (0.016)
Log worldwide employment	−0.279[a] (0.007)	−0.320[a] (0.007)	−0.317[a] (0.007)	−0.303[a] (0.011)	−0.314[a] (0.014)	−0.063[a] (0.020)
Foreign employment share	–	0.772[a] (0.039)				
Emp. share in LICs	–	–	0.914[a] (0.055)	0.889[a] (0.068)	1.310[a] (0.092)	0.549[a] (0.078)
Emp. share in HICs	–	–	0.619[a] (0.057)	0.512[a] (0.092)	0.250[a] (0.074)	0.254[b] (0.098)
Residual change	0.536[a] (0.034)	0.498[a] (0.034)	0.50[a] (0.034)	0.271[a] (0.027)	0.289[a] (0.012)	−0.106 (0.097)
Sample	All	All	All	1965–79	1980–90	Elect.
Number of observations	25 108	25 108	25 108	13 573	11 535	3605
R^2 (within)	0.286	0.297	0.298	0.205	0.19	0.228

Notes: Standard errors in parentheses; a and b indicate significance in a two-tail test at the 1 per cent and 5 per cent levels. Each regression is estimated with a fixed firm effect. Year effects are included but not reported in each regression.

independent of scale as well as the characteristics of foreign workers. By adding the sum of domestic and foreign workers as a measure of scale and variables representing the HIC and LIC share of total employment, we test if this restriction is valid. If this is the case, Table 4.3 indicates that it would be consistent with our replication process. However we might also obtain sign patterns shown in the table that support the branching or fragmentation process of FDI.

Table 4.4 shows the results of the estimation of Equation 4.2. In each specification we control for firm-specific fixed effects and year-specific effects. We sequentially include variables representing scale and foreign orientation. The first three columns respectively add worldwide employment, the total foreign (HIC plus LIC) share of worldwide employment and the HIC and LIC shares of employment. Columns four and five are the results of dividing the sample into the pre-1980 and 1980–90 periods. The last column focuses on the 154 firms in the electronics industry.

The first notable result is that scale has a negative effect on skill intensity. It enters negatively and significantly across all regressions. Capital intensity yields inconsistent signs and thus we do not draw strong inferences about this variable from these results. Rows three to five show the coefficient estimates for the foreign share of employment variables. There is a positive and highly significant relationship between the foreign employment share and our measure of skill intensity, as shown in column two. Moreover the degree to which skill intensity increases with foreign orientation depends on the income level of the host country. Column three indicates that establishing foreign manufacturing affiliates in LICs raises skill intensity at home to a greater degree than locating affiliates in HICs. The coefficient estimates are 0.914 and 0.619, respectively. The 'residual change' listed in the last row of coefficients reflects the average percentage change in the SGA–production payroll ratio, explained by the 1990 year dummy. Column three reveals that the 50 per cent increase in this ratio for the period 1966–90 is entirely accounted for by the 1990 year dummy. The reason is that the positive effect of international orientation is offset by the negative scale effect. The last three columns (the results for 1965–79, 1980–90 and the electronics industry subsample) reveal that the results are robust to these divisions of the observations. Overall there is a strong pattern of scale lowering skill intensity but foreign orientation, particularly LIC orientation, raising skill intensity.

We shall now examine an alternative measure of skill intensity: the ratio of SGA payroll to production payroll. We consider the average wage of the firm. The idea, expressed formally in Head and Ries (1999), is that if we control for economy-wide changes in the wages of highly skilled and low-skilled workers in Japan, changes in a firm's average wage correspond to changes in the skill mix. Specifically, if the average wage of a firm increases, then there has been an increase in the use of highly paid skilled workers relative to unskilled workers in the firm. We argue that this measure of skill intensity can capture types of skill upgrading associated with FDI that will not be reflected in the SGA–production worker payroll ratio. For example, suppose FDI transfers from Japan to the United States a parts facility requiring high skilled labour. We should expect a decrease in skill intensity as skilled workers are displaced in this example. However our data show a reduction in production labour relative to SGA labour and therefore a rise in skill intensity. Average wages may be a superior measure in this case as this variable may fall, reflecting the reduced use of highly paid skilled workers in Japan.

Table 4.5 shows the results of the same regressions when the dependent variable is the log of the firm's average wage. The results are very similar to those reported in Table 4.4. The scale effect is negative and the effect of foreign orientation is positive. The LIC share variable generally has higher estimated coefficients than does the HIC share variable, the sole exception being the electronics subsample (column six). Stronger results emerge in these regressions for capital intensity. Here capital is a 'friend' to workers and raises wages. One interpretation of this is that capital increases worker productivity, which is partly captured in the form of higher wages. Overall our results are robust to this alternative measure of skill intensity.

The results support a mixture of the branching and fragmentation process and strongly reject the replication process depiction of MNE activity. The negative scale and positive foreign employment share effects are consistent with what we expected in the case of branching. However the LIC coefficient estimate is consistently higher than the HIC coefficient. This suggests that the HIC coefficient is partly reflecting fragmentation where investment in HICs displaces highly skilled workers in Japan.

The literature on skill upgrading in the United States has generally used a translog cost specification to measure the influence of various factors on the demand for skilled and unskilled labour. Among these studies, those closest in topic to ours are Feenstra and Hanson (1996b, 1996c) and Slaughter (forthcoming). Both studies use industry-level data. Feenstra and Hanson show that foreign outsourcing

Table 4.5   Log average wage regressions

	(1)	(2)	(3)	(4)	(5)	(6)
	Dependent variable: $\ln[\hat{w}]$					
Log assets per	0.082[a]	0.079[a]	0.079[a]	0.079[a]	0.055[a]	0.083[a]
employee	(0.002)	(0.002)	(0.002)	(0.004)	(0.003)	(0.005)
Log worldwide	−0.027[a]	−0.038[a]	−0.037[a]	−0.075[a]	−0.121[a]	−0.134[a]
employment	(0.003)	(0.003)	(0.003)	(0.005)	(0.005)	(0.007)
Foreign employment	–	0.219[a]	–	–	–	–
share		(0.014)				
Emp. share	–	–	0.244[a]	0.304[a]	0.211[a]	0.277[a]
in LICs			(0.020)	(0.030)	(0.033)	(0.026)
Emp. share	–	–	0.190[a]	0.281[a]	0.180[a]	0.372[a]
in HICs			(0.021)	(0.041)	(0.028)	(0.033)
Residual change	2.278[a]	2.265[a]	2.266[a]	1.820[a]	0.408[a]	2.431[a]
	(0.013)	(0.013)	(0.013)	(0.012)	(0.004)	(0.032)
Sample	All	All	All	1965–79	1980–90	Elect.
Number of	25 222	25 222	25 222	13 636	11 586	3 608
observations:						
R^2 (within)	0.974	0.974	0.974	0.968	0.77	0.985

Notes: Standard errors in parentheses; a indicates significance in a two-tail test at the 1 per cent level. Each regression is estimated with a fixed firm effect. Year effects are included but not reported in each regression.

accounts for a minority of observed skill upgrading in the United States, and Slaughter finds no significant relationship between various measures of MNE activity and skill intensity across industries. In Head and Ries (1999) we provide estimates based on the translog cost specification fit to our 25-year panel of 1070 firms in Japan.

To begin, following Feenstra and Hanson (1996b, 1996c) and Slaughter (forthcoming), we consider two variables: skilled and unskilled labour. In this specification, capital is assumed to be a quasi fixed factor that does not freely adjust over time. Under these conditions the translog cost function is expressed as:

$$S_H = \frac{\omega_H E_H}{\omega_H E_H + \omega_L E_L} = \gamma_0 + \gamma_H \ln \omega_H + \gamma_L \ln \omega_L + \gamma_K \ln K/Q + \gamma_Q \ln Q$$

$$(4.3)$$

The dependent variable, S_H, is skilled labour's share of the total labour payroll. As before, the SGA payroll is the skilled worker payroll and we use year dummies to capture annual variations in both types of wage. We measure Q as value added and γ_Q reflects the effect of scale on skill intensity. A positive intercept in this regression has been interpreted in the literature as evidence of skill-biased technological change. Feenstra and Hanson add to this base specification a measure of foreign outsourcing, defined as purchased inputs from abroad. Like Slaughter we add a measure of MNE activities, namely the foreign share of worldwide employment. The coefficients of these variables will reflect a systematic relationship between the variables and the residual of the base specification. This new specification is quite similar to our initial specification. The only difference is that the dependent variable is a share rather than a ratio and we now substitute domestic value added for worldwide employment as our scale measure.

The first three columns of Tables 4.6 and 4.7 contain the results for the full sample and the subset of firms in the electronics industry. The column one estimates are based on the entire 25 years of data while the next two columns show the estimates for the sample split at the year 1980. The results are very supportive of our earlier ones, but with some differences. In this specification capital intensity consistently enters negatively and significantly, indicating that as the firm adds machines it tends to use more unskilled workers relative to skilled workers. The scale effect is still generally negative, but it is positive in the case of the sample of electronics firms over the full time period. The LIC share is positive and significant but less consistent results emerge for the HIC share, which tends to be insignificantly different from zero and is actually negative and significant in one instance (the 1980–90 period for the full sample of firms). The lower coefficient on the HIC share may be partly a consequence of our use of domestic value added instead of worldwide employment as a measure of scale. This new scale measure fails to capture expansion that is due to increased overseas production. Thus the foreign employment share variables may partly reflect negative scale effects associated with FDI and will therefore have lower coefficient estimates.

Using the results in column one of Table 4.6, we calculate the change in SGA labour share of total payroll that is attributable to increases in HIC and LIC share. Over the 1966–90 period, when the SGA share rose 10 percentage points, only 0.8 percentage points, or 8 per cent of the observed increase, can be associated with investment abroad. Thus the vast majority of skill upgrading is not explained by our FDI variables.

What is the mechanism by which overseas activities affect domestic skill composition? In Head and Ries (1999) we quote a *Time Magazine*

Table 4.6 Translog cost functions: all manufacturing firms

| | | | | Dependent variable: $(\omega_j E_j)/C$ | | |
Factors	(1) H, L	(2) H, L	(3) H, L	(4) H, L, G, M	(5) L, H, G, M	(6) G, H, L, M
Log of assets/output	−0.0381[a] (0.0012)	−0.0281[a] (0.0016)	−0.0346[a] (0.0016)	0.0098[a] (0.0004)	0.0323[a] (0.0007)	−0.0652[a] (0.0017)
Log of output	−0.0334[a] (0.0013)	−0.0181[a] (0.0017)	−0.0393[a] (0.0021)	−0.0159[a] (0.0004)	−0.0388[a] (0.0008)	0.0208[a] (0.0019)
Emp. share in LICs	0.1969[a] (0.0104)	0.1018[a] (0.0127)	0.2570[a] (0.0180)	−0.0234[a] (0.0031)	−0.0889[a] (0.0062)	0.2296[a] (0.0142)
Emp. share in HICs	0.0315[a] (0.0112)	0.0163 (0.0173)	−0.0461[a] (0.0148)	−0.0159[a] (0.0033)	−0.0116 (0.0067)	−0.0144 (0.0153)
Residual change	0.1671[a] (0.0069)	0.0696[a] (0.0055)	0.0754[a] (0.0024)	0.0655[a] (0.0021)	0.0820[a] (0.0042)	0.0410[a] (0.0096)
Sample	All	1965–79	1980–90	All	All	All
Number of observations:	25 131	13 551	11 580	25 222	25 222	25 222
R^2	0.28	0.168	0.198	0.264	0.229	0.158

Notes: The factors included in the variable cost shares are listed above each column with the factor in the numerator listed first. Standard errors in parentheses; a indicates significance in a two-tail test at the 1 per cent level. Each regression is estimated with a fixed firm effect. Year effects are included but not reported in each regression.

Table 4.7 Translog cost function: electronics firms only

			Dependent variable: $(\omega_j E_j)/C$			
Factors	(1) H, L	(2) H, L	(3) H, L	(4) H, L, G, M	(5) L, H, G, M	(6) G, H, L, M
Log of assets/output	-0.0096[a] (0.0031)	-0.0161[a] (0.0038)	-0.0104[a] (0.0048)	0.0068[a] (0.0010)	0.0263[a] (0.0021)	-0.0423[a] (0.0051)
Log of output	0.0072[b] (0.0032)	-0.0066 (0.0039)	-0.0211[a] (0.0061)	-0.0240[a] (0.0010)	-0.0639[a] (0.0021)	0.0564[a] (0.0052)
Emp. share in LICs	0.1397[a] (0.0143)	0.1096[a] (0.0149)	0.2355[a] (0.0231)	-0.0344[a] (0.0043)	-0.1384[a] (0.0088)	0.3687[a] (0.0216)
Emp. share in HICs	0.0248 (0.0178)	0.0259 (0.0212)	0.0255 (0.0308)	-0.0032 (0.0053)	-0.0006 (0.0110)	-0.0058 (0.0270)
Residual change	-0.0164 (0.0199)	0.0001 (0.0146)	0.0498[a] (0.0073)	0.0710[a] (0.0061)	0.1939[a] (0.0125)	-0.0945[a] (0.0307)
Sample:	All	1965–79	1980–90	All	All	All
Number of observations:	3606	1933	1673	3608	3608	3608
R²	0.231	0.236	0.148	0.326	0.382	0.204

Notes: The factors included in the variable cost shares are listed above each column with the factor in the numerator listed first. Standard errors in parentheses; a and b indicate significance in a two-tail test at the 1 per cent and 5 per cent levels. Each regression is estimated with a fixed firm effect. Year effects are included but not reported in each regression.

article stating that Japan imports 23 times as many televisions as it exports and that these televisions come primarily from foreign affiliates in low-income countries. Thus we think that finished goods purchases from overseas subsidiaries may be an avenue through which FDI influences skill intensity. To investigate this proposition, we add final goods purchases and materials purchases to the translog specification. This gives rise to separate expressions for the share of highly skilled labour (H), low-skilled labour (L), materials (M) and purchased final goods (G) in total variable costs ($C = \omega_L E_L + \omega_H E_H + \omega_M E_M + \omega_G E_G$):

$$S_j = \frac{\omega_j E_j}{C} = \gamma_{oj} + \sum_{i=1}^{4} \gamma_{ij} \ln \omega_i + \gamma_{Kj} \ln K/Q + \gamma_{Qj} \ln Q \qquad (4.4)$$

Here j is equal to H, L, G and M. In this specification, Q is total sales. The fourth equation is a linear function of the first three, so we will focus on H, L and G. We assume that greater foreign orientation lowers the cost of sourcing finished goods from abroad and thus the HIC share and the LIC share are inverse proxies for ω_G.

The last three columns of Tables 4.6 and 4.7 show the results. Columns four and five list the results of regressions explaining skilled labour's share and unskilled labour's share of total variable costs. Both scale and foreign orientation lower these shares. The coefficients on scale and LIC share are always significant, whereas the HIC share coefficient is often insignificant. The results for the HIC and LIC share variables indicate that as a firm becomes more foreign oriented, it uses a relatively smaller amount of both types of worker's with the greatest relative fall in employment born by low-skilled workers. This is consistent with our earlier findings for skill upgrading since it will give rise to an increase in the ratio of skilled to unskilled workers employed by the firm. On the other hand, increases in output are associated with a higher cost share for purchased goods (column six). Thus expansion appears to be accompanied by a disproportionate increase in goods purchased. In addition, greater foreign orientation in LICs raises the share of goods purchased, particularly for electronics companies. In contrast, there is no significant relationship between HIC share and the goods share. Thus the results indicate that one mechanism by which FDI affects workers in Japan is through the purchase of finished goods from overseas affiliates in low-income countries.

CONCLUSION

During the 1966–90 period Japanese firms had to cope with dramatic changes in the economic environment. Trade liberalization meant more competition at home. At the same time, trade barriers such as voluntary export restraints on cars in the United States and Europe restricted export access to foreign markets. Over the period, Japanese wages rose relative to those in many foreign countries. The dramatic rise of Japanese outward FDI was partly attributable to this changing global economic landscape. The question we have investigated is how outward investment affected domestic labour in Japan.

The results reported in Head and Ries (1994) suggest that those firms and industries which were most active in investing abroad fared at least as well as other firms and industries. Apart from textiles firms, firms engaging in FDI were able to increase their employment share and maintain their wage levels. The results in Head and Ries (1999) indicate that FDI is associated with an increase in the relative use of skilled workers in Japanese manufacturing firms. However we only associate a small proportion (8 per cent) of skill upgrading with FDI.

We conclude that despite the rapid growth of overseas production by Japanese firms, FDI has had a limited effect on workers in Japan. To the extent that we can measure the consequences of FDI on workers, it appears to be beneficial. As protectionism and cost conditions have undermined Japan as an economically feasible production site for some activities, FDI may be viewed as a means to shift some stages of production to locations where production can take place more efficiently. Since this process lowers costs and can increase sales, it increases employment opportunities in the stages of production that remain in Japan. Thus FDI may make Japanese workers, particularly skilled workers, better off.

Notes

1. We appreciate the comments of Masanori Hashimoto and other participants at the UBC Centre for Japanese Research Interdisciplinary Research Conference on Japanese Business and Economic System: History and Prospects for 21st Century, UBC, February 1999.
2. Our sample includes both acquisitions and greenfield investment.
3. For studies of skill upgrading in the United States that justify the use of the non-production worker share as a measure of skill intensity

see, for example, Berman *et al.* (1997). The average SGA shares in our sample of firms is highly consistent with the non-production wage shares reported in Japan's *Labor Force Survey* (see Head and Ries, 1999).

References

Arndt, S. (1997) 'Globalization and the Open Economy', *North American Journal of Economics and Finance*, vol. 8, no. 1, pp. 71–9.

Berman, E., J. Bound and Z. Griliches (1994) 'Changes in the Demand for Skilled Labor within Manufacturing: Evidence from the Survey of Manufacturers', *Quarterly Journal of Economics*, vol. 109, no. 2, pp. 367–98.

Berman, E., J. Bound and S. Machin (1997) 'Implications of Skill-Biased Technological Change: International Evidence', *NBER Working Paper* no. 6166 (Cambridge, Mass.: NBER).

Blomstrom, M., G. Fors and R. Lipsey (1997) 'Foreign Direct Investment and Employment: Home Country Experience in the United States and Sweden', *The Economic Journal*, vol. 107, pp. 1787–97.

Brainard, L. and D. Riker (1997) 'Are U.S. Multinationals Exporting U.S. Jobs?', *NBER Working Paper* no. 5958 (Cambridge, Mass.: NBER).

Carr, David, James Markusen and Keith Maskus (1998) 'Estimating the Knowledge-Capital Model of the Multinational Enterprise', manuscript, University of Colorado.

Feenstra, R. and G. Hanson (1996a) 'Foreign Investment, Outsourcing and Relative Wages', in R. Feenstra and G. Grossman (eds), *Political Economy of Trade Policy: Essays in Honor of Jagdish Bhagwati* (Cambridge, Mass.: MIT Press).

Feenstra, R. and G. Hanson (1996b) 'Globalization, Outsourcing, and Wage Inequality', *American Economic Review*, vol. 86, pp. 240–5.

Feenstra, R. and G. Hanson (1996c) 'Errata to Globalization, Outsourcing, and Wage Inequality', op. cit.

Feenstra, R. and G. Hanson (forthcoming) 'The Impact of Outsourcing and High-Technology Capital on Wages: Estimates for the United States, 1979–1990', *Quarterly Journal of Economics*.

Head, K. and J. Ries (1994) 'Causes and Consequences of Japanese Direct Investment Abroad', in Steven Globerman (ed.), *Canadian-Based Multinationals*, Industry Canada Series (Calgary: University of Calgary Press), pp. 303–39.

Head, K. and J. Ries (1999) 'Offshore Production and the Home Employees of Japanese Manufacturers', Faculty of Commerce, University of British Columbia International Business, Trade and Finance Working Paper 99–03.

Head, K. and J. Ries (forthcoming) 'Overseas Investment and Firm Exports', *Review of International Economics*.

Jones, R. and H. Kierzkowski (1997) 'Globalization and the Consequences of International Fragmentation', Unpublished manuscript.

Markusen, J. (1995) 'The Boundaries of Multinational Enterprises and the Theory of International Trade', *Journal of Economic Perspectives*, vol. 9, pp. 169–189.

Markusen, J. and A. Venables (1997) 'The Role of Multinational Enterprises in the Wage-Gap Debate', *Review of International Economics*, vol. 5, no. 4, pp. 435–51.

Sachs, J. and H. Shatz (1994) 'Trade and Jobs in U.S. Manufacturing', *Brookings Papers on Economic Activity* (Washington, DC: Brookings Institution).

Slaughter, M. (1995) 'Multinational Corporations, Outsourcing, and American Wage Divergence', *NBER Working Paper* no. 5253 (Cambridge, Mass.: NBER).

Slaughter, M. (2000) 'Production Transfer within Multinational Enterprises and American Wages', *Journal of International Economics*, vol. 50, no. 2, pp. 449–472.

Toyo Keizai Inc. (1992) *Japan Overseas Investment: A Complete Listing by Firms and Countries 1992/93* (Tokyo: Toyo Keizai).

Comments on Chapter 4

Masanori Hashimoto

Chapter 4 increases our understanding of how foreign direct investment (FDI) affects the labour market. The authors focus on the effect of outsourcing production rather than on portfolio investments – the outsourcing of production transfers technology and human resource management skills, so it is more likely to affect employment in both the recipient and home countries.

The chapter examines three Japanese industries: electrical equipment, transportation equipment and textiles. The main conclusion is that foreign direct investment (FDI) has not reduced employment or wage rates in Japan, except perhaps in the textile industry. However FDI in low-income countries has had a positive effect on skilled Japanese workers. Thus a hollowing out (*kudoka*) of employment has not occurred in Japan as a result of FDI. If anything FDI, especially in low-income countries, seems to have resulted in some skill upgrading in Japan, that is, an increase in the relative share of workers in sales and general and administrative employment. These findings are timely in view of the ongoing discussion on the role of production outsourcing in the economic deterioration of low-skilled US workers.

The findings reported by Head and Ries are quite interesting but prompt two important questions the authors have left unanswered: what is really behind these findings, and can these findings be generalized? The issue of whether the findings have general applicability is especially important. If the findings cannot be generalized, then their study is best viewed as a case study. If they can be generalized, then the study is applicable to countries other than Japan. I believe the findings can be generalized if one examines the motives for FDI, and analyzing the motives might offer a better understanding of what is behind their findings, for example differences in their findings on the effects of FDI between low-income (LIC) and high-income (HIC) destinations.

The following is a list of some of the primary motives for FDI that one might keep in mind when interpreting the Head–Ries findings.

- Foreign exchange rates.
- Political factors, for example formal import barriers (tariffs, domestic content requirements) and informal barriers (jawboning).
- Lower production costs abroad.
- Proximity to the markets for the products.

Some of these factors are relevant for FDI in a certain set of countries, some for other sets of countries. Consider, for example, Japanese FDI in the United States in the late 1970s and into the 1980s. Ray (1988) suggests that Japan timed its investment in US subsidiaries to take advantage of the appreciation of the yen against the dollar. Ray has also found that the unemployment rate, income per capita and business incentive programmes played little part in determining Japanese FDI in different states. In addition to the exchange rate factor, I believe political factors also played a role in the increased Japanese FDI in the United States. It is well known that car imports were the major factor in the US trade deficit with Japan in the 1980s and that the United States tried to persuade Japan to curb its exports.

The above considerations suggest that Japan's primary motives had little to do with wanting to take advantage of the lower production costs in the United States. It is also worth noting that Japanese investment evidently had the effect of transferring technology from Japan to the United States rather than the other way round (Ray, 1998). These considerations may be part of the story behind the Head–Ries finding that the coefficients on the scale variable tend to be insignificant for HICs.

To probe further into their findings, one needs to link the LIC and HIC distinction to the geographical and political aspects of Japanese MNCs' decision to go overseas. For example Honda operates factories in the United States primarily because of the exchange rate and political factors. On the other hand Toyota established factories in Thailand because of the cost advantage in that country as well as Toyota's expectation of expanding markets in Southeast Asia. This is an example of the geographical aspect of MNC behaviour. Operations in Mexico by Sony, Nissan and others are also likely to reflect geographical considerations. Since the authors can identify the countries where each firm's foreign affiliates operate, it would have been useful to control for these countries in their regression analysis.

Their definitions of LIC and HIC are clearly arbitrary. Are such countries as South Korea, Singapore, Taiwan and Hong Kong LICs or

HICs? Whether a country is low income or high income may depend on which year the income data are referring to. I think that some of the above countries might have switched from LIC to HIC, even using the authors' definition. Also, if the LIC definition of 'less than half of Japan's per capita GNP' is changed, their findings may change.

Finally, Head and Ries suggest that FDI in textiles may have reduced employment and wages in Japan. This is a potentially important finding. I conjecture that this finding reflects the fact that the motivation for FDI in this particular industry was the low cost of production in certain countries. The authors are in a position to probe deeper here, since it contrasts with their findings for the other two industries.

References

Belderbos, Rene, Giovanni Capannelli and Kyoji Fukao (1999) 'Local Procurement by Japanese Electronics Firms in Asia', in Takatoshi Ito and Ann O. Krueger, *Role of Foreign Direct Investment in Economic Development* (Chicago, Ill.: NBER University of Chicago Press).

Ito, Takatoshi (1999) 'Capital Flows in Asia', *NBER Working Paper* no. 7134 (Cambridge, Mass.: NBER).

Ray, Edward John (1998) 'Takeover and Transplants: Reassessing FDIUS', in Douglas Woodward and Douglas Nigh (eds), *Foreign Ownership and the Consequences of Direct Investment* (Westport, Connecticut: Quorum Books), pp. 69–96.

Part II

Transfer of Japanese Technology to Asia and North America

5 Technology Transfer in Asia in Transition: Case Studies of Japanese Companies

Takubumi Hayashi

INTRODUCTION

This chapter focuses on recent technological developments in East Asian countries, with particular attention to technology transfer from Japan. In particular the chapter argues that human-embodied technology transfer has played a critical role in technological accumulation in modern Japan, as it has in the Asian region as a whole. In this respect, technology transfer systems that emphasise the OJT (on the job training) for workers and engineers in overseas units and home factories seem to have been effective.

We shall first examine how and the degree to which international intrafirm technology transfer by Japanese companies has been conducted in the Asian regions. Second, light will be shed on cross-border transfers by Japanese companies that are in transition from a one-way flow to multiflow in the region. Finally, it will be argued that as a consequence of technology transfer, the time lag between the launching of a new product in Japan and its transfer to East Asian units has been drastically shortened.

EMERGENCE OF ASIAN NIEs AND TECHNOLOGY TRANSFER

From the 1970s many developing countries began to shift their industrialization policy from import substitution to export promotion. In addition, a large number of multinationals based in the US established production and assembly operations on a global scale along the lines of various export promotion measures by these governments. So why did only some Asian countries succeed in emerging as NIEs (newly industrializing economies)?

We should not, of course, make light of internal factors that can affect the success of industrialization policies. We should keep in mind, however, that the export-oriented policies taken together with those building the national R&D infrastructures, in order to keep pace with the conversion of the international industrial structures, have played critical roles in the industrialization policies of those countries.

However, such policies were put into practice in almost all developing countries, centering on the establishment of export-processing zones to induce foreign direct investment. It seems appropriate to conclude, therefore, that successful industrialization did not depend on whether the policies were implemented skilfully, but on some external factor. What will be examined next is the common key factor that has made some Asian countries rise as NIEs in the world economic system at the end of the 20th century and not others.

Since the oil shock in the 1970s, Japanese manufacturing sectors introduced robots and NC (numerically controlled) and CNC (computerized numerically controlled) machine tools. By the end of the 1980s, while the percentage ratio of numerically controlled machine tools to the overall shipments of machine tools in the United States was around 42 per cent, the same percentage ratio in Japan reached 70–80 per cent. In addition, about 60–70 per cent of the operating industrial robots in the world was concentrated in Japan. The fact that the so-called mother machines are numerically controlled is historically important for the following reasons: whereas the conventional automation work is done by machine tools which merely repeat the same operations continuously, different types of processing work can be done for 24 hours by automatically reprogrammable computer controlled machine tools. In other words, the emergence of programmable automation since the 1970s has transformed the technical basis from the system of mass production of only a few products to a flexible system which allows production of many products in small quantities. Japanese production systems are based on flexible job organizations and particularly suited to multiproduct, small lot production. They have acquired international competitive advantages (Fujimoto, Hayashi *et al.*, 1992).

The historical shift from the United States-based mass production system to multiproduct-based flexible production systems has allowed many countries other than the United States to enter the international competition. Rivalries became intense on a worldwide level and companies have been forced to set up their own overseas production (or assembly) operations or to secure cost competitive suppliers in order to establish competitive advantages, especially in price. This new international competitive structure enabled some East Asian countries to emerge as suitable production and procurement sites since these countries were in a position to develop their industrial infrastructures and export-oriented industrialization policies. In summary, the first reason that some East Asian countries emerged as NIEs was that a new international competitive structure was created when the shift from mass production systems to flexible production occurred. The second reason is concerned with technology transfer from Japan and will be discussed in the next section.

TYPES OF TECHNOLOGY TRANSFER

There are two methods to identify trends in technology transfer. The first is to analyze technology transfer from the flow of technological information in each of the R&D stages. Using this method we examine every technology transferred in each of the R&D stages: basic research, commercialization, mock-up (or prototype) and mass production. Through this method we can examine the technological information in the flow from upper to down stream in each R&D stage. The other method is to cut the flow of technology and examine the contents of it in cross-sections. This chapter employs the second method where technology transfer (TT) is classified into the following three types:

- Transfer of technology embedded in documented information; patents, designs, specifications, layout charts, manuals and so on.
- Transfer of technologies embedded in equipment, machine tools, components, materials and so on.
- Transfer of person- (or organization-) embodied technologies.

The important types of TT, especially for developing or industrializing countries, are type 2 and particularly type 3, although type 1 is vital for developing new products. It seems appropriate to note that type 2 has played important roles in supplying capital goods essential to the industrialization processes of the Asian countries. In these processes, capital goods such as machine tools, equipment, components and materials were successfully procured from Japan in a so-called JIT (just in time) way. In other words, Japan played a role as a key logistic base, namely as a TT 2 base, in their industrialization processes. Next, I examine TT 3 (a personal [organizational]-embodied TT) which is required to make final products taking full advantage of TTs 1 and 2.

TRANSFER OF PERSON (ORGANIZATION) EMBODIED TECHNOLOGY

European and Japanese historical experience

Historically, the movements of personnel who have embodied technologies and skills have played a more fundamental role than TTs 1 and 2. During industrialization in Europe in the 16th and 17th centuries, technologies were diffused mostly by the fact that skilled workers moved to regions where those workers were scarce (see for example Scoville, 1951, and Rosenberg, 1993). At the beginning of the 19th century, when continental European countries introduced newly developed technologies from Britain, although emigration of British artisans was forbidden until 1825, at least two thousand British skilled workers played a major role in providing skills there in the same year (Landes, 1969, pp. 148–9). The greatest contribution in transferring technology by these immigrants 'was not what they did but what they taught... [and] the growing technological independence of the Continent resulted largely from man-to-man transmission of skills on the job' (Landes, 1969, p. 150).

In shipbuilding, for example, 'many workers and foreman in French, German, Danish and Russian yards were British', (Jeremy, 1991, p. 80) and R. Fulton who is famous for the steamship which was built by him in the United States, was also an engineer from England. In developing its technological processes, the Japanese shipbuilding industry relied heavily on European engineers. A French naval engineer had planned the shipyard built at Yokosuka in 1864.[1]

Outlined next is the Japanese technology policy that the government put into practice in the rising era of Japanese capitalism in order to found her industrial technology base.

It was the Ministry of Industry, founded in 1870, that played a leading role in establishing Japan's industrial technology bases. This ministry, which could be thought of as being a founder of the Japanese industrial base, held the authority to import technologies from

Western countries for 15 years until it was abolished in 1870. The two important policies that the ministry adopted to strengthen technological levels in such industries as shipbuilding, mining, communication, railroad, machine tools and so on, of which it was in charge, were dispatching outstanding officials to study overseas and hiring foreign specialists from abroad. As Table 5.1 shows, the number of foreign specialists (*oyatoi-gaikokujin*) that the Meiji government hired was 2299,[2] of which ministry staff accounted for 764. The largest number of these foreign specialists were from Britain, followed by France, Germany, United States and Italy. Excluding non-skilled or non-engineering personnel (for example, cooks, sailors and so on), and including foreign specialists hired by the private sector, the total number of foreigners in charge of TT seems to have been around 2000.

Table 5.1   Number of foreign specialists (1867–89)

Country of origin	No.	Of which ministry employees
UK	928	514
USA	374	10
France	259	77
China (Shin)	253	42
Germany	175	22
Netherlands	87	1
Austria	21	1
Denmark	21	14
Italy	18	10
Russia	16	–
Sweden	9	1
Portugal	6	1
Swizerland	n.a	1
Finland	n.a	1
Norway	n.a	1
Philippines	n.a	70
Others	24	8
Unknown	80	–
Multinational	28	–
Total	2299	764

Notes: Most of the Chinese and Philippine nationals reported here are non-skilled personnel (e.g. cooks, farmers). Foreign Specialists hired in the private sector (not included here) are estimated to be about 2000.
Sources: UNESCO (1975); Ouchi and Tsuchiya (1964).

Interestingly, the number 2000 is equivalent to that of skilled immigrants from Britain who worked in continental Europe in the early 19th century to transfer technology. As mentioned above, in the processes of the international transfer and accumulation of industrial technologies, person-embodied TT through the movement of skilled and engineering personal played a critical role. I will now examine the role of TT, through personal movement between Japan and East Asian countries, in their industrialization processes since the end of the 20th century.

Technology transfer (TT) systems between Japan and Asian countries

Japanese TT systems in Thailand, focusing on the car industry

This section discusses the Japanese TT systems between Japan and Thailand in the case of Japanese-based Thai car manufacturers. The three most interesting points on Thai industrialization are as follows: while Thailand's industrialization policies for the electric and electronics industries have been conducted based on the export-oriented policies, the government has adopted import-substitution industrialization policies in the development processes of its car industry; since a car comprises around 20–30 000 components, the industry consists of many types sectors; and lastly, the Thai car output and market have become the largest in size among ASEAN countries. We note that the building of technological infrastructure of a car industry leads to the establishment of a wide range of supporting industries on a national level.

TT Channels to Thailand by Japanese-based car companies

When we look at the TT to Thailand by Japanese-based car companies, the following six transfer channels seem to be indicated:

• Intrafirm TT by Japanese-based supplier and assembly companies.
• TT from Japanese-based suppliers to Thai local suppliers.
• Organizational TT through local *Kyouryoku-kai* (a loose *keiretsu* system at a local level) set up by Japanese-based assembly companies.
• Licensing-based TT from Japanese-based supplier companies to local supplier companies.

- TT through spin-offs by local engineers from Japanese car companies.
- TT through spin-offs by Japanese engineers from Japanese die-casting (moulding) companies.

The first channel is that of intrafirm-based TT from main plants (factories) in Japan to Thai local plants (factories). The first channel will be examined in detail in the next section because of its importance. The second channel, 'TT from Japanese-based suppliers to Thai local suppliers', is the one in which Japanese-based suppliers give technical advice or guidance to local suppliers in order to raise local procurement, causing their production cost to fall and quality to improve. It usually becomes essential for local suppliers to get technical assistance from the Japanese-based suppliers in order for them to meet the QCD (quality/cost/delivery) standards required by the Japanese assembly makers.

The third channel is organizational TT through local *Kyouryoku-Kai*, which is set up by Japanese-based assembly companies, as the technology transfer channel. *Kyouryoku-kai* consists of local and Japanese-based suppliers and sets up regular technical training courses, arranges model member company tours, sends trainees to Japan and so on. The fourth channel is licensing-based TT from Japanese-based supplier companies to local supplier companies. When the Japanese assembly makers procure some components directly from local suppliers, they require them to introduce technologies and skills from Japanese suppliers who manufacture the same kind of components. The assembly makers subject first-time local suppliers to very strict QCD standards. Typically the assembly makers require local suppliers to agree to technology licensing contracts with Japanese suppliers providing the same kinds of components to these assembly makers.

The fifth channel, TT through spin-offs by local engineers from Japanese car companies, has become of a significant importance and position not only in the Thai industrialization but also in other East Asian countries. It would seem that the most important factor of the fifth channel is that local engineers, after getting sufficient technical training at some Japanese companies, quit the companies and set up their own businesses taking advantage of their embodied skills and technologies. We observed this during our research visit to Thailand. A Thai local engineer who graduated from a local college of engineering worked for 17 years as a die-casting and moulding specialist for a Japanese car assembly firm. He was sent to Japan to get technical training. After that he resigned from the company and set up his own business to manufacture body parts and engine parts in order to supply several Japanese-based and local companies. Whereas this kind of TT through spin-offs by local engineers that set up their own businesses has a negative effect on the Japanese companies, in the long run it becomes an essential TT channel to boost the local industrial base. Finally, the last channel, which is still exceptional but of greatest interest to the author, is TT through spin-offs by Japanese engineers who used to work for Japanese die-casting/moulding companies. Even if some local companies succeed in winning contracts with Japanese car companies, without having die-casting and moulding-related technologies, they could only undertake simple work such as bending, cutting, pressing and so on with low value. When they produce products in large quantities, it is essential for them to obtain die-casting/moulding-related technologies. In recent years we can find Japanese engineers in this field working for local suppliers who have contracts with Japanese-based companies. These engineers are more or less immigrants from Japan who are hired out as technical advisers by the local companies, and who teach technologies and skills to the local employees. After working for more than 10–30 years for Japanese companies, these engineers have resigned or retired and emigrated to do this sort of job under the condition that their wages are assured to be nearly the same as in Japan. In other words, they could nowadays be called foreign experts.

The previous six TT channels seem to have had a great impact on the technological basis of Thailand's car and other manufacturing industries. It could well be that these TT channels can be applied to the whole ASEAN region. According to survey research which was conducted by the author in 1993 and 1995, the most effective TT channels for Thai car companies seem to be TT through the movement of engineering (and skilled) personnel especially by transborder intrafirm TT, between Japan and Thailand.

In all six TT channels mentioned above, person-embodied TT through movement of skilled-personnel plays a critical role. The next section deals with the contents of the training system delivered to the local trainees in Japan by Japanese car companies.

Technical training systems in Japan by Japanese car companies

Table 5.2 shows the outline of the technical training system for trainees from the inspection division of Proton (a Malaysian-based car company), which was carried out for six months by a Japanese car assembly firm (Kobayashi and Hayashi, 1993, ch. 5).

Table 5.2 Training programme of a Japanese car company (section: press
              inspection; period: 6 months)

Programme items	Training content	Training hours
Practical training	Trial production and inspection training of components	652
Making inspection manual of new model	Making inspection manual by examining structures of new models	88
Repair and maintenance of machines	Examining the troubles and taking countermeasures	64
QCC activities	Understanding of aims, methods and tools and effects of QC activities and participating in real QC Circle activities	64
Safety	Basic rules for safe movement or motion, case studies of accidents	32
Meeting	Knowing each other through meeting with foremen and chiefs	24
Factory visiting tour	Understanding overall car industries	24
Sightseeing	General knowledge about Japanese history and culture	48
Orientation and guidance	General knowledge about life in Japan	32

Source: Interview survey, 1994.

Table 5.3 shows that the common characteristics of the contents that Japanese companies as a whole incorporate into the technical training system are as follows: firstly, the emphasis of technical training is placed on practical training mainly consisting of OJT (on the job training). It is structured for acquiring skills not only in how to operate or inspect, but also to maintain and repair machines to work well. As Table 5.2 shows, it is designed also to train workers for taking countermeasures (troubleshooting) against machine problems. This means that local trainees who obtain multifunctional and technical skills through this sort of training system can easily adapt to new and flexible production lines. A second point is that in the Japanese training system, the subject of quality control (QC) circle activities is included together with an understanding of scientific QC tools and methods. The table also indicates that 64 training hours for QC activities are set aside, the same duration as for troubleshooting. This has a significance in that understanding QC activities and

Table 5.3 Training measures for local operators and engineers

	Total	Training in Japan	Sending Japanese engineers	Training at local plant	Manual in local language	Setting up QCC	Activating Teian system	Scouting from other companies	Recruiting Asian students in Japan	Other
Total	213	187	158	151	71	45	19	14	14	6
(%)	(100)	(100)	(100)	(100)	(100)	(100)	(100)	(100)	(100)	(100)
Manual base	25	22	16	18	9	3	1	–	2	2
(%)	(11.7)	(11.8)	(10.1)	(11.9)	(12.7)	(6.7)	(5.3)	–	(14.3)	(33.3)
OJT base	151	132	116	109	49	33	16	10	8	2
(%)	(70.9)	(70.6)	(73.4)	(72.2)	(69)	(73.3)	(84.2)	(71.4)	(57.1)	(33.3)
Can not be identified	34	30	24	22	12	9	2	4	4	2
(%)	(16)	(16)	(15.2)	(14.6)	(16.9)	(20)	(10.5)	(28.6)	(28.6)	(33.3)
Unknown	3	3	2	2	1	–	–	–	–	–
(%)	(1.4)	(1.6)	(1.3)	(1.3)	(1.4)	–	–	–	–	–

Sources: Results of questionnaire survey of Japanese manufacturing companies in the machinery, electrical, car and precision instrument industries (received from 342 companies in October 1990). Nikkei (1991, p. 71).

methods by the trainees would allow independent *kaizen* activities on a local level to occur, speeding up localization of management.

Figure 5.1 shows the number of foreign trainees that some Japanese car parts company (supplier) accepted from its overseas operations from 1974 through 1993. Each number of trainees is limited to those who got formal trainee visas and stayed for more than three weeks in Japan between 1974 and 1993.

According to an interview survey the author conducted in 1995, the total number of trainees from its overseas operations had reached a little more than 7000 by 1993.[3] In addition, the company had also accepted a large number of engineers from its overseas operations without any formal trainee visas and they received training within three weeks in Japan. These foreign engineers without any formal visas are excluded from the table. As the figure shows, the Thai and the Philippine operations apparently hold important positions among Japan's global operations. In these two operations, the quality levels are the same as in Japan and most of the trained engineers remained with the company playing leading roles.[4]

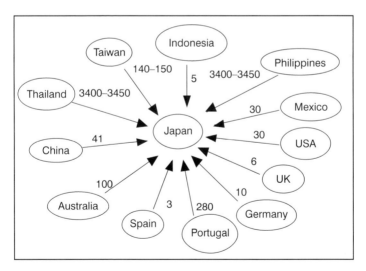

Figure 5.1   Number of trainees from overseas operations, Japanese component company, Japan, 1974–93
Note: The number of trainees are limited to those who stayed for more than three weeks on an official trainees visa.
Source: Interview survey, October 1994.

To summarize this section, the Japanese-style TT system based on an intrafirm international TT through personal movement appears to function effectively to improve the technical standards of the local operators and engineers particularly in terms of process technologies and skills.

Japanese engineers in Asia and Asian trainees in Japan

Under the Japanese-style TT system, technology information transferred is apt to have personally embodied features. Thus Japanese technology and skill-training systems centre on OJT regardless of the geographic location. One of the fundamental characteristics of the Japanese-style TT system, especially as far as TT for developing or industrializing countries is concerned, is found in *teian* or *kaizen* activities based on QCC and TPM (total production management).[5]

In the era of flexible production systems corresponding to diversified and changing market needs, dynamic production processes require much more multifunctional jobs than before. As a consequence, it seems reasonable for the Japanese companies to rely on OJT, rather than fix the mode of operations by the documented manual.

Whereas it rather tends to be more time-, cost- and manpower-consuming, person- (and/or organization) embodied technologies and skills can be constantly improved and continuously accumulated. As a result of this TT mechanism, intrafirm TT to East Asian countries among others, appears to have structured technological foundations of the industrialization of these countries.

In a positive sense, it seems appropriate that Japanese companies are called vocational technical training colleges (Chen and Hayashi, 1995, p. 67) and that Japan has played the role of a vocational technical training college for East Asian countries.

Next, I will examine how many Japanese engineers work abroad, particularly in East Asian countries. Table 5.4 shows the number of Japanese employees in the main Asian countries that are dispatched by Japanese manufacturing companies.

According to the interview survey, about 70–80 per cent of the Japanese employees working abroad serve as technical advisors in such areas as production technology, production management, quality control and so on. The number of Japanese employees and executives dispatched to East Asian countries exceeded 10 000 in 1994, of which 70–80 per cent, or approximately 7000–8000 Japanese engineers, were

Table 5.4   Number of Japanese employees in East Asia, manufacturing sector, 1991–96

	1991	1993	1996
Thailand	1 736	2 112	3 063
Malaysia	1 093	1 606	1 911
Taiwan	1 533	1 378	1 230
Singapore	1 256	1 217	1 303
Indonesia	850	1 074	1 563
China	459	811	2 897
Hong Kong	607	772	1 204
Philippines	287	349	563
Korea	425	387	343
India	73	88	101
Pakistan	–	17	13
Sri Lanka	–	13	24
Vietnam	–	10	100
Others	31	5	12
Asia total	8350	9839	14 327
East Asia total		9721	14 315

Sources: Chen and Hayashi (1995); Toyo Kei Zai (1997).

under long-term contracts. The number does not include, however, those engineers who were sent to these countries over a short time period to establish new production lines or expand existing production lines without formal working visas. When considering this, the number of Japanese people engaging in TT could amount to several times as many as 7000–8000. Although the absolute number of Japanese engineers abroad has increased, the percentage ratios of them to the total number of local employees working for Japanese-based companies in Asia are gradually declining, for example 0.89 per cent in 1991 and 0.88 per cent in 1994. Lastly, I examine how many Asian trainees have received technical training in Japan over the last decade. Table 5.5 shows the number of foreign trainees who visited Japan from overseas with formal trainee visas from 1983 to 1996.

As the table indicates, the number of foreign trainees is approximately 10 000 on an annual base from the first half to the middle of the 1980s, and has drastically increased to 30–40 000 since the end of the 1980s. Nearly 90 per cent of these are Asian trainees. Many more people who did not get formal training visas have undergone technical training for several weeks in Japan so, considering the number of

Table 5.5   Number of trainees from overseas, Japan, 1983–96

	1983	1987	1991	1993	1996
China	1 525	2 851	11 343	15 688	17 904
Thailand	933	3 529	6 414	4 075	3 298
Korea	1 517	3 183	6 233	3 224	2 710
Philippines	706	1 280	5 183	2 942	4 446
Indonesia	1 929	1 333	3 939	3 433	5 098
Malaysia	898	787	4 472	2 174	1 675
Taiwan	436	510	1 883	448	737
Singapore	371	236	462	148	110
India	274	347	638	544	737
Vietnam	–	–		292	1 313
Sri Lanka	–	–		400	501
Pakistan	–	–		220	242
Hong Kong	–	–			17
Asia total	9 400	14 463	42 755	34 799	40 201
Europe	672	959	2 109	1 282	1 078
North America	502	805	1178	766	662
South America	1 008	1 230	1 602	1 523	1 605
Total	12 612	18 613	48 868	39 795	45 536

Notes: Columns do not sum to the totals because some regions are not reported in this table.
Source: Compiled from immigration annual statistics, Ministry of Justice.

technical trainees without this sort of visa, approximately a hundred thousand people have come to Japan in order to receive technical training each year over this decade.

TECHNOLOGY TRANSFER SYSTEMS IN TRANSITION

Flying geese style or networking style

It seems inadequate that we examined TT to Asia by the Japanese companies only from the standpoint of the number of technical trainees sent to Japan from East Asian countries. The main reason is that intrafirm TT by Japanese-based companies is not a one-way flow from Japan to these countries any more. The following are examples of new types of intrafirm TT flows utilized by some Japanese-based companies in the Asian countries. When a Japanese-based electric and electronics company set up TV production lines in Vietnam, it sent some Vietnamese operators not to Japan but to Thai operations in order to get them technically trained. Also a Japanese car maker was planning to send Vietnamese operators not to Japan but to a Malaysian car company (Proton) for the same reason, and a Japanese electric and electronics parts company sent Chinese-Malaysian engineers to China when it set up a new factory in China. As Japanese companies increasingly transfer out production of their standardized products to Asia, to cut production costs and to aim at local markets, the number of intrafirm TT flows within the Asian regions appear to be increasing. With these new trends the number of Asian trainees who are sent to such Asian countries as Singapore or Taiwan should also be increasing. The case studies of Matsushita Electric give us an interesting insight into the new intrafirm TT flows within Asian countries. In 1990 the company established a human development centre in Singapore, which is called the AMS-HDC (Takeno, 1998).[6] AMS-HDC functions as a regional human development centre which trains employees at several levels of technology management. Their training courses are aimed at all of their subsidiaries and regions where they operate and cover several levels of difficulty from novice to advanced classes. It has accepted, on average, 3000 Asian trainees each year mainly from Singapore and Malaysia, but some trainees came from Thailand, the Philippines and Indonesia. (Note that the number of employees of Matsushita's operations in Singapore and Malaysia is around 48 000 as of 1996, accounting for more than 50 per cent of its total employees in Asia.[7])

As the cases of the Matsushita Electric and other Japanese companies indicate, the one-way flow of intrafirm TT by Japanese companies from Japan to Asian operations has gradually created another flow within the Asian regions. Other Asian NIEs companies likewise have conducted intrafirm TT inside Asia. Daewoo Electronics, a Korean electronics multinational company, has sent more than 200 Vietnamese operators and engineers from the Vietnamese operations to Korea for technical training. The more Asian companies internationalize their operations to other Asian regions, the more intrafirm TT flows within Asia are expected to increase.

As a result of these multi-TT flows by Asian companies in the Asian regions, a closer TT network in the region is being established. Although the so-called 'flying geese TT model' is still more or less effective, the model seems to have been changing in nature to a more network type TT model. Such TT networks often accelerate development of new products as discussed below.

**Time lag between the period of launching new products in Japan
and that of intrafirm import from their Asian operations**

As the TT flows get more complex, it will take less time for Japanese firms to transfer their products out from Japan to overseas operations. Table 5.6 shows how many years some products had been produced in Japan before they were transferred to overseas operations.[8]

The most striking feature is that 36.1 per cent of those products produced after 1997 will be transferred out within two years, reaching the highest percentage ratio of all time.

The reasons why these Japanese companies now wait for less time before they transfer out products to their foreign operations are the competitive environment facing the global market place and the enhancement of the R&D and production capabilities of their foreign operations.

Table 5.6   Age of Japanese products transferred to overseas
operations, 1985–97

	1985–89	1990–96	1997
Under 2 years	12.9	18.9	36.1
2–5 years	11.3	21.1	14.8
5–10 years	27.4	23.2	13.1
10–20 years	24.2	22.1	26.2
More than 20 years	29	24.2	23

Source: Questionnaire survey by the author.

Table 5.7   Location of research and development of products transferred to
East Asian countries: fractions in per cent (number of incidences)

	Totally in Japan	Totally at local	Mainly at local	Partially at local	Other*	Total
1990	85.8 (91)	0 (0)	3.8 (4)	7.5 (8)	2.8 (3)	100 (106)
1996	70.4 (88)	3.2 (4)	5.6 (7)	18.4 (23)	2.4 (3)	100 (125)
2001	38.5 (45)	4.3 (5)	10.3 (12)	43.6 (51)	3.4 (4)	100 (117)

*Transferred products developed partially in Japan in collaboration with another country.
Source: Questionnaire survey by the author.

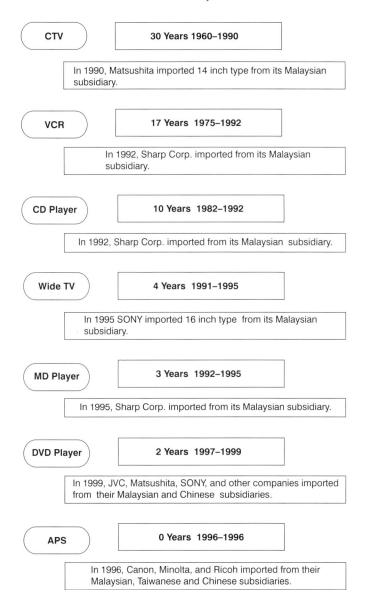

Figure 5.2   Time lags between the year of launching new AV products in the Japanese market and intrafirm imports from Asian operations by Japanese companies

Source: Compiled from Nikkei Newspaper (various dates) Shinbun.

Table 5.7 shows which products were (and are planned to be) transferred out to East Asia and which were (and are planned to be) developed in 1990, 1996 and 2001, respectively. Of the products transferred to East Asian countries in 1990, 85.8 per cent were totally developed in Japan; however, the percentage ratio is expected to drastically decline to 38.5 per cent in 2001.

On the other hand, while only 7.5 per cent of those products transferred in 1990 were partially developed locally, the ratio is expected to rise to 43.6 per cent in 2001, which will be the highest ratio of all. More interestingly, while the sum of the ratio of 'totally developed at local' and that of 'mainly developed at local' was 3.8 per cent in 1990, it rose to 8.8 per cent in 1996 and is expected to increase to 14.6 per cent in 2001. This means that one product out of 6–7 products produced in these regions is expected to be totally or mainly developed by the East Asian R&D units.[9]

Finally in this section, Figure 5.2 illustrates the time lags for certain consumer electronics products in Japan between the year these products were launched and when intrafirm imports began from Japanese-based operations in East Asian countries. As for colour TV sets, they had been produced for nearly 30 years in Japan until Matsushita Electric began to import them (14 inches type) from its Malaysian subsidiaries in 1990. Regarding home VCR sets, they had been produced for 17 years in Japan until Sharp began to import from its Malaysian subsidiary in 1992. Next, it took ten years for CD Players to be imported by Sharp from its Malaysian subsidiary in 1992. Sony imported wide-TV sets from its Malaysian subsidiary in 1995, while they were first launched in Japan in 1991. It took four years until they were imported to Japan through an intrafirm trade.

After MD (mini-disk) players were first mass-produced and launched in Japan in 1992, Sharp imported them from its Malaysian subsidiary to Japan in 1995. The time lag was shortened to three years. As for the APS (advanced photo system), it was almost at the same time when Canon, Minolta and Ricoh launched this new camera system into the Japanese market in 1996, and imported from their subsidiaries in Malaysia, Taiwan and China in the same year. As these examples show, it seems apparent that the time lag between launching new products in Japan and importing them from Japanese subsidiaries in East Asia has drastically shortened from several decades to being almost simultaneous. Therefore the international product life-cycle model does not necessarily seem to hold in Asia where production capabilities are diversified internationally.

Irrational features of the Japanese TT systems

As the Asian NIEs began to shift from process technologies in the so-called downstream of the R&D processes into product technologies in the upperstream, irrational aspects of the Japanese TT system have become apparent. I first note that, in transforming technological information into documents such as manuals and specifications, American (Western) TT systems appear to be superior to the Japanese system. When transferring technologies, the American system does not rely so much on personal functions as the Japanese system. For example, the American TT system performs better in TT of operational skills on machinery and equipment, which do not have to rely on personal factors. (Most of these sorts of technical information are standardized enough for the general public to understand, and hence can be documented well.)

Furthermore, the American TT method functions more smoothly than the Japanese method under circumstances where the turnover rate of employees is high, or linguistic and cultural differences exist. The Japanese system is beginning to experience more problems as TT gets into the realm of product development in the upper stream of R&D, since design concepts are not written clearly in such documents as manuals and specifications in Japan. Typically only a limited number of technical persons in charge belonging to the exclusive *keiretsu* group can understand the technical specifics well. (Technical documents are not properly standardized either.) Making contracts based on undocumented technology information which is not standardized well is difficult and would be costly. This aspect of the Japanese TT system, therefore, may limit future TT from Japan to Asia.

CONCLUSION: HOLLOWING OUT OF INDUSTRIES OR COLLABORATION SYSTEMS

As we have argued, in the historical processes of industrial revolutions starting from Britain and from the industrialization in each country, technology transfer through personal movement has played a key role. The processes of industrialization and technology transfer through the personal movement in East Asia involved industrialized countries, and Japan in particular. We have not, however, discussed future implications of TT to East Asia or to Japan.

Notes

1. When building the shipyard in Yokosuka, F. L. Verny, a French engineer, came to Japan in 1865 as a technical adviser. In 1866, 45 French engineers who were selected by Verny came to Japan to begin construction on a large scale (Yamada, 1968, p. 206).
2. The other main governmental organ which hired many foreign specialists was the Ministry of Internal Affairs. It mainly hired foreign specialists in the fields of agriculture and spinning technologies.
3. Since the number is cumulative, those trainees who trained three times in Japan, for example, get three counts. Most of the foreman class foreign engineers working for its overseas operations had more than 2–3 rounds of training.
4. This was indicated at interviews with the head of the personnel division at the HQ in 1995.
5. TPM basically centres on activities by operators under the guidance of engineers. Engineers teach operators how to control production lines efficiently by maximizing the workability of several machines. The purpose of TPM activities is to let operators themselves understand machine mechanism, repair and maintain machines, and design layouts of the lines to maximize the productivity of the whole line system.
6. The author would like to thank Prof. T. Takeno for providing valuable material on AMS-HDC.
7. The total number of employees in its Asian operations was about 79 000 in 1996, excluding Japan and China (Takeno, 1998).
8. The author conducted a questionnaire survey in October 1996 and February 1997 in collaboration six other researchers with the financial support of Nihon University. The questionnaires were sent to 1000 Japanese manufacturing companies, excluding chemicals, drugs, food and beverage companies. We received replies from 139 companies mainly assembly and component companies in the electric, electronics, transport, precision and other machinery sectors.
9. As for US and European R&D units by Japanese companies, 'totally or mainly developed at local' accounted for 14.5 per cent in 1990 and 19.2 per cent in 1996, and is expected to rise to 31.0 per cent in 2001.

References

Agmon, T. and M. A. V. Glinow (eds) (1991) *Technology Transfer in International Business* (Oxford: Oxford University Press).
Chen, B. and T. Hayashi (eds) (1995) *Technological Development and Technology Transfer in Asia* (in Japanese) (Bunshindo).
Cohen, S. and J. Zysman (1987) *Manufacturing Matters* (Basic Books).
Fujimoto, M., T. Hayashi, Y. Kawakami and T. Murakami (1992) *International Competitiveness of Japanese Companies* (in Japanese) (Zeimukeiri-kyoukai).

Hayashi, T. (1989) *Multinationals and Intellectual Property Rights* (in Japanese) (Moriyamashoten).

Hayashi, T. (1999) 'R&D Capabilities of Eastern Asian Countries – Focusing on Asian NIEs', in A. Inzelt and J. Hilton (eds), *Technology Transfer: From Invention to Innovation* (Kluwer Academic).

Henderson, W. O. (1992) *Britain and Industrial Europe 1750–1870* (Leicester: Leicester University Press).

Hirakawa, S. (1992) *NIES – World System and Development* (in Japanese) (Doyukan).

Imai, K. (1989) *Technological Conditions in Modern Japan* (in Japanese) (Yanagiharashoten).

Jeremy, D. J. (1991) *International Technology Transfer – Europe, Japan, and the USA, 1700–1914* (Aldershot: Edward Elgar).

Kiyokawa, Y. and K. Minami (eds) (1987) *Industrialization and Technology Development in Japan* (in Japanese) (Toyokeizaisinposha).

Kobayashi, H. and T. Hayashi (eds) (1993) *Industrialization of ASEAN Countries and Foreign Companies* (in Japanese) (Chuokeizaisha).

Komoda, F. (1987) *The Economics of International Technology Transfer* (in Japanese) (Yuhikaku).

Komoda, F., K. Nishiyama and T. Hayashi (1997) *The Economics of the Technology Paradigm* (in Japanese) (Tagashuppan).

Landes, D. (1969) *The Unbound Prometeus* (Cambridge: Cambridge University Press).

Mansfield, E. and A. Romeo (1980) 'Technology Transfer to Overseas Subsidiaries by US Based Firms', *Quarterly Journal of Economics*, August.

Mansfield, E. and A. Romeo (1984) 'Reverse Transfer of Technology from Overseas Subsidiaries to American Firms', *IEEE Transactions on Engineering Management*, vol. EM-31, no. 3.

Nakaoka, T., T. Ishii and H. Uchida (eds) (1986) *Technology and Technology Policy in Modern Japan* (in Japanese) (UN University Press).

Nikkei (1991) *Technology Transfer to Asia* (in Japanese) (Tokyo: Nikkei).

OECD (1979) *The Impact of the Newly Industrializing Countries on Production and Trade in Manufacturers* (Paris: OECD).

Ouchi, K. and M. Tsuchiya (eds) (1964) *The Meiji Period Finance* (in Japanese) (Tokyo: Meijibunken Shiryo Kankokai).

Piore, M. and C. Sabel (1984) *The Second Industrial Divide* (Basic Books).

Rosenberg, N. (1976) *Perspectives on Technology* (Cambridge: Cambridge University Press).

Rosenberg, N. (1993) 'Economic Development and the Transfer of Technology: Some Historical Perspectives', in E. Mansfield (ed.), *The Economics of Technical Change* (Aldershot: Edward Elgar).

Rosenberg, N. and C. Frischtak (eds) (1985) *International Technology Transfer* (New York: Praeger).

Sagafi-nejad, T., R. Moxon and H. Perlmuter (1981) *Controlling International Technology Transfer* (Oxford: Pergamon).

Saito, Y. (1980) *Economic Theory of Technology Transfer* (in Japanese) (Bunshindo).

Saito, Y. (1990) *Building the Development Corridor in Asia* (in Japanese) (Bunshindo).

Scoville, W. C. (1951) 'Minority Migration and the Diffusion of Technology', *Journal of Economic History*, vol. 11, no. 4.

Takeno, T. (1998) 'Regional Management and Human Resource Development, Technology Transfer: Matsushita Electric Industrial Company's Case, *Bulletin of Nagoya Institute of Technology*, vol. 50 (in Japanese).

Toyo Keizai (1997) *Japanese Overseas Investment* (in Japanese) (Tokyo: Toyo Keizai Shimposha).

UNESCO (ed.) (1975) *Foreign Specialists* (Oyatoi Gaikokujin), (in Japanese) (Tokyo: Shogakukan).

Yamada, N. (1968a) *Oyatoi-Gaikokujin: Transportation* (in Japanese) (Kashimashuppankai).

Yoshida, M. (1968b) *Oyatoi-Gaikokujin: Industry* (in Japanese) (Kashimashuppankai).

Comments on Chapter 5

Teri Ursacki

One of the paradoxes of academic life is that an interesting paper often begets more questions than it answers, requiring further research to deepen our understanding. We thus end up with more work than when we started. While a pessimist might despair that we may never achieve full understanding, an optimist such as myself looks at the positive side: job security for academics. Chapter 5 is like that: it raises some tempting questions that whet our appetite for more.

The chapter highlights the role of the movement of personnel in technology transfer within Asia. If such movement is indeed important, there are important policy implications at both the national and international levels. Nationally, host government policies to restrict inward movement of foreign companies' personnel to preserve jobs would be perverse: by impeding the flow of technology they would be undermining the competitiveness needed to generate lasting gains in employment. Internationally, it would suggest that trade negotiations need to devote much greater effort to freeing the cross-border flow of managerial and technical staff.

The questions Chapter 5 raises bear on how important the flow of personnel is in technology transfer. The chapter documents the flow of personnel between Japan and East Asia, but it would be useful to know more about the actual results of these transfers, particularly in light of press reports that many of the 'trainees' taken to Japan were simply cheap labour being brought in under a loophole created to release some of the pressure from what was once a very tight Japanese labour market. The decline in the number of trainees in 1991–92 after the bursting of the bubble economy lends particular interest to this issue. The chapter suggests at the beginning that the reliance on personnel-driven methods is a distinguishing characteristic of Japanese technology transfer. Demonstrating this would really require a cross-sectional study, while the chapter is based on a one-industry, one-country study.

Most importantly, we must ask how much technology was transferred and how well. The key question here is whether an indigenous

137

technological capability was developed. This answer bears on whether fears of 'hollowing out' are justified, for example. While technology embodied in people has the possibility of being more effectively transferred, it also has the potential to be simply a means of preserving technological secrets. While the chapter alludes to Japan's Meiji-era experience, in that case the importation of people-embodied technology was largely government driven; dissemination was therefore an important goal. Given that the process in Asia is largely driven by the private sector, which faces rather different incentives, can we really expect the same results?

There are several indicators we might find of interest in considering these issues. The chapter suggests that there is networking technology transfer going on among affiliates. Is this actually technology that has been newly developed by the affiliate, or simply a case of one affiliate passing on the same technology it received either unaltered or with minor modifications? There is also a reference to spin-off firms. It would be enlightening to have some quantitative data on the number and size of such firms to assess their likely impact. Where products are described as 'locally designed', what definition is being used? Is the product really new, or simply a local rearrangement of the knobs?

The reference to the shorter delay between innovation and the introduction of new products to these offshore markets leads one to consider a number of alternatives to the notion that this acceleration is due to higher technological levels in the offshore markets. Could it not be due to higher income levels in those markets, with a resultant increase in demand for more leading-edge goods? Or to straightforward economic factors such as high wages in the home market, the strong yen, or reductions in Japanese import barriers?

Chapter 5 raises interesting and important questions and points to the need for more systematic, quantitative evidence. Any one of the research directions suggested above could constitute a study in itself. Students of this topic are thus assured of a rich research agenda.

6 Japanese-Owned Car Suppliers in North America: A Review of the Literature and Prosposal for Research

Susan Helper

INTRODUCTION

Since the late 1970s, 1400 Japanese-owned manufacturing plants have been set up in the United States. In 1994, 322 of these plants supplied the car industry in some way.[1] These firms (the automotive ones in particular) have inspired a great deal of research. Their experience is variously cited as proof that Japanese-inspired 'lean production' methods can be successfully transplanted to the United States with virtually no adaptation (Kenney and Florida (1994)), as proof that Japanese dualist methods can be transplanted (Howes, 1993a) and as evidence that moving the Japanese production system abroad is slow, difficult and requires much hybridization (Liker *et al.*, 1999).

The next section discusses several theories of how Japanese transplants might perform in the United States and Canada. The third section looks at articles that examine the performance of Japanese-owned suppliers in the United States in light of these theories. It is found that, contrary to the expectations generated by lean production enthusiasts, their performance in general has not been far superior to that of US-owned plants in the same industry. The third section looks at some of the reasons why this might be so. The chapter concludes with suggestions for future research.

TRANSPLANT PRODUCTION: THEORY

The arrival of a large number of Japanese plants on US and Canadian shores created an opportunity to test theories about the effect of national institutions and culture on management practice. Even better, much of this investment was concentrated in one industry (cars), so technological factors could be controlled for. Japanese investment also brought with it some important policy questions: was the investment something to be encouraged, because it would create new jobs and bring improved management techniques, or was it part of a bad tendency to undermine both highly skilled engineering jobs and well-paid, unionized, blue-collar work in the United States and Canada?

The work on this question addresses two separate questions. First, are the Japanese replicating their production system here, or are they adopting the practices typical of their host countries? Second, have the Japanese plants been successful in terms of private profit and/or social benefit?

Much of the research has studied the nature of the practices adopted by Japanese transplants and has not examined the question of performance. This seems an important omission, since it would be interesting to know not only whether Japanese practices are being used in North America, but also whether they are effective.

Also, much of the work focuses on car assembly rather than supply. For both theoretical and policy reasons, it is important to study suppliers as well. Many studies have found that the size and access to resources of both sender and receiver are important determinants of the success of technology transfer (see for example the sources cited in Liker *et al.*, 1999, and MacDuffie and Helper, 1999). Suppliers tend to be smaller companies with less organizational slack (in terms of both management and capital) and less international experience than the automotive assemblers, which have many billions of dollars of sales annually. And in aggregate, Japanese-owned transplant suppliers employ more people than do transplant assemblers.

This chapter will discuss three bodies of work that examine both the practices and the performance of transplants and discuss suppliers as well as assemblers. They are: (1) lean production advocates, (2) dualism/management by stress and (3) hybridization. We shall consider each in turn.

Lean production advocates

This group believes that the Japanese are replicating their system here, and that this brings benefits both to the firms and to the host countries. Womack *et al.* (1990) argue that Japanese firms are more likely to be characterized by 'lean production', a system in which managers and employees work continuously to improve the process by reducing buffers between production stages and finding and fixing the root cause of defective products. Lean production

> is a superior way for humans to make things. It provides better products in wider variety at lower cost. Equally important, it provides more challenging and fulfilling work for employees at every level, from the factory to headquarters. It follows that the whole world should adopt lean production, and as quickly as possible (ibid., p. 225).

This diffusion will occur naturally,

> since this mode of production achieves its highest efficiency, quality, and flexibility when all activities from design to assembly occur in the same place.... Lean producers in the 1990s will need to create top-to-bottom, paper-concept to finished-car manufacturing systems in the three great markets of the world – North America, Europe, and Asia (ibid., p. 200).

Similarly, Kenney and Florida (1994, p. 8) state: 'of course the Japanese production system is efficient'. The Japanese transplants are 'rebuilding the rust belt [by]...making long-term commitments where US business leaders had seemed to give up hope' (Kenney and Florida, 1991).

Dualism/management by stress

Like the lean production advocates, this group argues that the Japanese are transferring a substantial part of their production system to North America, and that this is beneficial for firms. However the agreement stops there. The authors in this camp say that the Japanese production system in Japan includes a large measure of exploitation, and it is largely such unfair aspects that the Japanese are taking to the United States and Canada. For example Howes (1993a, p. 31) argues that an important component of the Japanese production system comprises the 'contingent workers and suppliers [who] build cost flexibility into a system otherwise characterized by high fixed costs'. It is this 'market' system that the Japanese are taking to North America. For every hour spent producing in a US-located transplant, almost twice as many hours are worked in Japan, doing design, engineering, high-technology parts fabrication, and research and development. 'There is no reason why the creative parts of the system should be transferred and a lot of reasons why the exploitative parts of the system would fit well in the United States' (Howes, 1993b, p. 76).

Arguments in this vein are also made by the Economic Strategy Institute (1992) and McAlinden (1991), which characterize Japanese cars assembled in the United States as having little more US content than imports. Kearns (1992) says that the Japanese are creating a 'separate auto economy' in the United States, one which imports high-value-added parts from Japan and uses low-wage, non-union workers to produce standard parts. In this view, the expansion of the transplants comes at the expense of the traditional US car sector, which has been a large employer of well-paid production workers and highly educated engineers.

These authors also have a different view of lean production from the first group. Worker participation does not lead to fulfilment for workers. Instead it means that workers provide free consulting to management, giving up their detailed knowledge about how to do their jobs quickly so that management can speed up production and hire cheaper replacements. Productivity is high, but this is achieved through rigid adherence to standardized work procedures that also leads to repetitive strain injuries as workers repeat the same motion again and again in a fast-paced, high-stress work environment (Parker and Slaughter, 1995; Lewchuk and Robertson, 1998).

Hybridization

In contrast to the first two groups, these authors believe that the Japanese are not transferring their unique production system to North America, or at least not without substantial modification. And unless they go through an arduous process of 're-contextualization'[2] (figuring out which parts of the system to keep, and which are simply not applicable in a new environment), they are not particularly successful either.

Authors in this school emphasize that the 'Japanese management system' is not a single, consciously designed set of techniques. Rather it is a philosophy that has evolved over time in a number of different ways in response to the pressures of and opportunities available in a much different society from those of the United States and Canada. Much of the system was (and remains) tacit; it was unclear (particularly at the beginning of transplant investment in the early 1980s) which features were inextricably linked to the excellent manufacturing performance obtained in Japan, and which could be (or had to be) dropped in order for the system to function elsewhere. In particular, Japanese managers have had to figure out how to adapt their practices to a more individualistic and legalistic environment in which workers have little trust in the management (Liker *et al.*, 1998; Abo, 1994.)

TRANSPLANT SUPPLIERS: EVIDENCE ON PERFORMANCE

The above theories exhaust the set of possible answers to the two questions posed at the beginning of this chapter. According to at least one set of authors, Japanese car suppliers either have or have not taken their system to North America, and either have or have not performed well. This section reviews the evidence on performance in the following areas: quality, productivity, inventory and worker outcomes. The subsequent section relates this evidence on perform-ance to evidence on the nature of production practices used by transplants.

Quality

Cusumano and Takeishi (1991) found that Japanese transplant sup-pliers had far fewer defects than their American counterparts, in a small matched sample of parts. US-owned suppliers to Japanese car-makers provided those customers with higher-quality parts than they supplied to their US customers.

This feeling about the superior quality of Japanese parts (whether the factory was located in the United States or Japan) was echoed as late as 1996 by Toyota's vice CEO, who was quoted in a major Japanese newspaper (*Nihon Keizai shinbun*) as saying that 'Japanese suppliers are still better [than Toyota's US-owned suppliers] in con-tinuous kaizen movement and product quality' (quoted in Nakamura *et al.*, 1999, p. 379).

However Helper (forthcoming) could find no significant differences in the 1993 defect rates between US suppliers to Japanese customers and the Japanese transplant suppliers supplying those customers. In contrast to Cusumano and Takeishi (1991), the data set was large, but was not matched by part type.

Productivity

A careful study by Okamoto (1997), using a variety of measures, has found that Japanese transplant suppliers are no more productive than their US counterparts. Using 1992 data from the US Census of Manufactures, she found that Japanese-owned car suppliers had significantly lower total factor productivity than did their US-owned counterparts, and value-added per worker was not significantly different.

A measure related to productivity growth is cost reduction. Helper (1998) looked at the extent to which Japanese-owned firms were able to reduce their costs on a given product between 1989 and 1993. After controlling for the nature of the product and changes in capacity utilization, it was found that Japanese-owned firms on average suffered cost *increases* of more than 2 percentage points compared with US- and Canadian-owned firms. The adoption of employee involvement practices such as a suggestion system reduced but did not eliminate the difference. By contrast, having a Japanese carmaker as a firm's 'most important' customer led to almost a 3 percentage point *decline* in cost compared with serving a US carmaker. In contrast, data from the same survey showed that Japanese firms in Japan had reduced their costs far more than the US average (Helper and Sako, 1995).[3]

Inventory

Lieberman *et al.* (forthcoming) found that Japanese transplants had no significant overall differences in inventory holdings. However, when 'lean' practices such as worker involvement was controlled for, Japanese-owned firms did worse than US- and Canadian-owned firms. By contrast, Okamoto (1997) used census data and found that in 1992 Japanese suppliers had lower levels of work in progress and finished goods, but higher levels of raw materials. In contrast Lieberman and Asaba (1997) have found that Japanese car suppliers in Japan have far less inventory holdings than do US suppliers in the United States.

Worker outcomes

Helper (forthcoming) has looked at a variety of measures and found that Japanese suppliers pay similar wages, have less unionization, hire better educated workers and train them more, and have more worker-involvement programmes. Jenkins and Florida (1998) have also found that in 1993 Japanese-owned plants received more suggestions per worker, and a greater percentage of workers were involved in statistical process control.

Without further analysis it is difficult to tell if the employee involvement is of the empowering or sweated variety. However preliminary analysis by Helper *et al.* (1999) suggests that once the level of employee involvement is controlled for, wages at Japanese owned-plants are significantly lower. Also, Jenkins and Florida (1998, p. 343) have found that while work teams are more prevalent at transplants than at US-owned suppliers, the US work teams have more authority.

These averages, however, mask significant differences in strategies among plants. Almost 30 per cent of the Japanese transplants (100 per cent Japanese-owned and US–Japanese joint ventures) surveyed by Jenkins and Florida (1999) had a work system that the authors characterized as 'Taylorist' – that is, had low capital intensity, no union, a high rate of managers to workers, a large inventory and little process improvement activity. This percentage was not significantly different from that for 100 per cent US-owned suppliers.

Similarly, 52 per cent of both groups were classed as 'innovative', having 'mid-range' wages, high capital intensity, a low ratio of managers to workers, a low inventory ratio and a high level of process improvement activity. (The unionization rates for the innovative group did not differ from the average for the sample as a whole.)

Florida *et al.* (1998, p. 207) have found that Japanese-owned suppliers in the United States locate in counties with larger minority populations, larger overall populations, higher wages and more manufacturing. The unionization rates were not significantly different in counties with and without Japanese-owned car suppliers.

These findings appear to run counter to the 'separate car economy' thesis. However there are two caveats. First, they do not address the question of unionization and minority employment rates in Japanese plants themselves (and the evidence presented above suggests that the former rate is consistently lower in Japanese-owned plants). Second, it appears that the above results are taken from a multiple regression in which a measure of the counties' proximity to a transplant assembler is included. According to the authors, this variable was 'far and away, the most powerful influence on location' (ibid.) Given the rural location of almost all Japanese-owned assembly plants, this suggests an alternative, perhaps opposite interpretation of the results. That is, that among the set of counties near transplant assemblers, transplant suppliers chose the more urban counties. Since the set of counties near transplant assemblers is more rural than the US average, it may well be that counties with Japanese investment are more rural than the US average. The correct test of the dualist thesis would appear to be to compare the mean rates of minority population, manufacturing employment and so on in counties with and without Japanese investment.

Comparable data on safety are hard to come by. There is some data (Fairris, 1998) that suggests that lean production plants have higher injury rates than other plants. However lean production advocates say that these higher rates are entirely due to better reporting, which is a direct result of the lean production philosophy's view that good data is essential to continuous improvement. On the other hand, time lost due to injuries in lean plants may look low compared with traditional plants, since most traditional plants simply send workers home if they are unable to do their normal jobs, while lean plants (especially Japanese-owned plants) assign such workers to lighter tasks (Adler and Landisbergis, 1996).

Conclusions

These results present a much more mixed picture of the adaptability of Japanese suppliers to their new environment than one finds in *The Machine that Changed the World* (Womack *et al.*, 1990). Only in quality performance do the Japanese transplants stand out as probably better. They appear to have lower productivity. The inventory results are mixed, but it seems clear that transplants hold more raw materials. The worker outcome results are also mixed, largely because of the large number of variables that affect it and the disagreement among the schools about the direction of some of the desired effects (for example more unionization and less employee involvement is held to be good by the management by stress school, whereas many lean production advocates would hold the opposite view). What seems clear is that unionization is lower, employee involvement is higher and wages are similar at US-owned and Japanese-owned plants.

As noted above, these results cast significant doubt on the lean production advocates' view that lean production is both clearly superior and easily transferred. It appears that at least one of these assertions must be wrong. The management by stress school would argue that the problem is with the first of the two. Given that almost all of the research conducted at car supplier plants had management approval, there is a surprising amount of support for this view. There is at least a significant subset of Japanese plants that fight unionization while asking for high levels of employee effort (both in suggestions and fast-paced work) and without paying higher wages. (However a lean production advocate could counter that having a suggestion implemented is its own reward, and that a faster pace is possible with the same effort in a lean plant due to reductions in wasted motion, higher-quality parts and so on.)

The hybridization school would suggest that the problem is with the second assertion: that lean production is superior, but it is not quickly diffused because of the time required to figure out the core principles and implement those principles in an environment different from the one in which they were developed. The next section looks at the available data on what practices have actually been adopted.

TRANSPLANT SUPPLIERS: EVIDENCE ON THE ADOPTION OF LEAN PRACTICES

The case study research reported in Abo (1994) and Liker *et al.* (1998) suggests that Japanese firms have had to go through a significant learning period in the United States and have adapted their production methods. For example NSK had little success with a quality circle programme in the early 1980s, but did enjoy significant performance improvements once it had designed and implemented self-directed work teams jointly with its local United Auto Workers Union.

In some cases, transplants initially adapted too much to local conditions, sacrificing what turned out to be key elements of lean production. For example Sumitomo Electric Wiring Systems (SEWS) initially left almost all plant management and human resource policy in the hands of Americans, who set up what one interviewee called a 'traditional Southern paternalist antiunion strategy', which among other things meant that workers could schedule themselves for overtime whenever they wanted, which wreaked havoc on just-in-time production (MacDuffie and Helper, 1998).

On the other hand, survey data in Helper (1998) and Jenkins and Florida (1998) suggest that both Japanese and US plants in the United States have adopted a fair number of lean practices with respect to supplier–customer and labour–management relations. However large-scale surveys cannot pick up the nuances of the effectiveness with which practices such as worker involvement in total quality management are carried out.

Also, there are some issues of interpretation. Abo (1994) and Kenney and Florida (1994) report similar levels of employee involvement at transplant suppliers. Abo sees this as evidence of adaptation by the Japanese to local conditions (a performance-decreasing move, in his view), while Kenney and Florida see it as evidence of easy diffusion.

Were the performance difficulties just a temporary phenomenon caused by start-up costs, or does the mixed performance continue? The answer is important, both for what it says about the interaction of national culture and production techniques, and for whether the huge efforts by some US firms to adopt lean production are likely to bear fruit.

The evidence is mixed. Case studies of Honda of America's efforts to improve its suppliers (MacDuffie and Helper, 1998) suggest that these difficulties are only temporary, and that with the help of a committed, experienced customer, Japanese suppliers can figure out how to adapt their system. They may even learn some things they can transport back to Japan.

On the other hand Okamoto (1997) has not found that transplant productivity has improved over time relative to the productivity of US-owned plants. But it is not possible to tell from census data alone whether or not the adoption of lean practices by either group increased over time.

According to survey research by Nakamura *et al.* (1998a, 1998b), when JIT practices such as small-group problem-solving and the establishment of a *kanban* system are implemented by either US-owned or Japanese-owned manufacturing plants, performance improves (for example inventory turns increase and lead time decreases).[4] However, many plants have not adopted such practices. These findings are consistent with the hybridization view that lean production is effective, but adoption is hard.

Interestingly, on a variety of measures the best performers in the industry are US-owned suppliers to Japanese carmakers. As mentioned above, their costs have fallen significantly more than those of other groups of suppliers. Also, they have fewer inventory items of some types (Lieberman *et al.* forthcoming).

This finding supports the suggestion by Liker *et al.* (1998) that transferring lean production requires (1) a great deal of commitment and resources, and (2) a large degree of familiarity with the local environment. Pil and MacDuffie (1998) show that transplant assemblers clearly perform better than US assemblers in terms of productivity, quality and variety, and are undistinguishable from their counterparts in Japan in respect of productivity and quality.[5] These assemblers, particularly larger firms such as Honda and Toyota, put a great deal of effort into transferring lean production to their suppliers in the United States and Canada. These efforts may have paid off more at firms that understand the local context than they have at firms that understand how lean practices work in Japan but have had little experience in the West.

SUGGESTIONS FOR FUTURE RESEARCH

There are other possible explanations for lacklustre transplant productivity besides the ones considered so far. These explanations suggest that either (1) the performance problems are more apparent than real; (2) the adaptations that the Japanese have made to the US system have had the effect of reducing productivity (though perhaps increasing profits); or (3) the system just doesn't work in North America. These explanations are detailed below, and are in principal testable.[6]

First, Japanese-owned suppliers hold a larger raw-materials inventory than their US counterparts. (Okamoto, 1997, has found that larger inventories do explain some of the total factor productivity differential.) Is this due to greater distance from raw materials suppliers (some of whom may be in Japan), greater distance from car assembly plants in the United States or less confidence in the ability and willingness of a US workforce to produce 'just-in-time'?

Second, Japanese-owned parts suppliers have a lower capacity utilization than did their US counterparts. Takeishi (1992) says that Japanese firms had hoped to achieve minimum efficient scale by selling to US-owned carmakers as well as to Japanese-owned firms, but orders from US-owned firms turned out to be hard to obtain.

Third, Japanese-owned firms have less market power than their US counterparts. The observed productivity differences, then, are caused by the reduced ability of Japanese-owned firms to appropriate rents, rather than by a lack of technical efficiency. In support of this idea, Okamoto (1997) finds that Japanese-owned firms have slightly lower price–cost margins than their US-owned counterparts.

Fourth, many researchers have found that Japanese firms have performance advantages due to their close customer–supplier relations (for example Nishiguchi, 1990; Sako, 1992; Smitka, 1991). Two possible reasons for the lacklustre productivity performance of Japanese-owned suppliers are that these practices were not transferred to the United States, or that they were transferred but did not lead to increased productivity in the US context.

Another related possibility is that Japanese customers demand parts with fewer defects. If (in contrast to the lean production literature) there is a tradeoff between quality and productivity, this might explain the observed lower productivity of Japanese-owned firms.

Fifth, Japanese firms are often held to reap performance advantages due to their human resource practices (Florida and Kenney, 1991; Womack *et al.*, 1990). Again a plausible hypothis would be that either these practices were not transferred to the United States or they did not lead to improved productivity in the US context.

Finally, largely because of their desire to avoid unions, Japanese plants were built outside the traditional agglomerations in the United States. (In 1975, 50 per cent of US car assembly and parts production took place in just 16 of 3000 or so counties. Most of these counties are in Ohio and Michigan near the Great Lakes. In contrast, Japanese-owned plants are disproportionately located in Kentucky, Tennessee, western Michigan and southern Ohio. See Helper, forthcoming.) This locational decision may have made it more difficult to gain access to specialized skills, many of which continue to be useful, even to a 'lean' producer. For example MacDuffie and Helper (1998) visited one supplier that kept an extra day's worth of inventory supplies because of its lack of access to die maintenance services, and found that organizing training was difficult because there was no community college in the area.

CONCLUSIONS

A few firm conclusions can be drawn from this review of the literature:

•   The optimism of the lean production advocates that lean production techniques developed in Japan can be easily transferred to the United States and Canada seems misplaced. These techniques can be transferred, but the transfer in most cases requires the human and financial resources of a large, world-class company such as Honda or Toyota.

- The optimism of the lean production advocates that lean production techniques almost always benefit everyone seems unsupported. There is wide variation in the effects of employee involvement programmes on workers, and the effects of standardized work on workers' health and safety is unresolved.
- At least some lean practices have been adopted in North America, and some hybridization (more in the labour–management area than in the supplier–customer area) has taken place.

However several important questions remain unresolved:

- Is the fact that Japanese suppliers have not performed better than other suppliers due to (1) excessive adaptation to the local environment, (2) insufficient adaptation to the local environment, (3) superior adoption of lean practices by domestically owned suppliers or (4) factors that affect measured productivity and happen to be correlated with ownership, but are unrelated to true efficiency?
- Under what conditions do management-sponsored continuous improvement efforts lead to improvements for all stakeholders?

Appendix 6.1: the data

The data I used in the papers discussed above draw on three surveys of car suppliers in the United States and Japan, all conducted with the sponsorship of the MIT International Motor Vehicle Program.

In 1993 I conducted two surveys of automotive suppliers. The first survey was sent to the divisional directors of marketing at automotive suppliers in the United States and Canada. This questionnaire asked about customer relations and product characteristics. The second survey was sent to plant managers, and asked about operations policies and relations with workers. Each answered the questionnaire for their most important customer regarding one product that was typical of their business unit's output. A questionnaire was sent to every automotive supplier and component division named in the *Elm Guide to Automotive Sourcing* (available from Elm, Inc. in East Lansing, Michigan). This guide lists the major first-tier suppliers to manufacturers of cars and light trucks in the United States and Canada.

The response rate was 55 per cent for the sales manager survey and 30 per cent for the plant manager survey.

The survey respondents were representative of the population in terms of firm size and location, as compared with data from the *Elm Guide* and from County Business Patterns for SICs 3714 (automotive parts) and 3496 (automotive stampings). However the vertically integrated business units of the carmakers were underrepresented. Also, due to the small number of Canadian transplant suppliers it was not possible to analyze them separately.

The analysis in the cost-reduction study required data from both the plant manager and the marketing director survey; 207 business unit/plant pairs provided these complete data. This subsample did not differ from the full samples on the variables used in the analysis. The respondents had a wealth of experience; they averaged 18 years in the car industry and 11 years with their company. Combining the datasets reduced common measure bias; in particular, worker relations and customer relations were measured independently of each other.

The inventory data reported above came from the plant manager survey, as did the data on worker outcomes.

Also, in 1993 Professor Mari Sako, now of Oxford University, surveyed first-tier car suppliers in Japan using an instrument similar to the US–Canada sales manager questionnaire. The response rate was 30 per cent; 471 surveys were received (for further details see Helper and Sako, 1995).

Notes

1.   These numbers are calculated from Florida *et al.* (1998, p. 191) and Kenney and Florida (1994, p. 126). They based their estimates largely on data collected in 1993 by JETRO (the Japan External Trade Organization). Few new Japanese-owned car supplier plants have been opened since then.
2.   This term is from Brannen *et al.* (1998).
3.   For a description of this data, see Appendix 6.1.
4.   The data, on 42 plants for machinery, car parts and electronics, was collected in 1990.
5.   Even at assemblers the worker outcome variables are mixed. Employee surveys conducted at NUMMI, the GM–Toyota joint venture in California, suggest widespread satisfaction (Adler *et al.*, forthcoming). However surveys carried out at car assembly plants in Canada show that the percentage of workers reporting problems such as 'physical

workload too heavy' and 'increased monitoring' rose with the degree of adoption of lean practices, most prominently at a GM plant and a Suzuki–GM joint venture (Lewchuk and Robertson, 1998).

6. I have matched my survey data to census data that is similar to Oka-moto's, so in future it should be possible to answer the question of whether firms (US or Japanese-owned) that have adopted lean practices also have higher productivity growth.

References

Abo, Tetsuo (ed.) (1994) *Hybrid Factory: The Japanese Production System in the United States* (New York: Oxford University Press).

Adler, P. and P. Land is bergis (1996) 'Dialog on Lean Production and Workers', working paper (Los Angeles, California: University of Southern California).

Adler, P., B. Goldoftas and D. Levine (forthcoming) 'Flexibility versus Efficiency? A Case Study of Model Changeovers in the Toyota Production System', *Organization Science*.

Brannen, Mary Yoko, J. Liker and W. M. Fruin (1999) 'Recontextualization and Factory to Factory Knowledge Transfer', in J. Liker, W. M. Fruin and P. S. Adler (eds), *Remade in America* (New York: Oxford University Press).

Chung, W., W. Mitchell and B. Yeung (1997) 'Foreign Direct Investment and Host Country Productivity: The Case of the American Automotive Components Industry', University of Michigan Business School Working Paper, May.

Clark, Kim (1989) 'Project Scope and Project Performance: The Effects of Parts Strategy and Supplier Involvement on Product Development', *Management Science*, vol. 35 (October), pp. 1247–63.

Cusumano, M. and Akira Takeishi (1991) 'Supplier Relations and Management: A Study of Japanese, Japanese Transplant, and US Auto Plants', *Strategic Management Journal*, vol. 12, pp. 563–88.

Dyer, Jeffrey (1996) 'Does Governance Matter? Keiretsu Alliances and Asset Specificity as Sources of Japanese Competitive Advantage', *Organization Science*, vol. 7, no. 6, pp. 649–66.

Economic Strategy Institute (1992), *The Case for Saving the Big Three*, (Washington, DC: Economic Research Institute).

Fairris, David (1998) 'Lean Production and Workplace Health and Safety', in Huberto Juarez Nunez and Steve Babson (eds), *Confronting Change: Auto labor and lean production in North America* (Detroit: Wayne State).

Florida, R. and D. Jenkins (1998) 'Japanese Transplants in North America: Production Organization, Location, and Research and Development', in Robert Boyer, Elsie Charron, Ulrich Jurgens and Steven Tolliday (eds), *Between Imitation and Innovation: The Transfer and Hybridization of Productive Models in the International Automobile Industry* (Oxford: Oxford University Press).

Florida, R. and M. Kenney (1991) 'Transplanted Organizations: The Transfer of Japanese Industrial Organization to the US', *American Sociological Review*, vol. 56, (June), pp. 381–98.

Helper, Susan (1991) 'How Much Has Really Changed Between US Automakers and Their Suppliers?', *Sloan Management Review*, vol. 32, no. 4, pp. 15–28.

Helper, S. (1998) 'Complementarity and Cost Reduction', NBER working paper, revised (Cambridge, Mass.: NBER)

Helper Susan (forthcoming), 'Japanese 'Transplant' Supplier Relations: Are they Transferable? Should They be?', in Massimo Colombo (ed.), *The Firm and Its Boundaries* (New York: Oxford University Press).

Helper, S., D. Levine and E. Bendoly (1999) 'Employee Involvement and Pay at U.S. and Canadian Auto Suppliers', working paper (Cleveland, Ohio: Case Western Reserve University).

Helper Susan and Mari Sako (1995) 'Supplier Relations in Japan and the United States: Are They Converging?', *Sloan Management Review*, vol. 36, no. 3, pp. 77–84.

Herzenberg, S. (1991) 'Continental Integration and the Future of the North American Auto Sector', US Department of Labor photocopy.

Howes, C. (1993a) *Japanese Auto Transplants and the US Automobile Industry*, (Washington, DC: Economic Policy Institute).

Howes, C. (1993b) 'Constructing Comparative Disadvantage: Lessons from the US Automobile Industry', in Noponen, H., J. Graham and A. Markusen (eds), *Trading Industries, Trading Regions* (New York: Guilford Press).

Ichniowski, C., Kathryn Shaw and G. Prennushi (1997) 'The Impact of Human Resource Management Practices on Productivity', *American Economic Review*, July.

Kato, Takao and Motohiro Morishima (1997) 'The Productivity Effects of Human Resource Management Practices: Evidence from New Japanese Panel Data', Colgate University Working Paper.

Jenkins, Davis and R. Florida (1999) 'Work System Innovation among Japanese Transplants in the United States', in J. Liker, W. M. Fruin and P. S. Adler (eds), *Remade in America* (New York: Oxford University Press).

Kearns, R. (1992) *Zaibatsu America* (New York: Free Press).

Kenney, M. and R. Florida (1991) 'How Japanese Industry is Rebuilding the Rust Belt', *Technology Review*, Feb./March.

Kenney, M. and R. Florida (1994) *Beyond Mass Production: The Japanese System and its Transfer to the US* (Oxford: Oxford University Press).

Kenney, Martin, Richard Florida and Andrew Mair (1988) 'The Transplant Phenomenon: Japanese Auto Manufacturers In the United States', *Economic Development Commentary*, vol. 12, no. 4, pp. 3–9.

Lewchuk, Wayne and David Robertson (1998) 'Work Reorganization and the Quality of Working Life in the Canadian Automobile Industry', in Huberto Juarez Nunez and Steve Babson, (eds), *Confronting Change: Auto labor and lean production in North America* (Detroit: Wayne State).

Lieberman, M. B. and S. Asaba (1997) 'Inventory Reduction and Productivity Growth', *Managerial and Decision Economics*, 18, 73–85.

Lieberman, M., S. Helper and L. Demeester (forthcoming) 'The Empirical Determinants of Inventory Levels in High-Volume Manufacturing', *Journal of the Production Operations Management Society*.

Liker, J., W. M. Fruin and P. Adler (eds) (1999) *Remade in America* (New York: Oxford University Press).

MacDuffie, J. P. (1995) 'Human Resource Bundles and Manufacturing Performance: Organizational Logic and Flexible Production Systems in the World Auto Industry', *Industrial and Labor Relations Review*, vol. 48, no. 2, pp. 199–221.

MacDuffie, J. P. and S. Helper (1999) 'Creating Lean Suppliers: Diffusing Lean Production through the Supply Chain', in J. Liker, W. M. Fruin and P. S. Adler (eds), *Remade in America* (New York: Oxford University Press).

MacDuffie, J. P and T. Kochan (1995) 'Do US Firms Invest in Human Resources? Determinants of Training in the World Auto Industry', *Industrial Relations*, vol. 34, no. 2, pp. 145–65.

McAlinden, S. (1991) 'The U.S. Japan Automotive Bilateral 1994 Trade Deficit', Transportation Research Institute Report No. 91–20 (Ann Arbor, Michigan: University of Michigan).

Nakamura, Masao, Sadao Sakakibara and Roger Schroeder (1998) 'Adoption of Just in Time Manufacturing Methods at US and Japanese-owned Plants', *IEEE Transactions on Engineering Management*, vol. 45, pp. 230–40.

Nakamura, Masao, Sadao Sakakibara and Roger Schroeder (1999) 'Just in time and Other Manufacturing Practices: Implications for US Manufacturing Performance', in J. Liker, W. M. Fruin and P. S. Adler (eds), *Remade in America* (New York: Oxford University Press).

Nishiguchi, T. (1990) *Strategic Industrial Sourcing: The Japanese Advantage*. (Oxford: Oxford University Press).

Odaka, K., K. Ono and F. Adachi (1988) *The Automobile Industry in Japan: A Study of Ancillary Firm Development* (Oxford: Oxford University Press).

Okamoto, Yumiko (1997) 'Multinationals, Production Efficiency, and Spillover Effects: The Case of the US Auto Parts Industry', Kobe University Working Paper, December.

Parker, M. and J. Slaughter (1995) 'Unions and Management by Stress' in S. Baron (ed.), *Lean Work* (Detroit, Michigan: Wayne State University Press).

Pil, Frits and J. P. MacDuffie (1998) 'Transplanting Competitive Advantage Across Borders: A Study of Japanese Auto Transplants in North America', in J. Liker, W. M. Fruin and P. S. Adler (eds), *Remade in America* (New York: Oxford University Press).

Piore, M. and C. Sabel (1984) *The Second Industrial Divide* (New York: Basic Books).

Sako, M. (1992) *Prices, Quality and Trust: Interfirm Relations in Britain and Japan* (Cambridge: Cambridge University Press).

Schonberger, R. (1984) *Japanese Manufacturing Techniques* (New York: The Free Press).

Smitka, M. (1991) *Competitive Ties* (New York: Columbia University Press).

Takeishi, A. (1992) 'A Study of Supplier Relationships in the American and Japanese Automotive Industries', Master's Thesis, Sloan School of Management (Cambridge, Mass.: MIT).

Womack, J., D. Jones and D. Roos (1990) *The Machine that Changed the World* (New York: Rawson Associates).

Part III

Technology in Japanese Economic History

7 Japanese Technological Development: The Technological Gap Hypothesis and Its Implications

Yukihiko Kiyokawa

PROBLEMS RAISED BY THE JAPANESE EXPERIENCE

As research continues on the factors responsible for Japanese economic development since the Meiji Restoration, the most commonly accepted explanations of Japan's success have been questioned. One such explanation is that the driving force behind Japanese economic development was an abundance of low-wage labour, since this made it possible to import capital goods paid for by the earnings from labour-intensive, light-industry exports.

While this is the most common explanation of Japan's success so far, it is obvious from the difficult problems faced by today's developing countries that low-wage labour in itself is not sufficient to promote successful economic development.[1] What must be understood, even in the case of Japan, is that low-wage labour is just one of several factors needed to achieve competitiveness in the international market.

From the end of the Tokugawa period, when Japanese ports were opened to the West, Japan strove to import and utilize Western technology and to create the necessary institutional infrastructure by employing foreign experts to facilitate the assimilation of that technology. From a relatively early stage this was a critical factor in long-term technological development. Moreover the development of indigenous Japanese technology, the adaptation of Western technology and the development of so-called 'appropriate technology' were also important in enabling Japanese exports gradually to become competitive in the international market. Put simply, the most important factor in Japan's rapid economic development after the Meiji

Restoration is considered here to be technological development. (In this chapter the term technological development includes the importation and copying of foreign technology, the improvement of indigenous technology and the growth of technical staff to support such activities.)

Despite this, to date there has not been a great deal of research into the contribution made by technological innovation and development to Japanese economic development. Though the two approaches applied so far to analyze technological development – indirect analysis of aggregate productivity and archeological analysis of industrial technology – have made some contribution, new approaches are needed.

The aggregate productivity approach has attempted to grasp technology development indirectly by measuring the total factor productivity of the manufacturing industry within an accounting framework – any residual that cannot be explained by growth in factor inputs is taken to be technological progress.[2] However, what this approach regards as technological development and innovation is merely an abstract, residual factor contributing to changes in productivity. That is, this approach fails to grasp actual technological development in the sense defined above.

Archeological analysis of industrial technology, on the other hand, has examined in detail various examples of imported and indigenous technologies since the beginning of the Meiji era, and the results have revealed the vivid path of Japan's technological development. However this approach does not necessarily provide an economic analysis of technological development, and often only amounts to a description of the technological innovations themselves.[3] Specifically, this approach tends to neglect the problems of supply and demand. In other words the archaeological approach does not sufficiently consider the unique characteristics of technologies as marketable goods.[4]

The hypothesis presented here is designed to overcome the deficiencies of these traditional approaches by revealing the common characteristics of technological development in different industries, and by interpreting those characteristics within an economic framework. In doing so, our analysis will reveal some empirical rules of technology transfers and adaptations in general. Although these are common patterns observed in Japan, they might have some limitations for generality since we extract them from the experiences of typical industries in Japan.

We shall first define some of the terms and concepts used in this analysis, and briefly review some of the characteristics of Japanese technological development.

TECHNOLOGY CHOICE AND TECHNOLOGICAL ADAPTATIONS

The term 'technology choice' has two different meanings that reflect very distinct perspectives. In the first usage, technology choice has been narrowly defined as deciding whether or not a particular technique should be chosen from a basket of available production methods, under given market conditions and with a subjective risk evaluation. Attention is paid to the reasons for that decision with respect to risk evaluation, entrepreneurship, the existing technological level and so on.

The second definition involves broader processes, that is, not only the decision maker's optimizing behaviour but also the sequential process of adopting a particular technology as a result of a distinct change in market conditions (for example changes in relative factor prices stemming from a wage increase). Here the focus is on the adaptive process of technology selection, hence the terms 'adaptive technology choice' or 'induced technology choice' may be appropriate.

One might also think of the two definitions as involving *ex ante* and *ex post* choices at a particular point in time.[5] In any event it is important to note that the same term is used for these two divergent concepts. Which of the two concepts is adopted will depend on the object of the analysis.

Let us now consider the level of the decision-making units and the optimizing criteria that prevail at the time when technology choices are made. Once again, as might be expected, there are various levels and criteria, depending on the objective or framework in question. For example the government is a representative decision-making unit that aims for optimization at the macro level, while an individual firm is a typical decision-making unit at the micro level. It is important here to make a clear distinction between the different optimizing behaviours of technology choice at each level.[6] This is mainly because the aggregation possibility condition can hardly be met in the dynamic and complicated real world, and the optimal choice at the micro level rarely coincides with that at the macro level. Thus the difference between aggregation levels leads to differences in choice criteria.

Technology choice at the macro level is usually explained on the basis of the national factor endowment ratio. There are, however, two problems with this. First, in the short run the static factor endowment ratio is not an appropriate standard for technology choice at the micro level of the firm, which is constantly faced with dynamic technological innovations. Second, technology choice at the macro level should be combined with *choice of industries*, since the range of alternatives for factor intensity is strictly limited within one industry. In this case, however, the factor endowment ratio does not serve as a useful criterion for technology choice.[7] While these reservations should be kept in mind, the significance of the macro perspective for labour-intensive technology should not to be overlooked, especially when considering the seriousness of the current unemployment problems in less developed countries.

In the case of technology choice at the micro level, the profit maximization criterion is generally accepted. This criterion reflects plausible behaviour by the firm in respect of technology choice, and is particularly effective for its applicability to adaptable technologies with wide scope for improvement (for example indigenous technologies). On the other hand, in the case of imported technologies, which are usually sophisticated and capital-intensive, the profit maximization criterion is not necessarily useful as decision makers have to consider the indivisibility of capital equipment, insufficient adaptive capability and the prospect of related technological innovations. Nonetheless such capital-intensive technologies are frequently chosen with a view to future profitability, despite the fact that they may not facilitate higher profits in the short run.[8] Thus we still have some conventional problems to be solved with regard to choice criteria and behaviour by decision-making units.

Usually, significant disparities can be expected between technologies chosen according to macro criteria, such as the factor endowment ratio, and those based on micro criteria, for example profit maximization. It is the role of technological adaptations immediately or gradually to reduce these disparities. Technology referred to as 'appropriate technology' is intended to fill this gap by applying indigenous production methods to modern technology to change factor intensity when technology chosen according to micro criteria does not meet the optimal conditions based on macro criteria.[9] Yet, as we shall see, not all technology can be adapted in such a way. Some technologies can be adapted only under certain conditions. Furthermore it should be noted that adaptation is not limited to machinery and the production process, but also includes product quality adjustments through the introduction of cheaper raw materials and operational methods. The latter factor – a reduction in quality to lower the price – played an important role in increasing Japan's competitive edge in the world market.[10]

Finally, foreign technology was crucial to the development of Japanese industrial technology. One might even say that there is hardly any Japanese technology that has not been influenced in some way by transferred technology. When introducing foreign technology it is important to bear in mind that it has been developed in a different technological environment (different technological systems and levels of development) with different market conditions, and therefore will have to be adapted and modified. If it is successfully adapted to the new environment, 'appropriate technology' will have been created. When this is not possible the markets (particularly the product market) may have to adjust to meet the supply conditions of the product produced by the transferred technology.[11] Thus adaptation by the market itself as well as the adaptability of technology is crucial for the assimilation of transplanted technology into the new economy.[12] Market adaptation is more often observed for transferred technology that is difficult to modify than for indigenous technology. If neither the technology nor the market is able to adapt, the transferred technology will fail to take root in the new environment.

It is not individual producers that modify this technology and transform it into intermediate technology (although this sometimes happens). Rather it is the technology supply sector (that is, machinery-related industries) that normally perform such modifications. The next section will briefly discuss the characteristics of the supply sector in the Japanese experience of technological development.

FROM TECHNOLOGY IMPORTATION TO DOMESTIC TECHNOLOGY PRODUCTION

Before investigating the production of technology it is necessary to define the word technology. In this chapter industrial technology is understood as a systematically gathered set of knowledge and information organized to achieve a specific aim of production. Such production knowledge and information is constructed according to two norms: engineering efficiency and economic efficiency. Technology therefore reflects not only the national industrial technological level and the degree of market development but also the characteristics of the society that produces the technology.

Within this abstract definition it is useful to point out two specific forms of technology: technology embodied in the form of human beings, such as engineers and skilled workers; and technology embodied in non-human form such as machines, machine specifications, manuals and the like.

The first type of technology, the level of which depends in large part upon the attributes of individual human beings, is relatively difficult to systematize and objectivize. It is often called skill or craftsmanship. As for the second type, technology is not exactly the physical embodiment of a machine, but a set of knowledge and information for production. These distinctions are important to understanding the intrinsic properties of license-agreement production, know-how, the patent system and technological assistance.

While imported machinery and other equipment is quite valuable for developing countries during the initial stages of industrialization, a more vital and decisive factor in economic development is human-embodied technology or high-quality human capital because it is needed to establish the organizational structure and system for receiving large amounts of technology transfer.[13] Such human capital is indispensable for decisions about which technology is most suitable for the level of economic development. During the early stages of development, however, it is common for these human resouces to be in short supply. Japan solved this problem by inviting foreign experts (*yatoi*) and entrusting them with very wide-ranging powers of discretion.

Once the necessary infrastructure for transferred technology has been developed the importation of non-human technology, particularly machinery and other equipment, can begin. When high-quality machines are introduced to developing countries, foreign manufacturers usually send engineers and fitters to help their clients install the machines and train their workers to operate them. For clients that have accumulated adequate technological knowledge, suppliers provide only a detailed manual or specifications and a supply of spare parts. The aim of developing countries with this type of technology transfer is to import the information embodied in the machinery.

When looking at historical trends in the importation of machinery, two types of technology transfer can be identified. The first, of which cotton-spinning equipment is a well known example, involves the transfer of an entire production system whose main facilities are updated with new imports over a long period of time. The other type, exemplified by early Japanese imports of the power loom, is an import-substitution-induced type in which the imported technology is soon copied by domestic producers. With the exception of a few sophisticated models, such imported machines are rapidly replaced by domestically adapted models. Even with the first type, although the main facilities continue to be imported the technology embodied in the machines is steadily transferred to and mastered by the importers. Thus the recipient firms gradually master the machines' operations, learn the basic maintenance skills and make appropriate improvements.

Various methods of copying imported machinery are used, ranging from production following a rough sketch, to reproduction by dismantling and recasting, to an almost perfect copy by means of specifications. The method chosen is largely governed by the level of technological education and knowledge accumulated from past R&D activities.

Finally, two points deserve some clarification. First, although the copying of technology has been viewed in the economic literature in a negative sense, it is almost unavoidable for late industrializing countries. That is, they have to start by copying imported technology in order to accumulate sufficient technological knowledge to produce more appropriate indigenous technology in the future. By making minor improvements and developing similar technologies they can eventually achieve technological self-reliance. Thus the copying of imported technology has great significance for technological development in developing countries. Furthermore, fostering such imitative capabilities is closely linked to the promotion of entrepreneurship.[14]

Second, it is viewed as paradoxical that prewar Japan concentrated on the development of labour-saving technology despite having an excess supply of labour. We, however, consider that the importation and development of labour-saving technology was rational even though the wage rate and labour costs were markedly lower in Japan than in Western countries. For a start, when viewed from the macro perspective, capital equipment is much more easily reproducible in the short term than is labour. Secondly, when viewed from the micro perspective, since labour is *de facto* a more fixed factor of production than capital, firms in the midst of rapid industrialization reasonably aim at developing (or importing) labour-saving technology to avoid the pressure of wage increases, and hence maintain only well-trained workers. Thirdly, industrialized countries are constantly producing more labour-saving technologies with higher labour productivity. Hence it is entirely reasonable for countries with a relatively abundant labour supply to adopt modern labour-saving technology to achieve a competitive edge in the international market.[15] The comparative advantage afforded by low-wage labour gradually diminishes as labour-saving technology progresses.

A NEW PERSPECTIVE ON TECHNOLOGICAL DEVELOPMENT IN LATE INDUSTRIALIZING COUNTRIES: A TECHNOLOGICAL GAP HYPOTHESIS

So far we have confined ourselves to sketching the characteristics of Japan's experience in the supply of and demand for technology. In this section a slightly more systematic analysis is provided. To this end we have to return to the unique properties of 'technology' to establish a perspective that best reflects the qualities of Japan's technological development as a late industrializing country.

As previously defined, technology is a systematically gathered set of knowledge and information organized to achieve specific production goals. That is, the accumulated amount of technological knowledge and information reflects the technological level attained. This stock of knowledge and information is considered to contain conceptually qualitative factors as well, including the precision and durability of machinery, the machinery's structural stability and material quality, and its economic efficiency. Although the precise measurement of these qualities is difficult, it is possible roughly to measure information quantitatively and qualitatively through the use of 'entropy' or similar concepts.

The stock of knowledge and information that determines the technological level has two essential properties. First, the development of technological knowledge is unidirectional and accumulative, although the speed at which it is accumulated varies. Second, the production of new technology is always accompanied by an expansion of technological knowledge and information, and abrupt production of sophisticated technology that requires a sudden leap in technological knowledge and information cannot be successful. Production should be based on a continuous build-up of technological information, thus a principle of continuity must be presumed to be at work for the production of technology.

When a technology developed in an economy with a qualitatively different technological level is transferred to a target economy, the response to the transfer in this economy depends on the extent of the 'technological gap', that is, the difference between the amount of information contained in the transferred technology and that in the technology already established in the target economy. Whether or not the technological gap can be bridged depends on the size of the gap and the research and development capability of the importing economy.[16]

This technological gap concept makes it possible to look at Japanese technological development from a new angle. The technological gap framework is particularly effective for analyzing the technological development of late industrializing countries that have to carry out large-scale technology transfers. This was the case with Japanese industrialization, since there were few fields that were not affected, either directly or indirectly, by Western technology after the Meiji Restoration. Where intrinsic traditional technology exists, innovations in such technology can be treated in our framework as a case in which the technological gap is zero. Similarly, when technology is introduced for which there is no existing counterpart in the target economy, this can be treated as a case in which the technological gap is extremely large. The remainder of this section will use the technological gap hypothesis as a stylized model to understand Japan's experience (see also Appendix 7.1).

Generally, the assimilation of transferred technology takes place in three stages. In the first stage the practical properties of the technology are learned during the process of installation and operation. It is essential to examine the extent to which productivity can be improved given the quality of the labour force and the technical level of engineers in the target economy. In Japan, several types of power supply and raw materials, as well as various combinations of old and new technology, were almost always tested, and potentially profitable modes of production were usually investigated. Such trial-and-error efforts were not limited to government factories, but were also carried out by a wide range of private enterprises.

During the second stage, when the optimal scale of production has been found, similar projects are undertaken all over the country. That is, similar technologies are imported according to the level of financial resources, the level of managerial skills and the size of potential markets. Thus the diffusion of new technology involves the process of establishing a marketing network and cultivating a demand in domestic and foreign markets.

During the third stage individual companies begin to compete with each other. This leads either to the making of technological

		Introduction stage	$\Rightarrow$	Diffusion stage	$\Rightarrow$	Adjustment stage
Present technology gap	Large	L		S		S
	Small			S		L

Key: S=Short period of time; L=Long period of time

Figure 7.1   Adaptation patterns of transferred technology

improvements in order better to meet market conditions, or to the market structure being reorganized to meet the supply conditions under the new technology. Which of the two takes precedence depends on the qualities of the imported technology and the gap between it and the existing technology.

Whether the three stages (trial introduction, diffusion and macro-level adjustment) occur sequentially or overlap largely depends on the size of the technology gap. Figure 7.1 illustrates this point (see also Appendix 7.1).[17] As can be seen, the pattern of adaptation or assimilation of transferred technology differs sharply according to the size of the technological gap. When there is a large gap between the newly imported technology and the existing domestic technology the three stages of the adaptation process are clearly defined (the introduction stage, the diffusion stage and the adjustment stage). By contrast, when the technological gap is small, technology diffusion begins earlier, the adjustment stage tends to overlap the diffusion stage and the demarcation between stages is less distinct.

In the former case, various trial-and-error experiments are carried out during the first stage since it takes time to accumulate technical knowledge of and experience in operating the machinery and the shift system, and to find the optimal factory size.[18] When this has been accomplished, rapid diffusion of the technology begins. During this diffusion stage, similar technologies are imported, and adjustments are often made to the quality of raw materials and finished products. The second and third stages are completed within a relatively short time.

When the technological gap is small the introduction stage is brief and diffusion begins quite quickly. However, full diffusion and the adjustment stage take relatively longer, and it is quite common for gradual adaptations to be made to the imported technology at this point.

Industries characterized by large technological gaps are generally modern industries based on large-scale production, such as iron and steel, cotton spinning, shipbuilding, transportation equipment and chemical fibres. Industries characterized by relatively small technological gaps are generally traditional rural industries such as silk reeling, weaving, paper manufacturing, timber, tea processing, and fermenting and brewing. A large number of Japan's indigenous industries are included in this category.

Secondly, depending on the size of the technological gap there is a clear difference in the form of adjustment and adaptation at the final stage of transfer in strengthening market competitiveness. In the case of technology with a large gap, adaptation by the relevant market through its reorganization (for example market stratification or oligopolization of the product market) is the main form of adjustment. Conversely, when the technological gap is relatively small the transferred technology is adapted to the market. These phenomena can be understood in terms of the abovementioned continuity principle of technological change. That is, when the technological gap is large it is difficult to adapt the technology in question because of insufficient technological knowledge in the recipient economy. And the development of appropriate technology (successful adaptation of technology to the local market) is possible only when the technological gap is small. In other words, when the technological gap is large there is little scope for the development of appropriate technology, and even if intermediate technologies are developed, many of them will not offer competitive edge in the market. Thus adaptation takes the form of market adjustments, including changes in product quality or the operating mode of the factor markets.

Thirdly, the different effects of transferred technology on existing technology have to be mentioned. Since transferred technologies with a large technological gap usually allow much higher productivity than do existing technologies, once the transferred technologies take root the existing technologies are quickly driven out of the market. Furthermore these technologies have a stronger linkage effect because they embody much greater technological knowledge. In contrast, when the technological gap is small the existing technology can be improved. As a result the old and new technologies coexist for some time.[19] However the existing technology, which in most cases is less productive, is gradually weeded out as the market develops.

These three mutually related characteristics are commonly observable features of technology transfers. The technological gap hypothesis is particularly applicable to late industrializing countries, where large transfers of technology and the adaptation of transferred technologies are central concerns. It should be reemphasized that indigenous technology that has not been affected by foreign technology can be considered as small-gap technology. Under the terms of the technological gap hypothesis, the Japanese experience is a successful example of evolutionary progress towards technological self-reliance. The overall technological gap in Japan was steadily reduced as the process from importation to assimilation to the domestic production of copied Western technologies took place in a variety of industries.

IMPLICATIONS OF THE JAPANESE EXPERIENCE

Japan's technological development, the first example of successful industrialization in a non-Western country, has important implications for today's developing countries in the sense of transferring technology a cross cultural barriers. Before drawing out the policy implications of this for developing countries, however, it is important to mention three reservations.

First, the technological gap between developed and less developed countries is far greater than it was a century ago when Japan began its rapid development. In the 19th century industrial technology and technological knowledge was insufficiently advanced to present an insurmountable problem. Thus Japan was able to move towards import-substitution industrialization by first exporting primary and processed goods such as raw silk, tea, marine products and coal, and then simple manufactured goods such as matches, cotton yarn, fabric, paper, glass, chinaware and simple machinery. Today the technological level in industrialized countries is far higher and the technological gap is continuously increasing due to accelarated innovations in those countries. This suggests that developing countries will have much greater difficulty catching up with the advanced countries.

Second, at the time when Japan began its large-scale importation of Western technology, not only was the technological gap smaller but also the initial conditions for economic growth were relatively better in Japan than in today's developing countries, particularly in terms of its relatively high educational level,[20] the rapid diffusion of primary education, the high productivity of agriculture, a well-developed market and fairly equal income distribution.

Third, Japanese society was highly adaptable to drastic social change. Whether this was due to a competitive nature based on social homogeneity, an ideology of civilization or a desire for social mobility fostered by the education system is a matter for future research. What is not in doubt is that in the case of Western technology, Japan exhibited an extremely high degree of adaptability and absorptive capacity. At the same time these unique Japanese characteristics were just one side of the coin, the other being a sense of national exclusivitity and aggression towards neighbouring countries.

Despite the above reservations, many valid policy implications can be gleaned from Japan's experience as a late industrializing country. First, Japan's experience illustrates the importance of industrial and technical education, and of human resources in general. In other words the promotion of technical education is indispensable to technological development, as are good rates of pay for engineers, a promotion system based on educational achievements, and the participation of engineers and technical managers in the making of vital decisions (for example technology choice).

Second, Japan's import-substitution process started with technologies that produced low-quality industrial goods. This is of great significance, because when a new technology is first introduced the production low-quality goods is relatively easy, but the appropriateness of this production depends on whether it boosts price competitiveness by reducing the production cost to a level commensurate with that quality. Less developed countries can learn from Japan's experience and start by producing lower-quality goods at lower prices, and then improving the quality by strengthening quality control and industrial standards. This would allow them in subsequent years to shift to high-quality products with high prices.

Third, Japan's experience offers a clear answer to the problem of appropriate technology. That is, the development of appropriate technology – intermediate technology that allows an adequate degrees of market competitiveness – should be limited to cases where the technological gap is small.[21] In today's less developed countries the seriousness of the unemployment problem often leads to the inappropriate transformation of large-gap technology into labour-intensive intermediate technology. The Japanese experience suggests that despite the short-term benefits it may offer, such an adaptation policy is not an effective way of promoting long-term technological development.

Fourth, Japan's experience strongly suggests that the formation and development of markets in parallel with the assimilation of transferred technology is essential to technological development. Market development in this sense includes not only the development of infrastructure, such as an effective transportation and communications system, but also institutional arrangements for upgrading market organization. Such improvements were realized in the case of prewar Japan by organizing a network of local trade and producers' associations, providing institutional support for the formation of a futures market and a financial market, integrating the markets by setting uniform industrial standards, and upgrading the patent system. Hence the current problem of relative technological stagnation in developing countries should be reexamined from a broad, long-term perspective that includes market development.

Finally, a few related and important topics that have not been touched in this chapter should be briefly mentioned. Research on Japanese technological development has tended to analyze only the success stories, yet many lessons can be learned from the few cases of failure. Black tea production and sugar manufacturing were typical cases of failure in the saga of Japanese technological transfers. Examination of these cases would provide precious information on the implicitly assumed reasons for the success stories.

For reasons of space we have not been able to analyse the effect of technological transfers on Japanese production and management systems, but the role of engineering managers and the absorption of technological information into the production system, as well as sources of entrepreneurship, are worthy of further examination. Similarly the exact causal relationship between general and technical education on the one hand and technological development on the other has not yet been sufficiently addressed in macro and micro analyses. The concrete effects of technological education should be analyzed within a rigorous causative framework in order to reveal more fully the effects of R&D investment, which presumes some effects of technical education even under great uncertainty.

There are still many unexplored topics, but it is hoped that the hypothesis provided above will serve as a first step towards a more detailed empirical analysis of these issues in technological development.

Appendix 7.1: a stylization of textile industries

Table A7.1   Technological transfers: large-gap industries

	Trial and error stage 1867–86	*Diffusion stage* 1887–1900	*Adjustment stage* 1900–10
Cotton spinning	1. 2000-spindle mills (about 20) 2. Government initiative 3. Not enough knowledge from books and manuals 4. Water power 5. Maintenance difficulty 6. Established Osaka CSM 'model mill', 2-shift system, steam power, 10 000 spindles, electricity	1. 1887, 21 mills; 1992, 39 mills; 1900, 79 mills 2. One company/one factory system 3. Traditional technique (*Gara-bo*), improved after 1876. Water wheel (throttle type)	1. Amalgamation: 1904, 49 mills; 1909, 31 mills (including the 'Big Six') 2. One company with four factories; 1909, 134 factories 3. 50% of spindles belonged to 8 mills; 'Big Six' absorbed 27 factories 4. Competitive oligopoly 5. Millowners' Association: active interaction to promote competition and control
	Characteristics: • blending technique • copied machinery • sales from government to private sector • rapid diffusion of new knowledge among engineers	Characteristics: • Mule → ring frame • Export to Korea, Manchuria and North China • Domestic market expanded for high-count yarn	Characteristics: • curtailments • discount shipment system for Indian cotton • futures market started

	1915–23	*1924–28*	*1929–32*
Rayon	1. Small chemical firms with indigenous technologies, Teijin (1918) 2. Asahi Benberg (1919) with German technology from chemical industry	1. Entry of cotton spinning companies with German, Swiss and Chzeck technologies 2. Bigger size with higher technology	1. Some domestic machines introduced for mass-production 2. Japan Rayon Association: curtailments 3. Oligopolistic market 4. New products

Table A7.2	Technological transfers: small-gap industries

	Trial–error and diffusion stage 1870–82	Diffusion and adjustment stage 1884–1902
Silk-reeling	1. Failure of Tomioka model filature plant (government); steam power; steel machinery; French methods 2. Combination of foreign and indigenous technologies (treadle machines, hand-reeling system)	1. Appropriate technology; water power; smaller size (30–50 units); half-wooden, half-steel; ceramic; Italian 'croisure' system 2. Cooperative firms organized by smaller filatures 3. Market development; National Silk Conditioning House (1896); Direct Export Promoting Act (1899); silk export tax (abolished 1899) 4. Japanese-style factory system
	1885–1896	*1897–1924*
Weaving (power looms)	1. Hand looms and treadle looms developed 2. Power looms: not diffused rapidly, only for plain cloth 3. Jacquard machine; flying shuttle diffused quickly 4. Combined mills developed after 1896	1. Domestic loom production by Toyoda Loom Co. and others; intermediate technology: half-wooden, narrow-beam; small weaving sheds 2. Foreign market expansion

Notes

1.	In the case of products for export there are a number of technological requirements that must be met, including uniformity of quality within a lot, reliable means of international transport and packing specifications in accordance with international customs and standards. These requirements are very important, but not always easy to meet.
2.	For examples of these approaches, see Shigeru Ishiwata, 'Source approach no tembo' (A survey of the source approach), *Keizai kenkyu*, vol. 22, no. 1 (January 1971); Ryoshin Minami, *Nihon no keizai hatten* (Japanese economic development) (Tokyo: Toyo Keizai Shimposha, 1981), ch. 5; Yasukichi Yasuba, *Keizai seicho ron* (A theory of economic growth) (Tokyo: Chikuma Shobo, 1980), ch. 5.
3.	A more detailed explanation of this view can be found in Yukihiko Kiyokawa, 'Obei gijutsu no juyo o meguru shomondai' (Issues regarding

transfers of Western technology), in *Shakai Keizaishi Gakkai* (ed.), *Shakai keizaishigaku no kadai to tembo* (Tokyo: Yuhikaku, 1984).

4. Since technology does not, by its nature, possess the property of exclusiveness that is observable for almost all ordinary goods and services, technology is necessarily subject to imitation and diffusion.

5. Government policies on so-called 'technology choice' in today's developing countries concentrate on *ex ante*, macro-level choices due to serious unemployment and poor adaptive capabilities. In this analysis the term 'technique' is not rigorously distinguished from the term 'technology' because the concept of technique should be interpreted a little more broadly in the case of developing countries to discuss the problem of adaptation.

6. The government is treated here as a decision-making unit at the macro level since its behaviour and decision-making criteria are constructed on the basis of aggregated data.

7. For a more detailed explanation see Kiyokawa (1984), op. cit.

8. For example such a choice is entirely rational under the expectation of a rapid wage increase in the long-term for a less mobile factor of production, labour. Furthermore the actual choice of technology tends to be between the various conventional technologies and new advanced technologies that embody the latest innovations.

9. Cases where the optimal choice from the micro perspective coincides with the choice suggested by macro standards, such as the adoption of ring spinning machines, are quite exceptional. It is more common for there to be a divergence between the optimal choices. What is often seen is the adaptation of minor technology with a relatively small technological gap, for example the transformation of such technology into a labour-intensive type and changes in the mode of machine operation (such as the adoption of a two-shift system). For a more detailed analysis of the choice between mule and ring machines in Japan, see Y. Kiyokawa, 'Technology Choice in the Cotton-Spinning Industry: The Switch from Mules to Ring Frames', in R. Minami, K. Kim, F. Makino and J.-H. Seo (eds), *Acquiring, Adapting and Developing Technologies* (New York: St Martin Press, 1995).

10. In such cases it is crucial that the price be lowered in accordance with the reduction in quality to ensure international competitiveness. For an analysis of this issue see Shigeru Ishikawa, 'Appropriate Technologies: Some Aspects of Japanese Experience', in H. Robinson (ed.), *Appropriate Technologies for Third World Development* (London: Macmillan, 1979).

11. For example multiple stratification of the market. For examples of oligopolization of the product market see Y. Kiyokawa, 'Gijutsu kakusa to donyu gijutsu no teichaku katei' (Technology gap and adaptations of transferred technology) in (Economic development in modern Japan) K. Ohkawa and R. Minami (eds), *Kindai Nihon no keizai hatten* (Tokyo: Toyo Keizai Shimposha, 1975).

12. This phenomenon of either the market adapting to the technology or vice versa has great significance at the adjustment stage of technology transfer. In India and China, however, where the same technologies were imported at almost the same time, this phenomenon was not

evident. Or perhaps this characteristic is simply peculiar to Japanese technological development.

13. In Japan the early factory system had a distinctly Japanese style. As the economy developed and scientific management was gradually introduced, both the system and the equipment were modernized. The fact that the factory system was first adapted and then improved was certainly one of the factors that enabled modern industry to break out of its isolation.

14. For a detailed analysis see Y. Kiyokawa 'Entrepreneurship and Innovations in Japan: An Implication of the Experience of Technological Development in the Textile Industry', *Developing Economies*, vol. 22, no. 3 (September 1984).

15. In the case where technological innovations continue for an extended period, because of the unidirectional accumulation property of technological information and the continuity principle of technology level the potential for future development is often lost when the quantity and quality of information embodied in the new technology cannot be followed up.

16. Intuitively this gap can be thought to reflect differences between the capital–labour ratio and labour productivity.

17. Kiyokawa (1975, op. cit.) describes in more detail the chronological characteristics of the textile industry.

18. In the case of Japan, the plants that were built during the introduction stage were normally small and were aimed at demonstration and experimentation (the government's model factories were something of an exception). In India and China, however, large-scale factories by Western standards were constructed from the beginning, and trial-and-error experiments were not evident.

19. When the technological gap is small the transformation of the production system into a modern factory and corporate system is very slow, and the traditional system prevails for a relatively long period of time.

20. The early establishment of a modern education system bolstered the quality of management, which was a decisive factor in industrial progress.

21. For example the clattering *gara-bo* spindle (a kind of throttle machine) was a typical example of intermediate technology in the case of large-gap technology – except in the initial stages of technology transfer it could not compete against more modern spinning technology. There are many examples of failed intermediate technology in the recent history of China, particularly during the Great Leap Forward and the Cultural Revolution.

Comments on Chapter 7
Mukesh Eswaran

As a development economist, what I find most interesting in Chapter 7 are the suggested lessons that developing countries can learn from the technological development of Japan. In this regard I shall focus on three issues, not all of which are raised in Chapter 7.

First, Kiyokawa claims that Japan's development was not led by abundant and cheap labour. I find this claim intriguing and quite plausible, even though it runs counter to the traditional view that Japan's growth was led by the exportation of labour-intensive goods. Kiyokawa offers two reasons for his hypothesis. The first is that Japan was importing capital-intensive equipment from the labour-scarce developed countries of the West, so Japan could not use its cheap labour even if it wanted to. The second is that firms wanted to maintain a long-term competitive advantage and therefore concentrated on capital-intensive production processes so as not to bid up the wage rate. I do not find this second reason persuasive because it presumes that all firms across the country adopted a concerted policy of not using labour-intensive technologies even though each firm would have gained a short-term advantage by using cheap labour.

I think it is possible that individual firms did in fact choose not to adopt labour-intensive technologies, but for a different reason. It is conceivable that Japanese firms were very quality-conscious and realized that their long-term survival in international markets depended first on meeting the high quality requirements of the West and then on improving that quality. It is very likely that there was very little trade-off between labour and capital in the determination of the quality of industrial products. Quality was largely determined by the sophistication of the capital equipment used in production so firms aiming for high-quality products probably had no choice but to go in for capital-intensive technologies despite the fact that labour was quite cheap.

The author's suggested lesson from this for the developing countries of today is, I think, quite important. It is possible to exaggerate the importance of exploiting comparative advantage based on cheap labour.

177

Second, another lesson that Japan can offer to the developing countries of today that is not discussed in Chapter 7 is as follows. When Japan sought to industrialize after the Meiji Restoration, the income distribution was such that a substantial proportion of the Japanese population was poised to consume industrial products. The income elasticity of demand for food was only around 0.2. This, no doubt, was because Japanese agriculture was sufficiently productive, and much of the income generated by agriculture was translated into a demand for industrial goods. This would have provided the test market needed to improve the quality of those goods. While it is theoretically possible to export high-quality industrial goods directly to the world market, I believe it is more feasible first to use a captive domestic market to gain experience in producing such goods. I think this was the route that Japan took, and this was made possible by an agricultural sector that was reasonably productive, although the supply of cheap food from the colonies of Taiwan and Korea cannot be discounted. The lesson that improvements in agricultural productivity can benefit industrial productivity is not an obvious one but it is one that the developing countries of today should take note of.

Third, the chapter mentions that three stages can be observed with regard to imported technologies. I believe that these three stages are quite general. They are the adoption of technology, the diffusion of technology, and the adaptation or improvement of technology. The chapter briefly mentions that diffusion leads to intense competition, and this in turn generates improvements to the imported technologies. I think domestic competition played an important role in Japan's technological development and export orientation for an additional reason, which I shall briefly discuss. Most of the developing countries that sought to promote import substitution by offering protection that was intended to be temporary eventually stumbled. Japan did not, and there is an important lesson to be learned from Japan in this regard.

In general the domestic industrial market is concentrated during import substitution. When there is a large and lucrative domestic market, there is a temptation for firms with market power to produce only for the domestic market. They do not make the R&D expenditure needed to bring about technological innovations that would render them export-competitive. Seeing the technical incompetence of domestic firms, the government is then averse to removing its protective measures because the rents from the domestic market would then go to foreign firms. In other words the temporary protection offered to domestic firms is time-inconsistent, and as a result protection has been provided for much longer periods than intended in most developing countries. Japan is one of the few countries to avoid this outcome. I believe that a contributing factor has been the intense competition that Japan has maintained in the domestic market. This has lowered the returns to just serving the domestic market. By eroding rents in the domestic market, competition has essentially forced firms to look to world markets in search of profits. This is yet another lesson that Japan can offer the developing countries of today.

8 Osaka and Tokyo[1]

Carl Mosk

INTRODUCTION

In this chapter I wish to argue two points: the first concerns the role played by great metropolitan centres such as Osaka and Tokyo as engines of Japanese economic development; and the second involves the shift from an Osaka-centred economy to a Tokyo-centred economy, a shift that occurred between the two world wars.

On the first point, it is the burden of this chapter that the urban sector – especially the great cities of the Tōkaidō industrial belt, which stretches along the Pacific coastline of the main island of the Japanese archipelago, Honshū (see Map 8.1) – played a crucial role in Japanese economic growth, a role that was shaped by powerful technological, political and environmental imperatives.[2] Cities were at the forefront in creating the physical and human resource infrastructure and the institutional innovations that were the primary vehicles for the importation and adaptation of Western technology. They were at the forefront because they offered economies of scale that were eagerly exploited by developers of capital-intensive infrastructure; and they were at the forefront because municipal administrations gave priority to infrastructure in shaping their fiscal outlays and served as coordinating agents for infrastructure-related activities initiated by private parties.[3]

The importance of infrastructure for long-term growth is clearly visible in the timing of foreign-technology-absorbing capital formation spurts between the late 1890s and the late 1930s, a period that was crucial for Japanese development because it was during this era that the expansion of electrical generating capacity revolutionized manufacturing. Capital formation involving the innovation and diffusion of hitherto untapped technology, first taken up by the infrastructure sector and initially heavily concentrated in the urban sector, laid the groundwork for investment spurts in manufacturing. In turn the expansion of manufacturing and the urban population growth that accompanied it created the conditions for the next infrastructure-focused capital formation spurt. The resulting technological innovation and diffusion created hybrid forms of infrastructure in which old and new

180

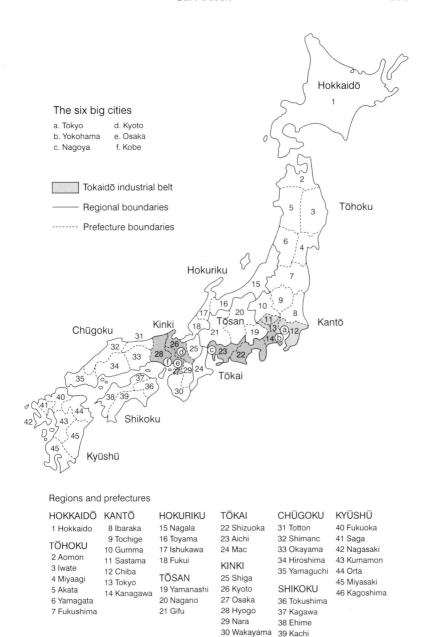

Map 8.1   The prefectures and regions of Japan, the Tōkaidō industrial belt and the six big cities

The six big cities

a. Tokyo   d. Kyoto
b. Yokohama   e. Osaka
c. Nagoya   f. Kobe

Tokaidō industrial belt

Regional boundaries

Prefecture boundaries

Hokkaidō
1

Tōhoku

Hokuriku

Chūgoku   Kinki   Tōsan   Kantō

Tōkai

Shikoku

Kyūshū

Regions and prefectures

HOKKAIDŌ	KANTŌ	HOKURIKU	TŌKAI	CHŪGOKU	KYŪSHŪ
1 Hokkaido	8 Ibaraka	15 Nagala	22 Shizuoka	31 Totton	40 Fukuoka
	9 Tochige	16 Toyama	23 Aichi	32 Shimanc	41 Saga
TŌHOKU	10 Gumma	17 Ishukawa	24 Mac	33 Okayama	42 Nagasaki
2 Aomon	11 Sastama	18 Fukui		34 Hiroshima	43 Kumamon
3 Iwate	12 Chiba		KINKI	35 Yamaguchi	44 Orta
4 Miyaagi	13 Tokyo	TŌSAN	25 Shiga		45 Miyasaki
5 Akata	14 Kanagawa	19 Yamanashi	26 Kyoto	SHIKOKU	46 Kagoshima
6 Yamagata		20 Nagano	27 Osaka	36 Tokushima	
7 Fukushima		21 Gifu	28 Hyogo	37 Kagawa	
			29 Nara	38 Ehime	
			30 Wakayama	39 Kachi	

techniques flourished side by side. But eventually the older modes were rendered obsolete by a process of creative destruction. In short the great conurbations of Japan, as exemplified by Osaka and Tokyo, served as the crucibles in which were forged and fashioned the hybrid techniques that made Japan into a mighty industrial giant.

The second proposition involves the shift from water-based infrastructure to land-based infrastructure, and the concomitant northward drift of the geographic centre of the Japanese economy from the southern to the northern pole of the Tōkaidō, from Osaka to Tokyo. I argue that with each successive infrastructure–manufacturing wave there was increasing emphasis on land-based infrastructure at the expense of water-based infrastructure, and on formal education at the expense of traditional skills (proto-industrial or craft industry). These are the two main reasons why the regional engine of the Japanese economy shifted from Osaka, the city famed as the Manchester of the Far East from the 1870s until the First World War, to Tokyo, which inexorably grew in terms of economic prowess, eventually emerging during the 1930s as the combined economic and political capital of the nation. To offer an American analogy for the sake of comparison and clarification: in the reshaping of the economic geography that accompanied the three infrastructure–manufacturing waves an analogous case would be the US political capital, Washington, DC and its immediate environs coming to outstrip New York as the primary financial and economic capital of the United States. Underlying the shift in the economic centre of gravity was a strong technological imperative; and flowing out of the geographic reorientation was an important consequence – the fashioning of an integrated unitary state, simultaneously unitary in both political and economic spheres, the political capital being overlaid by the economic capital. But why, at the outset of industrialization, was Japan not functionally unitary? And why did the logic of industrialization make it so?

Making sense of these questions is the burden of this chapter, which addresses the following two questions: why did Osaka become the Manchester of the Far East in the first place, and having concentrated tremendous economic power in its hands, why did that economic might slip away from it? The first question is addressed in the next three sections, where we shall briefly explore Japan's pre-industrial feudal background and the first of the three infrastructure–manufacturing waves between 1877 and 1938, which centred on the application of steam power. With this point established we shall move onto the second question. The fifth and sixth sections discuss the second and

third waves. We shall first consider the second infrastructure–manufacturing wave, which involved electricity and railroads, and then
the third wave, which was strongly shaped by the use of the internal
combustion engine – mainly in land transport, that is, lorries and
buses – and the utilization and improvement of roads. The principal
thrust of the analysis, which I hope will become clear from my
exposition, is that Osaka was perfectly suited for a water-based,
steam-power-driven economy. But its very advantage in water transport, as exemplified by its rich network of canals and waterways, came
to plague it when technological progress pushed the economy towards
reliance on land-based infrastructure. To cast the argument in evolutionary terms: technological development is restless, in the long run
ignoring past achievement and former glory, for it drastically reworks
the comparative advantage of different geographic locales. It ruth-
lessly turns what is a decided plus during one historical epoch into a
definitive disadvantage later on, driving out the old in order to replace
it with the new. Destruction is a necessary concomitant of and the
heavy price that must be paid for economic progress.

HISTORICAL AND GEOGRAPHIC BACKGROUND

Under feudalism the Japanese economy was an organic water- and
wood-based economy in the sense that most structures and imple-
ments were fashioned out of wood, a significant proportion of med-
ium- and long-distance trade was negotiated on wooden ships plying
rivers, seas and oceans, and the major sources of energy were organic:
wind, water and fire. Osaka – situated at a central point along the
north-west axis of the Japanese archipelago, nestled in the Inland Sea
at the point where the mighty Yodogawa River drains Lake Biwa and
the adjoining river basins, the sites where much of Japan's ancient
economy and culture flourished – naturally emerged under Pax Tokugawa as a merchant seaport, a Venice of the Far East.

As can be seen from Map 8.2, the comparative advantage of Osaka
– whose administrative heart under shogun rule was known as Sangō
(the darkly shaded area in the map) – was its capacity for conducting
commerce by water, as exemplified by its network of canals and rivers,
which turned Osaka into a veritable chessboard interlaced by east–
west and north–south waterways. This transport network had been
carved out in the aftermath of Hideyoshi's establishment of a mena-
cing castle in Osaka with the deliberate aim of concentrating

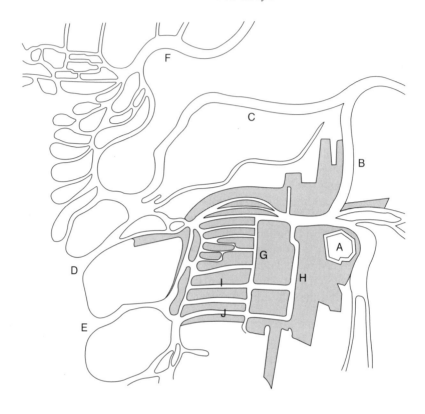

A Osaka Castle
B Yodogawa River
C Nakatsugawa River
D Mouth of Ajigawa River
E Mouth of Shirinashigawa River

F Kanzakigawa River
G Nishiyokobori Canal
H Higashiyokobori Canal
I Nagahori Canal
J Dōtonbori Canal

Sangō

Map 8.2   Osaka (Sangō) during the Tokugawa period

merchant activity at this point favoured by nature. For Osaka was centrally located, enjoyed access to an oceanic port that was generally more placid than the ports facing directly onto the Pacific Ocean, and was the *de facto* regional hub for the Kinai region, blessed with soils that were generally good for producing rice and a plethora of vegetables and fibres. In short, under feudal rule Osaka became a great seaport city whose economic destiny was tied to the waters along which most of its commerce flowed.

Osaka's most potent seaport rival was the shogun's capital, Edo (later to become Tokyo). Like Osaka, Edo lay on a plain and at the juncture of huge rivers and the sea; and like Osaka, Edo carried on a flourishing trade by water. But unlike Osaka, Edo's destiny was less strongly linked to the water, or rather its infrastructural development was far more balanced, resting equally upon land-based and water-based systems for transport and defence against natural disasters. The reasons for the difference were manifold, but the major causes were surely ecological, as captured schematically in Table 8.1. As can be gleaned from the table, Edo and Osaka, the actual urban settlements and their immediate hinterlands, differed markedly in terms of natural endowment – soil composition, frequency and type of natural disasters – and therefore ended up differing in preindustrial population density, land use and settlement patterns.

Edo became the chief transport hub and commercial centre for the Kantō plain, which lay in the shadow of volcanic ranges and was frequently rocked by earthquakes, and hence frequently gutted by conflagrations. For this reason the authorities, wishing to create fire breaks throughout the metropolis, stipulated that wide thoroughfares and boulevards should crisscross its environs. The Osaka authorities, meanwhile, were far more concerned with flooding than with fires, for the torrential monsoon rains in late spring, summer and autumn would often swell the rivers flowing into Osaka's waterway network, destroying homes and washing away the embankments lining the natural and artificial waterways and the myriad of wooden bridges spanning them. Thus Osaka developed a system of relatively wide canals and rivers for moving goods annexed to a network of narrow lanes and streets lined with shops, merchant house headquarters and residential structures. In Edo wide earthen boulevards cum fire breaks took the place of Osaka's canals and it ended up with a system of wide boulevards annexed to a network of narrow streets.

The build-up of canals, carefully channelled rivers and roads characteristic of early Tokugawa Osaka and Edo was typical of Japanese infrastructure construction during the first century or so of feudal rule, that is, from about 1600 until the 1720s. As a result of the massive construction effort a richly interlaced set of riparian, shipplying and road networks came into being, and in the wake of these a specialization and division of labour occurred, new crops (for example cotton) were introduced or flourished, and land reclamation proceeded apace as land that hitherto had not enjoyed irrigation became suitable for rice cultivation. Nor was land reclamation limited to areas

186

Table 8.1 Ecological contrast: Kinai-Osaka and Kantō-Tokyo

	Kinai–Osaka (Sango)	Kantō–Tokyo (Edo)
Climate	Mild winters (few days below freezing) except in Kyoto and Japan Sea district, hot summers	Mild winters (around 3 to 4 days below freezing), strong north-westerly winds, hot summers
Geology and soil	South and west of Fossa Magna, alluvial lowlands surrounded by diluvial borderlands; Yodogawa River formed from rivers flowing out of Kyoto, Lake Biwa and Nara basins flow into Osaka Bay; red soils with little volcanic ash	North and east of Fossa Magna, alluvial lowlands surrounded by diluvial terraces; Tone, Arakawa and Tamagawa rivers cross plain, empty in Tokyo Bay; Tokyo on low floodlands and delta of Sumida River; in vicinity of many volcanoes, brown soil laden with volcanic ash, infertile and deficient in basic minerals
Natural disasters	High frequency of flooding; occasional earthquakes	High frequency of earthquakes; occasional flooding
Tokugawa period: agricultural productivity/population density	Relatively high agricultural productivity, extensive double cropping of dry fields; high population density	Relatively low agricultural productivity, and relatively low population density
Agricultural land use	Rice fields dominant; land also supported cotton production and other industrial crops	Dry fields dominant – vegetables, fruits, mulberry, barley, potatoes, tea and tobacco
Settlement pattern	Small compact rural agglomerations, rectangular in shape, surrounded by moats and hedges	Rural agglomerations irregular in shape, typically surrounded by forest
Livestock	Cows dominant	Horses dominant

that could be converted from dry field agriculture to paddy production with the establishment of irrigation and drainage ditches. It also took place in lakes, wide rivers, bays and inlets. An example of this latter type of land reclamation can be seen in Map 8.2: the fields flanking the mouths of the waterways feeding into Osaka Bay were largely *shinden* (literally 'new fields'), that is, fields created at the behest of merchants, villages, peasant entrepreneurs or government authorities, fields that were largely put to agricultural use.

Resting upon the specialization and division of labour and the introduction and diffusion of new crops occasioned by the infrastructural improvements (which in turn promoted further infrastructural improvements in lagging regions) was the spread of craft-based industry, as exemplified by the proliferation of small cotton weaving sheds, silk filatures and hemp-producing operations.[4] This craft industry, long recognized as important for early Western European industrialization in the 18th and 19th centuries, has been dubbed 'proto-industrialization' by many historians. Two very important consequences of the spread of proto-industrialization after the early 1700s were the diversification of merchant activity into the promotion and trade of industrial products and the development of a skilled and semi-skilled labour force capable of working in the light industries, especially textiles, on both a full-time and a seasonal basis. And no region of Japan benefited as much from proto-industrialization as the Osaka region. As is apparent from Table 8.2, that industrial activity made particularly strong gains in the Kinai region, especially in the villages and small towns dotting the hills and plains near Kyoto and Osaka.

As can be seen, the Osaka region – 'Kinai, narrowly defined' (which included the five feudal domains in the immediate environs of Osaka and Kyoto), as distinguished from 'Kinai, surrounding area', which refers to an additional set of domains contiguous to the narrowly defined Kinai zone – was far more advanced in terms of economic development (for example high levels of urbanization, substantial diversification of economic activity and a shift away from dependence on farming) than the other regions of Japan, including the Kantō region, where Edo was located. It should be noted that the figures assembled in the table reflect the contrast between the environs of Edo and Osaka discussed earlier: the more thoroughgoing conversion of dry field to paddy field in the Osaka–Kyoto region than in the Kantō zone; the higher agricultural productivity of the Osaka environs compared with that in the Edo region and the greater population-carrying capacity of the Osaka–Kinai zone relative to that of Edo–Kantō.

Table 8.2   Industrial activity: Japanese regions, 1870

Region	Population density (per chō)	Urbanization (%)	Output in yen per chō		Index of village industrial activity	Ratio of paddy to dry fields (area)
			Cereals	Industrial crops		
Eastern Japan	6.21	17.8	29.5	7.0	0.236	1.11
Kantō East	5.83	8.5	28.3	3.8	0.135	1.13
Kantō West	7.59	33.2	30.9	11.6	0.376	0.59
Central Japan	9.24	17.9	38.8	6.4	0.165	2.22
Western Japan	9.24	14.7	41.0	7.8	0.191	1.64
Kinai, narrowly defined	15.7	34.8	60.4	28.6	0.474	3.16
Kinai, surrounding area	9.70	12.8	54.0	8.0	0.148	3.71
Japan	7.87	16.2	35.6	7.3	0.204	1.42

Notes: The estimates are approximate and are for circa 1870. A *chō* is a unit of land (about 2.45 acres). 'Kinai, narrowly defined' refers to the five domains in the immediate Osaka–Kyoto–Nara area, and 'Kinai, surrounding area' refers to the eight additional fiefs in the region. Today 'Kinai' roughly corresponds to the two subregions combined.
Source: Saito (1985), pp. 209ff.

That the Osaka region was more advanced than the rest of Japan had important implications for the level of skill formation, both in manufacturing and in wholesale/retail activities. Kinai region producers and wholesaler/retailers tended to be more experienced and more sophisticated in their capacity to work up textiles and processed foods such as soy sauce and spirits for sale elsewhere in the nation than were manufacturers and merchants in other regions of Japan. A good example of this was the 'putting-out' industry, in which Kinai merchants were active participants. They purchased raw materials from farmers and intermediaries and placed them with part-time farmers/part-time suppliers of craft labour services, who then worked the materials into finished products, which the merchants 'repurchased' and finally marketed through a chain of wholesalers and retailers. But while this advantage in skills came to characterize the Kinai as a whole during the 18th and 19th centuries, it is important to keep in mind that actual production did not come to be concentrated in Osaka, or more particularly within the Sangō boundaries. The technology being used was developed domestically and, insofar as spinning and weaving sheds were located in rural villages, was advanced by dint of experimentation and study amongst peasant households and/or at the suggestion of rural merchants rather than on the advice or at the behest of the great financial barons of Osaka. There were no obvious economies of scale to encourage proto-industrial manufacturers to concentrate themselves in metropolitan centres such as Osaka. This state of affairs changed and changed dramatically when the Western powers forced Japan to open its doors during the 1850s and treaty ports – Osaka became a treaty port in which Westerners enjoying extraterritorial privileges were allowed to reside in 1868, the year of the Meiji Restoration – became centres into which flowed the technologies of the Industrial Revolution and its aftermath. Producers wishing to utilize the latest techniques flocked to these locales. In cities such as Osaka was the new knowledge; in cities such as Osaka – enjoying ready access to raw material imports through its deep-water neighbouring port at Kobe – were assembled the coal, raw cotton and iron ore required for the new types of production; in cities such as Osaka assembled workers willing and able to work in mechanized plants; and in cities such as Osaka flourished banks and other financial institutions committed to funding industrial innovations. A new era in which the great seaport conurbations of the Tōkaidō came to enjoy sweeping advantages of economy of scale over their competitors, both rural and urban, was ushered in at the middle of the 19th century.

THREE INFRASTRUCTURE–MANUFACTURING WAVES, 1877–1938

With Japan's opening up to the West, the long evolutionary waves of institutional and technological progress that had already transformed or were in the process of transforming Western Europe (and certain areas of Western settlement such as the United States, Canada, Oceania and pockets of Latin America) became the new engine of economic growth in Japan, supplementing domestic sources of growth in agriculture and proto-industry. Three waves of about a half century in duration – known as Kondratieff waves since their classic characterization by Schumpeter (1939) – were associated with technological innovation and imitation.[5]

In initiating the upswing of a Kondratieff wave, risk-taking institutions draw from a wide range of potential innovations – for instance fresh techniques, new energy sources, products hitherto unavailable to consumers and untried methods of mobilizing capital and motivating and disciplining labour – and stimulate a wave of innovation and imitation. Successful innovations – those securing solid niches amongst producers and consumers – generate unusually high profits, which attract imitators. As other firms and non-profit institutions rush into the fray and attempt to secure a share of the highly profitable markets, capital construction surges as fresh plant, equipment and social overhead capital infrastructure supporting the innovations is put in place. But as imitation squeezes profits, as the position of institutions clinging to the older techniques is compromised and as the volume of bankruptcies grows, investment levels drop. The forward momentum of the wave dissipates because the expected rates of return on investment drop and because destruction goes hand in hand with innovation.

It is important to keep in mind that as more and more countries enter into the process of absorbing the technological waves, the speed with which they pass from technologies developed earlier to those developed later is truncated and in some cases – when all producers in a follower country elect to use the latest technique – is bypassed altogether. For this reason the duration of successive waves is often much shorter in follower countries than it is in the countries where the fundamental breakthroughs are actually accomplished. Moreover imitation is rarely a matter of slavish copying: most imitation involves some creativity, and in many cases true hybrids are generated through a process of derived innovation as adaptation takes place in response to varying relative factor prices, differing types of social institution and inbred consumer tastes. Consider if you will a snapshot of Osaka around 1915, in which is depicted the jostling of human-drawn carts with electrically propelled tramways. A hybrid transportation system is operating: passengers ride in a *jinrikusha* (a hybrid cart in which a Chinese pull-cart design was combined with rubber wheels of Western origin) to stations where they board electrically propelled trams.

The proliferation of hybridization that accompanies the spread of technology is a general process, extending into every nook and cranny of economic life. Consider the following schema for the (approximate) dating and characterization of the three pre-Second World War Kondratieff waves (Table 8.3).

As is apparent from the simple schema in Table 8.3, innovations such as investment banking and *zaibatsu* forms of organization were the result of experimentation in later industrializing nations, experimentation motivated in part because what had worked in the first industrializing nation, Britain, was less suitable for the factor market/institutional environments of follower countries and/or less efficient for generating the relatively rapid mobilization of capital that the rapid movement through the successive waves necessitated.

Table 8.3   Kondratieff Waves: Pre-Second World War Japan

Kondratieff Wave Dates	Some salient innovations	Approximate beginning of modern economic development involving shift to inorganic economy
1787–1842 (industrialization)	Coal, steam, iron and steel, canals, factory system; switch from organic to inorganic energy	Britain (1760–1800), France (1830s), Belgium and Netherlands (1830s), United States (1830s)
1842–1897 (railroadization)	Steam railways and ships, iron and steel infrastructure, investment banking, scale/scope economies in large integrated corporations	Germany (1850s), Switzerland (1860s), Norway and Sweden (1860s), Italy (1860s), Australia and Canada (1870s), Japan (1870s–1880s), Russia (1880s)
1897–1938 (electrification)	Electricity, internal combustion engine, motorized vehicles, chemicals, road networks, cartels and *zaibatsu* industrial groups	Argentina (1920s–1830s), Turkey (1920s–1930s), Brazil (1920s–1930s), Korea (1920s–1930s)

Notes: 'Organic energy' refers to energy generated by human or animal power, wind, water and fire. 'Inorganic energy' refers to energy from fossil fuels, electrical energy and the like. For other interpretations of long swing patterns that more or less overlap with the infrastructure–manufacturing waves discussed in the text, see Minami (1986, 1994) and Ohkawa and Rosovsky (1973).

Because of Japan's relative geographic isolation from the Atlantic economy, which was the geographic heart of 19th century technological progress and economic expansion, because of the relatively high level of development of Japan's proto-industrial economy and because the infrastructure supported a water–wood centred economy relying on organic sources of energy (wind, water currents, fire and so on), hybrid innovations were especially prevalent in the Japanese case. In each of the three technologically driven waves that transformed Japan between the 1870s and the late 1930s (Table 8.4), hybrid machines, hybrid transportation systems, hybrid energy generation and hybrid consumer products were characteristic of the Japanese economy. For instance *kobune* (small wooden boats known in common parlance as junks) and *niguruma* (wooden carts) were extensively used in conjunction with steamships, electric railways and lorries in interwar Japan. And craft industries that flourished in the heyday of the late Tokugawa proto-industrial economy survive even today. But once foreign technology began pouring into the country – first penetrating and establishing niches in the great metropolitan centres of the Tōkaidō and later diffusing into the countryside and hinterland – the engine of Japanese economic development came primarily to focus on the

Table 8.4   Infrastructure–manufacturing waves in Japan, 1877–1938

	First wave, 1877–1897	Second Wave, 1897–1919	Third Wave, 1919–1938
Phases	Simultaneous development of infrastructure and manufacturing, 1877–97	Infrastructure phase: 1898–1908 Manufacturing phase: 1908–19	Infrastructure phase: 1919–29 Manufacturing phase: 1929–38
Energy	Old: human/animal, water, wind, fire. New: steam, fossil fuels (coal), thermal electricity	New: hydroelectric power, internal combustion engine	Expansion in application of electrical power and internal combustion engine
Transportation and infrastructure	Old: *niguruma* and *kobune*. New: Steam ships and trains, *jinrikusha*, deepwater ports	Electric railway network expansion; lighting; electronic communication, land and water	Regional power grids; subways; lorries, buses and road networks; declining use of *niguruma*, etc.
Key manufacturing sectors	Textiles and food products; pig iron and shipbuilding, machinery	Textiles; iron and steel, shipbuilding, chemicals, machinery	Chemicals, machinery, shipbuilding and transportation vehicles
Raw materials demand	Raw cotton, ferrous metals, food, wood	Raw cotton, ferrous metals, wood, petroleum	Wide range of minerals (e.g. magnesium, zinc, lead, tin, chrome), petroleum, rubber
Regional focus	Tōkaidō, especially Kinki	Tōkaidō, Kantō and Kinki	Tōkaidō, pull towards Kantō
New Institutions and policies	*Shokusan kōgyō*, factories and prime movers, incorporation; banking, *zaibatsu*; stock issue	Subsidies for shipbuilding; nationalization of many local railway lines	Reforms in education and banking; systematic city planning; militarism and expansion of empire
Major exogenous factors	Gold standard established; Sino-Japanese War reparations	Anglo-Japanese alliance; First World War	Great Kantō earthquake of 1923; breakdown of gold standard and international trade; autarky

exploitation of inorganic sources of energy far removed from the human/animal/wind/fire-powered energy sources characteristic of the feudal and proto-industrial economy. For this reason the absorption and adaptation of the techniques and devices fashioned in the West for utilizing these inorganic energy sources became a major source of productivity growth for the economy.

And it is precisely for this reason that the cities of the Tōkaidō played a crucial role in Japan's economic development. Large-scale infrastructure investment was required in order to exploit the new energy sources; cities and geographically concentrated industrial zones enjoyed tremendous economies of scale (huge potential markets over which investors could spread the fixed costs of investment in infrastructure), which naturally enticed both private and public sector developers of infrastructure; and because movement through the technologically driven waves tended to increase the range of raw materials that manufacturers and utility companies required, seaport cities with access to deepwater ports enjoyed tremendous advantages in terms of securing requisite inputs. In short Western-style infrastructure and Western technology tended to take root first in the great cities of the Tōkaidō, thereby giving firms interested in exploiting this infrastructure (for example cheap hydroelectric power) a strong incentive to locate in the very same locales and increased the demands placed on that infrastructure as manufacturers and their workers congregated in these locales and further increased the demand for infrastructure in the region.

Indeed the kind of 'feedback' logic envisioned here, whereby infrastructure investment interacts with industrial sector investment in a 'lead–lag' fashion, is, I believe, characteristic of prewar Japanese economic development and constitutes a major part of the rationale for my characterizing the three prewar waves described in Table 8.4 as 'infrastructure–manufacturing' waves. For instance, as can be seen in the table, during the first wave infrastructure and manufacturing expanded in tandem. The manufacturing expansion in this wave led to a concentration of population in the great metropolitan centres of the Tōkaidō, which then established the economies of scale that were exploited by the developers of the railways, especially the intracity and intercity electric railway systems, and the developers of thermal and hydroelectric power grids during the infrastructure phase of the second wave. In turn the supply of relatively cheap electricity stimulated the rapid diffusion of electric motors, which gave a strong fillip to the mechanization of small and medium-sized factories,[6] thereby facilitating systematic import substitution during the First World War boom period, when the importation of capital goods and manufactured consumer products from the West was hobbled by the wartime embargoes imposed on shipping by the belligerent nations. And the resulting industrial expansion and attendant population concentration within the great metropolitan centres of the Tōkaidō put renewed pressure on the infrastructure sector and promoted the rapid adoption of lorries and buses during the interwar period, which helped – along with the development of huge power grids that brought hydroelectric power out of the alps to the three great Tōkaidō conurbations (Tokyo–Yokohama, Nagoya, and Osaka–Kobe) – lay the infrastructural groundwork for the massive manufacturing expansion of the 1930s.

In short, because technological progress was intimately tied up with exploiting inorganic energy sources, and because generating and distributing new energy required large-scale investment in infrastructure, the latter was essential to manufacturing expansion. Since investors in infrastructure naturally favoured large markets over which they could spread the relatively high fixed costs of putting in place the structures and other capital equipment needed to supply energy, infrastructural construction tended to first take place in the great Tōkaidō seaports where the demand and supply conditions were most favourable, that is, in the locales where raw materials, labour and population were concentrated and readily available. Thus a kind of 'feedback' logic was played out in prewar Japan, with technological progress, the construction of infrastructure and manufacturing expansion building one upon the other in the great metropolitan centres of the Tōkaidō industrial belt.

OSAKA DOMINANT: THE FIRST
INFRASTRUCTURE–MANUFACTURING WAVE, 1877–97

The argument concerning the feedback of technological progress, infrastructural construction and manufacturing expansion is key to explaining why the great cities of the Tōkaidō industrial belt played a particularly salient role in Japan's economic development. It is also essential to understanding why Osaka and the Kinai region became dominant as an industrial district during the late 19th century, only to see that preeminence slip away during the first half of the 20th century. Recall that Osaka's comparative strengths during the late Tokugawa period lay in its water-based infrastructure and the manufacturing and marketing skills tied up with the proto-industrial economy.

The introduction of steam power in Japan played into the hands of the Osaka business community for an important reason: the first economically viable applications of the new technology were to light industry, especially cotton textiles, and to steamships – two areas in which Osaka had a strong comparative advantage over potential Tōkaidō rivals such as Tokyo and Nagoya.

In cotton textiles Osaka was well positioned because, responding to the demand for proto-industrial raw materials in the Kinai, and reflecting the fact that its climate was perfect for spinning and the rich soil in its environs was ideal for growing fibres, raw cotton was abundantly produced in Osaka's hinterland. Moreover since proto-industrial production in the cotton textiles industry had reached advanced levels in the Osaka environs by the 1850s, the Kinai labour force was awash with the skills needed for the manufacturing and marketing of textiles. True, the wave of the future in the Osaka of the 1870s and 1880s was in steam-driven spinning and broad-loom cloth, not in the labour-intensive sheds producing narrow-loom cloth for kimonos and other traditional Japanese garb. Nevertheless its extensive experience of working with various grades of staple cotton, and its long-standing expertise in distributing clothing and sheeting to local markets all over Japan, surely stood Osaka in good stead as it negotiated the transition to an inorganic steam- and coal-based economy during the last quarter of the century.

But as important as light industry was for Osaka's emergence as the preeminent manufacturing conurbation in East Asia, the steamship industry was of more momentous long-term importance in terms of developing the pockets of skilled labour – the labour supply niche – that helped ease the transition to a Western-technology-oriented economy during the 1880s and 1890s. That is, the steamship industry helped pave the transition to an economy in which Western-style manufacturing was as profitable as Japanese-style manufacturing, and eventually more profitable.[7] Table 8.5 is instructive about the importance of steamships for Osaka–Kobe manufacturing. As can be seen, about 60 per cent of the steam-powered, wooden-hulled ships manufactured in Japan and registered in 1898 were manufactured in the Settsu region, that is, in Osaka and Kobe and the hinterland surrounding those two conurbations. This undoubtedly reflects the fact that since Osaka was a water-oriented metropolis under Tokugawa rule, a wooden shipbuilding industry had flourished there before 1850, an industry which had employed a huge cadre of individuals skilled in the art of wooden shipbuilding. Since Japanese craftspeople were inexperienced in wielding

Table 8.5 Steamers in the Japanese merchant marine fleet, 1898

A. Classified by locale of registration (626 ships)[1]

Hull Type	Number of ships (percentages in brackets)			Average registered Tonnage		Average Horsepower	
	Total	Outside Settsu	Inside Settsu	Outside Settsu	Inside Settsu	Outside Settsu	Inside Settsu
Wood	397 (100)	275 (69.3)	122 (30.7)	81.3	27.2	110.3	26.9
Non-wood[2]	229 (100)	128 (55.9)	101 (44.1)	1193.5	753.0	179.1	118.7

B. Classified by locale of construction/shipyard of origin (626 ships)

Hull type	Total (%)	Made in Japan%[1]		Made abroad[3]	Average Tonnage			Average horsepower		
		Outside Settsu	Inside Settsu		Made in Japan		Made abroad	Made in Japan		Made abroad
					Outside Settsu	Inside Settsu		Outside Settsu	Inside Settsu	
Wood	100	38.3	60.0	1.7	79.0	94.0	204.0	27.0	27.0	36.4
Non-wood[2]	100	5.7	12.2	82.1	341.8	292.9	1151.5	54.7	81.4	169.9

Notes:
1. The 'Settsu' category includes Settsu, Osaka, Kobe and Hyogo.
2. Non-wood includes iron, steel, combined iron and steel, and composite.
3. This category includes a small number of shipyards of unknown designation.
Source: Department of Communications, Mercantile Merchant Marine Bureau (1898): various pages.

and working with metal, having functioned in a wood-oriented economy before the country was opened up, the iron- and steel-hulled ships utilized in Japan were almost exclusively manufactured in Britain. Undergirding the argument about Osaka's primacy in the initial applications of steam in textile manufacturing and steamship construction is the fact that the other illustrious application of steam power – railways – was only in its infancy during the final quarter of the 19th century. This was not surprising. Japan is an island nation and almost all the newly burgeoning industrial centres were concentrated along the Tōkaidō industrial belt, where they enjoyed immediate access to deep-water ports (Kyoto and Nagoya were exceptions, and neither achieved the primacy of Tokyo, Yokohama, Osaka and Kobe in the new industries). For this reason, on the demand side coastal steamship fleets were highly competitive, holding their own against competition from land-based steam railways. And on the supply side, because Japanese craftspeople were not generally accustomed to working with metal, it was easier for the newly emergent producers of Western-style transportation equipment to build steam-powered ships (with wooden hulls) rather than railway rolling stock, which had a very high metal to wood content ratio. Indeed it was only after 1906–7, when most of the steam railways in Japan were nationalized, that an enterprise – the National Railroads, under a powerful Railroad Agency – was able to muster the economies of scale necessary to finance a huge reverse engineering project whereby designated companies were sufficiently subsidized to mount a campaign of import substitution within the rolling stock subsector of the capital goods industry.

Thus during the first infrastructure–manufacturing wave Japanese land transport was not mainly by railways but by *niguruma* (freight carts) and *jinrikusha* (human-powered passenger vehicles). For short-distance hauls *niguruma* and *jinrikusha* dominated, and for long-distance hauls ocean-going steamships accounted for a large share of traffic, especially freight traffic. Of course surges in demand for transportation were strongly felt everywhere, which can be seen in Figures 8.1 and 8.2. During the upswing of the 1880s the demand for *niguruma* and railway services surged. In the case of railways this eventually induced – with a lag – an expansion of rolling stock. The stock-flow adjustment pattern evident in Figure 8.2 is general. Indeed it helps explain why, in the first infrastructure–manufacturing wave, upswings in manufacturing output tended to move fairly close to upswings in infrastructural construction (in part because *niguruma*, which were easy and quick to construct, could be used on the narrow dirt roads and lanes

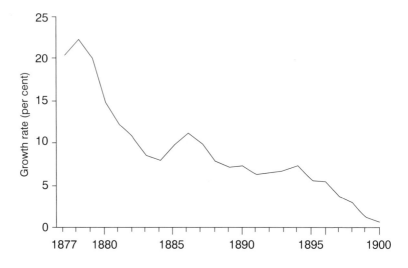

Figure 8.1   The growth of Niguruma, Japan, 1877–1900 (five-year moving averages)

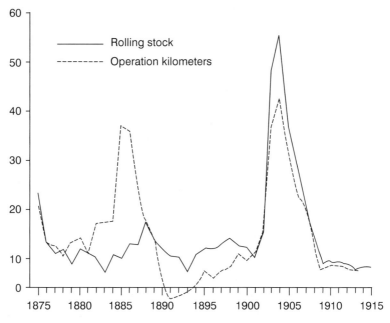

Figure 8.2   Japanese national railways: growth rates of rolling stock and operation kilometers, 1875–1915 (five-year moving averages)

that pervaded Japan at the time), and during the second and third waves (smoothed moving averages) fluctuations in infrastructural investment tend to move out of phase with fluctuations in manufacturing investment. As can be seen in Figure 8.2, which shows the growth rates of operation kilometers and the rolling stock used in the national railways, there is one prominent exception to the rule that in the Western-oriented, infrastructure-focused capital goods sector, surges in demand for services moved out of phase and, one presumes, elicited surges in the stock of capital goods: the period between 1905 and 1910. But during this period additions to the national rolling stock came about almost exclusively because the national railway was taking over lines that had hitherto been developed and managed by private enterprises, thereby simultaneously securing freight and passenger flows.

Because so much of the new activity connected with the infrastructure–manufacturing wave of the 1880s and early 1890s was concentrated in the Tōkaidō industrial belt, and especially in the six great cities – Tokyo, Yokohama, Nagoya, Kyoto, Osaka and Kobe – the populations of the great conurbations along the Pacific coastline of Japan's main island grew rapidly. This rapid growth was also reflected in the proliferation of suburban satellites, some of which were eventually incorporated into the city that had spawned them. Consider Tokyo and Osaka, which officially secured the 'city' (*shi*) designation in 1889. As can be seen in Maps 8.3 and 8.4, Tokyo and Osaka not only underwent the population expansion just discussed, they also expanded their boundaries. Osaka went through two major expansions before the Second World War, one in 1897, which was connected with the construction of a deep-water port for the city; and one in 1925, when the rapidly industrializing suburbs were brought under the city's administrative control, a move that was connected to the growing problems of inadequate water supplies and insufficient land transport for the suburbs. Tokyo went through only one major expansion before the war: a massive expansion towards the west.

It is important to keep in mind that as the two cities expanded their boundaries into the rural hinterlands they encompassed completely different types of land. In the case of the high-productivity, densely populated rural villages dotting the plains around Osaka, expansion was largely into paddy land, and as the city's population and manufacturing sites proliferated, land developers had to convert expensive paddy (which embodied valuable infrastructure in the form of irrigation ditches) into *takuchi* (non-agricultural/non-wasteland plots, upon which housing, shops and factories were erected. In the case of the

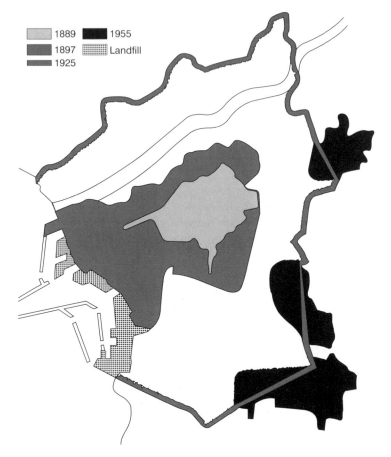

Map 8.3   Territorial expansion of Osaka, 1889–1955

Tokyo environs, relatively inexpensive and unproductive dry fields were interspersed with considerable patches of wasteland, so that Tokyo's population sprawl was less costly in terms of the direct and opportunity costs of land conversion.

ELECTRICITY, RAILWAYS AND THE SECOND INFRASTRUCTURE–MANUFACTURING WAVE, 1897–1919

Of the three infrastructure–manufacturing waves to sweep across the Japanese economic landscape the second was surely the most important

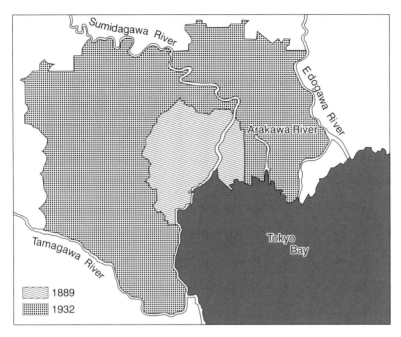

Map 8.4   Territorial expansion of Tokyo, 1889–1940

because it was associated with electrification, and electrification was instrumental in making Japan into a mighty industrial giant. But in the Japanese case electrification – a key sector in the third Kondratieff wave – occurred in tandem with a wholesale expansion of the railway network: the increased usage of electricity in rolling stock and communications facilitated the running of trains at night, when they were least likely to disrupt road traffic crossing the railway tracks; and a significant percentage of the new lines being laid after the turn of the century were for electrically powered trains, especially intra-urban tramway lines and interurban commuter lines. Following the nationalization legislation of the early 20th century, the (predominantly steam) railway network that fell into the hands of the central authorities formed a skeleton around and across the main islands of the nation. The development of shorter lines was given over either to the private sector, as was common in the case of commuter lines into city centres from the suburbs or between central cities, or to local municipal authorities, as was the case with many of the tramways built within cities. Thus the energy and transportation infrastructure that propelled Japan into its second major infrastructure–manufacturing wave was intimately tied up with interurban and intra-urban transportation, and with the diffusion of electrical power within the great metropolitan areas.

The overlap between the post-1900 expansion of the railways and electrical generation can be seen in Table 8.6. In appreciating why the overlap was so tight it is essential to keep in mind that many of the companies offering interurban and intra-urban train services also provided electrical power to the communities through which their lines passed. Evident in Panel C of Table 8.6 is the overwhelming importance of the Tōkaidō belt in the initial build-up of electrical power generation in Japan. As is clear from the indices during the early pre-First World War phase of this build-up, the Tōkaidō belt was far ahead of the rest of the country in supplying electrical lighting to its residential, industrial and commercial inhabitants. And it was also considerably ahead in terms of actual power generation, although when the great hydroelectric power grids were erected and put into operation between the world wars the generating plants were increasingly located in the vicinity of dams built in the alps, the power being supplied to the great industrial conurbations via high-voltage power lines.

As can be seen in Figure 8.3, the increase in electric railway usage during the first decade of the century was especially dramatic in the Kinai area (labelled 'Tōkaidō south' in the figure). Why was this surge not mirrored in the northern Tōkaidō district, that is in the cities of Tokyo and Yokohama and their suburbs? The reason is that prior to the introduction of electricity for powering trams and interurban railways a massive horse tramway network had been built up in the great conurbations of the northern pole of the Japanese industrial belt, and this system could be easily electrified. Why was this land-based infrastructure built up in Tokyo–Yokohama but not in the more industrially advanced Osaka–Kobe area? The answer is the road network, and in particular the existence or dearth of wide roads and boulevards. Recall that in the Tokugawa period in Edo emphasis was placed on the construction of wide boulevards in order to prevent the spread of fires, which were prevalent in that region because earthquakes were frequent. And recall that Tokyo was expanding out to the west into dry fields and wasteland that could be converted to other uses at relatively low cost. Thus at an early point Tokyo, Yokohama and their satellite cities could and did make the construction of wide boulevards a priority, and horses – which fouled the streets in their immediate path – could function in these wide streets but not in the

Table 8.6 Electricity and Railways: Japan, 1872–1941[1]

A. Railways: operation kilometers, rolling stock for national railways and rolling stock kilometers, indices, 1920–21 = 100

	Operation kilometers				Rolling stock (national railways only)			Rolling stock kilometers		
	National	Regional	Street	Total	Engines	Freight Cars	Total	Passenger	Freight	Total
1872–79	0.7	–	–	0.5	0.8	1.6	0.6	n.a.	n.a.	n.a.
1880–89	3.3	8.4	–	3.9	1.7	3.7	1.7	n.a.	n.a.	n.a.
1890–99	9.4	84.8	–	23.7	5.7	9.0	5.0	3.1	6.1	3.1
1900–9	35.6	104.4	–	45.1	30.0	32.6	29.7	16.7	20.5	16.7
1910–19	85.1	66.7	92.5	78.6	77.1	79.5	82.1	59.9	64.1	59.9
1920–29	115.9	141.8	113.2	120.9	113.5	119.3	114.2	94.8	110.3	94.3
1930–41	159.4	207.4	109.1	162.6	128.0	138.1	143.9	114.7	105.9	114.7

B. Railways electricity generated, electric lights, electrified carriages and electric lights in carriages: indices, 1920–21 = 100

	Electricity generated	Electric lights	Wattage – lights	Electrified carriages	Electric lights in carriages
1910–14	30.4	30.0	47.8	46.1	40.6
1915–19	93.8	63.9	77.5	75.0	68.3
1920–24	103.3	128.7	122.6	126.1	124.8
1925–29	143.4	232.0	247.2	179.9	178.3
1930–34	647.0	320.1	391.6	179.6	208.3
1935–39	724.2	450.1	610.9	190.4	235.8
1940–41	1494.2	555.0	732.2	210.1	269.8

Table 8.6 (continued)

C. Electrical lights and total electricity generated and supplied for Japan, the Tōkaidō belt and its sub-districts (indices, 1920–21 = 100); percentages of national lights and electricity generated within Tōkaidō, and percentages of Tōkaidō total in sub-districts

| | Japan | Indices (1920–21 = 100) | | | | % in Tōkaidō | % of Tōkaidō in sub-districts[1] | | |
| | | Tōkaidō[1] | | | | | | | |
		Total	North	Middle	South		North	Middle	South
Number of electrical lights									
1900–9	2.4	3.8	3.8	1.9	4.8	65.2	38.6	11.6	49.8
1910–19	41.7	51.4	54.4	39.1	54.8	54.5	42.4	14.5	43.2
1920–29	127.2	119.7	123.7	116.3	117.4	38.6	41.6	20.4	38.1
1930–37	163.1	160.4	174.7	149.8	151.3	40.2	44.0	19.4	36.6
Electricity generated and supplied[2]									
1915–19	70.4	74.7	79.5	70.0	70.0	45.3	53.9	10.5	35.6
1920–29	164.6	182.7	134.4	205.2	237.2	47.6	39.0	12.8	48.2
1930–37	339.6	386.7	270.8	503.4	500.2	48.9	34.5	14.7	50.8

Notes:
1. Sub-districts are defined in terms of the following groups of prefectures: north – Saitama, Chiba, Tokyo and Kanagawa; middle – Shizuoka and Aichi; south – Kyoto, Osaka and Hyogo.
2. Figures on electricity generated and supplied are in kilowatt hours.
Sources: Cabinet Bureau of Statistics, *Nihon teikoku tōkei nenkan*, (various dates); Ministry of Railroads, *Tetsudō tōkei shiryō to tetsudōin tōkei zuhyō*; (various dates); Minami (1965).

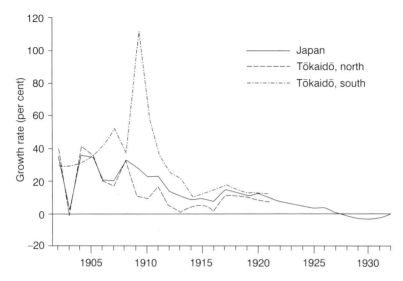

Figure 8.3   Electric railway passengers: growth rates for Japan and for the northern and southern districts of the Tōkaidō, 1902–32 (five-year moving averages)

narrow streets typical of the Kinai, where they presented a serious menace to public hygiene and safety. For this reason, in 1908 Tokyo–Yokohama had a huge advantage over Osaka–Kobe in terms of intercity and intracity electrical train service: for instance the two Kantō private companies operating in Tokyo–Yokohama – Tokyo Tetsudō and Keihin – between them had 68 per cent of all carriages and 34 per cent of all of the track used by the 18 companies providing an electrical train service that year (Mosk, 1998, p. 16).

What finally emerged in the Osaka region was a hub–spoke pattern for the electric railways, with the centre of Osaka acting as the hub. The private lines running out to Kobe in the south-west, Kyoto and Nara in the north and north-east, and Sakai, Wakayama and Nagoya in the west served as the spokes. In the centre, ringing the vortex of iron and steel lines, was the Osaka city-run tramway system. The skeleton of this network, in which the city transport services interacted with a powerful oligopoly of private railway line/electrical power supplier/land developer companies, is shown in Map 8.5. Osaka/ Umeda to the north of the city centre and Nanba to the south served as the key nodal points connecting the private lines that ran into the city from the other great cities of the Kinai to the tramway network,

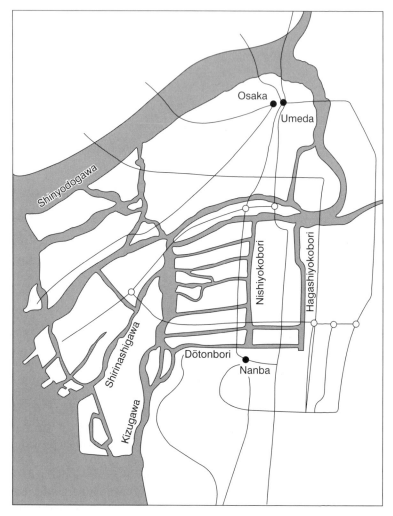

Map 8.5   Avenues of water, avenues of steel: major railway, river and canal
networks in Osaka circa 1930

which provided a link to important distribution points along Osaka's
extensive network of canals and rivers.

But as important as the urban demand for power and railways was
in stimulating the growth of the electrical power industry in Japan, an
equally important factor lay in the supply side, namely the harnessing
of hydroelectric power, first successfully achieved in North America

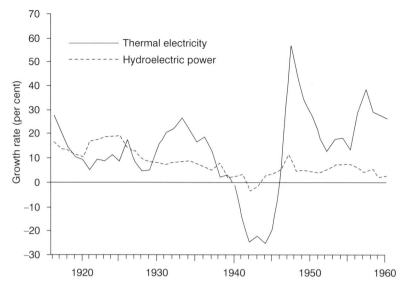

Figure 8.4   Hydroelectric and thermal power generation growth rates, Japan,
1915–60 (five-year moving averages)

but rapidly emulated on a global basis soon afterwards. As can be
seen from Figure 8.4, between the wars hydroelectric power generation tended to grow more rapidly than did thermal power generation.
Or to be specific, during the two great manufacturing sector surges
at the time of the First World War and in the 1930s hydroelectric
power grew especially vigorously. The fact that hydroelectric power
was crucial to the transformation of the Japanese economy from one
based on light industry and agriculture to one dominated by heavy
industry should come as no surprise. For Japan is mountainous and
during the monsoon season rainfall is abundant, so hydroelectric
power offered a relatively cheap way of providing the electricity
needed by heavy industry.

The impact of urban electrification and the elaboration of inter-
and intra-city railway lines during the infrastructure phase of the
second infrastructure–manufacturing wave put strong upward pressure on the price of heartland in the great metropolises of the
Tōkaidō. Since these areas now became extremely valuable for retail
ventures (there were massive daily flows of commuters through key
nodes such as Osaka/Umeda and Nanba) and service sector activity
(which required face-to-face contact, 24-hour operation capacity and

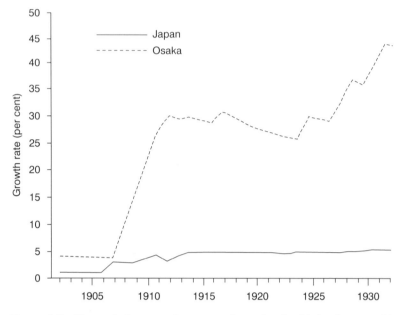

Figure 8.5 The relative per hectare price of *takuchi* land to paddy land (*takuchi* price/paddy land price ratio) Osaka city (inclusive of Nishinari-*gun* and Higashinari-*gun* before 1925) and Japan, 1902–32 (five-year moving averages)

up-to-date communications) urban land values skyrocketed. Consider Figure 8.5, which shows the *takuchi* land/paddy land unit price ratio. As can be seen, there was a surge in the price of *takuchi* land in Japan as a whole, but it was especially dramatic in Osaka. (Here the figures for Osaka include Nishinari-*gun* and Higashinari-*gun*, the two counties [*gun*] which were incorporated into Osaka city in 1925. Their inclusion enabled the construction of a consistent series from 1902 to 1932.) It is perhaps not an exaggeration to refer to this sharp upward rise in central metropolitan land prices in the wake of the infrastructure phase of the second infrastructure–manufacturing wave as the first modern Asian bubble. For as can be seen from Figure 8.5, during the industrial downswing of the 1920s central land prices did fall in Osaka, only to resume their upward march during the industrial surge of the 1930s.

Now the term 'bubble' hints at speculation in or strategic manipulation of the land market, and that certainly did occur in Osaka and its suburbs. For some of the most important local land developers were the private railway companies with lines into Osaka, and these companies had an astute long-term strategy. That strategy involved buying up land along the lines when it was relatively cheap, developing it for housing or recreational activities, and then opening a station in the vicinity of the developed land before selling off the real estate or making it available for rent. In this way land on the fringes of the great conurbations of the Tōkaidō underwent conversion to *takuchi* at points along the railway lines, the new stations serving as nodes from which spread the dormitory suburbs that sprang up chock a block amongst paddy fields and dry fields. To reiterate a point made earlier, because paddy land was relatively valuable compared with dry field land and the latter was easier to convert to *takuchi* since it embodied less water-related infrastructure, it was dry field land that tended to be used for residential or industrial purposes first. This can be seen for Osaka prefecture in Figure 8.6. But in this prefecture, where the vast bulk of land was paddy, urban sprawl eventually led to the widespread destruction of paddy. And herein lies an important difference between Osaka and Tokyo, for the latter was mainly expanding outwards into dry fields and therefore faced less of a problem in converting paddy. This difference has already been discussed in the context of inter- and intraurban railways during the infrastructure boom in the

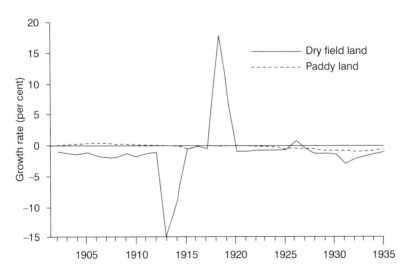

Figure 8.6   The conversion of agricultural land in Osaka prefecture: growth rates for paddy and dry field land, 1902–35 (five-year moving averages)

first decade of the century, and it had an even more momentous impact on the relative pace of industrial expansion in the two poles of the Tōkaidō during the third infrastructure–manufacturing wave.

LORRIES, BUSES, THE INTERNAL COMBUSTION ENGINE AND THE THIRD INFRASTRUCTURE–MANUFACTURING WAVE, 1919–1938

The First World War manufacturing boom – buoyed by the fillip given to import substitution in machinery and heavy industry by the wartime embargoes on shipping – came to an end in 1919. While the boom and its abrupt termination were undoubtedly shaped by particular historical forces such as the war itself, the Washington Conference, which set decided limitations on the shipbuilding programme of the Japanese navy, and the bubble-like atmosphere in the land market, the logic of imitation squeezing down profits on new investment in industrial plant and equipment was inexorably working to bring the surge to a conclusion. Because the economy was also going through a pronounced structural shift as it moved through the second infrastructure–manufacturing wave (heavy industry was growing far more rapidly than light industry) the downswing in factory production and employment in the 1920s was especially deep in the case of textiles and food products. This can be clearly seen by comparing Figure 8.7 with Figure 8.8, which trace employment changes in factories with five or more workers in the prefectures of Osaka and Tokyo, the dominant industrial prefectures of the period. Perusal of the figures reveals a second factor that has a direct bearing on the fundamental argument of this chapter. In virtually every year the growth rate in Tokyo outstripped that in Osaka. The downswing in the 1920s was far deeper in Osaka than it was in Tokyo; and the upswing in the 1930s was far stronger in Tokyo than it was in Osaka.

My basic thesis is that underlying the pull towards the northern pole of the Tōkaidō was Tokyo's comparative advantage in the developing rent of land-based infrastructure. When innovations involving steam-powered technology were the engine of growth of the Japanese economy, the manifold applications of that technology to water-based transportation favoured Osaka. But the most important applications of electricity and the internal combustion engine were land based: electricity was mainly used for land-based activities, and lorries, buses and cars ran on roads. For this reason, locating in the Tokyo region

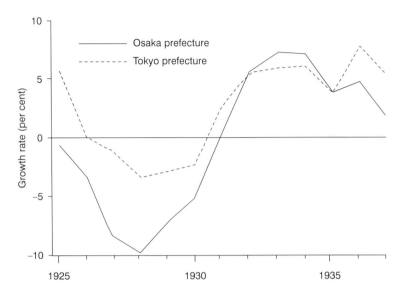

Figure 8.7 Factories with five or more workers in the light industrial sector: growth rates for employment in Osaka and Tokyo prefectures, 1925–37 (five-year moving averages)

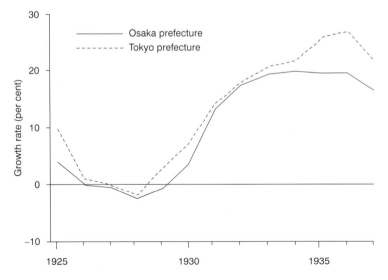

Figure 8.8 Factories with five or more workers in the heavy industrial sector: growth rates for employment in Osaka and Tokyo prefectures, 1925–37 (five-year moving averages)

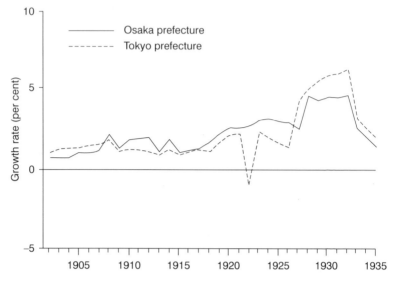

Figure 8.9   *Takuchi* land in Osaka and Tokyo prefectures: growth rates, 1902–35 (five-year moving averages)

held greater and greater appeal to investors in new industrial plant and equipment. So as Japan entered the third infrastructure–manufacturing wave, roads became key to Tokyo's comparative advantage. And this advantage involved both the inherited stock of roads and an elastic land supply for new road development. The importance of land conversion for Tokyo's rapid rise to industrial dominance is evident in Figure 8.9, which demonstrates how the Tokyo land conversion rates came to outstrip Osaka's, especially during the 1930s (the sharp downward fall during the early 1920s in Tokyo was due to the great Kantō earthquake of 1923).[8]

It should be noted that one reason why – after the first decade of the 20th century – an elastic supply of land within or surrounding a metropolis became an increasingly important element of industrial expansion was the strong upward pressure on city centre land prices in the great cities of the industrial belt, upward pressure occasioned by electrification and the growth of inter- and intracity electrical train lines. For the dramatic revamping of the real estate market forced many enterprises and households to move from the cities to the newly emergent suburbs. And the costs of that local relocation, weighed against the costs of a more wrenching move to a completely different metropolitan centre, surely penalized the post-1910 growth of manu-facturing activity in cities such as Osaka where the land conversion costs were extremely high. And of course for the newly formed enterprise contemplating a number of possible sites, the elasticity of the land supply in competing industrial-belt cities undoubtedly had a heavy bearing on the decision about where to set up business.

The explosion of central land prices had another very important consequence that worked against Osaka's comparative advantage, especially after the 1920s, when the third infrastructure–manufactur-ing wave commenced. For it rendered all the more expensive the widening of streets and boulevards in central districts: there was an escalation in the cost of buying out owners of property that needed to be removed so that a road could be widened, and the headaches attending the securing of local community group agreement on real-location of land use contiguous to the road mounted as well.

Tokyo's advantage in the pre-1910 stock of roads – especially wide roads – and the associated benefit this conferred on Tokyo in securing a massive lead in the use of lorries, buses and cars for transporting freight and passengers can be seen in Tables 8.7 and 8.8 and Figures 8.10 and 8.11.[9] Table 8.7 documents Tokyo's remarkable lead over Osaka in the use of lorries, buses and cars. It shows that Tokyo's vehicle stock not only began to grow at an earlier time than Osaka's, but that Osaka – a larger city than Tokyo between 1925, when Osaka expanded its boundaries, and 1932, when Tokyo took over adminis-trative control over its western suburbs and satellite cities – continued to lag far behind Tokyo as late as the early 1930s. Indeed, as can be seen from panel A of Table 8.7, the Osaka to Tokyo ratio for these vehicles in the early 1930s was less than 51 per cent.

That the dearth of wide roads was certainly acting as a constraint on the use of lorries, buses and cars in the Osaka region is indicated by Table 8.8. It is apparent that in Osaka, which enjoyed a larger land area and population than did Tokyo in 1930, a far smaller land area was devoted to roads even though the total length of Osaka's road network exceeded that in Tokyo. Indeed, as is clear from panel A of Table 8.8, the average road width in Tokyo was 10.7 meters as opposed to 7.3 meters in Osaka. And as is clear from panel C, a major reason for the narrowness of Osaka's roads in the 1930s lies in the fact that as it spread out into densely settled (and expensive) paddy areas it inherited a network of local suburban roads that were even narrower than those in the city centre, where the long-standing reliance on water transport, combined with *niguruma*, had discour-

Osaka and Tokyo

Table 8.7   Cars, buses and lorries, Osaka and Tokyo, 1907–40

A. Cars, buses and lorries in Osaka and Tokyo: indices, 1920–21 = 100 for total in each city; ratio of Osaka total to Tokyo total, Tokyo = 100

	1907–9	1910–14	1915–19	1920–24	1925–29	1930–32
Index for Tokyo city	0.6	7.6	34.4	124.8	338.5	535.6
Index for Osaka city	0.0	1.7	33.6	146.7	508.2	837.2
Osaka/Tokyo ratio	0.0	6.9	28.7	37.1	48.0	50.6

B. Buses and electric street railways in Osaka city: indices 1920–21 = 100 for kilometers of operation (KO), cars, daily operating kilometers (DOK), and passengers per day (PPD), for electric street railways and for buses and electric street railways combined

	Electric street railways				Buses and electric street railways combined			
	KO	Cars	DOK	PPD	KO	Cars	DPK	PPD
1921–24	113.1	120.8	107.0	110.6	113.1	120.8	107.0	110.6
Third period in city's history								
1925–30	132.3	133.0	110.2	115.2	199.5	157.5	127.7	120.0
1931–35	142.6	115.4	117.4	94.8	363.1	200.4	188.1	116.9
1936–40	146.2	115.0	136.3	125.6	383.9	258.6	229.3	177.5

C. Buses and electric street railways in Tokyo city: Indices, 1920–21 = 100 for electric street railway passengers (ESRP) and passengers on buses and street railways (PBSR); and percentage of total passengers on buses and street railways who are on buses (PBUS)

	First period in city's history						Second period 1932–37
	1905–9	1910–14	1915–19	1920–24	1925–29	1930–31	
ESRP	40.8	53.0	72.5	98.4	104.3	80.6	71.2
PBSR	40.8	53.0	72.5	98.4	123.3	99.7	105.8
PBUS	–	–	–	–	15.4	19.2	32.4

Sources: Osaka Shi Yakushō, *Osaka shi tōkeisho* (various dates); Tokyo city Hall, *Tokyo shi tōkei nenpyō* (various dates).

aged the more aggressive widening of roads at an earlier date. So the very prosperity of Osaka and its environs during the 19th century came to haunt it in the 20th century: as its rice fields were productive the opportunity cost of allocating land to roads was high; and its advantage in water transport discouraged improvements in land-transportation-supporting infrastructure. Osaka became a victim of its own past success.

The introduction of lorries, buses and cars into Osaka put tremendous pressure on the authorities in charge of conditions in the city, and they found themselves compelled to expand the width of existing thoroughfares and/or create new roads. This is evident from the 'lead

Table 8.8 Roads in Osaka and Tokyo, 1898–1938

A. Population, land area, total road length, total road area and average road width

			Roads[2]		
	Population[1]	*Area (sq. km)*	*Area (sq. m) (A)*	*Length (m) (B)*	*Average width (A/B)*
Osaka, 1900	695 297	55.7	2 220 414	404 966	5.5
Osaka, 1930	2 453 573	178.9	10 496 519	2 533 873	4.1
Tokyo, 1900	1 339 726	81.2	6 515 033	894 022	7.3
Tokyo, 1930	2 070 913	81.2	14 598 007	1 362 816	10.7

B. Growth rates of wide roads; growth rate of cars, buses and lorries combined; and ratio of wide roads, expanded Osaka relative to official Tokyo[2]

	Average annual growth rate of wide roads		*Average annual growth rate of cars, buses and lorries combined*		*Wide roads, ratio Osaka/Tokyo (base = 100)*
	Tokyo	*Osaka*	*Tokyo*	*Osaka*	
1900–4	0.23	2.36	–	–	67.3
1905–9	1.07	3.63	n.a.	n.a.	75.0
1910–14	0.38	−0.24	45.5	79.9	81.8
1915–19	0.35	4.02	38.5	52.9	82.7
1920–24	0.63	4.35	20.6	27.8	103.4
1925–29	4.47	2.38	17.8	20.7	113.0

C. Roads in Osaka's periphery: indices of road length and percentage distribution by road type in Nishinari-*gun* and Higashinari-*gun* combined[2]

	Indices of road length (1920–21 = 100)				*Percentage of total road length*		
	National	*Prefectural*	*Local*	*Total*	*National*	*Prefectural*	*Local*
1901–4	53.4	97.1	61.7	63.7	3.1	9.8	87.1
1905–9	53.4	97.1	66.2	67.7	2.9	9.2	87.9
1910–14	49.5	83.0	62.1	62.9	2.5	8.0	82.5
1915–19	57.3	89.7	66.8	67.9	3.2	8.6	88.2
1920–24	106.7	157.7	100.8	104.7	3.8	9.6	86.6

Table 8.8 (continued)

D. Roads in Osaka: indices (1920–21 = 100) for area and length; and percentage of total area of roads within the city that are city roads, are narrow and are paved [2]

	Indices				Percentage of total area		
Total in city	City-managed roads			Area of all roads in city	% of city managed roads	% of narrow roads	% of paved roads
	Wide	Narrow	Total				
Second period in city's history							
1900–4	59.2	59.7	15.8	56.8	43.9	87.0	1.9	–
1905–9	65.5	65.8	26.4	63.2	48.9	87.6	2.8	–
1910–14	75.9	75.4	46.7	73.5	60.9	87.7	4.3	–
1915–19	83.8	79.2	107.5	81.1	76.5	87.7	9.0	–
1920–24	103.2	103.1	99.4	102.9	106.1	81.9	6.5	–
Third period in city's history							
1925–29	346.6	157.4	2904.4	342.4	182.1	82.4	57.2	5.1
1930–34	337.6	155.8	2782.5	332.8	205.2	81.7	56.3	8.7
1935–37	340.4	n.a.	n.a.	n.a.	246.6	85.3	n.a.	13.9

E. Roads in Tokyo: indices of area (1920–21 = 100); average width (meters); and percentage of total road length by type [2]

	Indices of road area			Average width (meters)		% of total road length in types of road	
	National	Prefectural	Total	City roads	All roads	Wide	Narrow
First period in city's history							
1899–1904	61.3	16.2	73.3	7.1	7.4	95.4	0.6
1905–9	79.4	17.8	82.7	7.7	8.1	95.4	0.6
1910–14	100.6	19.2	92.8	8.1	8.6	95.5	0.6
1915–19	98.2	19.2	94.1	8.2	8.7	95.6	0.6
1920–24	100.0	101.6	101.2	8.4	9.1	91.2	0.0
1925–31	113.5	125.8	128.4	9.0	9.8	n.a.	n.a.
Second period in city's history							
1932–38	318.2	876.9	500.4	5.1	5.7	n.a.	n.a.

Notes:
1. 1900 population figures are actually estimates for 1895 and in the case of Osaka are based on boundaries established in 1897.
2. Roads are classified according to whether they are constructed and maintained by the national, the prefectural or local (city, town or village) authorities. In general national roads were supposed to be equal to or greater than three *ken* in width (one *ken* = 1.82 meters), prefectural roads were equal to or greater than two *ken* in width, and local roads were either classified as 'wide' (one *ken* or more in width) or 'narrow' (under one *ken* in width). For the purposes of this table wide roads are defined as those which are one *ken* or more in width. The term 'expanded Osaka city' refers to the city boundaries after the expansion of 1925. 'Paved' refers to both brick and asphalt. Panel D refers to Osaka within its officially defined boundaries. n.a. = not available.
Sources: Cabinet Bureau of Statistics, *Nihon teikoku tōkei nenkan* (various dates); Osaka Prefecture, *Osaka fu tōkeisho* (various dates); Osaka Shi Yakushō, *Osaka shi tōkeisho* (various dates); Tokyo City Hall, *Tokyo shi tōkei nenpyō* (various dates).

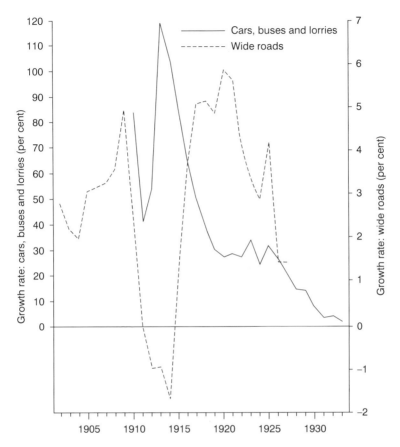

Figure 8.10   Road length (wide roads) and cars, buses and lorries: growth rates in expanded Osaka City (inclusive of Nishinari-*gun* and Higashinari-*gun* before 1925), 1902–33 (five-year moving averages)

and lag' pattern in Figure 8.10. It appears that in the case of Osaka a surge in the use of vehicles stimulated the widening of roads, but with a lag, a lag that was due to bureaucratic red tape, delays occasioned by the time required to negotiate and process the acquisition of land, technical planning and the time involved in constructing thoroughfares or additions to existing thoroughfares. But as can be seen from Figure 8.11, the situation in Tokyo was completely different: since Tokyo already had a well-developed network of wide roads and boulevards, virtually no widening was required to accommodate the growth in motorised vehicles.

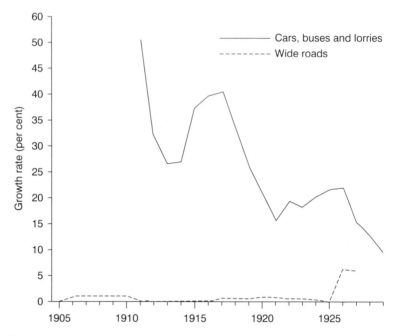

Figure 8.11   Road length (wide roads) and cars, buses and lorries: growth rates in Tokyo city, 1905–29 (five-year moving averages)

In sum, with the shift in focus from water to land in the technological revolutionizing of the Japanese economy, Tokyo's comparative advantage *vis-à-vis* Osaka in pre-existing and new land-based infrastructure increasingly gained force over time, and because of the close association between infrastructural investment and manufacturing investment Tokyo was ultimately able to wrest away Osaka's position of dominance in industrial affairs. The geographic concomitant of Japan's progress through the three infrastructure–investment waves was the shift from an Osaka-centred to a Tokyo-centred economy, from a water way-dominated economy to one focused on land communications.

CONCLUSIONS

Japanese industrialization was intimately linked to urbanization, or more specifically to the structure of the urban sector, dominated for centuries by the great seaport metropolises of the Tōkaidō industrial belt. The thesis of this chapter is that the great cities of the industrial belt played an exceptionally dynamic role after 1870 in the process of technological innovation whereby Japan absorbed, adapted and modified Western practices, structures and equipment. Undergirding this was the fact that the great cities of the Tōkaidō offered economies of scale – for infrastructure construction, for the creation of hybrid techniques and new product niches, and for the concentration of factors of production and energy supplies – that promoted expansion of manufacturing activity on both the supply and the demand sides. Economies of scale for infrastructural investment were especially important because in the second and third infrastructure–manufacturing waves, which drove Japanese economic growth between the 1870s and the late 1930s, periods of intense infrastructural investment preceded periods of heavy investment in manufacturing plant and equipment.

The emergence of Osaka as the Manchester of the East, followed by the steady erosion of its position and the eventual loss of its preeminence to Tokyo, well illustrates the importance of infrastructure (and therefore the importance of scale economies in infrastructure construction) for the progress of manufacturing activity. Osaka's initial advantage in water- and wood-based infrastructure, and in the proto-industrial labour skills required to construct and make use of that infrastructure, propelled it to a position of dominance during the first infrastructure–manufacturing wave (that based on steam power, textiles and coal), for water-borne transportation was favoured by the nature of the technology and the geography of the country. But when the second and third infrastructure–manufacturing waves (the second based on electricity and railroads and the third on the internal combustion engine) transformed the economy, land-based infrastructural development and the technical, Western-oriented knowledge required to master its construction and utilization moved into a position of dominance. And in land-based infrastructure Tokyo had an immense advantage over Osaka because the prevalence of earthquakes and fires in its environs had prompted the construction of wide roads and boulevards during the feudal period. Furthermore the outlying lands surrounding the conurbation were mainly given over to dry field agriculture or lay as wasteland, and could be converted for infrastructural purposes or residential or commercial use at much lower cost than could the paddy fields surrounding Osaka.

Technological change is ruthless, turning initial advantages and gains into detriments and losses. This is the sad moral to be drawn from this story of Osaka and Tokyo.

Notes

1. Earlier versions of this chapter were delivered at the International Research Center for Japanese Studies, at Kyoto Gakuen University in Kyoto, Japan, and at the University of Victoria. I am grateful to the participants at these various presentations for their comments and criticisms, which helped in the preparation of the present chapter. All remaining errors of fact and interpretation are my own.

2. The term 'Tōkaidō' (literally, eastern sea route) is used to describe both the coastline and immediate hinterland between Tokyo Bay in the north to the Osaka–Kobe Bays in the south (inclusive of Kyoto, which lies nestled between mountains in the vicinity of Lake Biwa), and a particular road or transportation system linking the Tokyo area to the Osaka–Kobe area and Kyoto. In this chapter the term is used to describe the nine prefectures of Japan, which include the six big cities of the Tōkaidō and their immediate economically developed hinterlands: the four prefectures of the Tokyo–Yokohama area (Chiba, Saitama, Tokyo, and Kanagawa); the two prefectures of the Nagoya area (Shizuoka and Aichi); and the three prefectures of the Osaka–Kobe–Kyoto area (Kyoto, Osaka and Hyogo). The northern axis of the Tōkaidō, which encompasses Tokyo and Yokohama, is known as the Kantō district; and its southern axis, which incorporates Osaka, Kobe and Kyoto, is known as the Kinai, Kinki or Kansai region.

3. This chapter focuses on the first proposition, which involves economies of scale. For a fuller treatment of this proposition, and an analysis that substantiates the second and third propositions, see Mosk (1998).

4. For a discussion of proto-industrialization in Japan see Saito (1985, 1987). Smith (1988) emphasizes the fact that farmers tried to lighten their tax burden by shifting from rice production (which was taxed as part of the village's stipulated rice tax burden due to the fief) to crafts, which were less frequently taxed.

5. The discussion here of Kondratieff waves and other related phenomena such as the long swing or Kuznets cycle is cursory. A much fuller treatment, demonstrating that long swings can be related to technologically driven Kondratieff waves in certain cases, and relating these themes to the infrastructure–manufacturing waves discussed later on in the text, is provided in Mosk (1998), especially in the Appendix to Chapter 1. On evolutionary interpretations of technological change see Mokyr (1990) and Nelson and Winter (1982). For the original interpretation of Kondratieff waves in terms of innovation and imitation, see Schumpeter (1939).

6. For the adoption of electric motors and their revolutionary impact on the organization of shopfloors and the mechanization of small and medium-sized companies due to the spread of the 'unit drive' system, whereby small motors could be operated on their own without drawing power from a central source such as a steam engine harnessed to smaller motors and machines through straps and pulleys, see Minami (1986).

7. Ohkawa and Otsuka (1994) show that firms using Western technology (that is, more capital-intensive, larger-scale operations) initially tended to generate lower profits than their Japanese competitors. One presumes

that it was only after they managed to develop a skilled labour force and a cadre of experienced managers that they were able to compete with enterprises using domestic techniques. In any event it is clear from the evidence in Ohkawa and Otsuka (1994) that eventually the more capital-intensive, mass-production-oriented mechanized plants did generate profits that exceeded those enjoyed by their traditional-technology-oriented rivals. In understanding why the opening up of Japan to a massive inflow of British, Dutch, German and American manufacturing methods dramatically improved the comparative advantage of metropolitan centres such as Osaka, it is essential to keep in mind that a major barrier to the international diffusion of technology was the dearth of labour capable of working with foreign styles of shopfloor organization, foreign machines and foreign scientific and engineering concepts. In cities such as Osaka, where Europeans and Americans congregated and to which migrated ambitious nationals interested in working with non-traditional methods, the barriers to the adoption of foreign technology were lower than in rural areas and in the medium-sized cities dotting those areas.

8. Tokyo also had an important edge over Osaka in terms of higher education and industrial research institutes. As the sophistication and range of technologies increased, Tokyo's advantage in engineering and science became increasingly important for the development of 'supply side' niches supporting new innovations. In addition Tokyo took the lead in city planning and municipal management after the turn of the century, and this had important implications for its growing comparative advantage in land-based infrastructure development. Limitations of space preclude a detailed discussion of these two issues, but they are discussed in detail in Chapters 5 and 6 of Mosk (1998).

9. For the definition of 'wide' roads see the notes to Table 8.8.

References

Cabinet Bureau of Statistics (Japan) (1882–1940) *Nihon teikoku tōkei nenkan* (Statistical Yearbook of the Japanese Empire) (Tokyo).

Department of Communications (Japan), (1898) *List of Merchant Marine Vessels of Japan, 1898* (Tokyo: Department of Communications, Merchant Marine Bureau).

Minami, R. (1965) *Tetsudō to denryoku* (Railroads and Electric Utilities) (Tokyo: Toyo Keizai Shinposha).

Minami, R. (1986, 1994) *The Economic Development of Japan: A Quantitative Study*, 1st and 2nd edns (Basingstoke: Macmillan).

Ministry of Railroads (Japan) (various dates) *Tetsudō tōkei shiryō to tetsudōin tōkei zuhyō* (Statistical Materials and Statistical Graphs and Tables Concerning Railroads) (Tokyo).

Mokyr, J. (1990) *The Lever of Riches: Technological Creativity and Economic Progress* (New York: Oxford University Press).

Mosk, C. (1998) 'Technology, Economy, City: Osaka and the Japanese Industrial Belt', unpublished manuscript.

Nelson, R. and S. Winter (1982) *An Evolutionary Theory of Economic Change* (Cambridge, Mass.: Harvard University Press).

Ohkawa, K. and K. Otsuka (1994) *Technology Diffusion, Productivity Employment, and Phase Shifts in Developing Economies* (Tokyo: University of Tokyo Press).

Ohkawa and Rosovsky (1973) *Japanese Economic Growth: Trend Acceleration in the Twentieth Century* (Stanford, CA: Stanford University Press).

Osaka Prefecture (various dates) *Osaka fu tōkeisho* (Osaka Prefecture Statistics) (Osaka).

Osaka Shi Yakushō (various dates) *Osaka shi tōkeinsho* (Osaka City Statistics) (Osaka).

Saito, O. (1985) *Purotokōgyō no jidai: Seiō to Nihon no hikakushi* (Age of Proto-Industrialization: Comparative History of Western Europe and Japan) (Tokyo: Nihonhyōronsha).

Saito, O. (1987) *Shōka no sekain, uradana no sekai: Edo to Osaka no hikaku toshishi* (The World of Merchant Houses: The Comparative Urban History of Edo and Osaka) (Tokyo: Riburopooto).

Schumpeter, J. (1939) *Business Cycles: A Theoretical, Historical and Statistical Analysis of the Capitalist Process* (New York: McGraw-Hill).

Smith, T. (1988) *Native Sources of Japanese Industrialization, 1750–1920* (Berkeley, CA: University of California Press).

Tokyo City Hall (various years) *Tokyo shi tōkei nenpyō* (Tokyo City Statistical Yearbook) (Tokyo).

Comments on Chapter 8

Terry McGee

My comments here will focus on the comparative relevance of Chapter 8 to the general field of urban studies, and particularly urban history. Two important questions have dominated the latter field for several decades. First, which historical processes lead to a shift in the dominance of one city to another city in the national economy? Second, what factors give a city a competitive edge in a national economy, and more recently the global economy?

The first of these questions has been addressed, for example, by Briggs and Smithson (1985) in Britain. The second question has come to be the focus of the 'world city literature', in which the writing of Sassen (1991) figures prominently. Mosk's chapter does not address this literature but focuses on these two questions in an empirical manner.

Mosk focuses on the shift in the geographic locus of economic power between Osaka and Tokyo between the 1890s and 1930s. His explanation is primarily technological, arguing that the shift from a water-based infrastructure (which characterized Osaka) to a land-based infrastructure (which characterized Tokyo) was accompanied by a shift from steam power to electricity and was closely related to changing investment priorities in both manufacturing and infrastructural development. Mosk provides a considerable amount of evidence to support his arguments and I will leave it to the scholars of Japan to determine its accuracy. However, I found the discussion of proto-industrialization in Osaka in the 18th century of very great value in formulating some more general ideas on the history of Asian urbanization. Thus, Mosk's chapter will certainly be a valuable source of information for those comparative urban historians, particularly those working on Asia, who are seeking to develop more rigorous theoretical explanations for the emergence of individual city dominance in national urban systems.

Finally, let me outline three issues on which the chapter leaves me unsatisfied. First, the chapter concentrates on technological and investment changes as the main reasons for the shift in economic power from Osaka to Tokyo. Surely, to be comprehensive, there should have been a discussion of the political economy of Japan, focusing on the emergence of the *zaibatsu*, increasing militarism and the growth of Japanese nationalism and imperialism, all of which encouraged the shift in power to Tokyo.

A second issue relates to the emergence of regional identity. Current research focuses on the role of regional factors (in many cases they are described as local versus national and global) in explaining the emergence of industrial districts. In particular the role of regional language, education and the clustering of geographic resources is seen as important in this process. Mosk, who has written a great deal about human skill development in Japan, mentions this factor at some point in the chapter but it is not followed up. What role did the emergence of the Tokyo-focused system of higher education play in developing the human skills basis for this shift from Osaka to Tokyo?

A third issue relates to the structure of the chapter. It would certainly benefit from an introductory paragraph to position the discussion in a wider context and perhaps address the reasons why issues of political economy were not included.

Mosk's chapter certainly contributes important information to fuel the current debates in the field of urban history and urban studies, but it may be much more contentious among historians of Japan.

References

Briggs, D.J. and P. Smithson (1985) *Fundamentals of Physical Geography* (London: Hutchinson).

Sassen, S. (1991) *The Global City: New York, London, Tokyo* (Princeton, New Jersey: Princeton University Press).

Part IV

US–Japan Relations and the Japanese Economy

9 Equity Markets, Political Markets and the Changing Framework of US–Japanese Economic Relations

Gary R. Saxonhouse

INTRODUCTION

For much of the latter half of the 20th century the Japanese economy grew far more rapidly than that of the United States, its major trading partner. This rapid growth was reflected in rapid changes in the structure of Japanese exports to the United States. Because the changes in Japan's export structure reflected rapid growth in industries that were already mature in the United States, and because – unlike most other advanced industrialized countries – Japan did not import large amounts of manufactures in the same industrial lines as its exports, its economic ascendance was viewed warily by the United States.

Rapid structural change in Japan triggered an often unwelcome acceleration in the pace of structural change in the United States. Many industries, adversely affected by such changes, sought to mitigate the impact of Japanese competition by calling on the trade policy resources of the US government. Unsurprisingly, this led to decades of diplomatic friction between the United States and Japan (Saxonhouse, 1986). Dissatisfaction with the state of US–Japanese economic relations led to unilateral and multilateral efforts to change the framework within which such disputes were resolved. Two of the most important of these initiatives were the enactment in the United States of the so-called 'Super 301' legislation in 1988, and the adoption of a significantly strengthened dispute settlement mechanism by the World Trade Organization, as laid down in the Uruguay Round Agreement of 1994. This chapter will assess the consequences for both Japan and the United States of these important initiatives. This assessment will rely primarily on equity market data.

It is only within the past dozen years or so that economists have begun to use equity market data to analyze the consequences of trade policy changes (Hartigan *et al.*, 1986). To date, virtually all this equity market literature has only assessed the impact on the market of the country initiating the change. Almost no attempt has been made to use equity market data to assess simultaneously the impact of policy changes on the welfare of trading partners.[1] Nor has this literature attempted to evaluate the impact of multilateral trade negotiations.[2] This chapter will address both these neglected areas, not only by examining the trans-Pacific equity market impact of the enactment of Super 301 and the strengthening of the dispute settlement mechanism, but also by assessing the impact of the Japan–US Automobile Agreement of June 1995. The latter is of obvious interest because it was the first important bilateral trade diplomacy to take place in the post-Uruguay Round international economic environment. As such it is able to throw additional light on the significance of Super 301 in light of the newly strengthened dispute settlement mechanism. The assessment of the negotiations will be political as well as economic, and use will be made of market evidence drawn from the Iowa Political Market (Forsythe *et al.*, 1991), which trades futures whose pay-off is based on the outcome of elections.

THREE EVENTS MARKING THE CONSTRUCTION OF A NEW FRAMEWORK FOR US–JAPANESE ECONOMIC RELATIONS

Event 1: the Super 301 clause of the Omnibus Trade and Competitiveness Act, 1988

The Super 301 clause of the Omnibus Trade and Competitiveness Act of 1988 changed existing trade law by requiring the United States Trade Representative (USTR) to identify countries with a 'consistent pattern of trade barriers and market distorting practices'. The USTR is required to enter into negotiations with countries so identified to remove all such practices within 15 to 19 months. Failing agreement, Section 301 cases begin. Any settlement reached must provide for the complete elimination of major barriers within three years. Super 301 also provides that while it is the USTR instead of the president who decides which retaliatory measures to impose, the president can block final retaliation by invoking overriding economic or security considerations.[3] Previous trade legislation allowed, but did not require the USTR to initiate Section 301 cases. Nor did previous legislation require such a strict timetable (Elliott and Richardson, 1997). Previous legislation also had a much narrower definition of unfair trade practices.[4]

Super 301, like the Omnibus Trade and Competitiveness Act itself, has a complicated legislative history. It arose, in part, out of a desire to put the onus on trading partners such as Japan to reduce bilateral trade imbalances between them and the United States. At the same time it built on a decade-long effort to amend the Trade Act of 1974 to strengthen Section 301.[5]

In 1986 Richard Gephardt, then majority leader of the US House of Representatives, proposed that countries with chronic bilateral trade surpluses with the United States be required to lower them by 10 per cent a year. This proposal, which was intended as an important element of the prospective Gephardt campaign for the presidency in 1988, was widely criticized. If the overall US trade imbalance reflected insufficient domestic savings relative to domestic investment, then requiring trading partners to reduce their bilateral surpluses – in the absence of any US adjustments – would simply lead to the shifting of these bilateral surpluses from one US trading partner to another (Saxonhouse, 1986).

The Gephardt Amendment (to the Trade Act of 1974) was effectively dead by the time the Ways and Means Committee of the US House of Representatives eventually debated it on 10 November 1987 (Lambsdorff, 1988). In its place, the Senate Finance Committee, in consultation with the Ways and Means Committee, crafted Super 301. By early January 1988 all the major provisions that would be included in the final legislation were present (Brookes, 1988a).

Ironically, even as Super 301 emerged from the Senate Finance Committee deliberations, Gephardt's presidential campaign was ending. This left Super 301 without an advocate among the major presidential candidates in 1988.[6] This changed in March, when Governor Dukakis, in advance of the Michigan primary, abandoned his previously stated position and announced he would support Super 301 (Brookes, 1988b). With Dukakis having changed his position, Vice President Bush prevailed upon the Reagan administration to base their opposition to the trade bill exclusively on the provision requiring 60 days' notice for plant closures and major layoffs. No emphasis would be placed on concerns about the Super 301 provision.

The period between early May, when the new Trade Act was first sent to the president, and 7 August, when the White House finally agreed to a different version of the bill, was characterized by intense lobbying. Following President Reagan's veto of the first version of the bill, sent to him in late May, the House of Representatives voted to override. As expected, the effort to override failed in the Senate. In the weeks that followed, whether Congress and the White House could agree on a trade bill at all remained in doubt (Swoboda, 1988).

While, as the Bush campaign intended, the focus of debate on the Trade Act was primarily on the plant-closure provision, public discussion of Super 301 continued. Senator Danforth argued that 'The underlying theme of the bill is reciprocity...[t]he "Super 301" provision of the bill provides us with a consistent means of addressing unfair trade practices.' In contrast Senator Evans complained that 'Any time you shrink that [flexibility], I think you're acting in a way detrimental to American general interests and also, specifically you're probably going to end up harming America's most competitive industries because other nations will clearly retaliate against the only industry they can, and those are the ones which are penetrating their markets, which are our most successful industries.'[7]

US trading partners, particularly Japan, were also quick to denounce Super 301. Japan's minister of international trade and industry, Hajime Tamura, went so far as to brand the provision 'racist' (Harbrecht *et al.*, 1988, p. 42). Otto Lambsdorff, Germany's former minister of economics, also complained that 'The Gephardt Amendment was designed to compel the surplus countries, among them the Federal Republic of Germany, to cut their trade surpluses with the U.S. by 10% a year, but the Senate proposal for...Super 301, which has been adopted in its place, is no less unpalatable to America's trading partners' (Lambsdorff, 1988). Nevertheless on 23, August 1988, after prolonged negotiations between the White House and the congressional leadership, Reagan finally signed the Omnibus Trade and Competitiveness Act of 1988 (Preeg, 1995, p. 78).

Event 2: the World Trade Organization's dispute settlement mechanism

It is widely agreed that the revised dispute settlement mechanism (DSM) is the most important instrument of the World Trade Organization (WTO). Indeed many believe that the revised DSM was the most important result of the entire Uruguay Round (*Inside U.S.*

Trade, 1993c, p. 6). Many also believe that, but for the enactment of Super 301, a revised DSM would have been no more part of the Uruguay Round than it was of the Tokyo Round (Preeg, 1995, p. 78).

The critical element of the revised DSM is the absence of single-country veto power over the formation of a dispute settlement panel or the adoption of panel findings. As the DSM had operated under GATT, veto power was held even by the accused party. Now panels go forward and panel findings are adopted unless the WTO Council decides otherwise by consensus (Jackson, 1994). This is the polar opposite of the previous *modus operandi*. At the same time, under the revised DSM an appellate review procedure is available upon request by one of the parties to the dispute, and a three-member appellate panel may uphold, modify or reverse the findings of the original dispute panel (Preeg, 1995, p. 208). Other important elements of the revised arrangements include a tightening of procedures to ensure prompt findings by dispute panels and a provision for cross-retaliation. Unlike the old GATT mechanism, a violation in one product area can be countered by a sanction in some other product area (*Inside U.S. Trade*, 1993b).

The US government's interest in a revised DSM was of very long standing. During the Tokyo Round the United States pressed both for an end to the single-country veto and for expedited procedures, but the European Community firmly resisted (Jackson, 1992, p. 182). Interest on the part of all parties was revived around 1985, when GATT member states began to use the DSM to resolve a number of significant trade disputes. As Preeg (1995, p. 77) notes:

> The surge in GATT dispute settlement was, in part, a reaction to the parallel growth in bilateral actions outside the GATT. It also reflected recognition by some countries, such as Japan, that unpopular decisions against vested political interests can be more palatable as part of an international adjudication process than as a result of bilateral political pressure.

This revived interest was such that, when the Uruguay Round commenced, a separate negotiating group on the dispute settlement process was established (Jackson, 1992, p. 183).

Despite the existence of a separate negotiating group on the dispute settlement process since as early as 1986, relatively little agreement was reached on revised procedures until as late as November 1993.[8] Had the Uruguay Round been successfully concluded as planned at the Brussels ministerial Meeting in December 1990, it is most unlikely that the single-country veto of a panel finding would have been approved as part of the dispute settlement process (Preeg, 1995, pp. 124–5).[9]

Hard bargaining on the final version of the revised DSM began only on 1 November 1993, when in response to US criticism that no significant progress had been made on this issue, GATT Director-General Peter Sutherland called on delegations to send higher-level representatives to the negotiations (Bergsman, 1993, p. 7). In the six weeks between then and the reaching of the final agreement on 12 December 1997, the bargaining was as much about the scope of the revised DSM as about its procedures. As bargaining proceeded the Clinton administration, under pressure from groups such as the Semiconductor Industry Association, seemed increasingly uncomfortable with the traditional US position of advocating a rigorous dispute settlement process (*Inside U.S. Trade*, 1993d, p. 51). For example the administration argued against giving dispute settlement panels the right to accept so-called non-violation cases (Bergsman, 1993, p. 6).

The Clinton administration also proposed, against the opposition of all its major trading partners, that dispute settlement panels be limited to ensuring that decisions by domestic authorities would involve a reasonable interpretation of the WTO rules. A reasonable interpretation would not have to be the interpretation most preferred by the dispute settlement panel. The Clinton administration's proposal would have limited the ability of dispute settlement panels to overturn interpretations of fact, arguing that 'reasonable minds could differ as to the significance to be attached to certain facts' (ibid., p. 1).

On many of the issues resolved during the final weeks of the Uruguay Round negotiations the US proposals prevailed, for example on research subsidies. Despite heavy pressure, however, the Clinton administration's proposed changes to the draft text of the DSM made no headway and were not incorporated into the final agreement (*Inside U.S. Trade*, 1993a, p. 5).

The increasing recognition that the Clinton administration had made no headway in its efforts to change the Uruguay Round dispute settlement text led industry groups in Washington, in the week just prior to the conclusion of the Round, to charge that 'The threat of unilateral action to protect U.S. interests has been repealed without changing a word of U.S. law' (ibid., p. 5). The most vocal critics of the new dispute settlement rules were private sector groups advocating aggressive trade policies against Japan. They pointed out that the United States would be restrained in its ability to enforce the results of the framework agreement that the administration wanted to negotiate with Japan, particularly if it sought to address anticompetitive practices (Jackson, 1994). The chief negotiator of the European Union (EU), Hugo Paeman, seemed to back this up, arguing that 'Section 301 will not be possible under the WTO as long as there are multilateral rules to settle disputes' (*Inside U.S. Trade*, 1993a, p. 6).

At the conclusion of the Uruguay Round, Japan's views on the revised DSM and Section 301 were summarized by its chief negotiator Nobutoshi Akao (*Inside U.S. Trade*, 1993c, p. 7):

> The American government has been saying [that the revised DSM] strengthens Section 301. But it's difficult ... to say how it is going to work. Perhaps ... if they first take the case to the WTO and ... if they lose they forget about it; if they win then they can use the strengthened dispute settlement mechanism with Section 301.... There is no reason for us to complain because retaliation would be based on a result of the dispute settlement procedure.
>
> What we have been afraid of in the past is that, without going through the GATT process, the US has invoked Section 301 and threatened us to concede. But the merit for our side is that once the WTO goes into effect, all countries, instead of resorting to unilateral action, have to go through the dispute settlement mechanism ...
>
> Under the new system, there is no reason for us not to negotiate on bilateral trade issues. If the US request is a reasonable one, then we should try to settle it bilaterally. At the same time, sometimes US requests are very unreasonable. For such unreasonable requests, we don't have to listen to the US, and we shouldn't worry about a threat by the US. If [the US takes] unilateral action in a case where we have more reason than the US, then we can go to the dispute settlement procedure. In the past, with the lack of that kind of multilateral system, we had to often compromise and sometimes accept something which from the multilateral viewpoint is not necessarily desirable. We have been major victims of Section 301 and Super 301.

At just the time when many significant interests in the United States came to doubt the wisdom of using multilateral institutions to deal with US–Japanese economic conflicts, Japanese diplomats had clearly changed their traditional position and embraced multilateral institutions as a means of containing US unilateralism.

Event 3: The Japan-US Automobile Agreement of June 1995

The first major Japan–US trade dispute to test the new multilateral framework came to a head in the spring of 1995, when the Japanese government refused to agree to measures that would have required Japanese car manufacturers to issue new foreign parts purchasing plans, whose fulfilment would be monitored by both the Japanese and the US governments (Alden, 1995, p. 1). In retaliation, on 16 May US Trade Representative Kantor announced that the United States, operating under Section 301 of the 1988 Trade Act, would impose tariffs of 100 per cent *ad valorem* on 13 Japanese-made luxury cars, valued at $5.9 billion at the entry prices prevailing in 1994. It was intended that a final sanctions list would be published on 28 June (*Inside U.S. Trade*, 1995b, p. 1). At the same time as Kantor was announcing sanctions under Section 301, he also confirmed that the United States would launch a broad challenge to Japanese practices in respect of cars and car parts under Article XXIII of the WTO (*Inside U.S. Trade*,1995c, p. 15). Despite filing this case, Kantor insisted that the US sanctions were in accordance with its obligations under the WTO because the practices targeted were not covered by the WTO (*Inside U.S. Trade*, 1995b, p. 2).

The prediction Ambassador Akao made at the conclusion of the Uruguay Round proved correct. Rather than caving in to US pressure, Japan challenged the US sanctions by filing its own case at the WTO, insisting it would not continue with the bilateral negotiations. Japan charged the United States with violating Articles I and II of the WTO. These provisions require countries to offer most favoured nation (MFN) treatment to imports from all WTO members and not to raise duties above those bound in their schedules of tariff concessions. Japan also argued that the announced sanctions were inconsistent with Article XXIII of the WTO dispute settlement understanding, which 'prohibits any Contracting Party from making a unilateral determination on remedial measures' (ibid., 1995b, p. 2).

The EU took Japan's part in the dispute, proclaiming that 'this is not the way to solve trade disputes.... These [sanctions], if implemented, would be contrary to U.S. obligations under the World Trade Organization.' The EU said it would continue to urge both sides to resolve their differences through the recently strengthened multilateral dispute settlement procedures (*Inside U.S. Trade*, 1995a, p. 3).

Echoing the EU's attack on the Clinton administration's trade policy, the speaker of the House of Representatives, Newt Gingrich, also denounced the decision to impose sanctions on Japanese luxury cars without first bringing a complaint to the WTO (Bergsman, 1995, p. 1). Even Alan Wolff, a lawyer representing the Semiconductor Industry Association, who in Geneva in December 1993 had argued strenuously in favour of limiting the scope of the DSM, predicted that Japan's case against the US decision to impose sanctions under Section 301 would be a 'slam dunk' victory for Japan (*Inside U.S. Trade*, 1995d, p. 1).

Other than an agreement to resume negotiations under WTO auspices on 22 June, little was accomplished in the four weeks following the announcement of sanctions (ibid.) On 15 June, Japanese government officials met with members of Congress, and congressional staff and indicated that Japan's car manufacturers would be willing to take a leadership role in resolving the bilateral dispute. While the manufacturers were not willing to announce purchasing plans for car parts, they were prepared to announce specific plans for increased car production in the United States and indicated that, in principle, increased localization of production should lead to increased purchases of US-made car parts over time. Since the plans for increased US transplant production had already been released previously, this was a concession that was easy for the Japanese car manufacturers to make. Neither they nor the Japanese government, however, were willing to permit US government monitoring of the implementation of these plans (*Inside U.S. Trade*, 1995f, p. 21).

During the week following the congressional meetings and the resumption of negotiations on 22 June, the USTR continued to insist that the Japanese car companies' purchase plans must include numerical targets either for the overall value of parts purchases, or for an increase in local content. The Japanese government continued just as strongly to reject this approach (*Inside U.S. Trade*, 1995g, p. 23). The agreement that was finally announced the morning of 28 June just before the sanctions were due to go into effect, embodied most of the principles that had been outlined by Japanese government officials to congressional members and staff two weeks earlier. The Japanese car companies would only announce transplant production plans, not their plans for parts purchases or local content. Likewise no mechanism for monitoring the fulfilment of even these limited plans was agreed upon. To make monitoring even more difficult, each of the major Japanese car companies announced transplant production plans of different duration and time periods, making the aggregation of results impossible.

US Trade Representative Kantor, at his joint press conference with MITI Minister Hashimoto, was permitted to announce an estimate of the increase in Japanese foreign car parts purchases under the agreement. Hashimoto immediately informed the gathering, however, that Kantor's estimates were his own and were not shared by Hashimoto himself or the Japanese government, and were not part of the agreement. Given the variation in the dates of the individual company plans, Hashimoto claimed to be surprised that Kantor felt the plans could be combined in a meaningful way (*Inside U.S. Trade*, 1995h, p. 17).

EVALUATION

The impact of each of the three events just discussed will be evaluated by examining their effect on the market evaluation of the equity of selected publicly traded US and Japanese firms. Such an approach assumes that in Japan, as in the United States, unbiased assessments of the effects of publicly released information are systematically incorporated into the value of publicly traded equities. A list of the Japanese and US firms whose equity valuation will be studied is presented in Table 9.1. In general, these are firms for whom it is expected an

Table 9.1   Japanese and US firms included in the Super 301, DSM and Japan–US Automobile Agreement event studies

Japan	US
Super 301 and DSM	
Hitachi	Chrysler
Honda	Federal Mogul
Matsushita Electric Industrial	Ford
Mitsubishi Electric	General Electric
Nippon Denso	General Motors
Nissan	Intel
NEC	Motorola
Oki Electric	National Semiconductor
Toyota	Texas Instruments
Japan–US Automobile Agreement	
Aisin Seiki	Chrysler
Koito Mfg	Exide
Honda	Federal Mogul
Nippon Denso	Ford
Nissan	General Motors
Toyota	Trinova

event would have a large impact. It is expected that the enactment of Super 301 would have negatively affected the valuation of Japanese firms. The reverse should be true for the valuation of US firms. If it is correct to say that the revised DSM greatly curtailed the use of Section 301, then the second event should have had a positive impact on the valuation of Japanese firms. The impact of this event on the valuation of the US firms in this study can be expected to be more ambiguous. Curtailing Section 301 should have had a negative effect, but over the time period being examined this effect may well have been swamped by other positive benefits that might have flowed to these firms from the enactment of the Uruguay Round and even from the DSM itself. Finally, if the conventional view of the 1995 Japan–US Automobile Agreement is correct, there should have been no impact at all on the valuation of the Japanese and US car and car parts companies in the sample being used here.

If an event is to have an impact on equity valuation, it must generate changes significantly above or significantly below those that would have been predicted given the firm's normal relationship with the market. If stock market returns follow a multivariate normal distribution, the following well-known equation holds:

$$R_{iw} - R_{fw} = a_i + b_i(R_{mw} - R_{fw}) + v_{iw} \tag{9.1}$$

where R_{iw} = the continuously compounded rate of return for security i in period w; R_{mw} = the continuously compounded rate of return for the market portfolio in period w; R_{fw} = the continuously compounded risk-free rate of return; $b_i = cov(R_{iw*}, R_{mw*})/var(R_{mw*})$ = the systematic risk of security i; $R_{iw*} = R_{iw} - R_{fw}$; $R_{mw*} = R_{mw} - R_{fw}$; a_i is a firm-specific constant; and v_{iw} is a normally distributed random error term that is uncorrelated with R_{mw} and has zero mean and constant variance.

Equation 9.1 is estimated for each of the three events using the firms listed in Table 9.1. This estimation takes place for the first event using weekly returns for the 78 weeks prior to 10 November 1987 and up until 26 weeks before that date, and for 26 weeks up until 78 weeks after the agreement between Congress and the White House was concluded. Likewise Equation 9.1 is estimated for the second event using weekly returns for the 78 weeks prior to 1 November 1993 and up until 26 weeks before that date, and for 26 weeks up until 78 weeks after the Uruguay Round Agreement was announced in Geneva. Finally, Equation 9.1 is estimated using weekly returns for the

78 weeks prior to 28 April 1995, when the first news reports on possible sanctions began to appear in press, up until 26 weeks before that date and for 26 weeks until 78 weeks after the Japan–US Automobile Agreement was announced by US Trade Representative Kantor and Minister Hashimoto. The parameters estimated from Equation 9.1 are used to compute excess returns for each equity for the period (e_1, e_2) when new information about each of the events, respectively, is thought to have reached the equity markets.

Just calculating excess returns for an arbitrary period (e_1, e_2) preceding the announcement of the projects ignores the gradual leakage of information that is so characteristic of legislative and diplomatic processes in both the United States and Japan (Halloran, 1969). Even newspaper reports of rumours about new negotiating positions for parties to a dispute may lag substantially behind the capitalization of such information by the equity markets. Unfortunately, if e_1 is set very far away from e_2 to allow for gradual information leakage, the test to check for statistically significant excess returns will have very low power (Morse, 1984; Brown and Warner, 1980). Alternatively, assume that the gradual leakage of information influences securities prices in the S-shaped pattern of the cumulative normal distribution (Ellison and Mullin, 1995):

$$
\begin{aligned}
E(G_{iw}/Y_w) &= g\left[\Phi\left(\frac{w-\mu}{\eta}\right) - \Phi\left(\frac{w-1-\mu}{\eta}\right)\right], \quad e_1 \leq w \leq e_2 \\
&= g\left[1 - \Phi\left(\frac{w-\mu}{\eta}\right)\right], \quad w = e_2 \\
&= 0 \quad w < e_1 \text{ and } e_2 > w
\end{aligned}
\tag{9.2}
$$

where g is reaction parameter; Φ is the normal cumulative distribution function with μ and η as first and second moments; e_2 is the time of the announcement of the agreement. The dependent variable in Equation 9.2 is the expectation of excess returns conditional on the vector of explanatory variables.

In order to avoid arbitrary decisions as to when the events first influenced equity prices, g, μ and η are estimated using observations for the period beginning 26 weeks before the first rumours about the nature of the final agreement for each event appeared in the press and ending with the official announcement of an agreement; g, μ and η are estimated separately for each of the events and separately for each national sample of firms.

Table 9.2   The impact of Super 301, the revised
DSM and the Japan–United States Automobile
Agreement on selected equity prices

	Japan	US
Super 301		
g	−0.0471	0.0087
	(0.0183)	(0.0160)
μ	36.5	34.1
	(2.8)	(3.6)
η	3.11	2.63
	(1.90)	(1.74)
Revised DSM		
g	0.0997	0.0285
	(0.0304)	(0.0196)
μ	29.2	30.8
	(3.7)	(2.4)
η	2.50	3.38
	(1.39)	(1.95)
Japan–United States Automobile Agreement		
g	0.0524	0.0188
	(0.0375)	(0.0216)
μ	24.4	25.2
	(1.6)	(2.5)
η	2.4	1.8
	(1.3)	(0.9)

Notes: Standard errors in parentheses. μ and η
are calibrated in weeks.

The results of the estimation are presented in Table 9.2. These
results highlight the rather different reactions of Japanese and US
equity prices to information about the three different events studied
here. Japanese equity values had a sharply negative reaction to the
passage of the 1988 Trade Act and the inclusion of the Super 301
clause. At the same time, and as expected, the successful conclusion of
the Uruguay Round with the revision of the dispute settlement process had a sharply positive effect on Japanese equity values. In contrast, US equity values reacted positively both to the passage of the
1988 Trade Act and to the adoption of the revised DSM by the WTO.
Neither of these reactions, however, was statistically significant. Nor
was there a statistically significant reaction by either the Japanese or
the US equity markets to the conclusion of the Japan–United States
Automobile Agreement in June 1995.

The first two moments of the cumulative normal distribution function φ (μ and η) characterize the path of the impact of information from the event: μ indicates the point in the distribution where new information about the projects had its maximum impact; η helps characterize how quickly such information diffused to the equity markets. Unlike the reaction parameter g in at least two of the events, μ and η are statistically significant for both the Japanese and US samples. Not surprisingly, given the resources devoted to monitoring each of these three events by political and economic elites in Japan and the United States, there was no statistically significant difference in the speed at which information about these events diffused to the equity markets in each country.[10] What is most interesting is how early the equity markets in both Japan and the United States appear to have reached the conclusion that whatever agreement might be reached in the case of cars it would be of little consequence. This conclusion appears to have been quite widespread even before the sanctions were formally announced.

POLITICAL INTERPRETATION

Unlike the first two events, equity market evidence suggests the Japan–United States Automobile Agreement had no impact on the major car industry participants on either side of the Pacific. There are a number of possible interpretations of this finding. First, the agreement, even as contemplated as early as February 1994, may never have been of a scale that could have had a substantial impact on the earnings of any of the companies whose equity values are being studied here. Second, it is also possible that the functional form being used in this study to characterize the impact of information on equity values is too limiting.

If neither of these factors is responsible for the findings here, and if it was obvious very early to all concerned that nothing of economic importance would result from an agreement, why is it that the Clinton administration pursued this case with such vigour and at such cost to amicable relations not only with Japan but also with many other US trading partners? In this connection, Figure 9.1 is most instructive. Evidence from the Iowa Political Market appears to indicate quite strongly, and in contrast to much press commentary, that President Clinton obtained considerable political benefit from pursuing this agreement. After having been relatively stable for the preceding

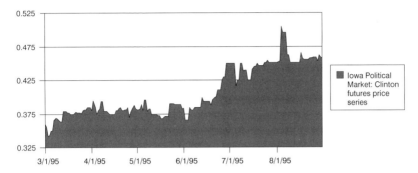

Figure 9.1   The price of Clinton futures, 1 March to 31 August 1995

three months, the price of Clinton futures rose by 15 per cent in late June when discussions of the Japan–United States Automobile Agreement dominated the news media.[11] Clinton futures hovered around this newly established level for most of the rest of the summer.[12] Whatever the economic consequences of these negotiations, the political market evidence does indicate that this agreement was viewed as highly favourable to Clinton's re-election prospects.

Notes

1. An exception may be Saxonhouse (1997).
2. For many years this has been the province of computable generated equilibrium modelling. See for example Brown *et al.* (1992).
3. The Super 301 clause had a sunset provision of three years, but the process was restored during the Clinton administration by executive order.
4. Super 301 expands the definition of actionable unfair trade practices to include lack of market reciprocity, export targeting, toleration of cartels, diversion of exports and restrictions on technology transfer.
5. For example it is only since 1984 that the USTR has had the power to initiate Section 301 cases without a private-sector plaintiff. This authority was not provided for in the Trade Act of 1974.
6. When the Omnibus Trade and Competitiveness Act was finally passed by the Senate, Gephardt voted against it, arguing that its final form had strayed too far from his original conception. See Wechsler (1988).
7. *Washington Post* (1988).
8. The mid-term Ministerial Review of the Uruguay Round, held at Montreal in December 1988, did make clear that under the contemplated agreement the establishment of a panel would normally be the right of a disputing complainant. Consensus to go ahead would not be necessary (Jackson, 1992, p. 183).

9.   The draft agreement put forward by Arthur Dunkel a year later (December 1991) contained a proposed DSM that included the provision that panel findings would be automatically adopted unless an appeals body or all members acting unanimously decided otherwise (Jackson, 1992, p. 183). At the time they were proposed, the provisions of the Dunkel draft were not accepted.
10. Contrast this with the asymmetric monitoring found in Saxonhouse (1997).
11. Holders of Clinton futures were to receive $1 per future in the event of President Clinton being re-elected in 1996.
12. The exception to this came in early August, when a Republican-sponsored welfare reform measure closely associated with Senate Majority Leader Dole had to be withdrawn. This, together with the almost simultaneous signing by Clinton of an executive order toughening toxic emission standards, resulted in a brief but unsustained rise in Clinton futures.

References

Alden, Edward (1995) 'Japan Auto Industry Fears Link Between Parts Plan, Government Deal', *Inside U.S. Trade*, 28 April, p. 1.

Bergsman, Michael (1993) 'U.S. Moves to Limit Dispute Settlement Panels' Scope of Review', *Inside U.S. Trade*, 5 November.

Bergsman, Michael (1995) 'Gingrich Slams Sanctions, but Says Congress Won't Step into Auto Fight', *Inside U.S. Trade*, 26 May.

Brookes, Warren T. (1988a) 'Senate's Trade Bill Provisions Spell Trouble', *The San Francisco Chronicle*, 5 January.

Brookes, Warren T. (1988b) 'Would President Bush Make US More Competitive', *The San Francisco Chronicle*, 21 September.

Brown, Drusilla K., Alan V. Deardorff and Robert Stern (1992) 'North American Integration', *Economic Journal*, vol. 102, pp. 1507–18.

Brown, Stephen J. and Jerold B. Warner (1980) 'Measuring Security Price Performance', *Journal of Financial Economics*, vol. 8, pp. 205–58.

Elliott, Kimberly Ann and J. David Richardson (1997) 'Determinants and Effectiveness of "Aggressively Unilateral" US Trade Actions', in Robert C. Feenstra (ed.), *The Effects of US Trade Protection and Promotion Policies* (Chicago, Ill.: University of Chicago Press).

Ellison, Sara F. and Wallace B. Mullin (1995) 'Economics and Politics: The Case of Sugar Tariff Reform', *Journal of Law and Economics*, vol. 38, pp. 335–66.

Feenstra, Robert C. (ed.) (1997) *The Effects of U.S. Trade Protection and Promotion Policies* (Chicago, Ill.: University of Chicago Press).

Forsythe, Robert, Forrest Nelson, George Neumann and Jack Wright (1991) 'The Explanation and Prediction of Presidential Elections: A Market Alternative to Polls', in Thomas R. Palfrey (ed.), *Laboratory Research in Political Economy* (Ann Arbor, Mich.: University of Michigan Press).

Grossman, Gene and Elhanan Helpman (1994) 'Protection for Sale', *American Economic Review*, vol. 84, pp. 833–50.

Halloran, Richard (1969) *Japan: Images and Realities* (New York: Knopf).

Harbrecht, Douglas, Steven J. Dryden and Barbara Buell (1988) 'Even if it Escapes a Veto, It Will Disappoint Almost Everyone', *Business Week*, 9 May, p. 42.

Hartigan, James, Philip Perry and Sreenivas Kamma (1986) 'The Value of Administered Protection: A Capital Market Approach', *Review of Economics and Statistics*, vol. 68, pp. 610–17.

Inside U.S. Trade (1993a) 'Administration Insists GATT Deal Section 301 Flexibility', 17 December.

Inside U.S. Trade (1993b) 'GATT Parties Settle Most Problems in New Dispute Settlement Text', 19 November.

Inside U.S. Trade (1993c) 'Japan's Chief Negotiator, in Interview Discusses GATT Round Endgame', 24 December, p. 6.

Inside U.S. Trade (1993d) 'SIA Opposes GATT Deal in Three Key Areas, Pushes for Tariff Cuts', 5 November, p. 17.

Inside U.S. Trade (1995a) 'Butler Warns Kantor against Unilateral Sanctions in Japan Auto Fight', 12 May.

Inside U.S. Trade (1995b) 'Japan to Charge U.S. in WTO with Violation of MFM Bound Tariffs', 17 May.

Inside U.S. Trade (1995c) 'U. S. Kicking Off Preparation of Japan WTO Case; EV Case Could Be Model', 12 May.

Inside U.S. Trade (1995d) 'U.S., Japanese Officials See Little Hope for New Round of Auto Talks', 19 May.

Inside U.S. Trade (1995e) 'U.S. Accepts Australia for Japanese Consultations, Balks on EU', 9 June.

Inside U.S. Trade (1995f) 'Japanese Government, Companies Signaling Flexibility in Auto Dispute', 16 June.

Inside U.S. Trade (1995g) 'U.S., Japan Resume Auto Negotiations amid Conflicting Signals', 23 June.

Inside U.S. Trade (1995h) 'U.S., Japan Auto Deal Still Unfinished on Monitoring, Enforcement', 30 June.

Jackson, John H. (1992) 'Strengthening of the Dispute Settlement Function and Future GATT Activities', in *The Uruguay Round: Appraisal and Implications for International Trade and Investment* (Tokyo: Fair Trade Center).

Jackson, John H. (1994) 'Testimony Prepared for the U.S. Senate Finance Committee Hearing, March 23, 1994 on Uruguay Round Legislation', University of Michigan, Research Forum on International Economics, Discussion Paper no. 353.

Lambsdorff, Otto Graf (1988) 'West Germany Awaits a Trade Bill Veto', *Wall Street Journal*, 27 April.

Leamer, Edward E. and Robert M. Stern (1970) *Quantitative International Economics* (Boston, Mass.: Allyn & Bacon).

Morse, Dale (1984) 'An Economic Analysis of the Choice of Daily versus Monthly Returns in Tests of Information Content', *Journal of Accounting Research*, vol. 22, pp. 605–23.

Preeg, Ernest H. (1995) *Traders in a Brave New World* (Chicago, Ill.: University of Chicago Press).

Saxonhouse, Gary R. (1986) 'Japan's Intractable Trade Imbalances', *The World Economy*, vol. 9, pp. 239–57.

Saxonhouse, Gary R. (1997) 'Optoelectronics in Japan: A Market Evaluation of Government High Technology Policy', *Managerial and Decision Economics*, vol. 18, pp. 1–17.

Swoboda, Frank (1988) 'Labor Won't Try for Compromise on Trade Bill', *Washington Post*, 3 June.

Washington Post (1988) 'The Trade Bill Battle: Two Senate Republicans' Perspectives: Danforth Sees Strong Need; Evans Sees Risk', 1 May.

Wechsler, Pat (1988) 'House Ok's Trade Bill but Reagan Threatens Veto over Plant-Closing Notice', *Newsday*, 22 April.

10 Global Duopolistic Competition between Fujifilm and Kodak: Corporate Strategy and Business–Government Relations

Yoshi Tsurumi and Hiroki Tsurumi

INTRODUCTION

Early in December 1997 the World Trade Organization (WTO) ruled unanimously in favour of Fujifilm and the Japanese government against Kodak and the US government. It was the first loss for the United States, which had won its six previous cases at the WTO. It was Japan's first win. The dispute between Kodak and Fujifilm went back to Kodak's legal action against Fujifilm and the Japanese government. In late May 1995 the US Trade Representative Office (USTR) accepted Kodak's complaint against Fujifilm and Japan 'Super 301' of the US Trade Act of 1988. Super 301 enables the US president to invoke unilateral trade sanctions against foreign countries accused of discriminating against US goods and services. The USTR and Kodak charged that Japan's Ministry of International Trade and Industry (MITI) and Fujifilm had conspired to restrict Kodak's access to Japan's distribution outlets of photographic films and papers. Fujifilm and MITI denied all charges.

The Japanese government asked Kodak to file its antitrust complaints with Japan's Fair Trade Commission (JFTC) because the alleged exclusion was illegal in Japan. Japan also urged the WTO to adjudicate the disputes. At first the US government refused to accept the WTO adjudication, contending that the WTO had no jurisdiction over market competition practices, but in September 1996 the Clinton administration accepted the adjudication.

Upon filing its USTR petition, George Fisher, Kodak's chief executive officer (CEO), went on public relations and lobbying campaigns in the United States and Japan (Kodak, 1995). In late July 1995 Minoru Ohnishi, Fujifilm's CEO, publicly refuted the Kodak/USTR allegations (Fujifilm, 1995). Fujifilm countered with public relations and lobbying in Japan and the United States. In the long history of US–Japanese relations, Fujifilm's open challenge to an American competitor and the US government was a notable first.

George Fisher of Kodak was said to be using 'political, public relations, and legal' tools to compete with Fujifilm in Japan and the United States (Baron, 1995). Thus Fujifilm–Kodak thrusts and ripostes across the Pacific were played out in the context of the strategic trade policies of the Clinton administration and the rising mercantilist/protectionist stance of the United States. Ever since Commodore Mathew Perry's 'Black Ships' forced feudal Japan out of its self-imposed isolation in 1853, US–Japanese relations have followed a 50-year cycle, alternating between cooperative and antagonistic phases (Tsurumi, 1993). Kodak's Super 301 action added another contentious page to US–Japanese relations, which had been unravelling due to the historical convergence of the aggressive phase of the US diplomatic cycle (Schlessinger, 1986) and the atrophying phase of Japan's political and economic system.

What really caused the decline in Kodak's market share in Japan from 1983 to 1995? How did Fujifilm manage to succeed in the United States? What can we learn from the Fujifilm–Kodak competition? To answer these questions we shall apply relevant theories of US–Japanese relations, international business and marketing, and combine a case analysis of the Fujifilm–Kodak competition with econometric time series tests of our core conclusions.

KODAK AND NEO MERCANTILIST AMERICA

Kodak's Super 301 complaint against Fujifilm challenged the myth of America as a free trader. Throughout its history since 1776 the United States has remained dominantly mercantilist and protectionist. The 25-year period from the end of the Second World War to the early 1970s was an aberration in that a free traders' agenda guided US foreign trade policy. Today, despite the illusion that the United States is the 'last remaining saint of free trade', the protectionist agenda dominates the country's domestic and foreign policies. As a result the WTO-based multilateral trading system is at risk (Bhagwati, 1990).

After the Second World War the United States took the initiative in the development of the international economic underpinning – the troika comprising GATT, the International Monetary Fund (IMF) and the World Bank. From the end of the war to the early 1960s the United States commanded monopolistic advantages in the world trade of manufactures and agricultural products. Politicians, business elites and the public had vivid memories of the devastating effects of the Great Depression. Many of them correctly believed that the most protectionist measure, the Smoot–Hawley Tariff Act of 1930, had aggravated the depression and spread it to the rest of the world. The United States hoped that freer international flows of goods and capital would avoid another Great Depression and a third world war.

However the United States' innate mercantilism/protectionism began to assert itself from the early 1960s as the manufacturing industries of Europe and Japan recovered from the damages of war and began to export their products to the United States. To avoid head-on challenges to protectionists, free traders used the tactics of diversion and appeasement, diverting the protectionists' attention by ignoring the benefits of imports and extolling the benefits of exports (Lindsey, 1998). The free traders also embraced the protectionists' mercantilist view of 'good exports and bad imports', and diverted protectionist pressure by reminding them of the United States' national security and foreign policy needs; Put simply, the United States had to grant its allies access to the US market in order to fight the Cold War with the Soviet Union and China. At the same time the free traders appeased the protectionists with trade remedy measures, namely antidumping and countervailing duties and other escape laws that protected firms and industries from harm by imports. The protectionists soon expanded these escape laws and protection criteria.

In the early 1970s, when US colour television sets and other products began to lose market share to Japanese products, the protectionists began to overwhelm the free traders. As President Richard Nixon's political influence waned due to the Watergate scandal and the Vietnam War, the protectionists successfully diffused 'Japanphobia' and had the Congress pass the Trade Act of 1974. This Act substantially shifted the trade policy focus away from the GATT-centred free and multilateral trade and embraced the US effort to pry open foreign markets for US goods and services while restricting imports of both agricultural and manufactured goods.

The Act also made it easier for narrow protectionist interests to exploit antidumping and other escape laws to restrict imports (Zicklin

Graduate School of Business, 1998). The United States defined 'dumping' flexibly to suit the protectionists and relaxed the protectionists' proof requirements for economic injuries. The burden of proof was shifted to foreign defendants and over 90 per cent of antidumping suits resulted in a guilty verdict against them. Protectionist and uncompetitive firms were found to be abusing the antidumping laws to harass imports, inflicting a severe cost on American consumers and businesses dependent on imports (Boltuck and Litan, 1991).

US–Japanese trade relations became antagonistic over the issue of colour TV sets. In the early 1970s the US market for colour TV sets was entering the mature phase of the product life cycle. American consumers were increasingly preferring Japan's compact and innovative products, whose defect rates were one-twentieth of that of the large and obsolete US console models. From 1968 to 1977 the income elasticity of demand for Japanese TV sets was 6.423 and significantly greater than 1.001 for American makes (Tsurumi and Tsurumi, 1980). To American consumers in the middle- to high-income groups, Japanese imports were superior goods and retail sales increased as the average US income rose. Mass merchandisers such as Sears were replacing Zenith and other US makes with more reliable Japanese imports. The oil-crisis-induced recession of 1973–76 promoted the American consumers' abandonment of US TV sets.

In 1976 the Zenith-led business and union alliance, COMPACT (Committee to Preserve American Color TV Sets), was formed to fight against Japanese imports. Zenith also used protectionist legal manoeuvres such as countervailing duty, antidumping and antitrust suits to harass Japanese imports. In 1977, to deflect the rising protectionist pressure from Congress, unions, businesses and the mass media, President Jimmy Carter instructed Robert Strauss, an influential former chairman of the National Democratic Party, to negotiate with Japan on voluntary export restraints (VER). However this did not save Zenith or other American TV manufacturers. Those who failed to improve their manufacturing and product development skills soon disappeared from the US scene.

Carter's VER opened the flood gates to other protectionist demands. In 1978, when Detroit's Big Three and the United Auto Workers Union sought to restrict the importation of Japanese compact cars, the Carter administration created the USTR, with Robert Strauss as its first chief representative. The USTR was to negotiate product-specific VERs or 'market opening measures' bilaterally with foreign governments. With such political mandates the protectionist lobbies captured the USTR

(Bovard, 1991). In 1981 President Ronald Reagan imposed a VER on Japanese cars. This cost American consumers $13 billion a year as both the Detroit manufacturers and Japanese importers increased their average price by $1500 per car (Tsurumi, 1984).

The social and economic costs of imports for import-competing firms and labour were visibly concentrated while the social and economic gains were invisibly spread throughout American society. This made it easier for protectionists to organize lobbying campaigns to enlist the support of the US Congress and sensation-seeking mass media against imports. The protectionists cultivated America's neo-mercantilist belief by graphically parading the plight of companies and workers allegedly hurt by Japanese imports.

Americans had another myth – that the United States was the most open market in the world. This was combined with the other equally deepseated myth that competitor countries, particularly Japan and other Asian countries, did not play fair. These two myths were so strongly held that Americans routinely ignored any credible factual evidence to the contrary. In spring 1983 the Institute for International Economics in Washington DC reported that non-tariff import barriers affected 34 per cent of the US markets for manufactured goods, compared with 7 per cent in Japan, 10 per cent in Canada, 20 per cent in West Germany and 32 per cent in France. American protectionists and the mass media simply ignored this. By the early 1980s, the Japanese markets were arguably more open than those in the United States, but the 'American perception of Japan's closed market persisted and generated massive complaints, bordering on paranoia and petulance' (Bhagwati, 1990).

During the presidential election of 1980, Motorola's Robert Galvin launched a massive anti-Japan public relations campaign through the mass media and lobbying in Washington. With President Reagan in the White House, Motorola intensified its campaign – 'if we let Japan waive the rules, Japan will rule the waves' – and despatched its executives and lobbyists to important positions in the Commerce Department, the USTR and Congress.

US–Japanese technological and economic competition shifted to the high tech and information areas of civilian/defence dual use technology. In 1986 – acting on behalf of Motorola, Texas Instruments and other semiconductor interests – the USTR forced the Semiconductor Agreement on Japan. This bilateral agreement not only involved VERs on microchips sold in the United States and the rest of the world, but also forced Japan to set aside 20 per cent of its microchip market for US products. The Reagan administration praised the agreement as the first 'numerical result-oriented market opening', which would increase US microchip exports to Japan and create jobs in the United States However, according to a 1990 study by Washington University the agreement eliminated at least 30000 computer-related US jobs, and failed to increase either US jobs or exports of US microchips to Japan.

This was because the 'magic 20 per cent market share for US microchips' was applied to Motorola, Texas Instruments and other US microchips made in Japan. Besides, Japan's VER on microchips increased their price in the United States by over 300 per cent, handicapping US computer and machine tools makers *vis-à-vis* Japanese and other Asian imports. Under Robert Galvin and his successor, George Fisher, Motorola exploited the semiconductor agreement to force Japan to buy Motorola's wireless telephones and exchange equipment even though this equipment was technically incompatible with Japan's NTT system.

In 1987, Cold War interests in the United States portrayed the 'Toshiba Incident' as betrayal by Japan, alleging falsely that Toshiba had sold sophisticated machine tools to the Soviet Union that made the screw of Soviet nuclear submarines 'undetectably quiet' (CBS Evening News, 1987). The resultant Japan bashing frenzy led to the enactment of the Omnibus Trade and Competitiveness Act of 1988. This Act turned Section 301 of the 1974 Trade Act into the 'Super 301'.

Both protectionists and free traders exploited this anti-Japanese phobia and 'Asiaphobia' in general for the purpose of advocating a managed trade regime of aggressive unilateralism – the restriction of Japanese and other Asian goods and a demand that Japanese and other Asian countries should set aside a share of their markets for US goods and services in the name of fair trade reciprocity. With the dissolution of the Soviet Bloc in 1989 and the Soviet Union itself in 1991, American free traders lost the Cold War as an argument for fighting against rising protectionism. Japan duly replaced the Soviet Union as America's 'archenemy'.

According to a Gallup Poll conducted in March 1989 (seven months before the collapse of the Berlin Wall), 31 per cent of Americans had an unfavourable impression of Japan. By February 1992 this had risen to 53 per cent. According to a Harris/Mirror poll in March 1990, only 8 per cent of Americans regarded Japan as the 'greatest danger to the US', but in a February 1992 poll that proportion rose to 31 per cent. Meanwhile the Reagan and Bush administrations had successfully forced Japan to accept the market-oriented, sector-specific (MOSS) market opening measure. This bilateral trade negotiation framework enabled the United States unilaterally to demand that Japan set aside a US-dictated market share (fixed-quota measures) for US goods and services.

Bill Clinton won the presidency in 1992 by calling, among other things, for 'results-oriented strategic trade' policies, particularly with Japan. He declared, that 'Trade and economic policy, rather than the traditional factors of defense and regional security, would be the basis for a new U.S.–Japan relationship' (Harvard Kennedy School of Government, 1997). However this results-oriented strategic trade was economic nonsense (Krugman, 1994). Strategic traders mistakenly equated trade deficits with US declining competitiveness. The US trade deficits were merely about 2 per cent of GDP, too small to hurt the economy. On a per capita basis, Japan's imports from the United States amounted to about $640 a year, while US imports from Japan came to $470. Japan's trade surpluses with the United States were recycled to the United States as direct and financial investment by Japanese firms. Between 1982 and 1997 Japanese direct investment created over 1.5 million jobs in the United States and accounted for net exports of over $10 billion a year to the rest of the world.

Besides, these imports were fuelling an already robust economy. The US trade deficits were mainly caused, not by Japan, but by domestic problems such as a chronic shortage of savings and US corporations' lukewarm commitment to exports. In its Super 301 complaint, Kodak argued that its 70 per cent market share in the United States should give it a much larger market share than the 10 per cent it held in Japan. Fujifilm replied that its 70 per cent market share in Japan would not automatically yield a larger market share than the 12 per cent it held in the United States.

In 1993 George Fisher left Motorola to become Kodak's CEO. He immediately filed a dumping charge against Fujifilm in respect of its graphic colour photo paper. But the International Trade Commission (ITC) ruled in favour of Fujifilm, mainly because independent wholesalers' photofinishers were switching from Kodak's paper to Fujifilm's, not for lower prices, but for better product quality and customer services (Fujifilm, 1995). In 1995 President Clinton and US Trade Representative, Mickey Kantor decided to 'bash Japan' in order to shore up Clinton's sagging popularity before the presidential election of 1996 (*Journal of Commerce,* 1996), whereupon Kodak and Federal Express pressured the Clinton administration to demand that Japan give the two corporations preferential market access.

Between 1994 and 1995 Kodak was confronted with three fundamental problems that were threatening its market competitiveness worldwide. First, Kodak had to divert over $750 million a year from R&D and market developments to costly write-offs of unprofitable diversification ventures. Second, its archrival, Fujifilm, was expanding its market share in the United States and Canada at the expense of Kodak. Fujifilm's market share in the United States passed the 10 per cent mark, while Kodak's market share in Canada fell from over 70 per cent in 1987 to 48 per cent in 1994. During the same period in Asia and Oceania, which were experiencing the fastest growth in photographic materials, Fujifilm's share soared from 20 per cent to 48 per cent while Kodak's once dominant position fell to 28 per cent from 70 per cent. Kodak's market shares also suffered at the hands of Fujifilm in Latin America and Europe. Third, digital imaging technology was forcing Kodak, Fujifilm and camera and electronics firms to scramble for new market positions. Kodak found its competitive position slipping against Fujifilm, which had strong in-house digital technology capabilities. It was these three problems that led Kodak to file the Super 301 complaint against Fujifilm in 1995.

Fujifilm's success in Japan, the United States and elsewhere was attributed to its single-minded 'exchange-of-hostage' strategy against Kodak. Such exchange-of-hostage behaviour by multinational firms has been particularly observed among competing oligopolistic multinationals (Graham, 1974; Tsurumi and Graham, 1977). In the case of the worldwide duopolistic competition between Kodak and Fujifilm, Fujifilm's exchange-of-hostage strategy against Kodak was a typical example of non-cooperative, game-theoretic competitive behaviour (Graham, 1998). Fujifilm's strategy in Japan, the United States and elsewhere depended on it anticipating Kodak's strategy. In particular Fujifilm's early entry into the United States, the home market of Kodak, was motivated by Fujifilm's planned exchange-of-hostage defence against Kodak. To defend its market leadership in Japan, Fujifilm needed to monitor Kodak's actions in the United States. Fujifilm was also hoping to make its market positions in the United States strong enough to retaliate against the anticipated competitive pressure by Kodak in Japan. In 1995, Kodak must have felt that the need to build up its market share and monitoring operations in Japan was strong enough to warrant a counterattack on Fujifilm's competitive pressures in the United States.

FUJIFILM–KODAK: DUOPOLISTIC COMPETITION IN JAPAN

To explain the persistent decline of Kodak's market share in Japan, Kodak alleged that Fujifilm and MITI had conspired from 1971 to

1975 to deny Kodak access to Asanuma, a large wholesaler of photographic film and paper. However the WTO found that from the 1960s to 1975 Kodak itself had rejected Asanuma's requests to handle Kodak products. Kodak did not explain why it had taken until 1986, almost 15 years after Japan had liberalized investment by foreign firms, to set up a fully owned marketing subsidiary directly to manage its marketing activities in Japan.

Kodak's market share of film in Japan nearly tripled from 6.1 per cent in 1971 to about 18 per cent in 1981–83. However, it persistently fell after 1983 to less than 10 per cent in 1995. During the post-trade liberalization period (1971–81) Kodak exploited its two distinct advantages over Fujifilm and eroded the latter's market share. First, Kodak had enjoyed a brand recognition of its products as superior goods since the prewar days. Second, Japan cut its import duty on film and photographic paper from 40 per cent (of the c.i.f. price in Japan) in 1971 to 5 per cent in 1976. Furthermore the yen continued to appreciate against the US dollar between 1971 and 1981. Kodak's Japanese importer exploited these two windfall opportunities for price cutting without reducing Kodak's dollar-based profits and aggressively cut the retail prices. Hence Kodak's quality brand image and aggressive price cutting threatened Fujifilm's dominant market position. How did Fujifilm hold Kodak in check and solidify its leadership in the quality segment of Japan's film market?

Cultural idiosyncrasies of Japanese consumer markets and Kodak's mistakes in Japan

In Japan one leading brand, whether Japanese or foreign, often dominates categories of consumer products that are related to upmarket and fashionable lifestyles. This leading brand often captures over 60 per cent of the market. For example Nescafe has garnered 80 per cent of Japan's instant coffee market while Maxwell House has stayed at around 10 per cent. Distant second- and third-place brands are crowded into the much smaller segment of 'inferior goods' whose retail sales are price-elastic. When a new brand replaces the leader, the previous brand leader falls precipitously to the 'inferior goods' segment. For example in 1998–99 Asahi replaced Kirin as the leader of Japan's beer market. For nearly half a century Kirin had held about 60 per cent of the beer market, but now it was on its way down to Asahi's previous position, with about 15 per cent of the market.

As discussed earlier in the case of the US colour TV market in the 1970s, retail sales of superior goods are more income- and brand-image-elastic (Pacific Basin Center, 1978). In 1995, contrary to the Kodak–USTR allegation, both Kodak and Fujifilm products were sold by over 85 per cent of film retailers in Japan. At these stores, however, Fujifilm outsold Kodak by seven to one even when Fujifilm's prices were higher than Kodak's (Japanese market research). Japanese consumers were attracted to Fujifilm's superior image and the availability of customer services. Since the retail sales of superior goods are not price-elastic, and since Japanese consumers equate higher prices with higher-quality products, Fujifilm used its price cuts to benefit its wholesalers and retailers. Meanwhile Kodak sought to expand its market share by cutting its retail prices, thus inadvertently convincing Japanese consumers of its inferior quality in comparison with Fujifilm.

Furthermore, in Japan, continuous firm-to-firm and person-to-person relationship marketing is a way of life (Morgan and Hunt, 1994). Direct management by a manufacturer of its distribution and retail networks is vital as its product goes through the rapid growth stage of its life and reaches maturity. The ultimate success of a manufacturer, Japanese or foreign, depends on how well it pushes its products through the multilayered distribution channels to fragmented retail outlets (Tsurumi, 1982; Takada, 1999).

To regain its leadership Fujifilm exploited Kodak's serious marketing error of ignoring the idiosyncrasies of the Japanese market. In 1971, rather than setting up its own marketing subsidiary in Japan, Kodak made the Japanese firm Nagase its exclusive import–wholesaler agent in Japan and left its marketing decisions to Nagase, which was an importer–distributor of industrial chemicals and lacked experience in photographic materials. MITI did not force Kodak to make Nagase its exclusive agent. Fujifilm was fully aware of the importance of continuous relationship marketing in Japan, and allowed four exclusive (Fujifilm products only) and three non-exclusive (multiple brand handlers) wholesalers to compete with one another for the job of opening and servicing their retail networks throughout Japan.

Unlike the US photo market, the Japanese photo market is dominated by amateur photographers, who are notorious for their impatience to see their developed pictures and demand quality processing and good customer services. Many Japanese regard picture taking as a symbol of a rising standard of living and fashionable lifestyle. By 1976 Japan had recovered from the severe economic recession caused by the oil crisis of 1973–74. With rising disposable income, Japanese consumers were embracing a fashionable life style that produced frequent photo-taking opportunities. Fujifilm's bid to dominate the superior goods segment rested on mini processing laboratories (mini-labs) consisting of on-site processing facilities that are compact and highly automated. One person can easily operate a mini-lab and provide a speedy, one-hour processing service. It took Konica, Fujifilm's Japanese competitor, until 1983 to respond with its own mini-labs, and it took Kodak until the late 1980s to follow suit. Fujifilm countered by expanding its mini-lab network and continuously updating its equipment. Fujifilm's mini-lab network embraced choice locations and photo shops, creating an effective barrier to entry for Konica and Kodak. The number of Fujifilm mini-lab installations in Japan grew from 10 in 1976 to 13400 in 1994, accounting for 45 per cent of mini-labs, 70 per cent of the film market and 60 per cent of the photographic paper market.

In the mid 1980s over 80 per cent of Japanese households owned at least one 35mm single lens reflex camera. The product life cycle of film entered its maturing stage, making Fujiflm's mini-lab networks all the more important for its market dominance. To extend its product life cycle, Fujifilm set out to persuade even camera-phobic consumers to take pictures. In 1987 it introduced a disposable 35-mm camera (a cheap, preloaded camera for one-off use) that took pictures of good quality and overcame customers' fear of film loading and removal. This created a 'party camera market' for spur-of-the-moment snap-shots among the fashionable younger generation. Fujifilm's disposable camera was ahead of Kodak's by two years in Japan and by eighteen months in the United States (Hammer and Champy, 1993).

By the time Kodak came up with its disposable camera, Fujifilm had expanded its retail outlets in Japan and elsewhere to include small tourist souvenir shops, restaurants, newsstands, theatres, coffee shops and even consignment placements in hotel rooms. The popularity of Fujifilm's disposable cameras and mini-labs persuaded many film retail outlets in Asia, Latin America, Canada and even the United States to carry Fujifilm's ordinary 35mm film. In this attack–counterattack duopolistic competition, this time Fujifilm's gain was Kodak's loss.

Econometric tests of Fujifilm–Kodak competition in Japan

From our observations of the Fujifilm–Kodak competition, we postu-lated that Fujifilm's marketing logistics and mini-labs first held Kodak's growth in check from 1976 to 1981 and then eroded Kodak's market share after 1982. To test this hypothesis, we applied annual time series data for Kodak's market share and Fujifilm's cumulative installation of mini-labs to a statistical analysis of two questions: (1) when did Kodak's market share begin to fall and (2) what caused the decline in Kodak's market share? Statistically, question 1 pinpoints the break point, or join point in Bayesian statistics, in the time trend of Kodak's market share

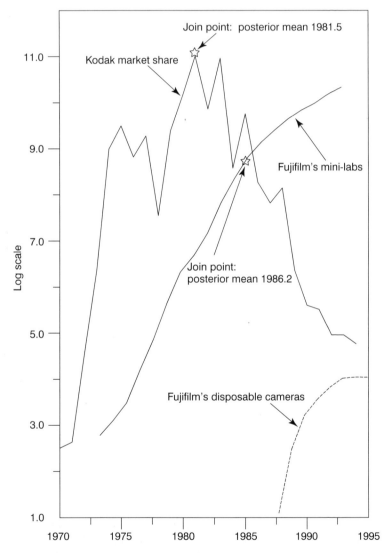

Figure 10.1   Kodak's market share, Fujifilm's mini-labs and disposable cameras, Japan, 1972–94

and Fujifilm's mini-lab installations (Tsurumi, 1976; Broemeling and Tsurumi, 1986). The join point identifies the changing phase in the product life cycle. Figure 10.1 shows the relationship between Kodak's market share and Fujifilm's mini-lab installations. The computed results are summarized in Table 10.1. As shown in Figure 10.1, the join point of Kodak's market share in Japan occurred in mid 1981, after which it fell persistently. The join point of the cumulative growth of Fujifilm's mini-lab installations was in early 1986.

To answer question 2 we used the Granger causality test, which uses an F-test procedure and is often used in macro-and monetary economic time series analysis (Judge *et al.*, 1985; Hamilton, 1994). Table 10.2 summarizes the results of the test of the relationship between the two variables: Fujifilm's cumulative installation of mini-labs and Kodak's market shares. At the 5 per cent significance level the test

Table 10.1 Posterior summary statistics of segmented linear trend regressions: Kodak's market share, Japan, 1971–94; Fujifilm mini-lab installations, Japan, 1976–94

	Intercept α	Slope β
Kodak's market share:		
Regime 1 (1971–81)	2.007 (0.122)	0.0812 (0.018)
Regime 2 (1982–94)	3.599 (0.113)	−0.0660 (0.006)
Fujifilm mini-lab installations:		
Regime 1 (1976–86)	−1.642 (0.186)	0.6520 (0.017)
Regime 2 (1989–94)	5.342 (0.192)	0.2120 (0.010)

Notes: The numbers in the table are posterior means and standard deviations, respectively. The join point t^* between Regimes 1 and 2 is 1981 for the Kodak market share and 1986 for Fujifilm mini-labs.

Table 10.2 Pariwise Granger causality test of Kodak's market share and Fujifilm's mini-lab installations, Japan, 1974–94 (with a computational lag length of 2)

	F- statistic	Probability value
Null hypothesis[1]	4.961	0.029
Null hypothesis[2]	0.718	0.509

1. Fujifilm mini-labs did not cause the Kodak market share to fall.
2. The Kodak market share did not cause the number of Fujifilm mini-labs to increase.

rejects the first null hypothesis that Fujifilm's mini-labs did not cause Kodak's market share to fall. The test does not reject the second null hypothesis that Kodak's market share did not cause the growth of Fujifilm's mini-labs. Hence the results of the test support our conclusion. The build-up and logistical support of Fujifilm's mini-lab network held Kodak in check from 1971 to 1983 and caused Kodak steadily to lose its market share in Japan after 1983. When Japanese film users became satisfied with Fujifilm's products and processing services, they increasingly came to regard Fujifilm as superior to Kodak, especially after 1981–83.

Hence just as Detroit's Big Three underestimated Toyota, Honda, and other Japanese car manufacturers, Kodak at first underestimated Fujifilm but then belatedly realized that Fujifilm had become solidly entrenched in the Japanese market. Avoiding head-on competition with Fujifilm in Japan, Kodak chose to invest mainly in world markets outside Japan from the mid 1980s to the early 1990s. Meanwhile Fujifilm transferred its mini-labs and disposable cameras to the United States and elsewhere and went after Kodak.

FUJIFILM'S EXCHANGE-OF-HOSTAGE ACTION AGAINST KODAK IN THE UNITED STATES

With Kodak continuing to ignore Fujifilm, the latter concentrated on counteracting the market pressure from Kodak in Japan. In 1958, anticipating Kodak's export drive to Japan (which did not actually materialize until 1971), Fujifilm opened a one-person office in Los Angeles to monitor Kodak's R&D, manufacturing and marketing operations. This intelligence work helped Fujifilm with its marketing moves against Kodak in Japan. Fujifilm made its film and paper compatible with Kodak's C-22 development process, which was accepted as the worldwide standard. Speaking about Fujifilm's reason for its entry into the United States in 1958, Minoru Ohnishi, the CEO of Fujifilm, recalled that 'we had to equalize our competitive conditions with Kodak to defend our dominant position in the superior goods segment of Japan's film market. We reached this decision from our market intelligence work about Kodak in the US' (Ohnishi, 1995). In 1965 Fujifilm set up a wholly owned marketing subsidiary, Fuji Photo Film (U.S.A.), in New York City.

What motivated Fujifilm to challenge Kodak, with its home-ground advantage and vast internal economies of scale, in the United States?

Unlike products such as Japanese compact cars versus American large cars, there was no real product differentiation between Fujifilm and Kodak. All that existed was Japanese and American consumers' perceived superiority of Kodak products. However in the late 1970s, with the success of Japanese electronic products, cameras and cars, both Japanese and American consumers came to recognize the superior quality of many Japanese products. In its advertising campaigns in Japan, Fujifilm emphasized American consumers' preferences for its products rather than Kodak's. This was the immediate payoff for Fujifilm's entry into the United States before it became strong enough to erode Kodak's market share. Fujifilm's exchange-of-hostage tactics against Kodak in the United States was spurred by its need to overcome Japanese consumers' treatment of Fujifilm as inferior to Kodak. Otherwise Kodak would dominate the 'superior goods' segment and therefore the Japanese film market.

Econometric tests of Fujifilm's exchange-of-hostage entry into the United States

What was the threshold market share that Fujifilm had to capture in the United States to make Kodak take action against Fujifilm? How long did it take Fujifilm to attain this market share, and how did it do so? To answer these questions we used a Bayesian inferential procedure to pinpoint the join point of Fujifilm's market share in the United States. Its share increased from 0.3 per cent in 1973 to 14 per cent in 1994, but it jumped to 25 per cent in 1997 after Kodak's intensive anti-Fujifilm campaign served to boost American consumers' awareness of Fujifilm. We pinpointed the join point year as 1984 (Figure 10.2). The computational results are summarized in Table 10.3.

When Fujifilm's market share reached the 10 per cent mark in 1984, almost 20 years had elapsed since the establishment of its wholly owned sales subsidiary. In order to conclude that Fujifilm's early direct investment in the United States was motivated by the company's exchange-of-hostage defence against Kodak in Japan, it is sufficient to point out evidence, albeit circumstantial, of exchange-of-hostage thrusts and counterthrusts between Fujifilm and Kodak across the Pacific. In 1984, when Fujifilm's aggressive price cutting gave it a 10 per cent market share in the United States (the join point in Figure 10.2), Kodak abandoned its price-cutting activity in Japan, relinquishing the price-cutting leadership to Fujifilm. In 1986, two years after Fujifilm's US market share passed the 10 per cent mark,

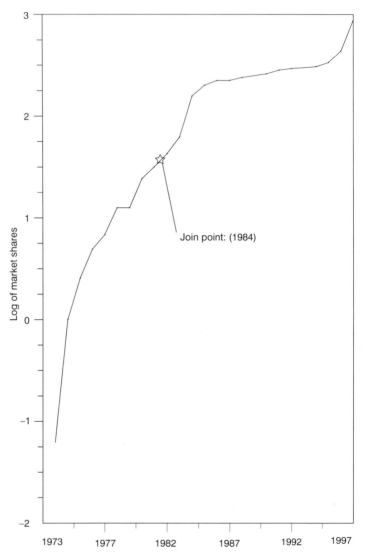

Figure 10.2   Log of Fujifilm's US market shares, 1973–97

Kodak acquired Nagase, its exclusive importer–wholesaler, and finally established a wholly owned sales subsidiary in Japan. In 1995, when Fujifilm's US market share passed the 13 per cent mark, Kodak suddenly filed a Super 301 complaint with the USTR. Until then

Table 10.3   Posterior summary statistics from segmented linear
trend regressions: Fujifilm's US market shares, 1973–97

	Intercept α	Slope β
Regime 1 (1973–84)	−0.5886 (0.2082)	0.2371 (0.0283)
Regime 2 (1985–97)	1.7962 (0.1344)	0.0358 (0.0069)

1. The numbers in the table are posterior means and standard
deviations, respectively.
2. The join point t^* between Regimes 1 and 2 is 1984.

Kodak had never complained about an alleged conspiracy by Fujifilm
and MITI against Kodak.

Part of Fujifilm's exchange-of-hostage strategy in the United States
was to capture the cine film market, which was not seriously defended
by Kodak. Fuji USA soon came to dominate the Hollywood movie
niche, and in 1982 Fujifilm won an Emmy and an Oscar for its A-250
cine film, clinching the word-of-mouth praise it had attracted from
professional photographers and boosting its consumer image in Japan
as superior to Kodak. Also in 1973, when Kodak was increasing its
market share in Japan, Fuji USA took over all sales and marketing
operations from independent distributors to go after the 35 mm film
market, which was dominated by Kodak. The timing and nature of
Fuji USAs actions were consistent with Fujifilm's exchange-of-hostage
defence against Kodak in Japan. Fuji USA was ready to transfer its
Japanese parent's relationship marketing (strategic logistics) to the
United States by building its own retail outlets.

US supermarket chains, which had been ignored by Kodak, were
shedding their food-only policy. Fuji USA hired former grocery suppliers as full-time sales personnel and taught them to service the film
retail and processing business of supermarket chains. In 1981 Fuji USA
became the official film supplier to the 1984 Los Angeles Olympics and
the US Olympic team (Kodak had failed to put in a bid). Fuji capita-
lized on this in its sales promotions, and by autumn 1984 it had over
70000 retail outlets throughout the United States. Fuji USA's official
sponsorship of the Olympics did so much to improve the image of
Fujifilm as a quality product both in the United States and Japan that
Kodak scrambled to win the official sponsorship of the Atlanta Olympics (1996) and the Nagano Winter Olympics (1998) in Japan.

Despite a rise in the value of the yen against the US dollar,
Fujifilm's manufacturing productivity enabled Fuji USA to keep its

retail film prices 10–15 per cent lower than Kodak's. This was necessary because Kodak's dominance of the quality segment of the US
film market was still strong and about 90 per cent of American
consumers would not even try out another brand if the price was the
same as Kodak's. In 1994, one year after Kodak's unsuccessful antidumping suit against Fuji USA, the latter opened a factory to produce
photographic paper and film in South Carolina, and improved its
delivery services to the growing network of wholesale processors,
retailers and mini-labs.

By December 1997 Fuji USA had become a full-fledged transplant
corporation. It had a network of 19 processing laboratories throughout the United States versus Kodak's 49. It had also expanded its
mini-lab networks in key city markets, it was engaged in a whole range
of operations from R&D ,and manufacturing to marketing, and it
employed over 8000 Americans. It had become politically and
economically resistant to Kodak/USTR threats of Super 301 trade
sanctions.

CONCLUSIONS

Fujifilm's success was made possible by its corporate culture and
structure (Tsurumi and Tsurumi, 1985; Tezuka, 1997), and both management and employees focused on the long-term goal of Fujifilm
becoming a worldclass player in the realm of photographic film and
processing. As shown in Figure 10.3, Fujifilm linked in a mutually
reinforcing way its public relations, marketing, manufacturing, R&D,
corporate finance and human resource activities. Meanwhile Kodak's
political and public relations counterattack failed to succeed as it
lacked an effective strategy for R&D, manufacturing and above all
international marketing. To refine its competitive strategy, Fujifilm
holistically used ten marketing variables (10 Ps) in Japan and the
United States – namely probing, price, product, placement, promotion,
productivity, people, plaintiff (legal), politics, and public relations.

Part of a corporation's competitive strategy is to differentiate itself
from its competitors. To achieve and maintain this differentiation, as
Fujifilm's success against Kodak teaches us, it is important to engage
in market and technology intelligence work at home and abroad. The
Fujifilm–Kodak competition in Japan and the United States revealed
asymmetric gaps in knowledge about each other's market. Fujifilm
exploited Kodak's tenuous knowledge of the Japanese market and

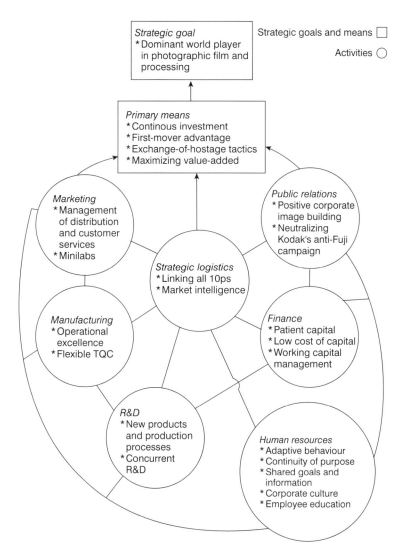

Figure 10.3   A schematic illustration of Fujifilm's holistic strategy

consumers while Kodak's knowledge of the US market and consumers was increasingly matched or even surpassed by Fujifilm. Under such dynamic duopolistic competition of asymmetric market knowledge, it is unlikely that there would be an equilibrium in which Fujifilm and Kodak would cease to compete with each other.

The WTO's ruling in favour of Japan set a precedent for the adjudication of disputes between the United States and other WTO members over market competition practices. For politically weaker countries such as Japan and other Asian countries, the WTO adjudication provides a viable defence against 'aggressive unilateralism' by the United States. Even if Japan had lost, the WTO ruling would have been politically more acceptable to the Japanese and other Asians than US unilateral pressure. The WTO shuns fixed-quota 'managed trade' (for example the US–Japan Semiconductor Agreement) that the United States tried to force on Asian countries in particular. Rather it supports fixed-rule market openings, such as Japan's abolition of the Large Store Law, which had prevented Toys 'R' Us from opening a retail chain in Japan. Since 1991 Toys 'R' Us has expanded rapidly in Japan, and other foreign retail chains are following suit. Fixed-rule market competition is what Japan and other Asian countries must undertake to open their last remaining markets. By pitting their firms against foreign competitors in their home markets, Asian countries can revitalize their economies.

The competitive pressure that Fujifilm put on Kodak in the United States forced Kodak to match Fujifilm's price cutting, product and marketing innovations. Before Fujifilm became strong enough to challenge Kodak's monopoly, the US Justice Department had not been very successful in enforcing Kodak's 1954 Consent Decree. Under this decree, Kodak was to refrain from anticompetitive practices, including price gouging and excluding its competitors from wholesaler–retail networks (US Justice Department, 1993). The United States and other countries should follow the lead of Japan's Fair Trade Commission and allow Kodak and Fujifilm to compete freely with each other.

Fujifilm and Kodak are not likely to moderate their struggle for market share now that they have to compete with camera and electronics manufacturers for worldwide market positions in the 'image capturing and transferring' industry. Just as Japanese imports forced US car, electronics and machine tool firms to improve their manufacturing productivity, product quality and customer services, Fujifilm imports helped improve Kodak's product quality and customer services. These are the visible benefits of imports that free traders should be publicizing in order to reduce the strength and influence of the mercantilists/protectionists in the United States.

References

Baron, D. P. (1995) 'Integrated Strategy: Market and Non-Market Components', *California Management Review*, vol. 37, no. 2, pp. 47–65.

Bhagwati, Jagdish (1990) *The World Trading System at Risk* (Princeton, NJ: Princeton University Press).

Boltuck, Richard and Robert E. Litan (1991) *Down in the Dumps: Administration of the Unfair Trade Laws* (Washington, DC: The Brookings Institution).

Bovard, James (1991) *The Fair Trade Fraud* (New York: St Martin's Press).

Broemeling, Lyle D. and Hiroki Tsurumi (1987) *Econometrics and Structural Change* (New York: Marcel Dekker).

CBS Evening News (1987) 'Soviet Subs Became Quieter before Toshiba Machinery Export', 1 July.

Fujifilm Co. (1995) *Rewriting History: Kodak's Revisionist Account of the Japanese Consumer Photographic Market* (Tokyo: Fuji Photo Film Co.).

Graham, Edward M. (1974) 'Oligopolistic Imitation and European Direct Investment in the U.S.', unpublished doctoral thesis, Harvard Graduate School of Business Administration, Boston, Mass.

Graham, Edward M. (1998) 'Market Structure and the Multinational Enterprise: A Game-theoretic Approach', *Journal of International Business Studies*, vol. 29, no. 1, pp. 67–83.

Hamilton, James D. (1994) *Time Series Analysis* (Princeton, NJ: Princeton University Press).

Hammer, Michael and James Champy (1993) *Reengineering the Corporation* (New York: Harper Business).

Harvard Kennedy School of Government (1997) 'Snapshot: Kodak vs. Fuji', teaching case material.

Journal of Commerce (1996) 'Dick Morris Helped Kantor Get Tough on Japan', 21 November, pp. 1A, 6A.

Judge, George C., W. E. Griffiths, R. Carter Hill, Helmut Lutkepohl and Tsoung-Chao (1985) *The Theory and Practice of Econometrics* (New York: John Wiley and Sons).

Kodak (1995) *Privatizing Protection: Japanese Market Barriers in Consumer Photographic Film and Consumer Photographic Paper* (Rochester, New York: Eastman Kodak Co.).

Krugman, Paul (1994) *Peddling Prosperity: Economic Sense and Nonsense in the Age of Diminished Expectation* (New York: Norton).

Lindsey, Brink (1998) 'A New Track for U.S. Trade Policy' (Washington, DC: The Center for Trade Policy, the Cato Institute, September 11).

Morgan, Robert M. and Shelby D. Hunt (1994) 'The Commitment-Trust Theory of Relationship Marketing', *Journal of Marketing*, vol. 9 (July), pp. 20–38.

Ohnishi, Minoru (1995) 'We Used to Respect Kodak', Ohnishi's opening statement at a press conference at the Foreign Correspondents' Club, Tokyo, 21 August.

Pacific Basin Center (1978) *American Style Trade War across the Pacific* (New York: Pacific Basin Center).

Schlessinger, Arthur Jr (1986) *The Cycles of American History* (Boston, Mass.: Houghton Mifflin).

Takada, Hirokazu (1999) 'A Cross-country Analysis of Marketing Channel Performance in Japan and the United States', *International Journal of Business Research*, forthcoming.

Tezuka, Hiroyuki (1997) 'Success as the Source of Failure? Competition and Cooperation in the Japanese Economy', *Sloan Management Review*, Winter, pp. 83–93.

Tsurumi, Hiroki (1976) 'A Bayesian Test of the Product Life Cycle Hypothesis applied to Japanese Crude Steel Production', *Journal of Econometrics*, no. 4, pp. 371–92.

Tsurumi, Hiroki and Yoshi Tsurumi (1980) 'A Bayesian Test of the Product Life Cycle Hypothesis Applied to the U.S. Demand for Color-TV Sets', *International Economic Review*, vol. 21, no. 3, pp. 583–97.

Tsurumi, Yoshi (1982) 'Managing Consumer and Industrial Marketing Systems in Japan', *Sloan Management Review*, Fall, pp. 6–14.

Tsurumi, Yoshi (1984) 'The Economics of Car Quotas: They're Merely a Subsidy for Detroit', *New York Times*, 16 December.

Tsurumi, Yoshi (1987) 'Adaptive Marketing for the Pacific Age', *EURO-Asia Business Review*, August, pp. 104–12.

Tsurumi, Yoshi (1993) 'Japan–U.S. Relations', in *The Oxford Companion to the Politics of the World* (Oxford: Oxford University Press).

Tsurumi, Yoshi and Edward Graham (1977) *Multinational Management* (Cambridge, Mass.: Ballinger).

Tsurumi, Yoshi and Hiroki Tsurumi (1985) 'Value-added Maximizing Behavior of Japanese Firms and Roles of Corporate Investment and Finance', *Columbia Journal of World Business*, vol. 20, no. 1, pp. 29–36.

United States Justice Department (1993) Letter to David Lascell, Esq., Kodak's Attorney, 4 November, reminding Kodak of the 1921 and 1954 Consent Decrees.

Washington University (1990) *The Impact of U.S.–Japan Semiconductor Agreement on the U.S. Economy* (St Louis, Missouri: Washington University Department of Economics).

Zicklin Graduate School of Business (1998) Fujifilm–Kodak Worldwide Competition (A): Government Relations and (B) Trade and Investment (New York: Cuny Baruch College, Department of Marketing).

Comments on Chapter 10

John Ries

Chapter 10 surveys the history of US–Japanese economic conflicts and argues persuasively against unilateral US trade action and managed trade. The latter part of the chapter argues that it was successful marketing that led to Fujifilm's increased market share in Japan and the United States, not anticompetitive practices as claimed by Kodak.

Many people would concur with the authors' opposition to unilateral US trade action and managed trade. Their focus on the Fujifilm–Kodak case in this context, however, is a bit peculiar as it was a case of neither unilateral US action nor managed trade. The United States chose a multilateral forum, the WTO, to litigate the case. Setting numerical market share targets was never a serious objective.

The authors also claim that concentrated and politically powerful industries in the United States are able to win trade concessions (voluntary export restraints on TVs, cars, semiconductors and so on) at the expense of US consumers. This argument cuts both ways – powerful Japanese special interests can influence policy to the detriment of Japanese consumers. Outside pressure on Japan (*gaiatsu*) has brought some benefits to Japanese consumers – US pressure to abolish the Large Retail Store Law has resulted in more competition and noticeably cheaper prices in retail stores.

With regard to the Fujifilm–Kodak dispute, the authors use their expertise in statistics and marketing to argue that Fujifilm's successful establishment of mini photo-processing labs explains the drop in Kodak's market share in Japan. They conducted Granger causality tests to show that the increase in mini labs 'Granger caused' the decline in Kodak's market share but not the reverse. This test is informative but not sufficient to establish causality; these statistics have to be supplemented with business analysis explaining the economic relationship between the mini labs and Kodak's market share.

On the marketing side the authors argue that the key to high film sales in Japan is establishing your product as being of high quality. According to them, Kodak's film was initially the superior product. However the establishment of mini-labs, market penetration in the United States and the introduction of the disposable camera by

Fujifilm combined to make the Japanese consumer view Fujifilm's film as superior.

I think the authors' case would be more compelling if they were to clarify a few points. What products underlie the market share statistics: film and photographic paper or just film? What is the economic connection between the mini photo-processing labs and the sale of film? What is the relationship between where film is developed and the brand that is purchased? Can Kodak film be developed in these mini-labs? If not, why? How do mini-labs influence consumers' perception of quality? The chapter does not clearly establish the link between Fujifilm's tactics and consumers' perception of film quality.

The authors also provide statistics on Fujifilm's gains in market share in different regions worldwide. Is not the fact that Fujifilm's market share is rising throughout the world evidence that competition policy was not the source of the increase in Fujifilm's market share in Japan? Kodak's problems seem not to be unique to Japan.

According to the authors, Fujifilm's and Kodak's investment strategies are a classic example of 'exchange of hostage' strategies, but these are not well defined. I presume they involve locating in the competitor's home market in order to 'punish' the competitor if it engages in 'hostile' behaviour. If firms are pursuing this type of strategy, are there predictions about performance that can be evaluated? I imagine the predictions would be (1) a very stable market where neither firm 'misbehaves' due to the threat of punishment; or (2) a price war in one location immediately followed by a price war in another market. Can we observe outcomes that are consistent with 'exchange of hostage' strategies? Perhaps the reason for the investment is more mundane: successful sales in a foreign market require a physical presence in that market.

Finally, the authors argue strongly against unilateral US trade actions against Japan. Their argument is largely based on a sound principle: such action is often costly both to Japan and to US consumers. The evidence supporting this position, however, may be selective and pro-US intervention advocates might select a very different body of evidence. This chapter should be considered as another salvo in a debate that is far from settled.

Addendum to Chapter 10: The Kodak–Fuji Dispute, the WTO and Trade and Competition Policies

Kaz Masui

THE KODAK–FUJI FILM DISPUTE: AN OUTLINE

I shall begin my discussion with a panel report submitted by the WTO in January 1998 on its ruling on the US–Japan dispute over photographic film and paper made in Japan.

History

The Kodak–Fuji case has a long history and presents a picture of a struggle for supremacy between the world's two largest film companies. In September 1993 Kodak filed a case against Fujifilm for allegedly dumping photographic paper. The US Department of Commerce (DOC) came to a provisional judgment that Fuji was guilty of dumping. Furthermore the dumping margin was the largest ever recorded by the DOC. Afterwards Fuji began construction on a manufacturing plant in South Carolina.

In July 1994 Fuji agreed to raise the prices of its colour printing paper in the United States in exchange for DOC withdrawing its judgement, and as a result Fuji's share of colour printing paper in the United States went down sharply in 1995.

In May 1995 Kodak filed another case against Fuji, this time in connection with its market share, agent system, rebate system and violation of the Japanese Anti-Monopoly Act.

Fuji's distribution system was the most serious of the issues in the dispute. Kodak Japan, Konica Marketing and Japan Agfa Gevaert all had sales dealers in Japan. Fuji had four independent agents that acted as the nodes of the distribution network: Asanuma Shokai, Kashimura, Misuzu Sangyo and Ohmiya Shashin Yohin. These agents handled only

Fuji products and distributed 95 per cent of the domestic share of films. Originally, conventional special agents distributed the products through small and medium-sized retailers, but then the manufacturers themselves started to get involved in the distribution process.

In June 1996 the US government brought a case before the WTO against the Japanese government, and in January 1998 the WTO rejected the US position.

INTERFACE BETWEEN COMPETITION POLICIES AND FOREIGN TRADE ISSUES

Japan's competition policy

I argue that the Kodak–Fuji case was really about the extent to which a foreign government and a film manufacturer could challenge another country's competition policy, specifically the Japanese government's competition policy towards the photographic film industry and Fuji's competitive behaviour. The following appeal measures were available to Kodak:

- Challenge the Japanese government and Fujifilm in a multilateral framework such as the WTO.
- Resort to domestic (US) laws such as Super 301 and extraterritorial application of the US Antitrust Act.
- Challenge Japan in a bilateral discussion.
- Appeal (through Kodak Japan, its subsidiary in Japan) to the Japanese FTC.

The question was how to correct the situation in Japan, where the country's anticompetition environment was hindering international trade. I would like to discuss some examples of the practice of competitive behaviour by both the Japanese government and Japanese firms.

In the Kodak–Fuji dispute the FTC judged that there was no problem with Japan's competition policy. The US discontent with this judgement has not disappeared. In fact the US discontent goes back for over ten years due to the frustration arising from a series of discussions on Japan's protective structure (for example the Structural Impediments Initiatives – SII – talks). Since then the United States has argued that Japan's protectionist environment is unacceptable. In fact many of the discussions that took place during the SII talks were about the application of Japan's Antimonopoly Law and improvement of the competitive environment in Japan.

For example the United States made specific requests in six areas: savings and investment patterns, land utilization, distribution, exclusive business practices, group (*keiretsu*) relationships and price mechanisms. Japan was to a large extent forced to carry out a number of promises in response to the harsh US requests.

The United States criticized the implementation of these promises in three particular areas: exclusive business practices, distribution, and *keiretsu* relationships. Furthermore, at the follow-up meetings the United States pointed out how closed the Japanese markets were with respect to individual sectors, such as feed grains, car parts, glass and insurance.

The problems raised by the United States were closely related to Japan's antimonopoly policies. Accordingly the United States continues to insist that Japan should strengthen the enforcement of its Antimonopoly Law.

Western-style economic systems

Japan's economic system is quite different from the Euro-American systems which have evolved over centuries. For instance the emphasis on seniority in worker management, labour–management harmony, a social structure that gives companies the highest priority, administrative guidance and other practices that connect the Japanese government to companies, cartel-like corporate structures and massive reciprocal shareholding among companies can be found only in the Japanese economic system.

The United States seriously wants Japan to assimilate its system. Japan, however, sees the unique characteristics of its system as originating in old cultural traditions and that the assimilation of a Western economic system would mean Westernizing Japan in terms of its culture too. Although Japan refuses to become culturally Westernized, one can say that it is trying to reform what must be reformed, as pointed out in the SII talks.

The success of Toys Я Us in Japan should also be pointed out. This involved a series of deregulation measures, especially in the case of the prohibition of large-scale chainstores. The Japanese government was forced to rescind this prohibition after negotiations in which President Bush was said to be directly involved. Very often, foreign-pressure-based changes do not lead to favourable acceptance domestically. However Toys Я Us, to the delight of the United States, achieved annual sales of 70 billion yen within six years, making it the number one toy retailer in Japan. Moreover, the sales revenues of the top 10 domestic toy retailers did not fall. No statistics are available on small and medium-sized retailers who went out of business due to falling sales, but it cannot be denied that Toys'R'Us generated a substantial new demand for toys in Japan.

Antidumping measures and Japan

Japan is vulnerable to foreign dumping charges, as exemplified by the Kodak–Fuji case. How effective is the Japanese government compared with other governments in terms of enforcing the antidumping aspect of its competition policy? The following figures illustrate this point:

Total number of antidumping charges for which investigations were initiated

Initiating country	1969–74	1975–79	1980–84	1985–89	1990–94	1995–98*	Total
US	125	140	146	219	249	75	954
EU	19	55	138	101	147	110	570
Canada	42	74	176	115	90	31	528
Australia	–	120	242	180	252	71	865
Japan	0	0	0	0	4	0	4
Other	39	64	10	74	227	395	809
Total	225	453	712	686	969	682	3730

Source: Compiled from various reports of the WTO Committee on Anti-Dumping practices (1998) available from http://WWW.WTO.ORG.

As can be seen Japan has filed far fewer antidumping cases than other advanced countries – just four to date. Two of these cases involved four countries and antidumping tariffs were applied to two exporting countries. Only one of these tariffs remains in force (that on Pakistani cotton yarn). In contrast investigations were initiated for over 500 cases each by the United States, the EU, Canada and Australia.

More recently the number of cases in which antidumping duties have been imposed has increased, remarkably in South Africa, Korea, India and Argentina. Moreover, since the WTO agreement Asian countries, such as Thailand, Malaysia and Indonesia, have developed and applied antidumping systems, and Brazil, Egypt, Israel, China and Peru have introduced antidumping measures. Tariffs have been reduced and non-tariff barriers such as import restrictions have been removed since the Uruguay Round of GATT and the establishment of the WTO.

Hence not only Asian countries but many other countries around the world seem to be utilizing antidumping measures to protect their domestic industries. On the other hand 80 tariffs, including 50 tariffs by the United States, have been imposed on Japan. The Ministry of International Trade and Industry argues that foreign countries are using antidumping measures as an administrative means of protecting domestic industries, leading to a trade distortion from which Japan is suffering.

The first investigation initiated by Japan took place in 1991 and concerned ferrosilicon-manganese. The highest hurdle when preparing a petition is ascertaining the selling price in the exporting country to determine the normal price. An antidumping tariff was imposed on China because dumping, damage and the casual relationship between the two were confirmed. The measure ended in 1998, as prescribed by the law.

The second case was made against Pakistan in respect of cotton yarn. It took almost two years to submit the case because of the difference between the time when Pakistani imports increased and the time when dumping margins occurred. A tariff was imposed and the measure is scheduled to end in July 2000. In both cases the Japanese government did not start its investigations until solid evidence of dumping was obtained.

Compared with other countries, Japan requires very stringent qualifications on the part of the parties making antidumping petitions to qualify. The parties also require sufficient evidence to back their claims. There is also some arbitrariness in Japanese law with regard to the implementation of antidumping tariffs.

Before the FTC proceeds with antidumping investigations, a responsible project group has to be set up in the relevant ministry. The Japanese government has a negative attitude towards antidumping measures, which it believes are abused by other countries. Therefore petitioners may find that when they take their petitions to the government there is no one to receive them or stamp the date of receipt. Japan's official position at the WTO has been to oppose the abuse of antidumping measures.

It is a national characteristic that Japanese companies try to avoid litigation by all means. In general companies are not sure that petitions are worthwhile, considering the tremendous effort required. Also,

Japanese firms have little information on past antidumping petitions and few experts exist whom the companies can consult about making a petition. For example there are very few Japanese lawyers who are able to handle or even understand the antidumping petition procedure.

In addition to the factors listed above, we should recall that Japan has historically maintained its high economic growth by exporting and has never suffered serious damage from imports. Nevertheless we can imagine that there may have been quite a few potential antidumping cases that Japanese companies had to abandon for the reasons stated above. In fact it is my view that foreign dumping is substantial in Japan and Japan's policy of not dealing with it properly through antidumping procedures may be impeding Japan's economic efficiency.

Since the beginning of 1999 dumping issues involving Japanese products, particularly steel products, have occurred and Latin American countries such as Mexico have filed suits against Japan. Even if Japanese products are not directly involved, measures taken against foreign products cannot be ignored because they set precedents that may be invoked in future situations regarding Japan. In North America, moreover, a decision made by one country often has a significant effect on another country's policies and corporate strategies. The North American Free Trade Agreement started with the aim of achieving free trade in products. This trend has accelerated on a global scale with the success of the WTO and the number of areas that need to be examined has rapidly expanded, including products, services, intellectual property and investments.

This gives rise to a new issue – the relationship between trade and competitive policies. Trade promotion is pursued on the implicit understanding that identical competitive conditions will prevail among the countries concerned. For example if there is a cartel in a certain region or country, a company attempting to enter that region would have to overcome tremendous barriers. The country to which the company belongs would find it difficult to apply its own competition laws outside its territory. Although some countries forcibly apply such laws, internationally coordinated rules are still under development. Competition policies vary among countries. This is why bilateral agreements have been promoted, centring on the United States. The agreement on the US–Japan competition laws that was announced at the US–Japan summit meeting was an extension of this trend. In terms of prices, coordinating competition conditions requires a different approach from that of antidumping policies. Competition laws are designed to prevent the use of predatory pricing to attain an advantageous position in the market. In principle, however, it is in the interest of the consumer if prices are lowered as a result of free competition.

Dumping is a practice where export prices are set lower than those in the exporter's country. The importing country tries to rectify the price imbalance by imposing import duties. This is not necessarily favourable to consumers in the importing country but the importing country weighs corporate protection against consumer benefits. Future measures include coordinating competition policies by eliminating predatory pricing and promoting free competition. However the discussions on this have gone on for a long time and there has been no policy harmonization. Even domestic coordination faces a great deal of difficulty because different ministries are involved and each tends to prioritize its interests over those of others. At the international level, coordination among countries would be even more complicated.

As I have argued, competition and foreign trade are closely intertwined. Consequently at the WTO, where the liberalization and equalization of intcrnational trade is promoted, competition policy must be included on the agenda.

ISSUES INVOLVING THE WTO

The WTO meeting in Seattle had to be adjourned before the adoption of a declaration. What effect will this have on the steel industry? The declaration was expected to include many subjects that were not foreseen when the General Agreement on Tariffs and Trade (GATT) negotiations first began. With the objective of bringing about free trade in products, two major principles were proposed national treatment (treatment applied to imports must not be different, apart from customs duties, from that applied to domestic products of the same kind), and most-favoured nation treatment (favourable treatment to certain counties that must be provided by all member countries).

Initially it was planned that social issues, such as environmental and labour issues, would be added to the agenda of the WTO meeting. It was absurd, however, to think it would be possible to come up with a coordinated declaration against non-governmental organizations (NGOs) and labour unions in such a short period of time. Who has been the greatest beneficiary of the meeting being adjourned without the adoption of a declaration? First, the United States, and in particular the Clinton administration, lost virtually nothing. US steel manufacturing unions conducted a large-scale opposition campaign, being apprehensive about a sharp increase in imports. The WTO, which is supposed to promote free trade, must not allow protectionists to emerge victorious. Second, developing countries and NGOs definitely gained the highest points. In particular NGOs will be actively involved in future WTO activities. It cannot be denied that their campaign has gathered momentum.

However the criticisms raised against the WTO by NGOs must not be taken at face value. NGOs assert that their opinions are supported worldwide, ignoring the fact that GATT has played a crucial role in raising global living standards and revitalizing the global economy. NGOs can only argue at a low level and will become an impediment to the WTO. The WTO is a forum in which benefits should be pursued on a macro scale. It was a political mistake to invite NGOs to such a forum – their opinions should be heard at a separate venue and then incorporated into WTO activities. The Japanese steel industry may be the greatest victim of this mistake. Improvements in areas that are addressed primarily by the WTO must be examined and evaluatedfully. The matter of deterring the United States from filing a series of antidumping suits should have been given the highest priority. What kind of world is it where protectionists emerge victorious from a meeting to promote free trade? The Japanese government is heavily responsible for this, although it made some people happy, in particular those who are influential in the areas of agriculture and fisheries. The losers include those who will suffer from a delay in the liberalization of telecommunications and high-tech industries.

The WTO will weaken if labour issues are involved. Rather the International Labour Organization should take the initiative in respect of labour issues. Impatience and disappointment with the WTO may provide grounds for the establishment of regional free trade agreements. Discussions have already begun with Mexico, to be followed by Korea and Singapore. There is concern, however, that this may lead to the opposite of liberalization of the steel trade. It is time for the WTO to go back to its basic principles.

The WTO will deal with competition factors as well as trade disputes, thus directly affecting our daily lives. Consider the example, of Korean and Japanese liquor taxes. Both Korea and Japan lost their cases, with the WTO intervening in domestic and cultural issues. Undoubtedly the WTO will play an even more important role in determining our standard of living in the future. The problem of competition and foreign trade will gain greater awareness among citizens when competition conditions become applicable on a domestic basis too.

In the Japanese Shochu case, the WTO Dispute Solution Panel recommended that the Japanese government take corrective measures because the difference in tax rates between Shochu and imported whisky amounted to protection and violated the WTO Agreement. This was the first case lost by Japan before the WTO Panel. The Shochu tax rate was duly raised in 1997. It was acknowledged, as the EU, the United States and Canada argued in their petition to the WTO, that Shochu, whisky and other spirits directly compete with one another and are substitutable, and hence it is appropriate to set the tax rate on whisky and other spirits at the same rate as that on Shochu.

Interface between foreign trade and competition

EU and Canada actively support the inclusion of competition policy in the WTO agenda. But as we have seen with the Fujifilm–Kodak dispute, there are difficulties in addressing competition issues even at the regional level. It would be virtually impossible to reach a consensus in a multilateral forum such as the WTO, which has more than 130 member countries. In addition the negative position of the United States is highly influential. There are numerous discrepancies between the competition laws and foreign trade practices of each country, leading to a bureaucratic nightmare. Furthermore, only a few countries have established competition laws and hence competition issues cannot be generally discussed as a part of an international agreement.

My personal view is that, at the WTO level, efforts should be made to reach a generalised, perhaps superficial agreement. In parallel with this, mutual agreements on the implementation of competition laws may be made on a bilateral or interregional basis. This way, problems will be identified during the course of discussions. In particular, a consensus on the problem of cartels and monopolists could easily be achieved. This problem causes substantial damage to foreign trade, which in turn affects the interests of citizens. Differences in the interpretation and application of competition laws in various counties will grow due to the expansion of international trade. It is vital for individual countries' competition law agencies to cooperate with one another. If international agreements can be reached on these points, the effort to achieve WTO-level agreements will be rewarded.

Once competition policy is incorporated at the WTO level, the next step will be for the WTO to tackle dumping. Japanese companies should be aware of the role and impact of the WTO when formulating their global strategies. This would be a step forward for Japan as a nation that has never signed a free trade agreement with any other country.

Reference

WTO (1998) *Various Reports* http://www.WTO.ORG (Geneva: WTO Committee on Anti-Dumping Practices).

Part V
Japanese Business Practices

11 Japan's Business Groups

David Flath

Business groups have been an important feature of Japan's industrial organization since at least the beginning of the 20th century. As early as the 1870s there had already emerged the Yasuda banking complex, Mitsubishi shipping conglomerate and Mitsui trading company, all of which later became the cornerstones of the vast commercial empires known as the *zaibatsu*, precursors of the current-day financial *keiretsu*. Each *zaibatsu* consisted of disparate firms, including banks, trading companies and manufacturing concerns, much of whose stock reposed in a common holding company *qua* head-office, which was itself controlled by a wealthy family. In Japan's First World War boom the *zaibatsu* expanded from their initial strongholds in mining, banking and the brokerage of foreign trade into new and diverse activities, including shipbuilding, iron and steel, and insurance. Nevertheless, in the 1920s and 1930s more than one half of the Japanese labour force continued to work in very small enterprises or were self-employed. Also, many of the large leading firms including cotton-spinning firms, remained outside the *zaibatsu* orbit and were diffusely held. The *zaibatsu* form of organization, in which a few families maintained concentrated ownership of diverse commercial holdings, was never the only viable way of financing and administering businesses in Japan.

After the end of the Second World War the US occupation authorities directed the dismantling of the *zaibatsu*. This included the divestiture of share interlocks, the dissolution and abolition of holding companies, and the appropriation and disbursement of shares held by the *zaibatsu* families. But by 1960 many of the constituent companies of the major *zaibatsu* had reestablished their earlier alliances. The new groups, known as the financial *keiretsu*, include many of the largest publicly owned corporations in Japan. At the centre of each of the six financial *keiretsu* is a single commercial bank, which is the largest debtholder and a significant stockholder in most of the other large firms affiliated with the group. In some ways these banks fulfil the same economic role of monitoring investments that the founding families undertook in the *zaibatsu*.

ZAIBATSU

Each *zaibatsu* (lit. 'property agglomeration') was a set of interrelated and interlocked commercial enterprises, closely held by the same family. The four most prominent *zaibatsu* – Mitsui, Mitsubishi, Yasuda and Sumitomo – had different origins, but the founding families of each of them acquired existing enterprises and established new ones throughout the Meiji era, all the while maintaining close ownership and ultimately consolidating controlling share interests in a family-owned holding company. As their commercial empires expanded, the *zaibatsu* families exercised control by selecting and monitoring the professional managers of the constituent enterprises.

The *zaibatsu* founders are as famous in Japan, and were as colourful, as their American equivalents and contemporaries: Carnegie, Rockefeller and Vanderbilt. The founder of the Mitsubishi *zaibatsu*, Iwasaki Yatarō (1834–85), started as the manager of a trading company set up in his home province (in Shikoku). After the Restoration the trading company and its ancillary ocean shipping fleet reverted to Iwasaki's private ownership. By providing ships for military expeditions, including the Taiwan expedition[1] and the Satsuma rebellion, Iwasaki eventually garnered generous government favours, subsidies and protection while artfully evading onerous government restrictions on his operations. By the time of Iwasaki's death in 1885 the Mitsubishi Mail Steamship Company was the largest and most profitable shipping line in Japan and had provided the necessary capital to purchase from the government the Takashima Coal Mine and Nagasaki Shipyard. In the ensuing decades the expanding Mitsubishi empire successively came under the direction of Iwasaki's brother, son and grandson. The last of these, Iwasaki Koyata (1879–1946), who directed the Mitsubishi *zaibatsu* from 1916 to 1945, was particularly able.

Both the Mitsui and the Sumitomo *zaibatsu* had as antecedents merchant houses founded in the late 17th century. Each owed its successful metamorphosis into a leading *zaibatsu* to the agency of hired managers with business acumen and political connections. The house of Mitsui operated dry goods shops in Edo and Osaka and dealt in currency exchange, including the discounting of government notes based on rice collected in taxes and stored in Osaka warehouses. Under the direction of Minomura Rizaemon (1821–77), hired by the eight Mitsui founding families to manage their affairs (a post referred to as *bantō*, lit. 'clerk'), the house of Mitsui performed lucrative banking services for the Meiji government, eventually leading to the establishment of the Mitsui Bank in 1876. The other Mitsui businesses at first fared less well under the new regime, but this began to change when in 1876 a collateral branch of the Mitsui family acquired a new company with influential political connections, renaming it Mitsui Bussan (lit. 'Mitsui products').

Government procurement and marketing contracts soon brought a stream of profits from foreign transactions, for example selling the coal from government mines to China, obtaining provisions abroad for Japan's new conscript army and so on. In 1888 Mitsui Bussan acquired the government's Miike Coal Mine, the beginning of extensive diversification. In 1892 the founders of Mitsui Bussan were welcomed back to the Mitsui fold, combining Mitsui Bank and its related enterprises with Mitsui Bussan under the joint control of eleven families. As Japan's cotton textile industry boomed in the last decade of the 19th century and first decade of the 20th Mitsui Bussan's business also expanded and it soon integrated itself into ocean shipping. By 1910 the company, in addition to its substantial domestic business, was brokering one fifth of Japan's exports and a sixth of its imports.

The Sumitomo family had specialized in copper trading and operated the shogunate's Besshi Copper Mine (in Shikoku) from 1691. After the restoration, Hirose Saihei (1828–1914), the delegated agent (*bantō*) of the Sumitomo family, persuaded the *dajokan* that the Besshi Copper Mine belonged to the family rather than to the government. Hirose successfully adapted superior foreign technology for use in the mine and developed effective channels of foreign trade, but resisted diversification of Sumitomo investments into banking and finance until his forced retirement in 1894.

Yasuda Zenjirō (1838–1921)[2] amassed a personal fortune as a moneychanger during the chaotic final years of the shogunate, then parlayed it further while a fiscal agent of the Meiji government. He used his wealth to found a banking empire that became the Yasuda *zaibatsu*, which was never as involved in industry as the other major *zaibatsu*.

Table A11.1 in the appendix to this chapter shows the four major *zaibatsu*'s principal enterprises as well as the date each was founded or acquired. The entries give a fair representation of the pattern of *zaibatsu* development. Each of them began in the 1870s or 1880s in a specific industry or activity, as already mentioned:

- Mitsui: banking and brokerage of international trade.
- Mitsubishi: shipping.

- Yasuda: banking.
- Sumitomo: copper mining.

Profits in the original *zaibatsu* lines of business in the 1890s and 1900s financed diversification into related lines:

- Mitsui: mining, textiles, iron and steel.
- Mitsubishi: shipbuilding and mining.
- Yasuda: insurance.
- Sumitomo: banking, coal mining, steel and copper wire.

Japan prospered during the First World War by taking advantage of the wartime boost in world interest rates to switch from net international borrower to net lender, and compounded its gains from doing so by expanding output. During the war boom the major *zaibatsu* reaped immense profits, emerging as the dominant forces in a wide range of industries. By around 1920 the owner families of the major *zaibatsu* had configured their respective commercial empires as disparate enterprises controlled by a holding company, a company whose assets consisted of equity shares in other companies. The principal enterprises so controlled had numerous subsidiaries.

Some idea of the overall place of the major *zaibatsu* in the economy can be gauged by the number of firms in the *zaibatsu* orbits and their paid-in capital. Paid-in capital refers to the cumulative receipts from the issue of equity shares and represents a crude measure of the economic scale of enterprise at best, but it does afford an approximate meter of the major *zaibatsu*'s importance in the economy. In 1928 the paid-in capital of the 191 firms in the orbit of the big four zaibatsu totalled 1,936 million yen, 15.2 per cent of the total paid-in capital of all Japanese firms (Nakamura, 1971). In the 1920s employment and output were still rather heavily concentrated in agriculture and textile manufacturing, neither of which much engaged the *zaibatsu*. In the remaining sectors the *zaibatsu* must have been rather dominating.

The distinguishing feature of the *zaibatsu* was their close control by the founding families. By this criterion there existed *zaibatsu* other than the four major ones, including Furukawa, Asano, Ōkura, Suzuki, Nomura, Fujita, Yasukawa, Kawasaki, Iwai and Kuhara. Behind each of them was an entrepreneur-founder,[3] who used success with one enterprise as a basis for branching into others, all the while maintaining close control. We can differentiate the *zaibatsu* from the numerous enterprises in Japan that were also closely held but did not spawn other ventures.[4] We can further differentiate the *zaibatsu* from diversified businesses that were not closely held including the so-called 'new *zaibatsu*', spawned by military procurement spending in the 1920s and 1930s and coaxed by the army into investing in the occupied areas, beginning with Manchuria.

The hostilities in Manchuria led in February 1932 to the creation of a new state, known as Manchukuo, with a puppet government completely subordinate to Japanese influence, a move that was condemned by the League of Nations and precipitated Japan's withdrawal from that body in March 1933. Later that year an economic construction programme for Manchukuo placed key industries under state control, each a government monopoly, managed by the Japanese army. Despite the army's best efforts, central planning of colonial enterprises proved disastrously ineffective in Machukuo and in 1936 the army invited private firms to enter the region with government guarantees. These so called 'new *zaibatsu*' included Nippon Sangyō (the antecedent of today's Nissan) and Nakajima Aircraft (the antecedent of Fuji heavy industries).[5] The new *zaibatsu* were diffusely held rather than closely controlled by their founders. In this sense the new *zaibatsu* can be distinguished from the others; they were in fact not *zaibatsu* at all. The new *zaibatsu* prospered on the basis of government procurement contracts and special subsidies, not on entrepreneurship and business acumen. Other than Nissan and Fuji Heavy Industries, few survived the Pacific War.

The economic rationale behind the *zaibatsu* form of organization

Close ownership was not an inevitable feature of business in Japan at the end of the 19th century and first half of the 20th. The numerous large cotton spinning companies were diffusely held and remained outside the orbit of the *zaibatsu*. The same was true of the private railways that predated the 1906 railway nationalization in Japan. The *zaibatsu* enterprises could also have chosen to be diffusely held, enabling the owner-families more fully to diversify their wealth portfolios, but the families chose to maintain close control, perhaps because the particular advantages of close control were more pronounced, or because the costs were lower in the industries in which the *zaibatsu* emerged than in others.

The advantages of close ownership reside in the superior economic incentives to monitor managers that close ownership entails. Such monitoring benefits all shareholders in proportion to their holdings.

Small shareholders have little to gain from actively aligning the interests of corporate managers with their own interest and rationally defer to large shareholders who have more of their own wealth at stake. Diffuse shareholding is viable where other considerations, such as the possibility of interruption or termination of managers' careers due to company bankruptcy or adverse labour market reputation effects, adequately constrain managerial behaviour without the active intervention of shareholders. To the extent that *zaibatsu* enterprises prospered because they were closely held firms, rather than in spite of that fact, they must not have exhibited the aforementioned characteristics.

The principal economic cost of maintaining concentrated share interests arose from the risk entailed in holding an incompletely diversified wealth portfolio. It was very natural, if not inevitable, that specialists in close ownership of companies were be the wealthiest investors, for they could attain a significant diversification of personal wealth even while maintaining large blocks of stock in specific enterprises. Not all *zaibatsu* prospered. Notable failures included Furukawa and Suzuki, neither of which survived the financial crises of the 1920s, which illustrates that the *zaibatsu* fortunes were indeed subject to a degree of risk.

Dissolution of the *zaibatsu*

The owners and managers of Japan's *zaibatsu* incurred the special wrath of the US occupation authorities. US antagonism was directed towards the founding families and leaders of both the original *zaibatsu* and the 'new *zaibatsu*'. To put it bluntly, in 1945 Americans embraced the notion that Japanese industrialists bore special responsibility for Japan's turn towards military government and armed aggression in the 1930s. In retrospect this attitude seems to have emanated from passions aroused by the war itself rather than from objective consideration of the facts. The principal *zaibatsu*, Mitsui and Mitsubishi in particular, had actually maintained close connections with the major political parties during the 1920s: the *seiyūkai* and *kenseikai-minseitō*. Hence the military fanatics who wrested control of the Japanese government from the political parties after 1932 would hardly have been the natural allies of Mitsui and Mitsubishi. The new *zaibatsu* did enjoy a close association with the Japanese armed forces, and initially profited from that association. Most of the new *zaibatsu* were effectively dissolved by the forced transfer of assets held outside Japan to the governments of the nations formerly occupied by Japanese troops, including the colonies of Taiwan and Korea, which were declared independent at the war's end. But the two largest new *zaibatsu*, Nissan and Nakajima, also had numerous installations in Japan itself.

The measures directed at the owners and managers of Japan's large industrial firms proceeded in three steps: (1) expropriation of all the securities holdings of designated individuals and companies (the latter including all the *zaibatsu* holding companies and their leading affiliates), dissolution of the main holding companies and the sale of shares in the remaining companies to individuals other than Members of the *zaibatsu* founding families or top managers; (2) purge of management personnel; and (3) forced liquidation of selected tangible assets of particular large companies. The last two of these steps became politically controversial in the United States itself and were scaled back as a result. The first step was fully implemented.[6]

As a result of consultations between the Supreme Commander of the Allied Powers (SCAP) and Japanese government officials, in November 1945 the Japanese cabinet proposed a law, enacted with modifications by the Diet in April 1946, that mandated the formation of a Holding Company Liquidation Commission to oversee the expropriation and redistribution of corporate equities. This commission expropriated all the securities held by 56 designated *zaibatsu* family members[7] and all the securities held by 83 designated companies, including the main holding companies and leading subsidiaries of the big four *zaibatsu* (Mitsui, Mitsubishi, Sumitomo and Yasuda), four of the lesser *zaibatsu* (Asano, Okura, Furukawa and Nomura) and the two largest new *zaibatsu* (Nissan and Nakajima). The main holding companies, nexus of family control of the original *zaibatsu*, were all dissolved. The expropriated shares of companies that were not dissolved were mostly sold to the public through underwriting dealers between May 1948 and December 1950. Finally, other companies in which the 83 designated companies had held a 10 per cent or greater share (1120 companies in all) were required by SCAP in 1949 to divest their own stock holdings in all other companies, eliminating the remaining vestiges of *zaibatsu* shareholding interlocks.

SCAP also initiated political and economic purges. In January 1946 SCAP issued a directive barring selected present and former political, military and bureaucratic officials from political or government posts. This involved more than 200 000 persons, including about 180 000 former military officers. In January 1947, in conformity with the US position that industrialists also bore responsibility for Japan's military aggression, 1535 officers of 28 government economic organs, about

60 industry control associations, 53 private economic associations and 283 private companies (85 of which had been based in Manchuria, Taiwan, Korea and elsewhere), including most of the larger companies in the orbit of the original *zaibatsu* or new *zaibatsu* (all during the period 1937–45), were identified by name and barred from holding any of the vacated positions in any of the companies for 10 years.[8] Finally, in January 1948 a similar purge was extended to the members of *zaibatsu* founding families and 2798 additional persons who, before the war's end, had held high-level managerial positions in an extended list of 1681 companies.[9] All these individuals were initially barred from any of the vacated positions for 10 years. But this 10-year limit on purgee activity was ultimately much shortened for most of the individuals affected, for in May, June and July 1951 the Japanese government, with the approval of SCAP, removed the restrictions on about half of the political purgees and nearly all of the economic purgees, including all of the *zaibatsu* family members. Even though the economic purges were short-lived, they resulted in the elevation of young and vigorous junior executives to top-level managerial positions in nearly all of Japan's leading companies. Many have suggested that this was a blessing in disguise as thereafter most companies in Japan voluntarily adopted a relatively low mandatory retirement age (55 years), institutionalizing the elevation of the young to top positions.

SCAP's original attempt at the widespread reorganization of large Japanese firms was derailed at about the same time as the purges were overturned. The policy and its ultimate denouement are worth a line or two. SCAP had already (in July 1947) forced the liquidation of most of the assets of Japan's two large trading companies, Mitsui Trading Company and Mitsubishi Trading Company, immediately spawning more than 200 much smaller successor companies. The next step was to empower the Holding Company Liquidation Commission (HCLC) to extend similar measures to Japan's other large companies. At the behest of SCAP, in December 1947 the Diet enacted a law empowering the HCLC to order the divestiture of tangible assets of any firm judged by it as having an 'excessive concentration of economic power'. And in February 1948, after close consultation with SCAP, the HCLC publicly identified 325 companies as targets for reorganization under the new statute.

This deconcentration policy differed fundamentally from the *zaibatsu* dissolution and economic purge in that its aim was not punishment but wealth redistribution, to allow wider economic opportunity for the smaller rivals of large firms. Perhaps this is why, unlike the measures directed specifically at the *zaibatsu*, this one became politically controversial in the United States. How could large firms in Japan have an unfair advantage over smaller rivals unless an analogous statement also applied to large firms in the United States? This was a policy to nip in the bud before it could be grafted on home soil. *Newsweek* magazine editorialized against the deconcentration policy, and US Senator William Knowland of California, with a critical eye on MacArthur's candidacy in the 1948 Republican presidential primaries, spoke out against it.[10] Both *Newsweek* and Senator Knowland argued, among other things, that by impeding economic reconstruction, the deconcentration measure and the economic purge might prolong or enlarge the burden on US taxpayers of humanitarian aid for Japan. Ultimately, between May and June 1949, the HCLC directed that 11 large Japanese companies be reorganized into 26 smaller ones, that two other companies divest their factories and that five other companies divest their securities.[11] None of this had much effect on market concentration in Japan,[12] and in 1954 the surviving remnants of the Mitsui Trading Company and the Mitsubishi Trading Company were reamalgamated. These two resumed their dominant positions in the brokerage of Japan's foreign trade, and they have also come to play a major role in the intermediation of funds to small and medium-sized Japanese businesses. So it appears that *zaibatsu* dissolution was the only one of the occupation era policies significantly to alter Japan's industrial organization, an alteration that was not necessarily for the better.

Zaibatsu dissolution disrupted an effective mechanism of corporate governance, based on concentrated ownership in holding companies and the pyramiding of control through interlocking shareholding. This probably had a detrimental effect on the performance of the affected firms. For instance Yishay Yafeh (1995) has shown that the greater the percentage of a firm's outstanding shares that were expropriated and resold by the HCLC, all else remaining equal, the worse its performance during the years 1951 and 1953.[13] To this extent, *zaibatsu* dissolution retarded Japan's economic recovery from the war rather than hastening it. But the disruption of corporate governance was only temporary. Soon after the occupation ended, and continuing until about 1960, many of the firms previously affiliated with the major *zaibatsu* or the successors of such firms reestablished their old shareholding interlocks. The large commercial banks among these firms became major stockholders in most of the other members of their respective reconstituted groups, playing the same role in investment monitoring and enterprise governance that was once performed by the zaibatsu founding families. None of the founding families of the *zaibatsu* ever reasserted a controlling interest in any of these reconstituted business groups, which today are known as the financial *keiretsu*, and under the Antimonopoly Law enacted by the Diet at the behest of SCAP in April 1947 (amended in June 1949 and again in September 1953) holding companies were prohibited.[14]

FINANCIAL *KEIRETSU*

By the early 1960s many of the companies previously associated with each of the four major *zaibatsu* had reestablished shareholding ties with one another. These groups are widely referred to as the financial *keiretsu*, or just *keiretsu* (but be warned that in Japanese the word *keiretsu* is also used to refer to other business groups, including subcontracting groups and directed marketing channels). *Keiretsu* defies exact translation, although a literal rendering into English might be 'succession', in the sense of a sequence of entities joined together as links in a chain. Besides the progeny of the big four *zaibatsu* – Mitsui, Mitsubishi, Sumitomo and Fuyo (formerly Yasuda) – the six financial *keiretsu* include the Dai-Ichi Kangyo group, consisting mainly of former members of the smaller Kawasaki and Furukawa *zaibatsu*, and the Sanwa group, which has no prewar antecedent.

There are different ways of ascertaining which companies belong to which financial *keiretsu*. The clearest evidence of affiliation is appearance on the roster of monthly 'presidents' club' meetings for any one of the six respective groups. These rosters are public, though the agendas of the meetings are not. The presidents' club members, as of October 1995, are listed by *keiretsu* affiliation and industry classification in Table A11.2 at the end of this chapter. A few companies belong to more than one presidents' club – Hitachi belongs to three – but these are rare exceptions. The rosters of the presidents' clubs change little from one year to the next, and the changes that do occur are mostly the result of mergers. Altogether the membership of the six presidents' clubs in 1995 ran to 185 companies, including most but not all of the largest companies in Japan. Some of the large companies not on the rosters of presidents' clubs include Honda Motors, Matsushita, Sony and Fujifilm.

The presidents' club companies span a wide variety of industries. In fact the economist Miyazaki Yoshikazu famously characterized the financial *keiretsu* as organized on the basis of the 'complete-set principle' (*wan setto shugi*), that is, each of them was composed of at least one company in each major industry.[15] It is readily apparent from Table A11.2 that in industry after industry the members of the differing financial *keiretsu* compete with one another. For instance Toyota, Mitsubishi Motors, Nissan, Daihatsu and Isuzu are each affiliated with a different *keiretsu*. Kirin Brewery belongs to the Mitsubishi presidents' club, but Sapporo Breweries belongs to the Fuyo presidents' club. There are many similar examples. The financial *keiretsu* are not simply cartels of coalitions of suppliers of similar products. Rather they are suppliers of differing products, and in many instances fellow members of the same presidents' club trade with one another. Japan's Fair Trade Commission has periodically surveyed the extent of transactions between fellow members. In 1980 it reported that 20 per cent of the sales of presidents' club manufacturing firms were to members of the same clubs, and 12 per cent of purchases were from fellow club members.[16] These are all very large companies, most of whose transactions are probably with smaller firms, outside the presidents' clubs, so the above Fair Trade Commission data does suggest a disposition towards trade between fellow members of the same financial *keiretsu*.

Presidents' club members borrow principally but not exclusively from fellow members. The single largest lender to each of them is usually the city bank that belongs to the same presidents' club as the company itself. In the usual pattern, loans from the presidents' club city bank account for 10–20 per cent of a fellow club member's total outstanding debt. The presidents' club trust bank holds another 5–10 per cent of each fellow member's debt and the life insurance company 1–5 per cent. The balance of a typical presidents' club company's total borrowing is from outside the group, including from financial members of other presidents' clubs than the one of affiliation. Presidents' club members also borrow from the three long-term credit banks, city banks not affiliated with the six financial *keiretsu* and regional banks. Since 1980 large Japanese companies have been allowed access to international financial markets as a source of funds, but still rely quite heavily upon domestic loans.

Another visible linkage among fellow presidents' club members is cross-shareholding. The average proportions of outstanding shares held within the respective clubs in 1997 were Sumitomo 22.2 per cent, Mitsubishi 27.3 per cent, Dai-Ichi Kango 11.3 per cent, Sanwa 15.8 per cent, Mitsui 15.1 per cent and Fuyo 15.5 per cent, but about half of these shares were held by the financial institutions of the respective groups. The Antimonopoly Law of Japan limits the extent of shares that banks and insurance companies may hold in any one company. Since 1987 this limit has been set at 5 per cent for banks and 7 per cent for insurance companies. Few banks or insurance companies hold share interests approaching these limits. The shareholding of banks in the companies to which they lend is an important aspect of Japan's bank-centred system of financial intermediation. In any case there does seem to be a bit more to the presidents' clubs than financial intermediation.

About one third of the (non-ordered) pairs of non-financial companies belonging to the same presidents' club are directly linked with one another by cross-shareholding, and in about half of these instances the cross-shareholding is reciprocal. Typically the share interest of any one presidents' club company in another is around 1 per cent. In other words the cross-shareholding ties are usually insufficient to confer a controlling interest. Cross-shareholding between non-financial members of different presidents' clubs is rare. A convincing explanation for cross-shareholding between non-financial firms – that they may be trading partners – would go a long way towards explaining the *raison d'être* of the financial *keiretsu* themselves, and indeed that of the other business groups in Japan.

The financial *keiretsu* occupy a sizeable niche in the Japanese economy. Together the six presidents' clubs in 1997 accounted for about one eighth of the sales of non-financial businesses, one seventh of paid-

Table 11.1   Scale of *keiretsu* presidents' club companies, excluding banks and insurance companies, in relation to the Japanese economy, 1997 (percentage of respective totals for all industrial companies in Japan, 2.4 million companies in all)

	Employees	Assets	Paid-in capital	Sales	Operating profit	Net profit
Mitsui	0.62	2.05	2.36	2.27	3.45	5.78
Mitsubishi	0.52	1.87	2.16	1.89	1.22	1.23
Sumitomo	0.29	1.17	1.51	1.43	1.06	0.73
Fuyo	0.68	1.97	2.67	2.10	1.87	0.00
Sanwa	0.89	2.50	3.05	2.41	2.40	2.88
Dai-Ichi Kangyo	1.03	3.32	3.55	3.60	2.99	2.80
All six	3.37	11.47	13.54	12.16	12.06	11.96

Source: Calculated using data from Toyo Keizai (1999, p. 33).

in capital and one eighth of net profits. These and other data, broken down for each of the six financial *keiretsu*, are presented in Table 11.1. Attempts have been made to broaden the classification of financial *keiretsu* beyond the rosters of the presidents' clubs by identifying all the important loan clients of the presidents' club banks, and identifying the broader web of cross-shareholdings linking presidents' club members to other companies. By focusing only on club members we may grossly understate their scale in relation to the Japanese economy.

ENTERPRISE GROUPS

The financial *keiretsu* are not the sole identifiable business groups in Japan. There also exist groups of firms that orbit around large industrial companies. These might be referred to as enterprise groups, but there is no standard term for them, and in Japanese the term *kigyō shudan* (lit., 'enterprise group') is also, somewhat confusingly, used to refer to the financial *keiretsu*. Here, we shall reserve the term enterprise group for this other category, a number of which are listed in the Table A11.3. Quite a few of the 40 firms identified there as leaders of enterprise groups are themselves members of a *keiretsu* presidents' club.

Enterprise groups generally include a myriad of subsidiaries as well as independent subcontractors and other suppliers, and some also include wholesalers and retailers of the group's products. Trading ties within the respective enterprise groups may be presumed to be considerably more extensive than is generally the case with the financial *keiretsu*. Also, the number of shares held by the enterprise group leader in the other members is typically large enough to confer *de facto* control, not merely a silent financial interest. The enterprise groups are more tightly knit than the financial *keiretsu*.

The combined assets of the 40 enterprise groups listed in Table A11.3 approached 10 per cent of the total assets of all industrial firms in Japan in 1994. In other words the scale of the 40 largest enterprise groups roughly corresponds to that of all the industrial members of the presidents' clubs of the six financial *keiretsu*.

THE ECONOMICS OF CROSS-SHAREHOLDING

Attempts to understand the economic rationale behind Japan's business groups have principally focused on cross-shareholding. The advantages of banks holding stock in the firms to which they lend are fairly well understood.[17] About half of the cross-shareholding within financial *keiretsu* presidents' clubs is of this sort, and roughly mirrors the pattern of lending by the banks. But bank stockholding in client firms is not confined to the financial *keiretsu*. For instance the smaller (regional) banks also hold clients' stock. Bank stockholding in client firms appears not to be a defining characteristic of the financial *keiretsu*. In fact the *zaibatsu* antecedents of the financial *keiretsu* predate Japan's bank-centred system of financial intermediation.

In the preceding discussion we speculated that the *zaibatsu* evolved as an efficient mode of corporate governance in selected industries, such as mining, trading and banking, in which close monitoring of managerial decisions was relatively productive. Consolidating their controlling share interests in close holding companies enabled the wealthy families of *zaibatsu* founders to monitor enterprise managers and capture the rewards from doing so. With the 1948 dissolution of the *zaibatsu* holding companies and the deconcentration of shareholding, governance of the former members of the *zaibatsu* was thrown into disarray. However, the enterprises had accumulated a number of valuable assets, including knowledgeable teams of employees, so perpetuation of the enterprises as going concerns was worthwhile.

One interpretation of the postwar reconfiguration of *zaibatsu* enterprises into the financial *keiretsu* is that it in some way established a new mechanism of corporate governance. Eleanor Hadley, an economist on MacArthur's staff during the early occupation era who had helped to implement the *zaibatsu* dissolution, later argued in an influential monograph that in the financial *keiretsu* the large city banks had essentially taken on the same role as that of the holding companies in the *zaibatsu*.[18] As banks became the dominant financial intermediaries – a consequence of particular regulations on the Japanese financial markets – it was natural that they should insinuate themselves into corporate governance. If this is true, then the organization of firms into bank-centred financial groups will have served an important purpose. Because companies belonging to the same group had ongoing dealings with one another, banks' information on each of them was improved if the same bank closely monitored them all. For many students of the subject this is a satisfactory explanation of the financial *keiretsu*. And tied as the explanation is to the unique history of *zaibatsu* evolution and dissolution, it answers the question of why groups like the financial *keiretsu* did not develop in the United States or other nations. But there remain puzzles. For example why are industrial members of a presidents' club so often linked to one another by cross-shareholding?

A leading explanation of *keiretsu* cross-shareholding (not altogether convincing) is that its purpose is to forestall any hostile takeover, the amassing of a controlling share interest by an outside investor that is opposed by the incumbent managers of the company. In one interpretation the prevention of such takeovers is merely in the selfish interests of the companys' managers, not necessarily in the interests of the company's shareholders.[19] In a more sophisticated version of the argument, the prevention of takeovers actually enhances the value of the firm by protecting the firm's long-term contracts from abrogation.[20] Takeovers are indeed quite rare events in Japan, but almost certainly not because company shares lie in the hands of fellow group members. For one thing, even companies outside the orbit of business groups in Japan are seldom acquired by other companies or outside investors. Takeovers, and the threat of takeovers, are simply not an important aspect of corporate governance in Japan.[21] And in the United States, where takeovers are frequent occurrences, many indisputable examples of takeover defences have been observed but the self-organization of firms into cross-shareholding groups is not among them. So if cross-shareholding in Japan is not to forestall hostile takeovers what is its purpose?

An explanation, developed by the author, is that cross-shareholding slants the terms of trade between two firms in favour of the firm in which shares are held, and so gives the other firm a way of penalizing it (by divesting the stock) should things go wrong, but trade between the two continues.[22] Bargainers may be presumed to set the terms of trade in such a way that they divide the gains equally. But if one firm holds stock in the other, then its own gains include a share interest in the other's gains. Consequently, equal division of the gains from trade actually enriches the party in which shares are held by the other, relative to the case in which there is no cross-shareholding. A small share interest in a trading partner might in this way impart a small bias to the terms of trade that is narrowly disadvantageous to the shareholder, but this can serve a useful purpose: it forces the other party to observe otherwise unenforceable stipulations. For instance presidents' club members may pay slightly higher prices when buying from fellow members in which they hold stock than if they purchase from outsiders, but they are assured of special consideration in terms of quality, service, truthful revelation of private information and the like, by the implicit threat that the stockholder will divest the stock if it ever becomes dissatisfied.

This explanation for cross-shareholding among presidents' club members is rather speculative, but it may explain why cross-shareholding is more likely to link trading partners than others (there is some evidence that it does).[23] It may also explain why cross-shareholding is often insufficient to confer anything other than a silent financial interest. The explanation does not account for the configuration of trading partners into (nearly) mutually exclusive, share-interlocked groups. So to account for the very existence of the financial *keiretsu*, we still need to invoke the fact that each of the large banks at the centre of each group economizes by insinuating itself into the governance of a set of mutually interacting companies, rather than unrelated ones. The existence in Japan of mutually interacting groups of firms owes a lot to the fact that, historically, each *zaibatsu* group of large companies was controlled by the same wealthy family. The Sanwa financial *keiretsu*, lacking any *zaibatsu* antecedent, remains something of an anomaly. In further explaining the many peculiar features of the financial *keiretsu*, historical inquiries and detailed case studies may prove helpful.[24]

The enterprise groups pose a different set of challenges for economists. Here the central issue is vertical integration.

VERTICAL INTEGRATION

Each enterprise group represents a less vertically integrated structure than would be the case if all its activities were organized within a single firm, but more vertically integrated than if each constituent enterprise was completely independent of the others, and not a subsidiary of the group leader or controlled directly by it. Vertical integration refers to the incorporation of successive steps of a production process within the same organization. Here production is defined in the broadest possible terms, including, for instance, the wholesaling and retailing of a product as well as its manufacture. The question of what determines the extent of vertical integration in an economy lies at the core of industrial organization, and also at the intellectual frontiers of it.

Because of the complicated web of technology, in which the output of each industry is also a productive input in every industry, complete vertical integration would require the entire economy to consist of a single enterprise, in which case it would become a command or centrally planned economy. The opposite extreme, the complete absence of vertical integration, would require each individual in the economy to be self-employed, his or her production behaviour being coordinated with that of others only through a decentralized price system. Economy-wide vertical integration (central planning) is cumbersome and wasteful of resources, as evidenced by its abject failure in every state in which it has been attempted. Yet the spontaneous self-organization of production into partially vertically integrated structures called business firms is a ubiquitous feature of every market economy.

If central planning at the national level wastes resources, then how can central planning on a small scale, which is the nature of a business firm, conserve resources? The Nobel laureate Ronald Coase long ago gave a definitive answer to this question.[25] Just as there are costs of directing production that can be avoided by allowing the price system to coordinate things, so too are there costs of employing a price system, avoidable by direct administration. The costs of employing a price system are the costs of activities that are either essential to trade or that facilitate trade in some way. Such activities include the search for a trading partner, negotiation of mutually agreeable terms of trade, assurance of ownership rights in the traded items, evaluation of the characteristics of the traded items, and so on. Advertising, negotiation, search and enforcement of exclusive ownership rights are all costly activities that can be dispensed with within a firm (not between firms), and so firms can be economical ways of organizing production, even though establishing and administering a firm gives rise to new costs.

In the market economy, the greater the costs of transacting through the price system and the lower the costs of administering a directed system of production, the further that vertical integration will proceed. One influence on the costs of transacting is the extent of the market. If a market is too small to allow middlemen to be profitable, or too small to allow more than a few sellers of similar goods to be profitable, then monopolistic distortions and limited gains from specialization in the costly activities that facilitate trading, elevate the costs of transacting and favour more complete vertical integration than would otherwise obtain. To put it another way, the division of labour is limited by the extent of the market.[26]

Vertically integrated production units are characteristic of a small economy with a limited demand for final products, not a large economy.

Japan's economy has grown large compared with those of most other nations, and so might have been expected to attain a quite decentralized organization of production. Whether the enterprise groups represent such a structure depends on the object of comparison. The Japanese car manufacturers that lead enterprise groups are clearly less vertically integrated than even their US counterparts. For instance Toyota relies on an extensive network of subcontractors to supply parts such as those which General Motors manufactures itself. Yet in thinking of the ways in which the Toyota group and Japan's other enterprise groups represent a more directed vertical structure than conceivable alternatives, one should be mindful of the added transaction costs that invariably accompany an expanded division of labour.

not vertically integrated

DO JAPAN'S BUSINESS GROUPS INEFFICIENTLY IMPEDE FOREIGN FIRMS' ENTRY TO THE JAPANESE MARKET?

The UCLA economist Harold Demsetz has argued with characteristic persuasiveness that the expression 'barrier to entry' in any sense relevant for public policy must refer to an inefficient organization of industry.[27] Some economically efficient arrangements may well contribute to industrial concentration or the entrenchment of incumbents. Japan's business groups perhaps represent such a structure, one that is economically efficient even if it impedes the entry of foreign firms into the Japanese market. Robert Lawrence's essay, 'Efficient or Exclusionist? The Import Behavior of Japanese Corporate Groups', poses a false dichotomy.[28]

Be that as it may, it is self-evident to many that the business groups do impede foreign sales in Japan. It should not be. The members of groups, both the financial *keiretsu* and enterprise groups, are inclined towards long and persistent trading with one another. When customers are loyal in this way to incumbents, entry will at first require a greater sacrifice but is also likely to be worth that sacrifice. The net effect on actual entry of these two offsetting considerations is ambiguous. Any net impediment to entry here is likely to rest on a first-mover advantage conferred by a general preference by customers for the known and familiar over the unknown. But to return to the crucial issue, even if the business groups do impede entry they may still represent efficient organizations of Japanese industry. For few would suggest that the loyalty of Japanese firms towards members of the same business group is motivated only by the desire to exclude competitors. In fact such 'naked exclusion' would have little basis in the logic of economics.

Customers would typically not agree to stipulations that confer monopoly on an incumbent supplier unless they were compensated in advance for the likely reduction in their own gains from trade that would result from monopoly pricing. But because monopoly pricing reduces customers' gains from trade more than it adds to the monopolist's profits, the compensation required for the customers to consent to foreclosing stipulations exceeds what the incumbent supplier is willing to pay. There are at least two exceptions to this argument. The first, following Rasmussen *et al.*,[29] is that where entry is unprofitable unless some minimum efficient scale is assured, the incumbent supplier need not obtain the consent of all its customers in order to block entry. In this instance, exclusive dealing stipulations can be profitable for the monopolist. The second exception, following Aghion and Bolton,[30] is that if an incumbent monopolist can join with its customers and levy fees on new entrants, they may profit from doing so, and if they do not know the entrants' costs exactly they may inadvertently but unavoidably set fees that block efficient entry.

Neither of these two examples applies to the Japanese business groups. One reason is the absence of monopoly. The financial *keiretsu* each span a broad set of industries in which they compete with one another, and the enterprise groups represent vertical structures in industries that may be oligopolistic at least in some stages, but none of which are virtual monopolies. A second way in which the arguments fail is in the absence of contractual stipulations of the sort specified. Downstream firms are not obliged to pay liquidation damages if they diversify their purchases. Neither would it be a breach of agreement for them so to diversify. Finally, exclusivity simply does not exist. Perhaps the firms have an inclination to patronize fellow group members, but it is not an absolute. The absence of monopoly, of contract and of exclusivity would seem to leave no play for naked exclusion by the business groups. Impediment to entry might well be a consequence but cannot be the fundamental rationale for the organization of Japanese firms into business groups. For that we must turn to the sorts of argument raised in the earlier sections of this chapter based on models of vertical integration, corporate governance and the economics of contracts.

DO JAPAN'S BUSINESS GROUPS HAVE A FUTURE?

The large banks at the core of the financial *keiretsu* have been profoundly and adversely affected by the ongoing deregulation of the Japanese financial markets and the decade of slowed growth and macroeconomic recession. But the implications of the banks' troubles for the viability of the financial *keiretsu* themselves are probably not great, for two reasons. First, the main bank system has shown remarkable resilience and may indeed be revived once the current recession is past. Second, the cross-shareholding, trading ties, common trademarks and all the other manifestations of intragroup cooperation are only tangentially related to financial intermediation anyway. In other words the financial *keiretsu* will still serve an economic purpose even if the main bank system does disappear and the large companies issue securities rather than borrowing from banks. The enterprise groups are even less identified with the main bank system than are the financial *keiretsu*.

The Japanese main bank system refers to a pattern of corporate financing in which Japanese companies have relied far more upon bank loans than upon the issuance of securities as the source of external funds, and in which each company has formed a close and durable relationship with the one bank that perennially is its largest creditor. For the members of the financial *keiretsu* these are typically the large city banks included in the presidents' clubs. But many of the Japanese companies that are not affiliated with a financial *keiretsu* also have main banks. The main bank is not only the leading supplier of loans to a firm but also a significant stockholder that insinuates itself into the governance of the company, dispatching directors for example, and undertaking a most active role in the company's affairs in the event of financial distress.

I suggested earlier that the *keiretsu* configuration of trading partners into (nearly) mutually exclusive, share-interlocked groups owes something to the fact that each of the large banks at the centre of the groups economizes by insinuating itself into the governance of a set of mutually interacting companies, rather than unrelated ones. To state the same point in a slightly different way, the main bank for one member of a financial *keiretsu* is naturally the main bank for all because, given the various group members' active commerce with one another, information about each one's creditworthiness bears on that of the others. This logic can be reversed. That is, information spillovers can be a reason to perpetuate the intragroup trading relationships in that they lower the cost of borrowing. If Japanese companies were to switch away from bank loans and rely instead upon securities markets for external funds, this particular advantage of business groups would disappear.

The main bank system owes a lot to regulations that cartelized and protected the banks and ensured that they would be the primary source of external funds for Japanese corporations.[31] When Japan's regulatory constraints on euromarket finance and domestic bond finance were lifted in the mid 1980s, many observers predicted that the main bank system would unravel. So far this has failed to happen, even in the face of the unprecedented solvency crisis faced by the banks since the 1990–91 fall in Japan's real estate and stock prices. Perhaps the massive infusion of public capital into the major banks has helped to perpetuate the main bank system. Its ultimate fate will not be known until the current recession ends and Japanese corporations again seek increased funds to finance their investments.

Table 11.2 shows the sources of funding for private investment in Japan in recent years. As of the end of December 1997, outstanding private loans to non-financial corporate businesses remained large relative to stocks, bonds and other securities, in spite of the fact that outstanding private loans actually diminished over the period 1995–97. Much of the reduction in outstanding loans may be attributed to the writing off of bad debt from the late 1980s. Between 1992 and 1997 the Japanese banks wrote off 45.7 trillion yen in bad debts.

The recent reduction in outstanding loans has not been accompanied by any significant expansion of outstanding securities. Rather, businesses have foregone added external funding of all kinds. This is depicted graphically in Figure 11.1. Journalists and other analysts have argued that the astringency of external funding, and of bank loans in particular, has caused the stagnation of private investment since 1990 that is also evident in the figure. But such a 'credit crunch' must not exist, for if it did then interest rates in Japan would be high, yet the opposite is manifestly true. In September 1998 the call rate reached the astonishingly low level of 0.25 per cent, while the short-term prime lending rate stood at 1.625 per cent and the long-term prime rate at 2.5 per cent. It appears that the demand for external funds, and not the supply, must be temporarily low in Japan. Only after private investment revives will we learn whether the Japanese banks have finally retained their place as the dominant source of external funds and the main bank system can persist.

Table 11.2 Sources of funding, non-financial corporate sector, Japan, 1965–97

	Percentage of private investment								Trillions of 1997 yen		
	Total corporate external fundraising	Private loans	Public loans	Commercial paper	Stock	Industrial bonds	Foreign bonds	Other foreign sources (FDI, trade credit and other)	Private investment	Total corporate external fundraising	Internal fundraising
1965–67	53.9	42.1	5.1	0.0	3.4	2.6	0.0	0.7	63.5	34.2	29.3
1968–70	47.8	36.5	4.0	0.0	4.0	1.4	0.2	1.6	115.6	55.2	60.4
1971–73	65.8	53.4	4.1	0.0	4.2	2.3	–0.1	2.2	147.0	96.8	50.2
1974–76	45.5	33.8	4.5	0.0	2.6	2.2	0.6	1.1	147.3	67.0	80.3
1977–79	30.6	20.8	3.7	0.0	2.7	1.7	0.5	0.7	154.8	47.4	107.4
1980–82	38.0	27.9	4.0	0.0	3.3	1.3	0.8	–0.2	171.4	65.2	106.3
1983–85	44.8	32.9	2.1	0.0	3.1	1.0	2.7	0.2	184.9	82.8	102.1
1986–88	59.9	34.9	2.7	4.0	4.9	2.4	4.5	2.0	237.7	142.4	95.3
1989–91	60.7	30.9	6.0	1.0	4.9	2.5	6.1	3.3	319.6	194.1	125.5
1992–94	14.7	6.6	8.1	–0.9	0.7	4.3	–1.4	–1.5	291.4	42.7	248.7
1995–97	4.1	–3.9	0.1	0.7	1.5	3.3	–2.3	6.6	305.4	12.6	292.9
1997	–	–	–	–	–	–	–	–	104.9	4.3	103.6
Outstanding, end of Dec. 1997 trillion yen	–	459.0	95.2	11.8	245.0	66.3	23.9	–	–	–	–

Sources: Bank of Japan, *Economic and Financial Data on CD-ROM 1998*; financial institutions' accounts; Bank of Japan web site (http://www.boj.or.jp/en/siryo/siryo_f.htm); Economic Planning Agency web site (http://www.epa.go.jp/e-e/eri/menu.html).

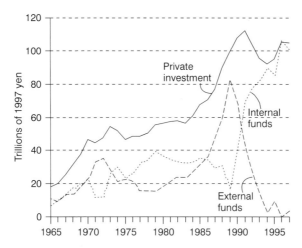

Figure 11.1   Sources of funds, non-financial corporate sector, Japan, 1965–97
Source: As for Table 11.2.

Within the financial *keiretsu* presidents' clubs, too, the companies have largely rolled over their bank loans, including those from the main banks and other financial institutions that are also members of the same club. As the Table 11.3 shows, the fraction of loans to presidents' club members by fellow members did not change dramatically during the 1980s and 1990s.

More detailed data on loans to the Mitsui and Fuyo presidents' club members in 1987 and 1997 affirms the same point. These data are presented in Table A11.4. The Mitsui and Fuyo financial institutions

Table 11.3   Average percentage of non-financial members' loans emanating from fellow presidents' club city banks, trust banks and insurance companies, 1983–97

	1983	*1985*	*1994*	*1997*
Mitsui	18.8	29.2	20.4	19.8
Mitsubishi	23.1	22.4	20.3	19.3
Sumitomo	27.0	27.3	20.5	20.3
Fuyo	17.5	19.4	16.8	14.4
Sanwa	19.9	19.2	16.6	16.3
Dai-Ichi Kangyo	12.4	11.5	13.5	14.3

Source: Calculated using data from Toyo Kerzai (1988), pp. 24–36 and (1999), pp. 40–9.

have largely rolled over their loans to fellow group members. The large Japanese firms that belong to the financial *keiretsu* have not so far abandoned loans as an important source of external funds, even though the regulations now permit them to issue industrial bonds, commercial paper and euromarket securities. Whether they will abandon loans and embrace securities when the Japanese economy expands again and macroeconomic investment revives is the big open question. But relational banking is not the defining characteristic of the financial *keiretsu*, nor of the enterprise groups, and it may not be crucial to their continued existence. As long as the reputations that the fellow group members have built up between themselves over their long histories remain valuable, the groups can survive.

Finally, the much predicted unwinding of cross-shareholding need not herald the end of Japan's business groups either. First, the extent of divestiture of cross-held shares has not been great and largely pertains to shares that were held by banks. Second, divestiture of share links between trading partners can be a rational response to the business cycle, perfectly consistent with the maintenance of business reputations.

Table 11.4 shows the cross-shareholding ratios within the respective *keiretsu* presidents' clubs in 1983, 1985, 1994 and 1997. The changes have not been very great. In fact *keiretsu* cross-shareholding exhibits considerable inertia. Neither has the extent of cross-shareholding among the broader set of Japanese firms changed much. For evidence on this we turn to data on the ownership composition of shares issued by Japanese companies (Table 11.5). As the figures in the table show, since 1970 about one fourth of all shares issued by Japanese companies have been held by other non-financial Japanese companies. The percentage of shares held either by ordinary banks or by the three

Table 11.4   Average percentage of shares held by other members of the same presidents' club, 1983–97

	1983	1985	1994	1997
Mitsui	17.7	17.6	16.5	15.1
Mitsubishi	24.4	27.4	27.5	27.3
Sumitomo	25.1	24.7	23.4	22.2
Fuyo	15.7	15.8	14.6	15.5
Sanwa	16.6	16.7	16.0	15.8
Dai-Ichi Kangyo	13.7	12.7	11.7	11.3

Source: Same as for Table 11.3.

Table 11.5 Percentage of unit shares of Japanese companies by type of shareholder, 1949–98

Survey year	Govt and local govt	Financial institutions	LTCB, city and regional banks	Trust banks	Investment trusts	Annuity trusts	Life insurance companies	Non-life insurance companies	Other fin. institutions	Business Corps	Securities companies	Individuals	Foreigners (companies and individuals)
1949	2.8	9.9	–	–	–	–	–	–	–	5.6	12.6	69.1	–
1950	3.1	12.6	–	–	–	–	–	–	–	11.0	11.9	61.3	–
1955	0.4	23.6	–	–	4.1	–	–	–	–	13.2	7.9	53.2	1.7
1960	0.2	30.6	–	–	7.5	–	–	–	–	17.8	3.7	46.3	1.3
1965	0.2	29.0	–	–	5.6	–	–	–	–	18.4	5.8	44.8	1.8
1970	0.2	32.3	15.4	–	1.4	–	11.1	4.0	1.8	23.1	1.2	39.9	3.2
1975	0.2	36.0	18.0	–	1.6	–	11.5	4.7	1.9	26.3	1.4	33.5	2.6
1980	0.2	38.8	19.2	–	1.5	0.4	12.5	4.9	2.2	26.0	1.7	29.2	4.0
1985	0.8	42.2	21.6	–	1.3	0.7	13.5	4.5	2.6	24.1	2.0	25.2	5.7
1986	0.9	43.5	16.1	7.1	1.8	0.9	13.3	4.4	2.6	24.5	2.5	23.9	4.7
1987	0.8	44.6	15.9	8.4	2.4	1.0	13.2	4.3	2.8	24.9	2.5	23.6	3.6
1988	0.7	45.6	16.3	9.9	3.1	1.0	13.1	4.2	2.1	24.9	2.5	22.4	4.0
1989	0.7	46.0	16.4	10.3	3.7	0.9	13.1	4.1	2.1	24.8	2.0	22.6	3.9
1990	0.6	45.2	16.4	9.8	3.6	0.9	13.2	4.1	1.8	25.2	1.7	23.1	4.2
1991	0.6	44.7	16.3	9.7	3.2	1.0	13.2	4.0	1.6	24.5	1.5	23.2	5.4
1992	0.6	44.5	16.2	10.0	3.2	1.1	13.0	4.0	1.3	24.4	1.2	23.9	5.5
1993	0.6	43.8	16.0	10.1	3.0	1.4	12.7	3.8	1.2	23.9	1.3	23.7	6.7
1994	0.7	43.5	15.9	10.6	2.6	1.6	12.2	3.7	1.1	23.8	1.1	23.5	7.4
1995	0.6	41.4	15.4	10.1	2.1	1.8	11.2	3.6	1.2	23.6	1.4	23.6	9.4
1996	0.5	41.3	15.1	10.8	2.0	2.3	10.9	3.4	1.0	23.8	1.1	23.6	9.8
1997	0.5	40.2	14.6	11.1	1.4	3.3	10.2	3.3	1.0	24.1	0.8	24.6	9.8
1998	0.5	39.3	14.0	11.7	1.2	3.8	9.4	3.2	1.0	24.1	0.7	25.4	10.0

Notes:
1. The number of shares has been calculated on a 'unit-of-share' basis since the 1985 survey.
2. The figures for trust banks are included in LTCB, city and regional banks upto and including 1985.

Source: Tokyo Stock Exchange, 1998 Share Ownership Survey (available on http://www.tse.or.jp/english/top/eframein.html.

long-term banks varied between 14 per cent and 22 per cent from 1970 and moved steadily downward from 16.4 per cent in 1990 to 14 per cent in 1998.

Cross-shareholding was brought to the fore of policy discussions in February 1999 when *Keidanren* proposed the creation of a government body to buy cross-held shares. Under the same proposal, within a period of a few years the companies that had sold the shares to the government body would then buy them back. This proposal amounted to a naked plea for government largesse and was immediately rebuffed by Prime Minister Obuchi and others. However, few disputed the proposal's fundamental premise that Japanese companies would continue to divest cross-held shares and that this would exert downward pressure on share prices. As already discussed, such divestiture as has occurred seems mostly to have involved shares that had been held by banks. This was probably related to the ongoing realignment of corporate finance in Japan due both to the relaxation of regulations and to the prolonged business slump. But the divestiture of cross-held shares between trading partners can also be precipitated by macroeconomic recession. This is because an expectation that trade will expand in the future if trading partners maintain their reputations for honesty towards one another, prevents them from engaging in opportunistic behaviour. Added inducements to behave honestly such as might be implied by cross-shareholding then become either redundant or no longer worth the cost.[33] At the trough of the business cycle firms should expect a large expansion of trade and so retrench their cross-shareholding, and at the peak of the cycle they should expect a smaller expansions of trade and so deepen their cross-shareholding.

Whether the effect just described will be large enough to matter is unclear, but there is at least one historical precedent for such a thing. The substantial deepening of cross-shareholding, including that within *keiretsu* presidents' clubs, that occurred in the late 1960s may actually have been symmetrical with the putative unwinding of cross-held shares at the trough of the business cycle, insofar as it reflected a rational expectation that the economic growth rate was bound to slow once the recovery from the war was complete. Of course many have suggested instead that the motivation for deepening cross-shareholding in the late 1960s was to preempt hostile foreign takeovers following the liberalization of international capital market transactions in Japan, but this is not convincing. The firms that deepened their cross-shareholding at that time included many that were not likely candidates for a hostile takeover. Nor is it at all obvious that cross-share-holding is an effective takeover defence – why should trading partners be any less likely than other stockholders to tender shares if confronted with an attractive offer?

If the above is correct, then even if *keiretsu* cross-shareholding does unwind once the Japanese business cycle reaches its trough, this need not mean the end of firms' bonds of reputation or loyalty to one another. Quite the opposite. It would merely reflect the fact that those bonds of trust no longer required the added buttressing of cross-shareholding.

CONCLUSION

The self-organization of Japanese firms into business groups originated with the *zaibatsu*: vast commercial empires, each controlled by a wealthy family though the pyramiding of closely held shares, that reached their fullest development soon after the First World War. The *zaibatsu* represented a form of corporate governance, highly effective and successful in some industries but absent and apparently unnecessary in others, for example cotton spinning. With the appropriation and disbursal of the *zaibatsu* founding families' shares by the US occupation government of Japan, the *zaibatsu* were dissolved. But when the occupation ended the constituent member firms of the old *zaibatsu* soon reestablished their former alliances. The members of each one of the new groups, called financial *keiretsu*, traded with one another and were linked by cross-shareholding. With the demise of the *zaibatsu* founding families, the large banks insinuated themselves into the governance of the former *zaibatsu* member corporations. Perhaps this was natural given the important role of the banks as suppliers of funds to the companies, a role that owed much to regulations that cartelized and protected Japanese banks. Deregulation has ended the bank cartel but the financial *keiretsu* nevertheless remain viable.

Appendix 11.1: data on the major *zaibatsu*, financial *kieretsu* and enterprise groups

Table A11.1 Formation of the four major *zaibatsu*: principal affiliated enterprises and their dates of entry into the *zaibatsu*[1]

	Mitsui	Mitsubishi	Yasuda	Sumitomo
Banking	Money exchange shops (1691) = MITSUI BANK (1876) MITSUI TRUST (1924)	119th National Bank (1885) = MITSUBISHI BANK (1895) MITSUBISHI TRUST (1927)	Yasuda shoten (1866–87) + Third National Bank (1876) = Yasuda Bank (1880)	SUMITOMO BANK (1895) SUMITOMO TRUST (1925)
Insurance	Taishō Marine & Fire Ins. (1918)[3] MITSUI LIFE INS. (1926)	Tokyo Marine & Fire Insurance (1944)[4] Meiji Life Insurance[4] MITSUBISHI MARINE & FIRE INS. (1919)	Yasuda Trust (1925) Tokyo Fire Insurance Co. Ltd (1893) Imperial Marine Insurance Co. Ltd (1893) Kyōsai Life Insurance (1894) = Yasuda Life (1929)	Fusō Marine & Fire Ins. (1917) = SUMITOMO MARINE & FIRE INS. (1940) SUMITOMO LIFE INS. (1925)
General Trading Companies	MITSUI BUSSAN (1876)	Bōeki Shōkai (1880) Dōshin Kaisha (1886) = MITSUBISHI TRADING COMPANY (1918)	Yasuda Motojime Yakuba (1874) = Yasuda Trading (1899)	None
Mining	Miike Coal Mine (1888)[2] + Kamioka Metal Mines (1886) = MITSUI MINING COMPANY (1892) Yamano Coal Mine (1895) Tagawa Coal Mine (1900) Hokkaido Colliery & Steamship (1913)[3] Ishikari Coal (1916)	Yoshioka Copper Mine (1878) Takashima Coal Mine (1878)[2] Shinnyū Coal Mine (1889) Namazuda Coal Mine (1889) Hashima Coal Mine (1890) Osarizawa Metal Mine (1887) Makimine Metal Mines (1889) Sado Gold Mine (1896)[2] Osaka Copper Refinery (1896)[1] Ikuno Silver Mine (1896)[2] Kyomip'o Iron Mine (1911), consolidated as MITSUBISHI MINING (1918)	Kushiro Sulphur Mine (1888–98)	Besshi Copper Mine (1691) = SUMITOMO BESSHI MINING (1927) Shōji Coal Mine (1893–1903) Tadakuma Coal Mine (1894) Sumitomo Kyushu Colliery (1928) + Sumitomo Ban Colliery (1921) = SUMITOMO COAL MINING (1930)

Foods	None	Kirin Brewery (1907)[4] Koiwai Farm (1904)	None	None
Textiles	Kanegafuchu Cotton Spinning (1890s)[3] Maebashi Silk Spinning Mill Shinamachi Silk Filature[3] Tomioka Silk Filature (1894)[2] Mie and Nagoya Silk Filatures, all sold in the 1900s Tōyō Rayon (1926)	None	Nishinari Cotton Spinning (1899–1905)	None
Paper and Pulp	Oji Paper, founded in 1873[3]	Mitsubishi Paper Mills[4] (1897)	None	None
Chemicals	First Nitrogen Industries (1926) Claude-Process Nitrogen inds (1929–35) = Miike Nitrogen (1931–37) + Oriental High Pressure (1933) + Synthetic Industries (1938) = MITSUI CHEMICAL INDUSTRIES (1941) Dai Nippon Celluloid[3] Electrochemical Inds[3] Miike Petroleum Synthesis (1934)	Nippon Nitrogen Fertilizer (1908) Nippon Tar Inds (1934) = Nippon Chemical Inds (1936) + Shinko Rayon (1942) = MITSUBISHI CHEMICAL INDS (1944)	None	Sumitomo Fertilizer Mfg (1925) = SUMITOMO CHEMICAL INDS (1934)
Oil and Coal Products	None	MITSUBISHI OIL (1931)	None	None
Cement, Glass, Ceramics	Onoda Cement[3]	Asahi Glass (1907),[4] consolidated with MITSUBISHI CHEMICAL INDS (1944)	None	Nichibei Sheet Glass (1918) = Nippon Sheet Glass[5] (1922)

Table A11.1 (continued)

	Mitsui	Mitsubishi	Yasuda	Sumitomo
Iron and Steel	Nippon Steelworks (1907)[3] Kamaishi Kōzan Company (1924–34)	Makiyama Coke Factory (1896) MITSUBISHI IRON AND STEEL (1917–34)	Yasuda Seichōsho (1897)	Sumitomo Steel Works (1901) = Sumitomo steel (1915) + Sumitomo Copper and Steel (1926) = SUMITOMO METAL INDS (1935)
Nonferrous Metals	None	None	None	Sumitomo Copper Rolling (1897) SUMITOMO ELECTRICAL WIRE (1911) Sumitomo Aluminium Refining (1934)
Machinery	Shibaura Engineering Works[3]	MITSUBISHI ELECTRIC (1921)	Tenma Tekkōjo (1900)	
Electrical Equipment	None	None	None	Nippon Electric Company (1899)[5]
Shipbuilding	MITSUI SHIPBUILDING (1942)	Nagasaki Shipyard (1884)[2] Kobe Shipyard (1905) Hikoshima Shipyard (1914) = Mitsubishi Shipbuilding and Engineering (1917) = MITSUBISHI HEAVY INDS (1934)	Toba zōsensho (1911–13)	None
Other transport equipment	None	Mitsubishi Internal Combustion Engine Works (1920) = Mitsubishi aircraft (1928), absorbed by MITSUBISHI HEAVY INDS (1934)	None	None
Real estate	None	Marounouchi Land (1890) = MITSUBISHI ESTATE CO. LTD (1937)	None	None

	Mitsui	Mitsubishi	Yasuda	Sumitomo
Transport	None	Mitsubishi Mail Steamship Company (1872) = Nippon Mail Steamship Company, 'NYK' (1885)[4]	None	Osaka Shōsen Kaisha (1884)
Shipping related businesses	None	Mitsubishi Ship Repair Facility (1875) = Mitsubishi Exchange Office (1876–85)	None	None
Warehousing	Toshin Warehousing (1909)	Tokyo Warehouse Company (1887) = MITSUBISHI WAREHOUSING AND TRANSPORTATION (1918)	Yasuda Unpan Jimusho (1894)	None
Services	Mitsui Dry Goods (1673) = Mitsukoshi dry goods (1904)[3]	None	None	Kobe Copper Sales (1871–82)
Utilities	None	Senkawa Water (1880–1908)	None	None
Holding companies; central control organs	Mitsui Gumi (1866) = Mitsui Motokata (1893) = Mitsui Board of Directors (1896) = Mitsui Gōmei Kaisha (1909), absorbed by Mitsui Bussan (1940)	Mitsubishi Company (1886) = Mitsubishi Ltd (1893) = Mitsubishi Inc. (1937) = Mitsubishi Head Office (1943)	Hozensha (1887)	Sumitomo Honten = Sumitomo Sōhonten (1909) = Sumitomo Ltd (1921) = Sumitomo Head Office (1939)

Notes:

1. Companies printed in capital letters were directly controlled subsidiaries of the holding company. In the table, + denotes amalgamation and = denotes a new company name.
2. Purchased from the government.
3. Independent company in which Mitsui gōmei kaisha was a major shareholder.
4. Independent company in which the Iwasaki family was a major shareholder.
5. Independent company in which Sumitomo Ltd was a major shareholder.

Source: Based on Morikawa (1992), passim.

312

Table A11.2 Presidents' clubs of the six financial *keiretsu*, October 1998

	Mitsui	Mitsubishi	Sumitomo	Fuyo	Sanwa	Dai-Ichi Kangyo
City Banks	8314 Sakura Bank	8315 Bank of Tokyo-Mitsubishi Bank	8318 Sumitomo Bank	8317 Fuji Bank	8320 Sanwa Bank	8311 Dai-Ichi Kangyo Bank
Trust Banks	8401 Mitsui Trust and Banking	8402 Mitsubishi Trust and Banking	8403 Sumitomo Trust and Banking	8404 Yasuda Trust and Banking	8407 Toyo Trust and Banking	None
Hazard insurance	8752 Mitsui Marine and Fire Ins.	8751 Tokyo Marine and Fire Insurance	8753 Sumitomo Marine and Fire Ins.	8755 Yasuda Fire and Marine Insurance	None	8756 Nissan Fire and Marine Insurance Taisei Fire and Marine Insurance
Life insurance	Mitsui Life Insurance Company	Meiji Life Insurance Co.	Sumitomo Life Insurance Co.	Yasuda Life Insurance Co.	Japan Life Insurance Co.	Fukoku Life Insurance Co. Asahi Life Insurance Co.
Forestry	None	None	1371 Sumitomo Forestry	None	None	None
Mining	1501 Mitsui Mining	None	1503 Sumitomo Mining	None	None	None
Construction	1821 Mitsui Construction 1961 Sanki Engineering	1996 Mitsubishi Construction	1823 Sumitomo Construction	1801 Taisei	1802 Obayashi 1811 Zenitaka 1890 Toyo Construction 1928 Sekisui House	1803 Shimizu Construction

Foods	2001 Nippon Flour Mills	2503 Kirin Brewery	None	2002 Nisshin Flour Milling 2501 Sapporo Breweries 2871 Nippon Reizo	2284 Itoham Foods Suntory	None
Textiles	3402 Toray Industries	3404 Mitsubishi Rayon	None	3105 Nisshin Spinning 3403 Toho Rayon	3103 Unitica 3401 Teijin	3407 Asahi Chemical Industry
Paper and pulp	3861 Oji Paper Company* 3863 Nippon Paper Industries*	3864 Mitsubishi Paper Mills	None	3863 Nippon Paper Industries*	None	3861 Oji Paper Company*
Chemicals	4061 Denki Kagaku Kogyo* 4183 Mitsui Chemicals	4010 Mitsubishi Chemical Industries 4182 Mitsubishi Gas Chemical 4213 Mitsubishi Plastics Industries	4005 Sumitomo Chemical 4203 Sumitomo Bakelite	4004 Showa Denko 4023 Kureha Chemical 4403 Nippon Oil and Fats	4043 Tokuyama Soda 4204 Sekisui Chemical 4208 Ube Inds 4217 Hitachi Chemical 4508 Tanabe Seiyaku 4511 Fujisawa 4613 Kansai Paint	4061 Denki Kagaku Kogyo* 4151 Kyowa Hakko Kogyo 4205 Nippon Zeon 4401 Asahi Denka Kogyo 4501 Sankyo 4911 Shiseido 4912 Lion
Oil and coal products	None	5004 Mitsubishi Oil	None	5005 Toa Nenryo Kogyo	5007 Cosmo Oil	5002 Showa Oil
Rubber goods	None	None	None	None	5105 Toyo Tire and Rubber	5101 The Yokohama Rubber
Glass and ceramics	5233 Taiheyo Cement*	5201 Asahi Glass	5202 Nippon Sheet Glass 5232 Sumitomo Osaka Cement	5233 Taiheyo Cement*	None	5233 Taiheyo Cement*

Table A11.2 (continued)

	Mitsui	Mitsubishi	Sumitomo	Fuyo	Sanwa	Dai-Ichi Kangyo
Iron and steel	5631 The Japan Steel Works	5632 Mitsubishi Steel Mfg	5405 Sumitomo Metal Industries	5404 NKK	5406 Kobe Steel* 5407 Nisshin Steel 5408 Nakayama Steel Works 5486 Hitachi Metals	5403 Kawasaki Steel 5406 Kobe Steel* 5562 Japan Metals & Chemicals
Non-ferrous metals	5706 Mitsui Mining & Smelting	5711 Mitsubishi Materials 5771 Mitsubishi Shindoh 5804 Mitsubishi Cable Industries Mitsubishi Aluminum	5713 Sumitomo Metal Mining 5738 Sumitomo Light Metal Ind. 5802 Sumitomo Electric Industries	None	5812 Hitachi Cable	5701 Nippon Light Metal 5715 Furukawa 5801 Furukawa Electric
Machinery	None	6331 Mitsubishi Kakoki	6302 Sumitomo Heavy Industries	6326 Kubota 6471 Nippon Seiko	6472 NTN Toyo Bearing	6011 Niigata Engineering 6310 Iseki 6361 Ebara
Electrical appliances	6502 Toshiba	6503 Mitsubishi Electric	6701 NEC	6501 Hitachi* 6703 Oki Electric Industry 6841 Yokogawa Hokushin Electric	6501 Hitachi* 6704 Iwatsu Electric 6753 Sharp 6971 Kyocera 6988 Nitto Denko	6501 Hitachi* 6504 Fuji Electric 6506 Yaskawa Electric Mfg. 6702 Fujitsu 6791 Nippon Columbia
Transport equipment	7003 Mitsui Engineering & Shipbuilding 7013 Ishikawajima-Harima Heavy Industries* 7203 Toyota Motor	7011 Mitsubishi Heavy Industries 7211 Mitsubishi Motors	None	7201 Nissan Motor	7004 Hitachi Zosen 7224 Shin Meiwa Industry 7262 Daihatsu Motor	7012 Kawasaki Heavy Industries 7013* Ishikawajima-Harima Heavy Ind. 7202 Isuzu Motors

Precision machinery	None	7731 Nikon	None	7751 Canon	7741 Hoya	7750 Asahi Optical
Commerce	8031 Mitsui, 8231 Mitsukoshi	8058 Mitsubishi	8053 Sumitomo	8002 Marubeni	8004 Nichimen, 8063 Nissho Iwai*, 8088 Iwatani, 8233 Takashimaya	8001 Itochu, 8063 Nissho Iwai*, 8020 Kanematsu-Gosho, 8110 Kawasho, Seibu Department Store
Miscellaneous financing	None	None	None	None	8591 Orix	None
Securities	None	None	None	None	None	8607 Nippon Kangyo Kakumaru Securities
Real estate	8801 Mitsui Real Estate Development	8802 Mitsubishi Estate	8830 Sumitomo Realty & Development	8804 Tokyo Tatemono	None	None
Transportation	9104 Mitsui O.S.K. Lines	9101 Nippon Yusen	None	9001 Tobu Railway, 9006 Keihin Electric Express Rail, 9126 Showa Line	9042 Hankyu, 9062 Nippon Express, 9105 Navix Line	9062 Nippon Express, 9107 Kawasaki Kisen
Warehousing	9302 The Mitsui Warehouse	9301 Mitsubishi Warehouse & Transport	9303 The Sumitomo Warehouse	None	None	9304 The Shibusawa Warehouse
Services	None	Mitsubishi Research Institute	None	None	None	9681 Tokyo Dome, 9871 Itoki

Notes: The number before the company name is the securities identification code number. * = affiliated with more than one presidents' club.

Source: Compiled using data from Toyo Keizai (1999).

Table A11.3   Companies that head the 40 most significant enterprise groups, as judged by Oriental Economist, 1996. Presidents' club memberships are shown in parentheses

1801	Taisei (Fuyo)
2503	Kirin Brewery (Mitsubishi)
2914	Japan Tobacco
3402	Toray Industries (Mitsui)
3407	Asahi Chemical Industry (Dai-Ichi)
3863	Nippon Paper Industries (Mitsui, Fuyo)
4010	Mitsubishi Chemical Industries (Mitsubishi)
4204	Sekisui Chemical (Sanwa)
4452	Kao Corp.
4502	Takeda Chemical Industries
4901	Fuji Photo Film
5001	Nippon Oil Co.
5108	Bridgestone Corp.
5201	Asahi Glass (Mitsubishi)
5401	Nippon Steel
5404	NKK (Fuyo)
5711	Mitsubishi Materials (Mitsubishi)
5802	Sumitomo Electric Industries (Sumitomo)
6326	Kubota (Fuyo)
6501	Hitachi (Fuyo, Sanwa, Dai-Ichi)
6502	Toshiba (Mitsui)
6503	Mitsubishi Electric (Mitsubishi)
6701	NEC (Sumitomo)
6702	Fujitsu (Dai-Ichi)
6752	Matsushita Electric Industrial Co.
6758	Sony Corp.
7011	Mitsubishi Heavy Industries (Mitsubishi)
7201	Nissan Motor (Fuyo)
7203	Toyota Motor (Mitsui)
7267	Honda Motor Co.
7751	Canon (Fuyo)
8031	Mitsui (Mitsui)
8058	Mitsubishi (Mitsubishi)
8263	Daei
8264	Ito-Yokado Co.
8591	Orix (Sanwa)
8801	Mitsui Estate development (Mitsui)
9501	Tokyo Electric Power Co.
9613	NTT
	JR-Higashi Nihon

Source: Compiled using data from Toyo Keizai (1996).

Table A11.4 Loans to non-financial members of the Mitsui and Fuyo presidents' clubs, as of March 1987 and 1997[1]

	Mitsui	Outstanding loans and loans held by Sakura Bank, Mitsui Trust and Banking, Mitsui Life Insurance, or Mitsui Marine and Fire Insurance (billions of yen, March 1987)	Outstanding loans and loans held by Mitsui Bank, Mitsui Trust and Banking, Mitsui Life Insurance, or Taisho Marine and Fire Insurance (billions of yen March 1997)	Fuyo	Outstanding loans and loans held by Fuji Bank, Yasuda Trust and Banking, Yasuda Life Insurance, or Yasuda Fire and Marine Insurance (billions of yen, March 1987)	Outstanding loans and loans held by Fuji Bank, Yasuda Trust and Banking, Yasuda Life Insurance, or Yasuda Fire and Marine Insurance (billions of yen, March 1997)
Forestry	None	–		None	–	–
Mining	1501 Mitsui Mining	159	154	None	–	–
		82	67	None	–	–
Construction	1821 Mitsui Construction	118	256	1801 Taisei	183	406
	1961 Sanki Engineering	48	100		68	96
		11	12			
		3	3			
Foods	2001 Nippon Flour Mills	14	26	2002 Nisshin Flour Milling	18	18
		4	8		3	3
				2501 Sapporo Breweries	10	148
					2	30
				2871 Nippon Reizo	24	56
					6	10
Textiles	3402 Toray Industries	178	124	3105 Nisshin Spinning	20	11
		37	38		4	4
				3403 Toho Rayon	15	32
					6	9

Table A11.4 (continued)

	Mitsui	Outstanding loans and loans held by Sakura Bank, Mitsui Trust and Banking, Mitsui Life Insurance, or Mitsui Marine and Fire Insurance (billions of yen, March 1987)	Outstanding loans and loans held by Mitsui Bank, Mitsui Trust and Banking, Mitsui Life Insurance, or Taisho Marine and Fire Insurance (billions of yen March 1997)	Fuyo	Outstanding loans and loans held by Fuji Bank, Yasuda Trust and Banking, Yasuda Life Insurance, or Yasuda Fire and Marine Insurance (billions of yen, March 1987)	Outstanding loans and loans held by Fuji Bank, Yasuda Trust and Banking, Yasuda Life Insurance, or Yasuda Fire and Marine Insurance (billions of yen, March 1997)
Paper and pulp	3861 Oji Paper Company*	118	447	3863 Nippon Paper Industries*	149	265
	3863 Nippon Paper Industries*	20	100	Paper Industries*	34[3]	–
		170	265	–	–	–
		30[2]	46			
Chemicals	4061 Denki Kagaku Kogyo*	142	99	4004 Showa Denko	383	213
		18[4]	22	4023 Kureha Chemical Industry	100	64
	4183 Mitsui Chemicals	198	123		14	30
		73[5]	31		2	8
		259		4403 Nippon Oil and Fats	25	22
		92[6]			8	8
Oil and coal products	None	–	–	5005 Toa Nenryo Kogyo	88	60
					12	8
Rubber goods	None	–	–	None	–	–
Glass and ceramics	5233 Taiheyo Cement*	133	199	5233 Taiheyo Cement*	162	199
		33[7]	39		55[8]	0
Iron and steel	5631 The Japan Steel Works	77	73	5404 NKK	1232	406
		27	29	–	254	17
Non-ferrous Metals	5706 Mitsui Mining & Smelting	174	151	None	–	–
		73	53	–	–	–

Sector	Firm (left)			Firm (right)		
Machinery	None	—		6326 Kubota	31	21
				6471 Nippon	3	2
				Seiko	39	63
					16	13
Electrical Appliances	6502 Toshiba	213	286	6501 Hitachi*	165	217
		38	35	6703 Oki	28	27
				Electric Industry	181	118
				6841 Yokogawa	53	23
				Hokushin	7	5
				Electric	2	1
Transport equipment	7003 Mitsui Engineering & Shipbuilding	191	187	7201 Nissan	422	360
		60	69	Motor	82	40
	7013 Ishikawajima-Harima Heavy Industries*	431	195			
		22	29			
	7203 Toyota Motor	—	—			
		—	—			
Precision Machinery	None	—	—	7751 Canon	24	18
		—	—		6	3
Commerce	8031 Mitsui	1719	2413	8002 Marubeni	1917	1668
		218	279		264	275
	8231 Mitsukoshi	—	97			
		—	37			
Miscellaneous Financing	None	—		None	—	
Securities	None	—		None	—	
Real estate	8801 Mitsui Real Estate Development	441	661	8804 Tokyo	28	183
		103	199	Tatemono	8	77

Table A11.4 (continued)

	Mitsui	Outstanding loans and loans held by Sakura Bank, Mitsui Trust and Banking, Mitsui Life Insurance, or Mitsui Marine and Fire Insurance (billions of yen, March 1987)	Outstanding loans and loans held by Mitsui Bank, Mitsui Trust and Banking, Mitsui Life Insurance, or Taisho Marine and Fire Insurance (billions of yen March 1997)	Fuyo	Outstanding loans and loans held by Fuji Bank, Yasuda Trust and Banking, Yasuda Life Insurance, or Yasuda Fire and Marine Insurance (billions of yen, March 1987)	Outstanding loans and loans held by Fuji Bank, Yasuda Trust and Banking, Yasuda Life Insurance, or Yasuda Fire and Marine Insurance (billions of yen, March 1997)
Transportation	9104 Mitsui O.S.K. Lines	310 39	159 22	9001 Tobu Railway 9006 Keihin Electric Express Rail 9126 Showa Line	303 50 224 34 117 17	432 61 286 32 43 8
Warehousing	9302 The Mitsui Warehouse	16 9	13 6	None	–	–
Services	None	–		None	–	–

Notes:
1. Number before company name is the securities identification code number. * = affiliated with more than one presidents' club.
2. Tujo paper; not a presidents' club member.
3. Sanyo-Kokusaku Paper.
4. Not a presidents' club member.
5. Mitsui Petrochemical Industries.
6. Mitsui Toatsu Chemicals.
7. Onodo Cement.
8. Nippon Cement.
Source: Compiled using data from Toyo Keizai (1988, 1999).

Notes

1. In 1873 a contingent of 54 shipwrecked Japanese sailors were attacked and killed on Taiwan and the following year the Meiji government conducted a retaliatory raid.
2. For a biographical sketch of the venal yet frugal Yasuda, see Yamamura (1968).
3. These included the following. Asano: Asano Sōichirō (1848–1930). Ōkura: Ōkura Kihachirō (1837–1928). Furukawa: Furukawa Ichibei (1832–1903), Nakajima Kumakichi (1873–1960). Yasukawa: Yasukawa Keiichiro (1849–1934), founder of Yasukawa *zaibatsu*, which he developed from coal mines in northern Kyushu. Fujita: Fujita Denzaburō (1841–1912), grew rich from government supply contracts and went on to found a business empire based on mining, land reclamation and forestry. Kawasaki: Kawasaki Shozo (1837–1912), vice president of the Japanese government mail steamship company 'YJK', unsuccessful rival of Mitsubishi mail steamship Co.; founder of Kawasaki shipyard company 1886; Matsukata Kōjirō (1865–1950, third son of the famous finance minister) took over Kawasaki shipbuilding in 1896 and the Kawasaki empire ultimately passed to the control of the Matsukata family. Suzuki: Suzuki Iwajiro (?–1894); Kaneko Naokichi (1866–1944). Nomura: Nomura Tokushichi (1878–1945). Iwai: Iwai Katsujiro (1863–1960). Hitachi/Kuhara: Kuhara Fusanosuke (1869–1965).
4. A few of the most famous entrepreneurs and the companies they founded are as follows. Itō Denhichi: Mie Textile Company. Tomiji Hirano: Ishikawajima Shipyard. Suzuki Tōzaburo: Japan Sugar Refining Company. Morinaga Taichiro: Morinaga Candy. Toyoda Sakichi (1867–1930): Toyota weaving looms, forerunner of the famous car manufacturer.
5. The founders of the so-called 'new *zaibatsu*' were as follows. Ayukawa Yoshisuke (1880–1967): Nissan. Mori Nobuteru (1884–1941): Shōwa Fertilizer, later Shōwa electric manufacturing company. Nakajima Chikuhei (1884–1949): Nakajima Aircaft. Nakano Tomonori (1887–1965): Nihon Soda Company. Noguchi Shitagau (1873–1944): Japan Nitrogen Fertilizer Company. Ōkochi Masatoshi (1878–1952): Riken Inc.
6. For details of the policies described in the next paragraphs I have drawn upon Bisson (1954) and Hadley (1970).
7. The owners of shares in pure holding companies, including members of the *zaibatsu* founding families, received partial compensation in the form of non-negotiable, ten-year Japanese government bonds, ultimately rendered almost worthless by the poster rise in prices.
8. All of the 85 companies based outside Japan, all of the economic associations and the like and a number of the companies based in Japan were dissolved with no successors, leaving only 187 companies (of the approximately 400 named entities) still in operation at the time of the purge order (Bisson, 1954, Table 8, p. 163).
9. Bisson (1954), Table 11, p. 175.
10. Extracts from both the *Newsweek* piece and a speech by Senator Knowland are reprinted in Livingston *et al.* (1973).

11. For a list of the companies affected by these directives see Hadley (1970).
12. On this point see Uekusa (1977).
13. Yafeh (1995) measures corporate performance by the price–cost margin (that is, profit-to-sales ratio), and controls for the effect of market share and capital intensity.
14. Under amendments to the antimonopoly law enacted in 1997, holding companies are once again permitted in Japan.
15. For an example of Miyazaki's dissection of the financial *keiretsu* in English, see Miyazaki (1967).
16. Executive office of the Fair Trade Commission of Japan (1980).
17. Flath (1993).
18. Hadley (1970).
19. For developments of this line of argument see Odagiri (1975), Kobayashi (1980) and Aoki (1984).
20. Examples of this kind of argument can be found in Ramseyer (1987), Aoki (1987) and Sheard (1991).
21. This, despite its title, is the essential theme of Kester (1991).
22. Flath (1996).
23. See Flath (1996) for details.
24. For a recent attempt by a sociologist rather than an economist, see Gerlach (1993).
25. Coase (1937).
26. The original author of this principle was Adam Smith, but it was Stigler (1951) who reinterpreted it in roughly the terms expressed here.
27. Demsetz (1982).
28. Lawrence (1991).
29. Rasmussen *et al*. (1991).
30. Aghion and Bolton (1987).
31. For details see Flath (2000).
32. Financial Supervisory Agency (1998).
33. For a detailed elaboration of this argument in terms of an algebraically specified model, see Flath (1996).

References

Aghion, Phillipe and Patrick Bolton (1987) 'Contracts as a Barrier to Entry', *American Economic Review*, vol. 35, pp. 38–401.

Aoki, Masahiko (1984) 'Shareholders' Non-unanimity on Investment Financing, Banks Versus Individual Investors', in M. Aoki (ed.), *The Economic Analysis of the Japanese Firm* (Amsterdam: North-Holland).

Aoki, Masahiko (1987) 'The Japanese Firm in Transition', in K. Yamamura and Y. Yasuba (eds), *The Political Economy of Japan, Volume 1, The Domestic Transformation* (Stanford, CA: Stanford University Press), pp. 263–88.

Bisson, T. A. (1954) *Zaibatsu Dissolution in Japan* (Berkeley, CA: University of California Press).

Coase, Ronald H. (1937) 'The Nature of the Firm', *Economica*, vol. 4, pp. 386–405.

Demsetz, Harold (1982) 'Barriers to Entry' *American Economic Review*, vol. 72, no. 1, pp. 47–57.

Executive Office of the Fair Trade Commission of Japan (1980) 'Kigyō shudan no jittai ni tsuite' (Concerning the state of business groups), *kosei torihiki*, 394, pp. 20–4.

Financial Supervisory Agency, Government of Japan (1998) 'The Current Status of Risk Management Loans Held by Deposit-Taking Financial Institutions', 17 July (Table: Loss on Disposal of Bad Loans of All Japanese Banks).

Flath, David (1993) 'Shareholding in the Financial Keiretsu', *Review of Economics and Statistics*, vol. 75, pp. 249–57.

Flath, David (1996) 'The Keiretsu Puzzle', *Journal of the Japanese and International Economies*, vol. 10, pp. 101–21.

Flath, David (2000) *The Japanese Economy* (Oxford: Oxford University Press).

Gerlach, Michael (1993) *Alliance Capitalism: The Social Organization of Japanese Business*, (Berkeley, CA: University of California Press).

Hadley, Eleanor (1970) *Antitrust in Japan* (Princeton, NJ: Princeton University Press).

Holmström, Bengt and Jean Tirole (1997) 'Financial Intermediation, Loanable Funds, and the Real Sector', *Quarterly Journal of Economics*, vol. 112, no. 3, pp. 663–91.

Kester, Carl (1991) *Japanese Takeovers, the Global Contest for Corporate Control* (Cambridge, Mass.: Harvard Business School).

Kobayashi Y. (1980) *Kigyō shudan no bunseki* (Economic analysis of enterprise groups) (Hokkaido University, Sapporo).

Lawrence, Robert Z. (1991) 'Efficient or Exclusionist? The Import Behavior of Japanese Corporate Groups', *Brookings Papers on Economic Activity*, vol. 1, pp. 311–41.

Livingston, Jon, Joe Moore and Felicia Oldfather (eds) (1973) *Postwar Japan, 1945 to the Present* (New York: Random House), pp. 107–15.

Miyazaki, Yoshikazu (1967) 'Rapid Economic Growth in Post-War Japan – With Special Reference to "Excessive Competition" and the Formation of "Keiretsu"', *The Developing Economies*, vol. 5, pp. 329–50.

Morikawa, Hidemasa (1992) *Zaibatsu, the Rise and Fall of Family Enterprise Groups in Japan* (Tokyo: University of Tokyo Press).

Nakamura, Takafusa (1971) *Economic Growth in Prewar Japan* (New Haven, CT: Yale University Press).

Odagiri H. (1975) 'Kigyō shudan no riron' (A theory of industrial groups), *Kikan riron keizaigaku*, vol. 26, pp. 144–54.

Ramseyer, J. M. (1987) 'Takeovers in Japan: Opportunism, Ideology, and Corporate Control', *UCLA Law Review*, vol. 35, pp. 1–64.

Rasmussen, Eric J., Mark Ramseyer and John S. Wiley Jr (1991) 'Naked Exclusion', *American Economic Review*, vol. 39, pp. 1137–45.

Sheard, Paul (1991) 'The Economics of Interlocking Shareholding in Japan', *Ricerche Economiche*, vol. 45, pp. 421–48.

Stigler, George (1951) 'The Division of Labor is Limited by the Extent of the Market', *Journal of Political Economy*, vol. 59, no. 3.

Toyo keizai (1988–99) *Kigyō keiretsu sōran (Handbook of keiretsu enterprises)* (Tokyo: Toyo Keizai).

Uekusa, Masu (1977) 'Effects of the Deconcentration Measures in Japan', *The Antitrust Bulletin*, vol. 22, no. 3, pp. 687–715.

Yafeh, Yishai (1995) 'Corporate Ownership, Profitability, and Bank–Firm Ties: Evidence from the American Occupation Reforms in Japan', *Journal of the Japanese and International Economies*, vol. 9, pp. 154–73.

Yamamura, Kozo (1968) 'A Re-examination of Entrepreneurship in Meiji Japan (1868–1912)', *The Economic History Review*, vol. 21, no. 1, pp. 144–58.

12 Japanese Corporate Governance and Macroeconomic Problems[1]

Randall Morck and Masao Nakamura

INTRODUCTION

North American academics became interested in Japanese economic institutions in the 1980s, when rapidly growing Japanese firms were seizing significant shares of the global market (long dominated by established US and European firms) for cars, electronics, electrical and general machinery and precision instruments. Japan's success seemed to many to have been achieved at the expense of declining US manufacturing industries. Thus, North American business schools taught Japanese practices in industrial relations (for example teamwork), manufacturing methods (JIT), industrial organization (*keiretsu*) and bank-based corporate control.

While research into the Japanese economy has a long history in the North American and European academic literature (see for example Patrick and Rosovsky, 1976, and the references given there), the massive effort on the part of North American scholars, particularly those from business schools, did not begin until the 1980s. For example the number of articles on JIT manufacturing written in the United States increased from essentially zero in the late 1970s to over 700 in the period 1985–1990.

Transfer of business practices

Much of the academic research in these areas has been devoted to the question of whether or not Japanese practices could be successfully transferred to North American industries. For example Morck and Nakamura (1995), Romano (1993, 1995) and Tschoegl (1995) discuss the feasibility of transferring Japanese corporate governance practices to the North American environment.

There is considerable empirical evidence that many aspects of Japanese manufacturing practices had been successfully adopted by US manufacturing industries by the early 1990s (see for example Nakamura *et al.*, 1998, forthcoming). But others were either unsuccessful or rejected. For example transplanting Japanese-style interfirm relations, such as supplier–assembler relations, has not taken place to any significant extent in the United States (not even in the case of Japanese transplants). Japanese long-term employment practice is also largely incompatible with the structure of the US labour market, and hence has not been widely adopted (Nakamura, 1993).

The generally perceived poor performance of the US economy, particularly in the case of certain key manufacturing industries, throughout the 1980s prompted scholars to question the effectiveness of the US system of corporate governance (see for example Jensen and Meckling, 1976; Mace, 1986). Critics of the US governance system argue that boards of directors are cosy reunions of old boys who are generally powerless to prevent, or even recognize, potentially disastrous corporate policies, and managers are self-interested, unhindered by effective board oversight and run corporations to suit themselves. Baker, Jensen and Murphy (1988), Morck *et al.* (1988, 1989, 1990) and many others, have found empirical evidence that many large US corporations suffered from corporate governance problems in the 1980s.

It is for these reasons that reformers began to speculate about alternative institutional frameworks that might work better.[2] The key theoretical argument for alternative frameworks is that the typical large US firm suffers from the lack of a large shareholder. Shleifer and Vishny (1988) argue that even a single large and sophisticated shareholder might provide a valuable counterweight to management. McConell and Servaes (1990) present some evidence that a large shareholder enhances firm value. Jensen (1989) compares the Japanese main bank system with (Leverage Buy Out) partnerships in the United States and argues that the joint ownership of debt and equity by large informed investors (such as Japanese banks) results in stringent managerial monitoring and creates strong incentives for managers to make value-maximizing decisions.

Outside the United States large shareholders are ubiquitous. Indeed the United States and Britain are the only countries in the world where widely held firms are prevalent. In Japan and Germany, banks control large blocks of shares in most large firms. In most countries, including Canada, most of Europe and Asia and all of Latin America, wealthy families hold dominant voting blocks in most large corporations, either directly or through control pyramids. US antitrust and banking policies were explicitly aimed at dislodging such 'robber barons' and their families from positions of economic power, so returning to this system appears retrogressive to many Americans. Morck *et al.* (1998) present empirical evidence justifying this view. The German and Japanese systems have thus become the main focus of US researchers, spurred on by the outstanding performance of those economies.

Assessment of the Japanese corporate governance system

There is considerable variance in the assessment of Japanese and German corporate governance mechanisms. Shleifer and Vishny (1997, p. 739), for example, note that 'corporations in successful market economies, such as the United States, Germany and Japan, are governed through somewhat different combinations of legal protection and concentrated ownership. Because all these economies have the essential elements of a governance system, the available evidence does not tell us *which one of their* governance systems is the best.'

Because of the superior performance of the Japanese and German economies prior to the 1990s, some authors favoured their governance systems over the US system (see for example Aoki, 1990; Charkham, 1994; Roe, 1993). As the 1990s drew to a close, Japan's prolonged recession and floundering banking sector suggested that these assessments should be reassessed.

Morck and Nakamura (1995) and Romano (1995) argue that transfer of essential aspects of Japanese corporate governance practices would probably not improve North American firms' performance. Perhaps successful US firms quickly adopted those Japanese practices that made sense, and the remaining differences are Japanese practices that US firms found undesirable.[3]

Contemporary policy issues in Japan

Mired in a prolonged and serious recession, Japan now seems to be looking abroad for solutions to its economic problems. For the past few years the Japanese business press and Japanese bookstores have been filled with articles and books describing all aspects of US business practices. For example a Japanese best-seller entitled *Those*

Who Can Become Anglo-Saxon Will Succeed (Itose, 1998) argues that the United States and Britain currently set the global standard. It therefore encourages Japanese corporations and workers alike to adopt 'Anglo-Saxon' practices in industrial relations and employment behaviour, work practices, corporate control and other business management areas. This US triumph is echoed by many US government officials, including President Bill Clinton and Deputy Secretary of Commerce Larry Summers, who have both argued on many occasions that US-style capitalism is the only way to go for other countries.

It remains to be seen whether the transfer of certain US business practices to Japan will indeed successfully end Japan's protracted recession. Certainly, Japanese business practices have *not* been the chief suspects in many economic analyses of Japan's post-bubble woes. Rather, Japan's macroeconomic policy makers and bank regulators are routinely blamed for stumbling into Keynesian employment and liquidity trap problems. We do not dispute this view. However we argue that Japanese corporate governance practices may also have played a critical role, both in pulling Japan's economy into its current muddle and in keeping it there. Our reasoning meshes well with historical explanations of Japan's current problems. For example some historians argue that the present Japanese business and economic system served Japan well as it caught up with the United States and Western Europe during the 20th century, but that Japan now needs a new system.

The next section develops our argument by examining the evolution of corporate governance in Japan and elsewhere to see how Japan (and Germany) ended up with bank-centred systems while other countries did not. The third section considers how creditors' interests differ from those of residual claimants, and how assigning corporate control to creditors distorts firms' investment decisions. The fourth section shows how such distortions at the microeconomic level might lead to macroeconomic problems of the sort Japan is now undergoing.

HOW CURRENT JAPANESE BANK-BASED CORPORATE GOVERNANCE PRACTICES AROSE

Best practice in 19th-century banking and corporate governance

In the 1860s, when Japan reopened its economy to the world after centuries of self-imposed quarantine, banks in most countries owned equity in non-financial firms and exercised considerable influence over the governance of those firms. The new Meiji rulers of Japan perceived these to be the best banking practices and adopted them in Japan.

The model for universal banks at the time was the Société Générale du Crédit Mobilier, established in November 1852 by Emile and Isaac Péreire, disciples of the utopian socialist Claude-Henri, Comte de Saint-Simon.[4] Banks, for these Saint-Simonians, were canals that could irrigate arid parts of the economy with capital. Crédit Mobilier took deposits, underwrote stock and bond issues, bought and sold stocks and bonds on its own account and for others, and securitized industrial loans as short-term bonds called *valeurs omnium*, which it sold to the public. To maintain its own share price, Crédit Mobilier routinely repurchased shares. Companies for which Crédit Mobilier underwrote securities had to maintain current accounts with the bank. It thus engaged in all the activities a full-service, one-stop financial services and banking firm would provide in the 1990s. Crédit Mobilier was a fully fledged universal bank.

Crédit Mobilier established replicas of itself in Amsterdam, Turin and London. Rival replicas were also established in London (the General Credit and Finance Company) and Paris (the Société Générale pour Favoriser le développement du Commerce et de l'Industrie en France and the Crédit Lyonnais). Heavy losses in equity investments by these banks (including Société Générale's 'guano affair' debacle in Peruvian bonds) and the spectacular collapse of Crédit Mobilier convinced French bankers of the wisdom of separating commercial banking from equity investment, and gave rise to the present division between *banques de dépôts*, such as Crédit Lyonnais, and *banques d'affaires*.

Imitators quickly sprung up throughout Europe. The Bank für Handel und Industrie was established in Darmstadt in 1853. The Rothschilds founded the Kaiserlich-Königliche Privilegirte Österreichische Credit-Anstalt für Handel und Gewerbe in 1855. Others include the Schweizerische Credit-Anstalt in Zurich (now one of the three main Swiss banks), the Allgemeine Deutsche Credit-Anstalt in Leipzig, the Vereinsbank in Hamburg, the Norddeutsche Bank in Hamburg, the Mitteldeutsche Credit-Bank in Meiningen, the Schlesischer Bank-Verein in Breslau, the Dessauer Credit-Anstalt, the Coburg-Gothaische Credit-Anstalt, the Preussiche Handelsgesellschaft in Königsberg and the Magdeburger Handelscompagnie.

In the United States, banks were also directly involved in corporate governance. In 1912, when US GNP was $39.4 billion, 18 financial institutions sat on the boards of 134 corporations with $25.325 billion in combined assets (Simon, 1998).

Why other countries abandoned universal banking

Stock markets in the 19th century were prone to repeated panics and crashes, and universal banks were often ruined when the value of their equity holdings collapsed suddenly. Kleeberg (1995) counts 20 bank collapses, 15 bank liquidations, one forced merger and 10 narrowly averted bank collapses in Germany between 1850 and 1910. Universal banks elsewhere fared no better. The General Credit and Finance Company was liquidated after 90 per cent of its capital was wiped out in the panic of 1866. Crédit Mobilier itself failed in 1867 due to reverses in the stock market and a disastrous investment in the North of Spain railway, a real estate firm.

A perception arose in Britain that equity ownership destabilised banks. When the General Credit and Finance Company was recapitalized after its spectacular failure, its managers renounced all 'financing' and transferred all commercial banking activities to the General Credit and Discount Company of London. An informal separation of commercial banking from equity investments has characterized British banking ever since.

This informal separation was inherited by Canada and other Commonwealth countries. The Canadian and US banking rules differ in a number of ways. Unlike US banks, which are prohibited from owning industrial firms' equity for active investment (control) purposes, since 1967 Candian banks have been allowed to own up to 10 per cent (compared with 5 per cent in Japan) of voting stock equity in non-financial firms, excluding stocks of small companies and stocks obtained as collateral. Prior to 1967 there were no laws prohibiting Canadian banks from equity blockholdings. Nevertheless Canadian banks have shunned equity ownership in non-financial firms. Canadian banks collectively have very little equity (C$10.4 billion) out of a total equity base of C$800 billion. The reason Canadian banks and the Bank of Canada give for this is that equity ownership is not part of banking.

Over a number of decades, and especially during the Great Depression, country after country separated banking from equity ownership. In Italy, universal banking existed until the banking crisis of April 1931, when the government imposed a legal separation of commercial and investment banking and took over banks' holdings of non-financial firms' shares. These were placed in a state-owned holding company, the Istituto per la Ricostruzione Italiana or IRI, one of the largest conglomerates in Europe. Similar legislation was imposed in Belgium.

Simon (1998) provides empirical evidence that the eviction of banks from corporate boards, which took place around 1910 in the United States, depressed firms' value by about 7 per cent. The United States legislated the separation of commercial banking from investment banking with the Glass–Steagall Act of 1933. The Bank Holding Act of 1956 forbids US banks from holding more than 5 per cent of their capital in corporate shares, and the corporate shares they own cannot be used for purposes of control.

Germany and a handful of small European countries retained the older banking model

Germany also had a severe banking crisis in 1931. German banks had extended large loans in the 1920s to highly levered industrial firms, especially those controlled by the industrialist heir Hugo Stinnes. As these companies failed the German banks accumulated their equity, which had been pledged as collateral. German banks also spent large amounts of their depositors' money buying their own shares to maintain their stock prices in the late 1920s. Since the share prices being maintained were artificially high, this probably contributed to their later insolvency. By 1931, when all the major German banks were recognized as clearly insolvent, the Deutsche Bank und Disconto-Gesellschaft owned 27 per cent of its own shares, the Dresdner Bank owned 34 per cent, the Commerz und Privatbank 50 per cent and the Darmstädter-Nationalbank owned 60 per cent of its own shares.

To bail them out, the Weimar government took over these blocks, effectively partially nationalizing the banks, and established a committee in 1933 to consider banking reform. The committee quickly recommended against any changes when the National Socialist Party came to power (Kleeberg, 1987). Hitler toyed with the idea of fully nationalizing the banks, but never implemented such a plan. Following the war, banks in the Soviet occupation zone were 'temporarily' closed in 1946 (Kleeberg, 1987), while those in West Germany were privatized and had reattained their prewar structures by 1957.

Banking reform was also on the back burner in Switzerland, Holland and the Scandinavian countries. The trade war that followed the Smoot–Hawley tariff, passed by the US Congress in 1930, virtually shut these small nations out of international trade.[5] Given the economic devastation wrought in these countries by the cessation of international trade, public policy attention centred on trade initiatives such as the Oslo Agreement; banking reform was of negligible importance. Thus various aspects of universal banking survived in these countries as well. In Switzerland especially, cosy cartels were established to protect the stability of the system. When barriers to entry were relaxed in 1990, 130 of the existing 625 either lost their independence or disappeared.

The circuitous history of Japanese banking and corporate governance practice

Despite the 1866 collapse of Crédit Mobilier, Japan's Meiji government chose to implement a universal banking system modelled on that of Germany. Economic historians such as Colomiris (1992) view heavy bank involvement in industrial firms in Germany as having played a key role in Germany's rapid economic development between 1870 and 1914. For example German banks were able to provide capital to industry during this period at a much lower cost than in the United States (about 4 per cent in Germany compared with 20 per cent in the United States).[6]

It is, however, unclear whether German bank involvement in corporate governance through equity ownership contributed to the fast economic growth in Germany during this period. Kleeberg (1987) presents evidence that German universal banks were remarkably poor at 'picking winners' during the country's industrialization, that they invested in a depressing series of financial debacles, and that they may actually have impeded Germany's development by sustaining poorly run firms. It is often argued in this regard that Germany industrialized rapidly because it was a latecomer and the path it had to follow was clear, not because of its universal banks.

In any case, Japan's choice of a universal banking system was certainly politically motivated as well. By owning a universal bank that in turn owned controlling stakes in a large number of companies, a Meiji family could magnify its wealth into control over corporate assets worth vastly more. Cross-holdings between controlled firms further reduced the actual values of the equity stakes the bank needed for control. Such family-controlled corporate groups, called *zaibatsu*, characterized Japan's economy until 1945.[7]

Like Europe and North America, Japan experienced economic crises in the 1920s and 1930s. The banks of the Mitsubishi, Mitsui and Sumitomo families survived this turbulence. They were well diversified, having invested their excess cash flows across many firms and industries. These banks also lent only 10–20 per cent of their loan funds to related firms. Other Japanese families had greater need for outside capital, and therefore used their banks primarily to raise money for their own firms. These 'organ' banks were poorly diversified. For example 94 per cent of the Nakazawa Bank's loans were to insiders, as were 75 per cent of the Watanabe Bank's loans. Prior to their collapse in 1927, 72 per cent of the loans of Suzuki's captive bank, the Taiwan Bank, want to Suzuki companies and 75 per cent of Matsukata's Jugo Bank's loans went to Matsukata family firms. In the crisis of 1927, triggered by the financial frauds by Ione Suzki and the closure of the Tokyo Watanabe Bank, 37 banks failed. All were 'organ' banks. It is of note that organ banks typically held less equity (about 15 per cent of the value of their loans) than did the highly diversified banks of the surviving *zaibatsu* (about 21 per cent).

Another wave of bank failures occurred as the Great Depression took hold in Japan. In 1930, 19 banks failed; 33 closed their doors in 1931; and 13 more failed in 1932. Again, large diversified *zaibatsu* banks survived and more 'organ' banks failed. Equity ownership was again lower in the banks that failed.

After the Second World War the US occupation force in Japan oversaw a full-scale revamping of Japan's financial system. Banks were forbidden to underwrite securities. Although the US government exerted considerable pressure for a complete ban on bank ownership of non-financial firms' stock along the lines of US practice, the Allied Forces ultimately decided against this. Banks' share ownership in other companies was limited to a 10 per cent stake, and *zaibatsu* firms were ordered to disgorge their shareholdings in each other in 1950. As a result, shares of large Japanese companies were mostly widely held in the immediate postwar period.

Postwar reconstruction entailed high interest rates, which lowered equity prices. This, in concert with the disgorgement of banks' former equity holdings to public shareholders, led to a collapse in the share prices of former *zaibatsu* firms, as illustrated in Table 12.1. Sheard (1991) documents a series of hostile takeover bids against firms formerly in *zaibatsu* groups, including Taisho Marine, Mitsubishi Real Estate and Mitsui Real Estate.

Just before the end of the US occupation in 1952, Japanese firms began to buy up each others' shares with the explicit purpose of preventing hostile takeovers (Sheard, 1991). This resulted in a considerable increase in intercorporate share ownership between the former Mitsubishi, Mitsui and Sumitomo *zaibatsu* firms and banks in 1949–51. A renewed spate of takeover bids and greenmail payments in the late 1960s accelerated Japanese firms' intercorporate stock purchases, particularly between the firms and banks in the newly

Table 12.1   Estimates of Tobin's q for Mitsubishi and Sumitomo group firms, 1949–53*

	1949	1950	1951	1952	1953
Mitsubishi group	1.61	0.46	0.39	0.72	1.00
Sumitomo group	1.96	0.34	0.35	0.78	0.86

*The Mitsubishi group includes 13 manufacturing firms and two marine transport firms; the Sumitomo group includes seven manufacturing firms and one warehouse firm. Tobin's q's for the corporate groups are value weighted averages of the q's of their member firms. The firm q values were calculated using the book value of fixed assets. Since book value is likely to underestimate true replacement cost during this period, these estimates of q are probably too large.
Sources: Miyajima (1990) and Morck and Nakamura (1992).

Table 12.2   Equity cross-holding, 1945–66* (percentage of outstanding shares owned by group firms)

	1945	1950	1952	1954	1958	1962	1966
Mitsui	57.3	0.44	5.44	6.87	7.42	12.40	21.77
Mitsubishi	46.1	2.18	10.09	12.61	13.82	17.39	26.12
Sumitomo	44.0	0.00	10.49	15.00	18.19	27.62	30.05

* The 1945 figures denote total ownership of the *zaibatsu* group of firms by the family holding company, family members and other *zaibatsu* firms. Later figures are total ownership of the successor *keiretsu* by its member firms.
Sources: Miyajima (1990) and Morck and Nakamura (1992).

emerging Sanwa, Fuji, Daiichi and Kangyo groups. Table 12.2 documents this transformation for three major *zaibatsu*.

The result was the grouping of Japanese firms into *keiretsu*, groups of firms that together owned controlling blocks of each others' shares. Aoki and Sheard (1992), Morck and Nakamura (1999) and Sheard (1989, 1991), propose that *keiretsu* arose primarily as antitakeover barriers. The following warning, taken from a Japanese guidebook on making firms public, shows that this use of cross-holdings is still explicitly acknowledged:

> Large corporations, foreign investors, and speculative investment groups holding large amounts of capital can acquire a majority of the shares in your newly listed firm, resulting in your losing management control. To avoid such a takeover attempt, it is

essential that you take the precautionary measure of locating stable shareholders [such as banks and related companies].
(Kato and Matsuno, 1991, p. 51, our translation)

The potency of *keiretsu* as antitakeover defences is illustrated by the American financier T. Boone Pickens' bid for the Japanese firm Koito in 1990. Pickens accumulated stock on the open market until he was by far the largest single shareholder, yet he was unable even to gain a seat on the board. Together, other firms in the *keiretsu* owned a majority of Koito's stock, and acting in concert they blocked Pickens' every move. Thus Japanese banks and their main client firms are effectively insulated from shareholder pressure.[8] Public shareholders thus have little or no voice in Japanese corporate governance.

THE IMPLICATIONS OF ASSIGNING CONTROL RIGHTS TO CREDITORS

Why corporate control should be in the hands of residual claimants

A firm's employees, managers, creditors and suppliers have contractual claims against the firm's assets. These claims are for fixed, prearranged monetary amounts: wages, interest payments or invoice amounts. In contrast its common shareholders have only a residual claim on its assets: the shareholders are entitled to the residual value left over once all the contractual claims are settled.

Contractual claimants, in maximizing the value of their claims, in general seek to minimize the probability of the firm defaulting before their contractual claims are paid. Meanwhile residual claimants seek to maximize the value of their residual claims. In general this is equivalent to maximizing the value of the firm's assets.

A fundamental consequence in corporate finance is that control rights are assigned to residual claimants. This is because the residual claimants, when maximizing the value of their own claims, must see to it that contractual claimants are paid. In contrast creditors, or other contractual claimants, in minimizing the firm's probability of default, see no need to raise further the value of the residual. This is why most countries give creditors little voice in corporate governance except when the firm is or is near to becoming bankrupt and general creditors usually become residual claimants.

Japanese banks are creditors first and shareholders second

Japanese banks are both creditors and shareholders. The webs of equity cross-holdings among *keiretsu* firms make Japanese banks influential in Japanese corporate governance. Do they use this influence to advance shareholders' interests or creditors interests, or a mixture of the two?

There are many reasons for thinking that banks are creditors first. First, banks' equity stakes were limited to 10 per cent in non-financial firms in the 1950s, and this was reduced to 5 per cent in the 1980s. In contrast banks' loans to non-financial firms are not limited. Second, the main banks in Japanese *keiretsu* implicitly guarantee the timely repayment of loans made to *keiretsu* member firms by other lenders. They make no such guarantee in respect of dividend payments to other shareholders. Third, Japanese banks, as stable shareholders, implicitly commit themselves to holding on to their equity stakes indefinitely. They therefore have little direct interest in the value of those stakes.

Kang and Shivdasani (1995) and Kaplan and Minton (1994) show that new bank representatives are appointed to the boards of Japanese companies when their financial performance lags, and argue that Japanese banks may exercise a corporate governance role that in some respects substitutes for shareholder pressure. Morck and Nakamura (1999) show that Japanese banks act primarily to protect their interests as creditors, responding to potential and actual debt repayment problems rather than more general indicators of financial health.

How creditors' and shareholders' interests diverge

The essential difference between creditors' interests and shareholders' interests in corporate governance can best be illustrated with a simple example. Let $V = D + E$ be the value of the firm, where E the value of its equity and D the value of its debt. Shareholders want to maximize $E(V - D)$ whereas creditors want to minimize $Prob(V < D)$. Suppose the firm has an investment opportunity that costs C and returns P with probability p and zero with probability $1 - p$, and let $pP > C$. Clearly, risk-neutral shareholders want the project to go ahead. In contrast, the creditors are indifferent about the project if $C < V - D$, and are opposed to it if $C > V - D$. Myers (1977) argues that shareholders, given sole control rights, can exploit creditors by launching projects for which $C > V - D$, and that this raises the cost of debt financing.

If creditors have control rights and shareholders are merely along for the ride, such a project would clearly not be approved if $C > V - D$. The problem with giving creditors control is that it might not be approved if $C < V - D$ either. Indeed a new set of criteria might come into play. Creditors might exploit shareholders by charging the firm artificially high interest rates. They might distort the firm's investment decisions towards low-risk projects, especially if this keeps cash flows stable and thereby lets the firm use more debt financing. They might also skew the firm's investment decisions towards projects that provide lots of collateral. These possibilities should increase the cost of equity finance and depress share prices in proportion to the probability of their occurring.

These predictions are consistent with the observed behaviour of Japanese banks and the client firms in which they exercise corporate control. Hoshi *et al.* (1993) show that firms in bank-centred *keiretsu* pay higher interest costs than other similar firms. They also use more bank debt and show a worse financial performance. There is also some empirical evidence that Japanese firms affiliated with *keiretsu* groups and/or main banks pay higher interest rates on their loans from their main banks than unaffiliated firms (Nakatani, 1984; Weinstein and Yafeh, 1998).

If Japanese banks could in fact extract money in these ways from their client firms, we should not necessarily expect banks to show an abnormally high financial performance or bank shares to rise. Banks, like other firms protected from their shareholders by equity cross-holdings, would presumably retain free cash flows. A more plausible use for such funds might be greater organizational slack, higher salaries and the like. Table 12.3 compares the hours worked and pay scales of Japanese bankers with those of comparable employees of other firms – banking appears to be a substantially more attractive career.

Regulatory capture

Related to the figures in Table 12.3, another potentially serious cost of having powerful bank investors in industry is their ability to influence public policy making to their advantage. This is particularly so in the banking and finance industry, which is generally regulated heavily in all developed economies. Such influence might also explain the figures in Table 12.3.

The relationship between Japanese banks and their regulators, the Ministry of Finance and the Bank of Japan, has been quite close. For

Table 12.3   Wages and working conditions for male employees with university education at firms with at least 1000 employees, 1990

	Manufacturing sector	*Banking sector*
Mean age	37.4 years	35.8 years
Mean years of service	12.1 years	11.7 years
Mean scheduled hours per month	172 hours	157 hours
Mean overtime hours per month	18 hours	13 hours
Mean annual regular contract pay	6 271 900 yen	7 289 600 yen
Mean annual bonuses and other special pay	1 707 100 yen	2 324 000 yen

Notes: Manufacturing sector data includes only non-production workers. Banking sector includes banks, insurance companies and other financial firms.

example since July 1998 eight (10) of the 96 Japanese regional banks have had former MOF (BOJ) officials as their CEOs; six (two) banks have had former MOF (BOJ) officials as chairmen of their boards; and 31 (20) banks have had former MOF (BOJ) officials on their boards of directors or serving as auditors (Toyo Keizai, 1998).

It is not implausible that these linkages between politically powerful banks and their watchers might have further distorted capital allocation. The serious lack of independent regulatory power may also explain why Japan has been reluctant to deal with corrupt banking practices.

How creditors' interests and employees' interests converge

Employees, like creditors, are contractual claimants, not residual claimants. What is good for creditors is therefore likely to be good for employees. The low-risk environment fostered by banks made possible the Japanese practice of lifelong employment, the cornerstone of industrial relations in many Japanese firms. This practice inhibited movement of personnel between corporations and, it is argued, encouraged employees to invest in firm-specific human capital. While such investments may have enhanced internal efficiency, they may have inhibited the development of industry-wide or economy-wide standards. It is also argued that highly developed, firm-specific practices discourage firms from hiring workers in mid career from other firms, except in very special cases. For example new technologies might require personnel with specific expertise.

THE MICROECONOMIC FOUNDATIONS
OF A MACROECONOMIC CRISIS

The conditions for an old-fashioned Keynesian recession

In a simple Keynesian model of the business cycle, excessive capital expenditure by firms leads to underutilized productive capacity and a consequent excess aggregate supply. Traditional Keynesian macroeconomic prescriptions are aimed at curing this imbalance by increasing aggregate demand with tax cuts, public works projects and the like.

It seems plausible that assigning control rights to creditors might produce precisely these conditions. Profitable capital projects might not be approved if they appear too risky. More marginal projects with lower but safer returns might displace them – especially if they provide abundant collateral. In short, creditor-controlled firms might excessively direct their capital investment towards the expansion of existing facilities, increased market shares in existing products, minor variations in product design and other low-risk, low-return ventures.

This strategy should work well as long as new markets open to provide a growing aggregate demand for such products. This characterized Japan's reconstruction during the postwar period and firms' explicit quest for market share rather than profits. It also explains the importance to Japan of the growing markets in East Asia in the 1980s as a source of increased aggregate demand, and the devastating impact on Japan of slowing growth in those markets and increasing competition from local firms.

Faced with persistent excess aggregate supply, Japanese firms have been forced to lay off huge numbers of workers in mid career. The practice of lifelong employment means that few firms know how to hire such workers. Consequently a serious social problem is developing.

Why not in Germany too?

German banks, like Japanese banks, are both creditors and shareholders in non-financial German firms. Why has a similar situation not arisen in that country?

German banks' corporate control role is arguably more explicit and more important than that of Japanese banks for several reasons. First, German banks' direct equity stakes are not legally capped. In contrast Japanese banks' equity stakes were limited to 10 per cent throughout most of the postwar period and are now limited to 5 per cent. Second, insurance companies and other financial firms in Germany are subsidiaries of large banks, which vote their subsidiaries' shares. This is often true in Japan too, but exceptions are more evident there. Third, German banks vote the shares that back US depository receipts. Japanese banks have no analogous role. Fourth, independent stockbroker firms are not important in Germany. German banks also act as stockbrokers for German investors, and hold the shares owned by their clients in trust. In contrast Japanese banks are barred from the brokerage and investment banking industry. When all of these stakes are combined, large German firms that at first glance appear to be widely held are actually fully and directly controlled by the country's largest four or five banks, as shown in Table 12.4.

Table 12.4   Voting rights exercised by German banks in widely held German Corporations, 1992 (per cent)

	Banks' direct stake	Subsidiary investment funds' stake	Bank-controlled proxy votes	Total bank control
Siemens	–	9.87	85.81	95.68
Volkswagen	–	8.89	35.16	44.05
Hoechst	–	10.74	87.72	98.46
BASF	0.09	13.81	81.01	94.91
Bayer	–	11.23	80.09	91.32
Thyssen	6.77	3.82	34.98	45.57
VEBA	–	12.82	78.23	91.05
Mannesmann	–	7.78	90.35	98.13
MAN	8.67	12.69	28.84	50.20
Preussag	40.65	4.51	54.30	99.46
VIAG	10.92	7.43	30.75	49.10
Degussa	13.65	8.65	38.35	60.65
AGIV	61.19	15.80	22.10	99.09
Linde	33.29	14.68	51.10	99.07
Deutsche Babcock	3.22	11.27	76.09	90.58
Schering	–	19.71	74.79	94.50
KHD	59.56	3.37	35.03	97.96
Bremer Vulkan	–	4.43	57.10	61.53
Strabag	74.45	3.62	21.21	99.28
Average	13.02	10.11	60.95	84.09

Notes: Includes shares on own accounts, depository rights as proxies held by subsidiary investment funds expressed as a percentage of all shares represented at the general meeting.
Sources: Baums (1995) and Morck and Nakamura (1995).

Table 12.5   Votes in the five largest German banks controlled by the five
largest banks, 1992 (per cent)

	Deutsche Bank	Dresdner Bank	Commerz Bank	Bayr. Bank	Bayr. Hypo	Total
Deutsche Bank	32.07	14.14	3.03	2.75	2.83	54.82
Dresdner Bank	4.72	44.19	4.75	5.45	5.04	64.15
Commerz Bank	13.43	16.35	18.29	3.78	3.65	55.50
Bayr. Bank	8.80	10.28	3.42	32.19	3.42	58.11
Bayr. Hypo	5.90	10.19	5.72	23.87	10.74	56.42

Notes: Includes depository voting rights and shares held by subsidiary investment funds. Figures are the percentage of all shares represented at the general meeting.
Sources: Baums (1995) and Morck and Nakamura (1995).

If German banks were to choose to run large non-financial firms primarily to maximize the value of their debt, no one could interfere. Moreover the banks are theoretically immune to shareholder pressure. This is because the banks collectively vote substantial majorities of their own shares, as Table 12.5 shows.

German banks have immense voting power in many large German firms, yet their actual ownership stakes are often trifling in comparison. German banks might therefore be even more likely than their Japanese counterparts to use their control rights to distort corporate decision making away from firm value maximization and towards the maximization of debt values.[9]

German law also assigns an explicit corporate governance role to employees. Employees' representatives make up half the members of the *Aufsichtsrat* (the supervisory board of a large German firm) and are represented on the *Vorstand* (the managerial board). Employees, like creditors, are contractual claimants. Their interests are largely aligned. Thus employee control rights should further distort corporate decisions towards stability and away from risk taking.

There are, however, some important reasons to doubt such a conclusion. First, West Germany was not forced to adopt a widely held US corporate governance system after the war. Coordinating policy across the French, British and US occupation zones proved too difficult. Consequently denazification left wealthy German families owning large blocks of equity in many companies. These may have provided corporate governance counterweights to banks that did not exist in large Japanese companies.

Second, German banks hold huge quantities of common shares in trust for public shareholders and foreigners, who invest in equities only via banks or their subsidiaries. Every time a shareholder buys or sells common shares, his or her bank charges about 1.5 per cent of their market value. One per cent of this is a commission fee, the rest is a stamp fee, theoretically paid to the stock exchange. In practice the bank typically settles customers' equity tradings against its own account and retains this fee. These brokerage fees are a significant part of total German bank revenues. Since these fees are proportional to the market value of the equities traded, German banks have a direct interest in high share prices.

In short the German model places bank equity ownership within a general regulatory context that gives banks a clear incentive to worry about value maximization as well as firms' creditworthiness. By imposing US-style separation of commercial and investment banking without permanently disabling banks' ability to exercise corporate control through equity markets, Japan's postwar financial reforms allowed an unbalanced financial system to develop over time. This is an example of the problem Romano (1993) warns of: business practices and laws are part of a system and may not work as expected when transferred piecemeal from one economy to another.

Prognosis

The standard Keynesian remedy for a recession caused by excess aggregate supply is to increase aggregate demand by lowering taxes, stimulating private consumption or undertaking public works projects. Such demand-side stimulation is also being prescribed by those who would inject large amounts of bailout money into the Japanese economy. Such prescriptions are valid, but may provide only short-term symptomatic relief rather than effect a complete cure.

Keynes argued that excess capacity results from bouts of 'animal spirits' on excessive optimism that lead to overinvestment. Such psychological factors were apparent in Japan's bubble economy of the 1980s. However we argue that Japan's excess capacity problem was also due to the dysfunctional corporate governance system's proclivity to encourage overinvestment in low-return, low-risk operations involving lots of physical assets. We propose that this microeconomic misallocation of capital triggered the overinvestment bubble in the first place and is now prolonging the resulting economic disarray.

While significant measures have been implemented to deregulate certain aspects of Japan's corporate governance law and its capital and foreign exchange markets since the mid 1990s, little change has been proposed for the role of banks as large investors (both shareholders and creditors) in Japanese industrial firms. For example no change in the antimonopoly laws has been proposed to end the long-standing stable shareholding or cross-shareholding practices. It is also far from clear that financial deregulation will make it unprofitable for banks and industrial firms to continue to engage in cross-holding. Also, except for a small number of failing firms being purchased by foreign firms, there seems to be no rush on the part of US or European corporations to purchase major Japanese firms despite their historically low market values.

Japanese banks appear to have used their lobbying influence to erect capital barriers and entrench their dominance over the domestic debt markets. Until 1972 Japanese banks actively opposed and successfully prevented the issuing of bonds without collateral. Thus only secured bonds existed. Japanese banks were the underwriters and primary buyers of these bonds, so they were essentially transferable bank loans. Securities firms, which had grown in relative power during the 1960s, won the right to underwrite unsecured corporate bonds in 1972, and Mitsubishi Corporation, Hitachi and Marubeni issued convertible debentures in that year. (Convertibles were allowed by the regulator – the Ministry of Finance – on the basis that they are closer in nature to equity than debt.) An active bond market has slowly developed since then. Unsecured straight corporate bonds became a financing option for Japanese industrial firms only recently. Such delay has forced Japanese firms to rely heavily on bank loans rather than capital market financing.

As this deregulation proceeded, high-net-worth Japanese firms began to raise significant funds in bond markets (Hoshi *et al.*, 1993). Thus the globalization and deregulation of securities markets appears to be eroding the financial hold that banks have on firms. These firms appear to have freed themselves from the corporate governance of banks.

Financial deregulation allowed Japanese banks to enter the securities business in the 1990s. They did so with vigour, and took a significant market share away from the traditional brokerage firms. This should increase banks' interest in promoting high equity values.

Thus banks are becoming less powerful in corporate governance matters in many firms, and at the same time are growing more interested in high share values. We therefore propose that continued financial liberalization should gradually nullify Japan's corporate governance problems, and should therefore be a public policy priority.

CONCLUSIONS

Japan's prolonged economic problems are due to more than faulty macroeconomic policies. We do not deny the importance of bungled macroeconomic policy, but argue that deeper maladies in Japanese corporate governance made that country increasingly vulnerable to such problems. We argue that Japan's main bank and financial *keiretsu* systems left corporate governance largely in the hands of creditors rather than shareholders. Thus Japanese governance practices did not assign effective control rights to residual claimants. This, we argue, led to a widespread misallocation of capital that mired Japan in excess capacity and liquidity problems.

There is significant interest in Japan in identifying aspects of the Anglo-American corporate governance system that can be incorporated into the Japanese system. Some measures have either been taken or proposed for serious consideration. Holding companies are now legal for large industrial firms. Toshiba, for example has already announced its intention to become a holding company and all the present production divisions are to be reorganized into separate companies. Hitachi and Toyota will follow suit. It is now legal for firms to purchase their own shares to prop up their stock prices. Tax and other legal conditions are being revised so that firms can offer certain types of stock options to their executives. These measures have been taken to a large extent to tighten the connection between firms' performance and their stock prices, and because of the policy makers' belief that implementing these measures might improve firm performance and bring Japan out of its recession.

Notes

1. An earlier version of this chapter was presented at the UBC Conference on Japanese Business and Economic System: History and Prospects for the 21st Century, 12–13 February 1999. The Research was in part supported by the Social Sciences and Humanities Research Council of Canada.

2. Two major types of comparative corporate governance system presented in the literature are the market-oriented (Anglo-Saxon or Anglo-American) type and the bank-oriented (European–Japanese) type, with some variants for each of the two types (Morck and Nakamura, 1995; Shleifer and Vishny, 1997; Tschoegl, 1995). Additional classifications include outsider (market-oriented), insider (bank-oriented) and ultra-insider (bank-oriented with cross-holdings) types (Rybczynski, 1984; Walter, 1992). Market-oriented and bank-oriented systems are broadly associated with, respectively, common-law-based and code-law-based legal systems. These types of alternative system also embed general societal and business culture.

3. In the 1980s there was a massive effort devoted by academics, business and government decision makers in the United States to studying Japanese practices and adopting those aspects deemed likely to improve the performance of the US economy. Looking at their economic achievement, some Japanese interpreted the translation of Vogel's (1980) book, *Japan as Number One*, to mean 'Japan is Number One'.

4. Much of the historical discussion here closely follows Kleeberg (1987), who gives a fascinating description of the history of universal banking in Europe, focusing on Germany. His work is not well known to economists, but should be.

5. The 'beggar thy neighbour' devaluations after the September 1931 collapse of sterling and the adoption of imperial preferences at the Ottawa conference were also key events.

6. Ando and Auerbach (1988) argue that Japanese banks similarly provided low-cost capital to industry after the Second World War to finance Japan's high economic growth period. It is not clear, however, that the particular structure of Japan's banking system caused this. Japan's very high savings rate and barriers to outward capital flow may been the vital factors.

7. The discussion of the prewar Japanese banking system follows Hoshi (1995) and Morck and Nakamura (1992).

8. The largest shareholders of the major Japanese banks tend to be their affiliated life insurance firms. Since these firms have a 'mutual' ownership structure (that is, the policyholders are *de jure* owners) they are unlisted and essentially are management controlled.

9. German directors have much more job security than their American counterparts and the turnover of industrial firms' management boards is somewhat related to sliding stock prices, but more to very poor earnings (Kaplan, 1993).

References

Ando, A. and A. J. Auerbach (1998) 'The Cost of Capital in the U.S. and Japan: A Comparison', *Journal of Japanese and International Economies*, vol. 2, pp. 134–58.

Aoki, M. (1988) *Information, Incentives, and Bargaining in the Japanese Economy* (New York: Cambridge University Press).

Aoki, M. (1990) 'Towards an economic model of the Japanese firm', *Journal of Economic Literature*, vol. 28, pp. 1–27.

Aoki, M., H. Patrick and P. Sheard (1995) 'The main bank system: An introductory overview', in M. Aoki and H. Patrick (eds), *The Japanese Main Bank System: Its Relevance for Developing and Transforming Economies*, (New York: Oxford University Press).

Aoki, M. and P. Sheard (1992) 'The role of the main bank in the corporate governance structure of Japan', working paper, Stanford University.

Baker, G., M. Jensen and K. J. Murphy (1988) 'Compensation and Incentives: Practice vs. Theory', *Journal of Finance*, vol. 43, pp. 210–228.

Baums, T. (1995) 'Universal banks and investment companies in Germany', NYU Salomon Centre Conference on Universal Banking.

Charkham, J. (1994) *Keeping Good Company: A Study of Corporate Governance in Five Countries*, Oxford: Clarendon Press.

Colomiris, C. (1992) 'The cost of rejecting universal banking: the American finance in the German mirror, 1870–1914', NBER Working Paper (Cambridge, Mass.: NBER).

Daniels, R. J., and R. Morck (eds) (1995) *Corporate Decision Making in Canada*, Industry Canada Research Series (Calgary: University of Calgary Press).

Denis, D. and J. Serrano (1996) 'Active investors and management turnover following unsuccessful control contests', *Journal of Financial Economics*, vol. 40, pp. 239–66.

Diamond, D. (1984) 'Financial intermediation and delegated monitoring', *Review of Economic Studies*, vol. 51, pp. 393–414.

Easterbrook, F., and D. Fischel (1991) *The Economic Structure of Corporate Law* (Cambridge, Mass.: Harvard University Press).

Flath, D. (1993) 'Shareholding in the keiretsu, Japan's financial groups', *Review of Economics and Satistics*, vol. 75, pp. 249–57.

Franks, J. and C. Mayer (1994) 'The ownership and control of German corporations', manuscript, London Business School.

Gilson, S. (1990) 'Bankruptcy, boards, banks, and block holders', *Journal of Financial Economics*, vol. 27, pp. 355–87.

Gorton, G. and F. Schmid (1996) 'Universal banking and the performance of German firms', NBER Working Paper 5453 (Cambridge, Mass.: NBER).

Grossman, S. and O. Hart (1980) 'Takeover bids, the free-rider problem, and the theory of the corporation', *Bell Journal of Economics*, vol. 11, pp. 42–64.

Hodder, J. and A. Tschoegl (1985) 'Some aspects of Japanese corporate finance', *Journal of Financial and Quantitative Analysis*, vol. 20, pp. 173–91.

Hodder, J. and A. Tschoegl (1993) 'Corporate financing in Japan', in S. Takagi (ed.), *Japanese Capital Markets* (Massachusetts: Basil Blackwell).

Hoshi, T. (1995) 'Cleaning Up the Balance Sheets: Japanese Experience in the Post-War Reconstruction Period' in M. Aoki and H.-K. Kim (eds) (1995), *Corporate Governance in Transitional Economies: Insider Control and the Role of Banks*, (Washington, DC: The World Bank).

Hoshi, T., A. Kashyap and D. Scharfstein (1990) 'The role of banks in reducing the costs of financial distress in Japan', *Journal of Financial Economics*, vol. 27, pp. 67–88.

Hoshi, T., A. Kashyap and D. Scharfstein (1991) 'Corporate structure, liquidity, and investment: evidence from Japanese industrial groups', *Quarterly Journal of Economics*, vol. 106, pp. 33–60.

Hoshi, T., A. Kashyap and D. Scharfstein (1993) 'The choice between public and private debt: An analysis of post-deregulation corporate financing in Japan', NBER Working Paper 4421 (Cambridge, Mass.: NBER).

Itose, S. (1998) *Those Who Can Become Anglo-Saxon Will Succeed* (anguro sakuson ni nareru hitoga seiko suru) (Tokyo: PHP Institue).

Jensen, M. (1989) 'Eclipse of the public corporation', *Harvard Business Review*, vol. 5, pp. 61–74.

Jensen, Michael (1993) The modern industrial revolution, exit, and the failure of internal control systems, *Journal of Finance*, vol. 48, pp. 831–81.

Jensen, M. and W. Meckling (1976) 'Theory of the firm: managerial behavior, agency costs and ownership structure', *Journal of Financial Economics*, vol. 3, pp. 305–60.

Kang, J. and A. Shivdasani (1995) 'Firm performance, corporate governance, and top executive turnover in Japan', *Journal of Financial Economics*, vol. 38, pp. 29–58.

Kang, J. and A. Shivdasani (1996) 'Does the Japanese Governance System Enhance Shareholder Wealth? Evidence from the Stock-price Effects of Top Management Turnover', *Review of Financial Studies*, vol. 9, pp. 1061–95.

Kang, J. and A. Shivdasani (1997) 'Corporate restructuring during performance declines in Japan', *Journal of Financial Economics*, vol. 46, pp. 29–65.

Kang, J. and R. Stulz (1997) 'Is bank centered corporate governance worth it?', working paper, Ohio State University.

Kaplan, S. (1992) 'Top executive rewards and firm performance: A comparison of Japan and the US', *Journal of Political Economy*, vol. 102, pp. 510–46.

Kaplan, S. (1993) 'Top executive turnover and firm performance in Germany', CRSP working paper, University of Chicago.

Kaplan, S. and B. Minton (1994) 'Outside intervention in Japanese companies: Its determinants and its implications for managers', *Journal of Financial Economics*, vol. 36, pp. 225–58.

Karp, E. and A. Koike (1990) 'The Japanese corporate bond market', in F. Fabozzi (ed.), *The Japanese Bond Market: An Overview and Analysis* (London: McGraw Hill).

Kato, M. and Y. Matsuno (1991) *Information about Going Public* (Tokyo: Nikkei).

Kleeberg, J. (1987) 'The Disconto-Gesellschaft and German industrialization', PhD thesis, Oxford University.

Kleeberg, J. (1995) 'Some notable German bank collapses, and why they happened', (New York: The American Numismatic Society).

Mace, M. (1986) *Directors: Myth and Reality* (Cambridge, Mass.: Harvard Business School Press).

McConell, J. and H. Servaes (1990) 'Additional evidence on equity ownership and corporate value', *Journal of Financial Economics*, vol. 27, pp. 595–610.

Miyajima, H. (1990) 'Historical formation of corporate groups' (in Japanese) (Toyo Kezai Kigyo Keiretsu Soran), pp. 18–27.

Miyajima, H. (1994) 'The transformation of Zaibatsu to postwar corporate groups – from hierarchically integrated groups to horizontally integrated groups', *Journal of the Japanese and International Economies*, vol. 8, pp. 293–328.

Morck, R. and M. Nakamura (1992) 'Banks and Corporate Control in Japan', University of Alberta, Institute of Financial Research Working Paper 6–92.

Morck, R. and M. Nakamura (1995) 'Banks and Corporate Control in Canada', in R. J. Daniels and R. Morck (eds), *Corporate Decision Making in Canada*, Industry Canada Research Series (Calgary: University of Calgary Press), pp. 481–521.

Morck, R. and M. Nakamura (1999) 'Banks and Corporate Control in Japan', *Journal of Finance*, vol. 53 (February), pp. 319–39.

Morck, R., M. Nakamura and A. Shivdasani (forthcoming) 'Banks, Ownership Structure, and Firm Value in Japan', *Journal of Business*.

Morck, R., A. Shleifer and R. Vishny (1988) 'Management ownership and market valuation: An empirical analysis', *Journal of Financial Economics*, vol. 20, pp. 291–315.

Morck, R., A. Shleifer and R. Vishny (1989) 'Alternative mechanisms for corporate control', *American Economic Review*, vol. 79, pp. 842–52.

Morck, R., A. Shleifer and R. Vishny (1990) 'Do managerial objectives drive bad acquisitions?', *Journal of Finance*, vol. 44, pp. 31–48.

Morck, R., D. Strangeland and B. Yeung (1998) 'Inherited Wealth, Corporate Control and Economic Growth' in R. Morck (ed.) *Concentrated Corporate Ownership* (Chicago: University of Chicago Press).

Myers, S. (1977) 'Determinants of Corporate Borrowing', *Journal of Financial Economics*, vol. 5, pp. 147–175.

Nakamura, M. (1993) 'Japanese Industrial Relations in an International Business Environment', *North American Journal of Economics and Finance*, vol. 4, pp. 225–51.

Nakamura, M., S. Sakakibara and R. Schroeder (1998) 'Adoption of Just-in-Time Manufacturing Methods at US and Japanese Owned Plants: Some Empirical Evidence', *IEEE Transactions on Engineering Management*, vol. 45, pp. 230–40.

Nakamura, M., S. Sakakibara and R. Schroeder (forthcoming) 'Just-in-Time and Other Manufacturing Practices, and Market Environment: Implications for Manufacturing Performance', in P. Adler, M. Fruin and J. Liker (eds), *Remade in America: Transplanting and Transforming Japanese Production Systems* (Oxford: Oxford University Press).

Nakatani, Iwao (1984) 'The economic role of financial corporate grouping', in M. Aoki (ed.), *The Economic Analysis of the Japanese Firm* (Amsterdam: North Holland).

Patrick, H. and H. Rosovsky (1976) (eds) *Asia's New Giant: How the Japanese Economy Works* (Washington, DC: The Brookings Institution).

Roe, M. (1993) 'Some differences in corporate structure in Germany, Japan, and the United States', *Yale Law Review*, vol. 102, pp. 1927–2037.

Roe, M. (1994) *Strong Managers Weak Owners: The Political Roots of American Corporate Finance* (Princeton, NJ: Princeton University Press).

Romano, R. (1993) 'A cautionary note on drawing lessons from comparative corporate law', *Yale Law Review*, vol. 102, pp. 2021–9.

Romano, R. (1995) 'Commentary on Part V', in R. J. Daniels and R. Morck (eds), *Corporate Decision Making in Canada*, Industry Canada Research Series (Calgary: University of Calgary Press), pp. 503–11.

Rybczynski, T. M. (1984) 'Industrial finance system in Europe, US and Japan', *Journal of Economic Behavior and Organization*, vol. 5, pp. 275–86.

Sheard, Paul (1989) 'The Main Bank system and corporate monitoring and control in Japan', *Journal of Economic Behavior and Organization*, vol. 11, pp. 399–422.

Sheard, Paul (1991) 'The economics of interlocking shareholding in Japan', *Richerche Economiche*, vol. 45, pp. 421–48.

Shivdasani, A. (1993) 'Board composition, ownership structure, and hostile takeovers', *Journal of Accounting and Economics*, vol. 16, pp. 167–98.

Shleifer, A. and L. Summers (1988) 'Breach of trust in hostile takeovers', in A. J. Auerbach (ed.), *Corporate Takeovers: Causes and Consequences* (Chicago, Ill.: University of Chicago Press), pp. 65–88.

Shleifer, A. and R. Vishny (1988) 'Value maximization and the acquisition process', *Journal of Economic Perspectives*, vol. 2, pp. 7–20.

Shleifer, A. and R. W. Vishny (1997) 'A Survey of Corporate Governance', *Journal of Finance*, vol. 52, pp. 737–83.

Simon, M. C. (1998) 'The Rise and Fall of Bank Control in the United States: 1890–1939', *American Economic Review*, vol. 88, pp. 1077–93.

Toyo Keizai (1981–88), *Kigyo Keiretsu Sokan* (Corporate Grouping) (Tokyo: Toyo Keizai Shimposha).

Toyo Keizai (1998) *Company Executives* (in Japanese), (Tokyo: Toyo Keizai Shimposha).

Tschoegl, A. E. (1995) 'Commentary on Part V', in R. J. Daniels and R. Morck (eds), *Corporate Decision Making in Canada*, Industry Canada Research Series (Calgary: University of Calgary Press), pp. 513–21.

Vogel, E. (1980) *Japan As Number One* (Cambridge, Mass.: Harvard University Press).

Wallich, H. and M. Wallich (1976) 'Banking and finance', in H. Patrick and H. Rosovsky (eds), *Asia's New Giant: How the Japanese Economy Works*, (Washington, DC: The Brookings Institution).

Walter, I. (1992) 'The battle of the systems: Control of enterprises and the global economy', *Journal of International Securities Markets*, vol. 6, pp. 309–17.

Weinstein, D. and Y. Yafeh (1998) 'On the costs of a bank-centered financial system: Evidence from the changing main bank relations in Japan', *Journal of Finance*, vol. 53, pp. 635–72.

Comments on Chapter 12

Murray Frank

INTRODUCTION

This comment is an attempt to place Morck and Nakamura's chapter into context. First it will be argued that Japan's performance during the 1990s was not as bad as is widely believed. However it was disappointing relative to its performance during the previous few decades. Second, it will be suggested that the evidence does not support the popular idea that misguided macro economic policy is the source of Japan's problems – at least not in the IS-LM sense in which the argument is normally presented. Third, it will be argued that Morck and Nakamura's focus on corporate governance problems is reasonable, but incomplete as an explanation of Japan's disappointing performance in the 1990s. They have identified one element of a larger problem in the Japanese financial system. Thus it will be suggested that Morck and Nakamura have revealed an important element of the problem. If they are right, and if the recent financial market reforms have the effects that many analysts are suggesting, then the prognosis for Japan's performance over the next decade is quite optimistic.

The currently leading account of Japan's problems in the 1990s is provided by Krugman (1998). He has argued that the miserable performance in the 1990s was due to the poor macroeconomic policy making in the face of a liquidity trap. The misguided policy makers refused to generate inflation. If only they had done so, all would have been well. Morck and Nakamura accept that poor macroeconomic policy may have been a factor, but suggest that the real problem lay at a deeper level. The real problem is that corporate governance is creditor determined. Accordingly firms pay too much attention to maintaining their payments to debt holders, and not enough attention to generating high returns for equity holders. As a result firms have undertaken too many investments that are excessively safe. Thus oversupply and inadequate demand follow in an old-fashioned Keynesian sense. In Krugman's purely macroeconomic interpretation, the solution is more enlightened macroeconomic policy. In the corporate governance interpretation by Morck and Nakamura the solution is to reform corporate governance so that corporate managers (and their bankers) will care more about generating high equity values.

HOW HAS JAPAN DONE IN THE 1990s?

Japan has not done nearly as badly as popular opinion seems to suggest. Consider Figure C12.1, which plots real GDP per capita for Japan and the United States for the period 1961–98. As is well known, Japan started very far behind the United States, but apart from a slow-down in the early 1970s it was closing that gap until about 1991. Over the period 1991–98 the US growth rate increased sharply while the Japanese growth rate declined. On closer examination it can be seen that Japan enjoyed an economic recovery during 1994–96, but it came to an end with the very sharp downturn of 1997–98. In 1998, for the first time since the early 1970s per capita GNP actually declined in Japan.

Where does this leave Japan? According to OECD figures for 1998, Japanese GDP per capita (purchasing power parity adjusted) was US$24 109. This was just behind Canada ($24 468) and just ahead of Belgium ($24 097) but significantly behind the United States ($30 514) albeit nothing like the poorer OECD countries such as Korea ($13 540) and Turkey ($6720) – to say nothing of the many poor countries in the world.

So Japan's the GDP per capita was not the stuff of tragedy, and neither was the unemployment rate. During course of the decade the unemployment rate very gradually drifted up from about 2 per cent to around 4 per cent, and by October 1999 it stood at 4.6 per cent. This may have been bad by postwar Japanese standards, but by international standards it was a remarkably good performance. The typical rate for the other OECD countries over the period was in the neighbourhood of 8 per cent.

Despite these figures there is a widely held perception that Japan has had a decade-long slump. Why is there such a perception? Most commentators believe that Japan could have done better. Krugman (1998) talks of a gap relative to potential output and claims that the gap is more than 5 per cent of GNP. But this is a purely notional calculation based on a particular theory of what might generate the potential. Potential output is not actually observable. Since the underlying theory is controversial, it is hard to know how much confidence ought to be placed in such calculations. It depends on your view of 'Okun's law', Hodrick–Prescott filters and other such things.

352

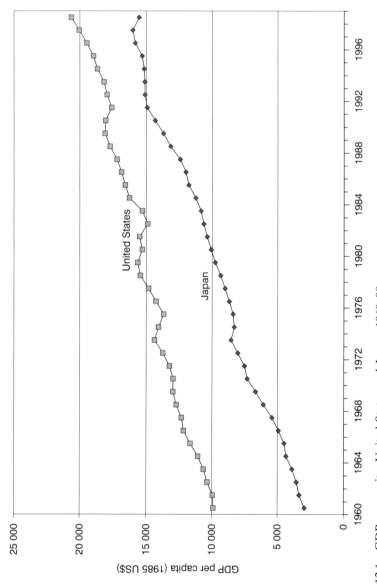

Figure C12.1   GDP per capita, United States and Japan, 1960–98
Source: Calculated data from Easterly and Yu (1999) and OECD (1999).

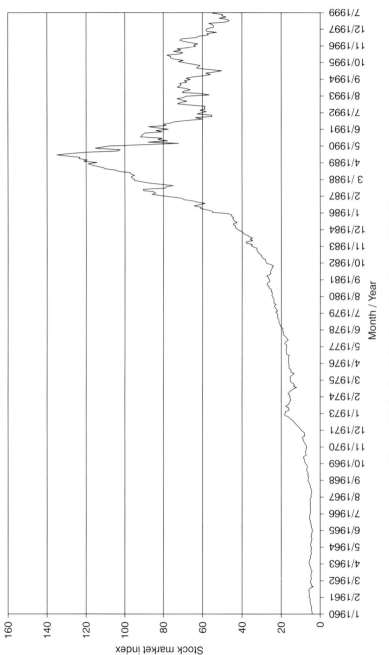

Figure C12.2   Stock Market index, Japan, 1960–99

However, as shown in Figure C12.1, there was a significant decline in the growth rate of GDP from 1991. What does have considerable policy resonance is a fairly simple calculation. If the growth rates of the 1970s and the 1980s had continued during the 1990s per capita GNP would have been much higher. Considerable attention has been focused on the bursting of the financial bubble in real estate and the stock market. As can be seen in Figure C12.2 the stock market had reached very great heights by the end of 1989, and ten years later it stood at less than half the peak value. The bursting of the financial bubble was accompanied by a sense of pessimism in popular accounts and the media. (there is a discussion of this change in mood in Chapter 12). So even if it was not a genuine tragedy, many find Japan's recent performance disappointing and they want it to do better.

MACROECONOMIC POLICY

Since there is wide spread disappointment about the performance of the Japanese economy in the 1990s, attention has naturally turned to the question of who to blame, and how to fix it. Morck and Nakamura appear to endorse the claim that Japan is in a liquidity trap.[1] In the IS-LM model there are two basic policy tools to get out of a slump: increase the money supply to shift out the LM curve, or increase government spending and government debt to shift out the IS curve. When an economy is in a liquidity trap, according to the textbooks the LM shift will not work because the LM curve is flat over the relevant range. So fiscal policy must be used.

In contrast to the textbook liquidity trap story, Krugman (1998) calls for a radical increase in the Japanese money supply in order to generate inflation. This is needed in order to have negative real interest rates. With a zero rate of inflation and an equilibrium requirement of a negative real rate of interest, the nominal rate of interest must be negative. But under the assumption that negative nominal interest are not permitted, inflation is Krugman's way out. The nominal rate can remain positive while the real rate turns negative. This actually happened in Japan in the early 1970s. Left inadequately explained is why the nominal interest rate cannot be negative. Why is the difference between 0.1 and 0 so very different from the difference between 0 and -0.1?[3]

As a matter of history there have been periods of negative nominal interest rates. These have often taken the form of service charges by banks. Particularly during earlier periods, when the main function of a bank was to offer protection for the depositor's money, there was nothing terribly strange or odd about charging depositors for this service. It does not seem far-fetched to imagine that Japanese savers might prefer the security of money in the bank rather than money in a mattress where it might be stolen.

IS-LM analysis, in either its textbook variety or its Krugman variety, calls for fiscal expansion, monetary expansion or both if we want to increase Japanese output. What has the Japanese policy stance been on each of these dimensions?

Perhaps surprisingly, given much of the rhetoric about misguided Japanese macroeconomic policy, during the 1990s Japanese fiscal policy was highly expansionary in the IS-LM sense. Using OECD figures for 1990 the general government gross public debt as a percentage of nominal GDP was 61.4 per cent in Japan and 55.3 per cent in the United States; the corresponding figures for 1997 were Japan 84.7 per cent and the United States 59.1 per cent. For 2000 it is forecast that Japan will surpass Italy on this dimension at 117.6 per cent while the United States will reach 51.7 per cent. Similarly, Japan's total government outlay as a share of GDP grew over the period from 31.3 per cent to 35.1 per cent and it continues to grow, while that in the United States fell from 35.2 per cent to 33.6 per cent and continues to shrink.

Thus by any reasonable standard Japan followed an extremely expansionary fiscal policy throughout the decade and failed to grow. The United States lacked an expansionary fiscal policy and yet it grew sharply. Looking at other countries makes the case even stronger. For example over the period 1990–98 Ireland had the highest average annual GDP growth rate of the OECD countries at 7.3 per cent in real terms. This compared with 3.0 per cent for the United States and 1.2 per cent for Japan. In 1990 the Irish debt to GDP ratio was 105.4 and by 1997 it had *fallen* to 66.9. There are many examples of intensionally expansionary fiscal policy, ranging from France under the socialists to the Canadian provinces of Ontario and British Columbia under left-wing parties. The record of these attempts to shift out the IS curve has not been pretty. During the late 1990s Japan seemed well on its way to adding another example to this sad list. It is very far from clear that increased government spending and government debt really serves to increase economic activity in the manner depicted in the textbook IS-LM model.

What about monetary policy? In the US Great Depression of the 1930s, M2 collapsed near the start. Many economists think that much

356

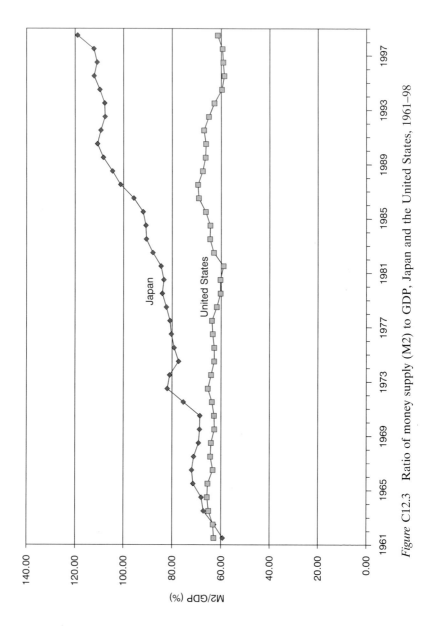

Figure C12.3 Ratio of money supply (M2) to GDP, Japan and the United States, 1961–98

of the devastation of the period could have been avoided if M2 had not been permitted to collapse by a third. Japan has not witnessed a major collapse of the money supply like that seen in the US depression. An indication of the Japanese monetary policy stance can be see in Figure C12.3, which plots the ratio of M2 to GDP. On average, since 1961 Japan has increased its money supply more than the United States has done. In the early 1990s both Japan and the United States decreased this ratio slightly, and from 1994 Japan increased the ratio to a greater extent than did the United States. In 1998 the Japanese even increased the ratio while experiencing a serious recession. From this evidence it seems hard to believe that US GDP per capita rose faster during the 1990s than Japanese GDP because of monetary policy. As with fiscal policy, these data would suggest that Japan ought to have performed at least as well as the United States over the period.

Thus the evidence suggests that Japanese policy makers in fact followed some thing not unlike textbook Keynesian policy measures to deal with the slump. The data really does not suggest that an IS-LM style remedy is really what has been missing in Japan. If one believes that increasing the money supply will generate real output, then the real mystery in Figure C12.3 is the US economic performance during the 1990s! And the real fiscal policy conundrum is why Ireland boomed while Japan did not during the period.

Perhaps in an effort to avoid controversy, Morck and Nakamura 'do not deny' the importance of poor macro policy in Japan. The evidence suggests that the Keynesian criticism of Japanese macroeconomic policy over the period is misplaced. The Japanese policy makers were more expansionary in the textbook Keynesian sense than were the Americans during the same period. It may even be that the textbook IS-LM models have the wrong signs on the fiscal policy variables, but this is not the place to investigate that possibility. The point here is that the main macroeconomic-oriented explanations that have been offered to account for Japan's performance over the period do not seem plausible. But is Morck and Nakamura's focus on corporate governance better?

THE CORPORATE GOVERNANCE PROBLEM

Morck and Nakamura provide a very interesting historical discussion of how the Japanese governance system developed. The incentive properties associated with *Keiretsu* have been widely discussed. In contrast to many of the discussions, Morck and Nakamura find the system problematic. For instance they state that 'Firms in bank-centered *keiretsu* pay higher interest costs than other similar firms.' In general they consider that firms pay too much attention to the interests of debt claimants and not enough to the interests of equity claimants. As a result firms overinvest in excessively safe projects. Thus there is excess supply. They interpret these incentives as feeding an 'old-fashioned Keynesian recession'. While they believe that stimulative macroeconomic policy will be helpful in the short run, they argue that it cannot cure the problem since it does not address the source of that problem. To fix the problem would require a change to the mode of corporate governance, in particular making changes that would result in banks becoming more interested in high equity valuations.

My concern with their approach is the question of timing. A complete story would explain why the economy did so well from 1960 to 1989. It would explain why the economy recovered so much better in the early 1970s. Why did the bubble burst? How was this related to the changes in unemployment and per capita GNP? To me their approach seems incomplete. While they do suggest that there is a connection, they do not explain how the connection works. Why did the bubble burst when it did? The timing is particularly odd since at about that time Japan's major export market (the United States) entered a period of particularly robust growth. As can be seen in Figure C12.2, between 1973 and 1975 the financial market also suffered a significant decline. Yet a couple of years later Japan resumed its high growth rate in per capita GNP. So why did it take so long in the 1990s? This seems to me to be the biggest missing piece in their otherwise rather convincing discussion.

It is not clear how best to answer these questions. On a speculative note, one possibility is that for many years the investment opportunities available were so rich that minor errors in judgement hardly mattered in most cases. As the easy pickings are reduced, it makes a much bigger difference if bad decisions are made. Under this interpretation, after the bubble economy it may have been that the available domestic investment opportunities became much leaner (although it is not clear why this happened). The initial reaction was to invest more in Asian countries. That turned out poorly when the Asian crisis hit. Overall the weaknesses of the Japanese financial system became much more apparent.

In the 1980s Japan was doing well and many in the West looked to Japanese methods for guidance. But in the 1990s it ran into difficulties, and now we are told that what had been seen as strengths (in particular the *keiretsu* system) may in fact have been weaknesses. According to Morck and Nakamura, Japanese corporate governance was inducing a poor choice of investment projects all along. However until the bursting of the bubble the problem had been hidden.

FINANCIAL PROBLEMS

It seems to me that there is good reason to believe that there are broader financial system problems in Japan than just the corporate governance problems identified by Morck and Nakamura. To understand this it is helpful to recall some basics.

What is a financial system supposed to accomplish? What can we expect to observe if the system is performing its tasks well? What kinds of things would indicate potentially fixable problems? In essence any financial system has two tasks. The most basic task is to take people's savings and invest them in productive opportunities. A good financial system is one that leads to high-value projects being undertaken, and low-value projects not being undertaken. This is vitally important to the welfare of a nation. It is the most fundamental of financial problems, and it arises whether or not there is any 'risk' in the system.

Of course there really is plenty of risk in the system. Thus the second basic problem that a financial system must resolve is how to allocate the risk. It is desirable that those people who are more capable of bearing the risk do so. This needs to be accomplished without doing too much damage to the effort incentives present in the system. It also needs to be accomplished without doing too much damage to the project choice decisions made by the people in the system. As might be imagined, coping with moral hazard and adverse selection are delicate problems.

In the real world all financial systems grapple with these problems. Sometimes the problems are solved better than at other times. In some countries the problems seem to be solved better than in other countries. When conditions change, what had previously appeared to be a good solution might suddenly appear to be a bad one.

How does the Japanese financial system fare on these basic dimensions? Not all that well. It has been difficult for individual investors to move their savings to higher-paying opportunities abroad for

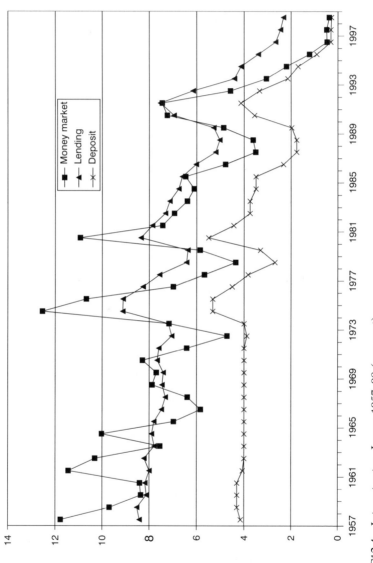

Figure C12.4   Interest rates, Japan, 1957–98 (per cent)
Source: Complied from IMF (1999).

institutional reasons. Since considerable saving was still taking place in the period in question the net effect was that interest rates declined substantially. Figure C12.4 shows the interest rates for Japan from 1957–98. By IMF definitions the money market rate is a short-term rate, the lending rate is a long-term rate and the deposit rate is what an individual can get on typical bank deposits. As can be seen, the short rate and the deposit rate came very close to zero towards the end of the 1990s. At the same time the US Treasury bill rate was about 5 per cent and the comparable rate in Britain was around 6 per cent. Thus better interest rates were available abroad. Yet the Japanese banks and other domestic financial institutions remained flush with funds throughout most of the 1990s.[3]

Thus a basic problem with the Japanese financial system is that it has not been offering investors as good a rate of return as possible. This is a crucial issue for the future welfare of the country. Turning to Japanese equities would not easily have solved the problem for Japanese investors either. Cai *et al.* (1997) have shown that Japanese mutual fund managers perform remarkably poorly.[4]

While the Japanese continued to save it may be that domestic investment opportunities worsened. As the available investment opportunities declined, borrowers were much less interested in borrowing since they did not have so many good uses for the funds. The banks had resources to lend, but they found less in the way of good investment opportunities. This may have been particularly acute for the types of investment opportunities in large firms that the banks had good experience in assessing.

As is well known, Japan had very serious banking problems in the late 1990s and this attracted considerable attention. Hoshi and Kashyap (1999) argue that the Big Bang deregulation played a big role in the Japanese banking crisis. They argue that large corporations quickly switched from depending on banks to relying on capital market financing. This suggests that the top managers will become more concerned about equity values, as indicated by Morck and Nakamura in chapter 12. When the financial market transition is complete in 2001 the Japanese financial markets will apparently be as unregulated as the US financial markets.

CONCLUSION

The evidence suggests that Japanese policy makers have not been nearly as naive as some seem to think. They have attempted to expand their economy in an IS-LM sense. Unfortunately the IS-LM model may be giving misguided policy advice. More stable fiscal policy might have served better than seemingly unsustainable fiscal 'expansion'. The money supply has not collapsed in the way it did in the United States during the Great Depression. Indeed it remained surprisingly high during the serious recession.

More importantly the policy makers do seem to be taking steps to reform their financial system. I think that Morck and Nakamura have probably correctly identified an important part of Japan's disappointing economic performance during the 1990s. They have certainly provided a much more believable explanation than the current high-profile macroeconomic policy explanations. Indeed I think that they err in giving too much credence to the macroeconomic policy interpretations. However their explanation as it stands is incomplete. They have not accounted for the timing and why the early 1990s differed from the early 1970s.

Suppose that Morck and Nakamura have correctly identified a crucial part of the problem. Suppose that they and Hoshi and Kashayp (1999) are right about the behaviour of large Japanese firms in reaction to the Big Bang. Then it may be that the first decade of the 21st century will again see a much better performance by the Japanese economy. We shall see.

Notes

1. 'A liquidity trap may be defined as a situation in which conventional monetary policies have become impotent, because nominal interest rates are at or near zero – so injecting monetary base into the economy has no effect, because base and bonds are viewed by the private sector as perfect substitutes' (Krugman, 1998).
2. In Krugman (1998) the answer has to do with people switching between alternative financial assets. The fact that such a massive switching of assets has not been observed, as a zero nominal interest rate has been approached over the last few years, ought to call the underlying model into question. Instead Krugman takes the fact that the nominal interest rate has not actually fallen below zero as evidence that it cannot do so.
3. It is worth noting that for the top income earners, Japan (at least in 1998, according to the OECD, 1999) gives a much bigger tax break for investors who get their returns in the form of interest on bank deposits. This may have encouraged continuing bank deposits, and been nice for the banks. But it does not seem to be a good way to encourage savings in forms that will generate the highest future per capita GNP.

4. It would seem that an important policy issue for Japan is to make better savings vehicles available to the citizens. An easy way to do this would be to encourage the creation of a menu of index funds based on a range of international stock and bond indexes. These should probably be offered both with and without exchange rate insurance clauses, so that individuals can decide whether to undertake such a risk. It is important that these indexed investment vehicles should be offered by financial institutions the Japanese people have long experience with and can trust. Unfortunately this is not the right place to go into greater detail about this issue.

References

Cai, Jun, K. C. Chan and Takeshi Yamada (1997) 'The Performance of Japanese Mutual Funds', *Review of Financial Studies*, vol. 10, pp. 237–74.

Easterly, William and Hairong Yu (1999) 'Global Development Network Growth Database', World Bank (http://www.worldbank.org/growth/GDNdata.htm).

Hoshi, Takeo and Anil Kashyap (1999) 'The Japanese Banking Crisis: Where Did It Come From and How Will It End?', NBER Working Paper W7250 (Cambridge, Mass.: NBER).

IMF (1999) *International Financial Statistics* (Washington, DC: IMF).

Krugman, Paul (1998) 'It's Baaack! Japan's Slump and the Return of the Liquidity Trap', working paper, MIT (http://web.mit.edu/krugman/www/bpea_jp.pdf).

OECD (1999) 'Economic Survey of Japan, 1999', policy brief (Paris: OECD).

13 Environmental Issues and Japanese Firms

Kozo Horiuchi and Masao Nakamura[1]

LOCAL ENVIRONMENTAL ISSUES

While the Japanese economy enjoyed unprecedentedly high growth in the late 1960s, Japan's natural environment deteriorated rapidly. Many Japanese factories dumped effluent containing harmful pollutants into rivers and oceans and emitted other pollutants into the air. The air pollution was worsened by car exhaust. The health problems caused by all this pollution became a serious problem in Japan.

In the 1960s and 1970s the pollution problem had two main characteristics. First, environmental damage was generally local and limited to the areas where those responsible for the pollution were located. Second, the local residents suffered serious health problems (Figure 13.1). Unfortunately the Japanese government was slow to take significant antipollution measures, and although the government introduced the Basic Law for Environmental Pollution Control in 1967 and the Air Pollution Control Law in 1968, both of these laws turned out to be ineffective. Pollution continued to cause life-threatening ailments such as Minamata disease (mercury poisoning) and severe asthma due to air pollution in cities such as Kawasaki and Yokkaichi.

When the damage to personal health became more obvious in the early 1970s the government at last implemented a number of measures to reduce the problem. These consisted of a series of amendments to the pollution control laws and some additional laws, including the Cost Allocation of Public Pollution Control Law and the Punishment for Environmental Pollution Crimes Relating to Human Health Law.

By international standards, extremely strict environmental requirements were introduced. Factories (particularly large factories) were forced to conform to legally set limits on the emission of airborne pollutants as well as pollutants contained in effluent. For example the Japanese pulp industry was responsible for most of the organic pollu-

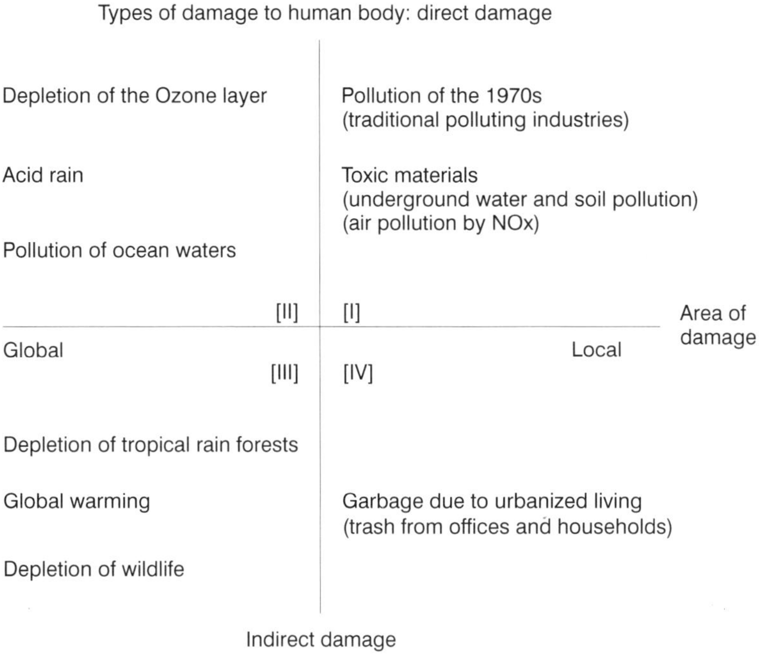

Types of damage to human body: direct damage

Depletion of the Ozone layer	Pollution of the 1970s (traditional polluting industries)
Acid rain	Toxic materials (underground water and soil pollution) (air pollution by NOx)
Pollution of ocean waters	

	[II]	[I]		Area of damage
Global			Local	
	[III]	[IV]		

Depletion of tropical rain forests	
Global warming	Garbage due to urbanized living (trash from offices and households)
Depletion of wildlife	

Indirect damage

Figure 13.1   Characteristics of environmental problems

tion in the Inland Sea, which was on the verge of irrecoverable decline in 1970 (Nishimura, 1995). The pulp industry was required by law to reduce the amount of discharged waste to a fifth of the previous level within two years and to a twentieth within seven years. The industry responded by completely abandoning the sulfite pulp (SP) production process used up until then in favour of the new Kraft pulp (KP) process. The KP process is not only environmentally clean but also energy-saving since it turns organic waste into energy to power the production process.

Regulatory agencies monitored the quantity of pollutants emitted by factories in real time using telemeter-based systems so that the agencies could help the factories to observe the pollution emission levels. Such governmental monitoring was unique to Japan in the early 1970s.

There are two types of policy measures by which governments can deal with environmental problems. The first of these consists of taxation, subsidies and other interventions to align the incentives of polluting firms with the well-being of the public. It should be noted that such an alignment was also promoted by the significant oil price increases after the oil shocks of the 1970s. The government's policy to promote the global competitiveness of Japanese industry despite rising energy costs resulted in a massive effort, financial and otherwise, to encourage Japanese firms to shift their investment to sectors that consumed less energy and also to deploy energy-saving production equipment, which tends to create less pollution (Mani and Wheeler, 1998). In fact because of Japan's persistent effort to encourage the adoption of environmentally friendly technologies and to reduce energy consumption, its per capita level of carbon dioxide emissions is already low by international standards (Hayami *et al.*, 1997).

Another type of policy measure consists of direct controls, such as those ones laid down in the new laws mentioned above. The cost of the antipollution and pollution-abatement equipment that these laws required manufacturers to purchase was significant.[2] Further more strict environmental requirements forced Japanese firms to develop new antipollution technologies, and those became the world's leading-edge antipollution technologies. Industrial investment in pollution control and energy-saving devices increased from a few per cent of total investment in plant and equipment in the late 1960s to a peak of 20 per cent in 1975, and then gradually declined to a few per cent in the mid 1980s, yielding an average of about 10 per cent in the 1970s. The corresponding figures for the United States, the Netherlands, Germany and Sweden in 1975 were considerably lower: 3.4 per cent, 2.7 per cent, 2.3 per cent and 1.2 per cent respectively (Nishimura, 1995). There was general agreement that Japanese industry had been successful in 'decoupling environmental degradation and economic growth, proving that environmental policies and economic growth policies can be not only compatible but indeed mutually supportive' (OECD, 1994, pp. 95–6). In fact, during the 1970s and 1980s Japan achieved the highest economic growth rate among the G7 countries while reducing its SO_2 and NO_x emissions at a higher rate than the other OECD members (OECD, 1994).

The Japanese government's measures to improve the quality of the natural environment were effective in minimizing the social costs that result from a deteriorating natural environment. Firms bore the cost of investment in water and air pollution control, and the direct measures were firmly grounded in the polluter-pays principle. The government's administrative costs were low, partly because the environmental measures and monitoring, which were implemented with the backing of powerful political forces, focused mostly on large-scale factories: the primary polluters.

However, since the 1980s the types of pollution have grown in number and now include those resulting from certain consumption practices. The most serious local environmental problems in Japan include the release of dioxin and similar poisonous contaminants.[3] There are also general concerns that, for example, the hormones released into the environment with waste products are damaging human health. Other serious human health problems are attributable to car exhaust. Despite Japan's stringent requirements on exhaust emissions, people living or working near major roads and highways are still suffering health problems. It can be expected that as long as mass production, mass consumption and mass waste continues Japan will continue to experience environmental problems, some new and some old (Figure 13.1, parts I and IV).

GLOBAL ENVIRONMENTAL ISSUES

In the 1980s, global environmental problems emerged as an important public policy issue. These problems were quite different from the traditional local water and air pollution problems Japan had suffered during the late 1960s through the late 1970s. For example the widespread use of chlorofluorocarbons (CFCs), halons and other chlorine- or bromine-containing compounds resulted in depletion of the atmospheric ozone layer, increasing the risk of skin cancer.[4] Thus damage caused by CFCs, halons and so on is not limited to the local area or country where the emissions take place. Rather the entire global community suffers from the damage.

Other causes of global environmental damage are the commercial destruction of tropical rain forests, the eradication of animals, plants and other types of wild life and the massive use of fossil fuels (II in Figure 13.1).

Depletion of the ozone layer

Health concerns about the depletion of the ozone layer in the 1970s led to a ban on the use of CFCs as aerosol propellants in several countries, including the United States. However the production of CFCs and other ozone-depleting substances grew rapidly afterward as new uses for these compounds were discovered, and the world's nations became increasingly concerned that these chemicals would further deplete the ozone layer. In 1985 the Vienna Convention was adopted to formalize international cooperation on this issue. Additional efforts resulted in the signing of the Montreal Protocol in 1987. The original protocol would have reduced the production of CFCs by half by 1998.[5] Because of measures taken under the protocol, emissions of ozone-depleting substances are already falling. Assuming continued compliance, stratospheric chlorine levels will peak in a few years and then slowly return to normal. The natural ozone production process is expected to restore the ozone layer in about 50 years.

In addition to regulating the production of the ozone-depleting substances, some government agencies have implemented several other programmes to protect the ozone layer. For example the US Environmental Protection Agency introduced programmes of this sort under Title VI of the Clean Air Act. These programmes include refrigerant recycling, product labelling, banning non-essential uses of certain compounds and reviewing substitutes.

In Japan the government has introduced a series of regulations since the Ozone Layer Protection Law was passed in 1988. For example, consistent with the Montreal Protocol, Japan banned the production and use of halons and CFCs by the end of 1993 and 1995 respectively. Production and use of other chemicals that damage the ozone layer have been either banned or regulated. Japanese firms that use CFCs, for example, are required to limit their emissions of CFCs and rationalize their use. But this is a voluntary requirement and there is no legal penalty for underachievers, although the Environmental Agency and the Ministry of International Trade and Industry (MITI) provide joint guidelines and advice to the firms concerned.

In order to promote the recycling of CFCs contained in cars and refrigerators, special councils for retrieving CFCs were established in all prefectures and certain large cities in August 1999. Certain appliance retailers and car dealers have become registered cooperators for the recycling of CFCs, and consumers can take unwanted appliances to them for salvaging. This service is subject to a fee, and to avoid this many consumers take their redundant appliances to shops that are not registered cooperators. Alternatively refrigerators can be collected for a fee by the local government refuse collection agency. The fees for this are lower than the fees charged by registered cooperators, and the local refuse agencies also recycle CFCs.

The estimated recycling rates for CFCs in 1998 are as follows: 29 per cent of total units of home refrigerators, 12 per cent in volume of CFCs contained in car airconditioners and 56 per cent in volume of CFCs contained in industrial freezers and refrigerators. These recovery rates are low but are increasing. (The amount of CFCs destroyed in Japan increased from 142 tons in 1997 to 537 tons in 1998.) Currently, special corporate income tax and accelerated depreciation subsidies are provided to firms that invest in washing, refrigeration and freezer facilities that use CFC substitutes. Firms that invest in these facilities are eligible for low-interest government loans.

The Japanese programmes for recycling CFCs are not yet internally consistent and do not take into account the cost–benefit calculations by consumers and recycling dealers such as registered cooperators. Unless the relevant costs of recycling CFCs are explicitly internalized within the Japanese programmes, the recovery rate for CFCs is not likely to rise very quickly.

Global warming

We have seen that even though the potential damage to human health from using CFCs is known to many Japanese, it is not easy to formulate and implement policy measures to encourage the recovery of CFCs. Unlike the ozone layer depletion problem, global warming does not cause any direct damage to human health (IV in Figure 13.1) and the issue is intertwined with production, consumption and foreign trade matters where nations' interests are not necessarily aligned. For example Japan imports natural resources such as coal, minerals and timber in large quantities from Canada. Because of the increased level of atmospheric CO_2 associated with the production of these products it is often argued that in effect Japan is exporting CO_2 to Canada. This is particularly the case since most of Japan's exports to Canada are manufactured goods whose production generates only relatively small amounts of CO_2. (See Hayami *et al.*, 1999, for a policy analysis of bilateral trade between Canada and Japan and global warming issues.) Similar issues exist in trade between developed nations and resource-rich developing nations. For these reasons there is much less public interest in promptly solving the global warming problem. It seems particularly difficult for the international community to form an agreement to curb global warming.

A characteristic of global environmental problems is that there is a significant time lag between the act that causes the damage and recognition of that damage. For example developed countries have taken several centuries to attain the high living standards now enjoyed by most of their citizens. During the developmental process the burning of fossil fuels such as coal and petroleum was (and will continue to be) an important source of energy. The consequent and massive emission of CO_2 gradually led to global warming, which appears to have accelerated in the last few decades. Atmospheric CO_2 is eventually absorbed by such sinks as oceans and plants, but the speed of absorption is slow and it is thought that it will take 50 years for the current volume of excess CO_2 to halve, and even longer for the remaining half.

Our highly developed, consumer-oriented society is likely to continue to depend on fossil fuels, the effects of which will bear heavily on future generations. The important question to resolve is how to live well now without lowering the quality of life of future generations. This is the notion of sustainable development, which provides a basic framework for analyzing global environmental problems.[6]

Uncertainty and irreversibility

There are two major problems when analyzing global environmental problems: uncertainty and irreversibility. Analysis of how human activities affect the global environment requires complex models of the mechanisms involved, the understanding of which is associated with a significant degree of uncertainty. How much CO_2 is emitted in each individual economic activity? (Hayami *et al.*, 1997, and Hayami *et al.*, 1999, provide estimates for the Canadian and Japanese economies for 1990). How many degrees will air temperature increase as a result? How will the Earth's weather patterns change? By how much will the sea level rise? Given our imprecise understanding of the dynamics between economic activities and environmental phenomena, even with the use of supercomputers the predictions these models provide for global environmental conditions over a period of 100 to 200 years are plagued by a high degree of uncertainty.

The UN IPCC report (1995) predicted that if the present level of economic activity were to continue, the mean atmospheric temperature would rise by 2 °C between 1990 and 2100, but the predictions upon which this mean was based ranged between 1.0 °C and 3.5 °C. Similarly the predicted average rise in sea level was 50 centimeters but its predicted range was between 15 and 95 centimeters. How global warming will affect specific local areas seems impossible to predict, but it is likely to cause serious harm to agriculture, forestry and fisheries. It is also predicted that the rise in sea level will seriously damage the ecosystems of islands and coastal areas in the South Pacific.

Another characteristic of global environmental damage is that it is often irreversible, or at best will not be reparable in the span of a human lifetime.

Hence global warming is characterized by a large time lag between cause and effect, together with a high degree of uncertainty and irreversibility. Also, because it is not yet causing direct harm to humans, widespread recognition of the seriousness of the problem may come too late. It is therefore essential for nations immediately to adopt effective policy measures that will allow future generations to have a wider range of policy alternatives and will promote sustainable development. Such policies are called 'no regret' policies.

JAPAN'S ENVIRONMENTAL POLICY SHIFT FROM DIRECT TO INDIRECT REGULATION MEASURES

Japan's policy for dealing with its own pollution problems in the 1970s consisted primarily of direct regulatory measures, but its current policy measures on the global environment are fundamentally different. Global environmental management extends to all areas of production, distribution, consumption and waste management. The breadth of both the objects and the origins of the environmental problems implies that the cost of monitoring direct regulations would be enormous. Also, direct government regulation of environmentally damaging production and consumption processes implies that governments would unilaterally determine the path of global society. This would not be a desirable outcome, given the uncertain and irreversible nature of environmental problems.

The direct measures that the Japanese government imposed on large polluting factories in the 1970s constrained firms' profit-maximizing decisions and made them less able to adapt promptly to changes in business conditions. At the same time, sectors that were not subject to direct regulations had no incentive to implement environmentally desirable measures. Because of these sorts of complications we believe that dealing with the current global problems will require indirect regulatory measures that make use of price mechanisms to influence behaviour. One such measure would be an environmental tax: a tax on activities that damage the environment, and subsidies and/or reductions in taxes for activities that improve the environment.

Indirect regulatory measures of this type, unlike direct measures, would force firms to reevaluate the economics of their polluting activities, because the latter would become more costly to undertake while activities to improve the environment would become relatively cheap. Under these conditions many firms would find it profitable to invest promptly in R&D for pollution-reduction methods. Firms would find inaction unacceptable for competitive reasons. In general, indirect environmental regulations would allow firms to choose among various alternatives so as to maximize their profitability when facing new input and product prices. Precisely the same argument can be made in respect of households in the case of indirect environmental measures such as petrol taxes.

Indirect environmental regulations would facilitate firms' response to the new environmental realities by requiring their business decisions to be based on the incentives offered. For this reason, indirect measures would be particularly effective when the environmental problems in question involved a large degree of uncertainty. Such measures would also encourage households, governmental and non-profit organizations to adjust their behaviour in response to the problem. Wisdom on the part of individual decision makers is particularly essential.

As discussed earlier, Japan's initial antipollution measures consisted of direct regulations and the development of environmentally friendly technologies as a package. It is fair to say that this policy succeeded in the 1970s and 1980s, since Japan's natural environment did improve during this period. Furthermore its economy continued to grow at a significant rate. We should also note the relationship between a nation's economic growth and the amount of pollutants it produces. There is some international evidence (Grossman and Krueger, 1991; Selden and Song, 1992) that pollution caused by SO_x, airborne particles and carbon monoxide is worse in the initial stages of a nation's economic development, but improves considerably as the economy grows and becomes more prosperous. On the other hand there is no evidence that the pollution problems caused by NO_x and CO_2 lessen with economic growth. These factors need to be incorporated into environmental policy measures.

In December 1997 the United Nations conference on the prevention of global warming took place in Kyoto, Japan. During the conference Japan promised a 6 per cent reduction in the emission of global warming gases from the level observed in 1990, to be achieved by 2008–2012. This reduction was similar to those proposed by the United States (7 per cent) and the EU (8 per cent). Nevertheless it will be very difficult for Japan to bring about this reduction in the time promised, given the already high level of energy-saving measures throughout society. In fact some energy specialists have pointed out that energy-saving measures alone will not allow Japan (and other developed nations) to achieve the emission reductions proposed in the Kyoto Protocol (Horiuchi, 1998b).

There are limitations in relying entirely on the development of new technologies to achieve the required reduction in global warming gases. We can see this by projecting the emission levels into the mid 21st century. Suppose that the world population has grown to 10 billion by then and that developing nations have achieved the standard of living currently enjoyed by the citizens of developed countries. Simple calculations suggest that the annual global emission of CO_2 will reach 4.7 times the current level by then. The Earth cannot absorb the current level of CO_2 emitted and this is already causing global warming. It is highly unlikely that the development of new technologies will be sufficient to remedy the problem, given the present patterns of emission. We therefore conclude that unless nations drastically reduce their emissions of CO_2 and other global warming gases by other means, sustainable growth will not be possible. Direct reduction of Japan's CO_2 emission will require changes to the current way of life and in this respect it is important to implement indirect environmental measures of the type discussed above.

GLOBAL ENVIRONMENTAL ISSUES AND CHANGING JAPANESE MANAGEMENT

One aspect of the post-Second World War Japanese management that attracted much attention in the literature was its bottom-up nature. Japanese bottom-up business practices such as team work and quality circles contributed significantly to manufacturing productivity. These bottom-up practices were particularly effective in allowing Japanese firms to catch up with advanced North American and European firms in terms of increased productivity and sales revenues. Now that they have achieved that goal, Japanese firms must tackle the other challenges facing them.

The deterioration of the global environment is one of the most important issues facing contemporary Japanese management, and Japanese firms are facing an uncertain future. Just as sustainable development has become the global goal for economic development, the creation of strategies to achieve sustainable development have become an important goal for firm management in Japan.[7]

Faced with a public demand for sustainability strategies, Japanese firms are now trying to develop, on a voluntary basis, their own corporate strategies, which require Japanese managers to become more decisive and exhibit leadership in their management. As stated above, bottom-up management has been the backbone of post-war participatory management practices in Japan, but this approach has limitations when it comes to creating and implementing sustainable development strategies. Many Japanese firms now recognize that times have changed and that significant aspects of top-down management must be introduced.

This by no means implies that bottom-up management has lost its usefulness. Nevertheless there are important areas in which this approach has failed to produce results that align with the macro goals of the Japanese economy or of the corporate sector itself. The top managers of Japanese corporations are recognizing the need to introduce, in a top-down manner, new management goals towards which bottom-up efforts can be directed. Once this alignment has been achieved, Japanese management practices based on the participatory efforts of workers will again become effective in achieving macro goals, including global environmental ones. (See Fruin and Nakamura, 1997, for a discussion of the recent trend in top-down management practices in Japan.)

In this new management paradigm, top executives have clear visions that are embodied in their firms' management principles. Management goals and strategic plans are formulated according to these principles and new management departments are being created in many Japanese firms to help top executives with managerial decisions. In fact global environmental problems have prompted many firms in the Japanese petroleum, electrical equipment, and manufacture and electrical power industries to establish top-down management procedures and implement organizational reforms along the lines described above.

About 48 per cent of listed Japanese firms had already introduced formal management principles in respect of the environment by 1995 (Japanese Environmental Agency, 1995) and the number is rapidly increasing. The existence of policies of this sort increases with firm size and more than 90 per cent of large Japanese firms with annual sales revenues of at least one trillion yen have introduced them. Fifty-six per cent of firms have a top executive who is responsible for environmental matters and the number of such firms is also increasing. Thirty-nine per cent of firms have special sections or departments to deal with environmental issues, or 78 per cent in the case of large firms with sales revenues of at least 1 trillion yen.

As these figures show, leading Japanese firms have responded quickly to the global environmental challenge and top executives understand that the survival of their firms is closely tied to their environmental strategies. Typically they lead middle managers and other employees in dealing with these issues. It is very important for firms to educate middle managers and other employees about the new environmental paradigm that they face, and the recent introduction of ISO 14001 by Japanese firms has helped them with this task. (The stated objective of ISO 14001 is continuously to monitor and improve firms' environmental management processes.)

GLOBAL ENVIRONMENTAL ISSUES AND THE JAPANESE CAR INDUSTRY

The Japanese car industry has been proactive in dealing with environmental issues. Car manufacturers in Japan, Europe and the United States face the same fundamental problems. They must find ways to reduce petrol consumption and NO_x emissions, and promote the recycling of used car parts. The survival of these companies in the global market may well depend on how well they perform in the keen competition to achieve these goals.

Toyota's environmental strategy is attracting considerable attention in Japan (Toyota, 1999). In 1992 Toyota adopted a formal policy on the environment, stating that it was Toyota's mission to provide clean and safe products and to contribute, through all its corporate activities, to the sustainability of the planet and a prosperous society. Based on this, Toyota formalized an environmental charter based on the following principles: (1) sympathetic treatment of the environment; (2) prevention of accidents; and (3) positive contributions to society. This led to the introduction of an environmental plan in 1993 that consisted of 22 specific targets, including the reduction of toxic emissions, improved mileage and the development of clean-energy cars.

Under the leadership of its top management, Toyota undertook an organizational reform to deal with global environmental issues. In 1992 the Toyota Environmental Committee, chaired by Toyota's CEO, was set up to discuss important environmental issues from the overall corporate perspective. Three subcommittees were also established: the Product Environmental Committee (to deal with issues at the product development stages), the Production Committee (to deal with issues at the procurement, production and logistics stages) and the Recycling Committee (to deal with issues of product distribution, sales and scrapping). In 1998 Toyota also established an environmental department, consisting of environmental experts who are changed with promoting environmental improvement activities. The environment department reports to and advises the office of the CEO. Its functions include guiding the company's overall environment policy, coordinating cross-functional conflicts in environmental policies, and serving as the secretariat to the various environmental committees. Through this framework Toyota transmits the strategies put in place by top management to the entire organization.

According to estimates by the Japan Automobile Association on the total emission of CO_2 that occurs during the production and lifetime of a 2000cc car, about 86 per cent of emissions occur during the driving stage and the remaining 14 per cent in the production and the scrapping stages. For this reason Toyota prioritized the development of an environmentally friendly engine, and in 1997 produced the Prius, which is powered by a hybrid petroleum–electric engine. The Prius attracted considerable attention in the Japanese car market and received the Car of the Year Award in 1997.[8] Toyota also set up a company committee on lifecycle assessment, which promotes the reduction of environmental damage during the procurement, distribution and scrapping processes.

In addition to the above reforms, Toyota implemented a procedure to monitor the costs associated with its environmental policies, including R&D, investment and the costs arising from environmental policies, such as scrapping parts. (Toyota's expenditure in 1998 on R&D and investment in plant and equipment were, respectively, 448 billion yen and 330 billion yen.) The estimated 1998 environmental cost for Toyota was 97 billion yen (9 billion yen for maintenance and 88 billion yen for investment in environment-related projects), which constituted about 1 per cent of its sales revenue for that year.

Since the early 1990s the top management of car manufacturers in Japan have recognized that global environmental problems may have a vital bearing on their firms' sustainability. For this reason they have established top-down organizations in which individual managerial responsibilities are clearly delineated and environment-related costs are monitored. It is our view that many of these firms are responding to the global environmental challenges voluntarily and to a greater extent than that required by government regulations. There are a number of reasons for this.

First, such voluntary actions are essential to survival in the highly competitive global car industry. Strategic alliances to develop fuel cells and other environmentally friendly engine technologies, for example between Ford, Daimler Benz and Chrysler since 1998 (Daimler now owns Chrysler) and between Toyota and GM since 1999, make it even more important for firms to build up their competence in environmental technologies so that they can benefit from these alliances.[9] The developer of a new technology that is adopted by the world car industry as an industry standard will benefit enormously and Japanese car manufacturers' voluntary environmental R&D investment expenditures are consistent with this objective.

Second, a significant change has taken place in the environmental awareness of Japanese consumers in general. In particular the Rio Earth Summit in 1992 and the Kyoto COP3 meeting in 1997 generated considerable sympathy among Japanese consumers for policy measures to deal with global warming. Toyota's domestic advertising campaign to promote the sale of the Prius was far more successful than anticipated and public relations experts agree that the Japanese public was impressed with Toyota as an environmentally friendly firm.[10]

Third, Japanese government policies towards the environment have changed. For example in 1999 the government reducted the sales tax on cars with a high mileage per gallon of petrol, such as the Prius. The government is also considering reducing the road tax on such cars. However this alone may not serve the stated objective of an environmental tax, since such tax reductions may promote the purchase of high-mileage cars without reducing the total emission of global warming gases. From an economic perspective it is more desirable and consistent with theory for such tax reductions to be combined with measurable reductions in the emission of CO_2 and NO_x.

Another noteworthy change in Japan's environmental policy is the implementation of direct regulations. For example, to control the emission of CO_2 the Energy Saving Law was revised and reenacted in 1999.[11] This law introduced a system of energy savings in the consumption standards for cars, home appliances and automated office equipment. Manufacturers of these products are now required to develop products whose energy consumption standards are at least as good as the best performer in each category of products. This means that the most energy-efficient product becomes the industry standard, and firms that perform best in this area gain a competitive edge. The Japanese government is able to punish firms that fail to meet the industry standards by means of warnings, the publication of company names and other explicit punishments. To establish a competitive advantage in the market in accordance with this law, Japanese carmakers and appliance manufacturers are implementing their own voluntary environmental policies.

NEW RELATIONSHIP BETWEEN FIRMS AND GOVERNMENT

Clearly there is a relationship between firms' approach to the environment and the Japanese government's environmental policy. The 1970s was the era of pollution prevention and dealing with industrial waste became an urgent problem. Environmental management by firms closely followed the government's regulations, which proved quite successful.

In the 1980s Japanese firms shifted their environmental policy emphasis towards the prevention of pollution. This meant controlling the amount of waste being produced rather than dealing with harmful waste after the fact. In the 1990s firms' environmental responses advanced even further. For example, reducing waste by improving the manufacturing process drew the attention of many Japanese firms in the wake of recognition that a reduction in waste would lead not only to a reduction in environmental costs but also to increased efficiency due to increased yields. This is, of course, the notion underlying the win–win strategy in environmental management (Porter and van der Linde, 1995).

The evolution of environmental management by Japanese firms reflects realities such as stricter environmental standards and penalties, the publication of information on firms' environmental performance, and more frequent environment-related law suits. Examples of stricter environmental standards include mandated reductions in the emission of dioxin and higher energy-saving goals. An example of stricter punishment is the strengthened enforcement by the Japanese police of laws on the dumping of industrial waste. The police now prosecute not only waste disposal companies but also the producers of the waste. In 1999 the government passed legislation that led to the institution of the Pollutant Release and Transfer Register (this can be viewed as the Japanese counterpart of the US Toxics Release Inventory Program). Firms are now required to report emissions of 200 chemical substances, including dioxin. This information is published.

Another important factor that has stimulated Japanese firms' interest in environmental management is the recent government discussion on proposed measures such as environmental taxes and the creation of emission rights markets. Some Japanese firms, especially firms in the energy industry, are opposed to the introduction of a carbon tax, but a number of large firms are already discussing the potential of trade in the right to emit CO_2.[12]

Many Japanese firms view environmental issues as a strategic subject of corporate management. This implies, among other things, that their response to environmental issues is not handled in an *ad hoc* manner as in the past, but rather in a company-wide, strategic manner (see Nakamura *et al.*, forthcoming, for an analysis of this). We have described earlier how car manufacturers are engaged in the design of environmentally friendly cars, and how many firms are tying their management plans, R&D and investment in plant and equipment to environmental policies in a top-down manner.

One procedure that is attracting attention in environmental management is life-cycle assessment of products. Leading firms are assessing the impact of their products on the environment at three stages – the production stage, the utilization stage and the scrapping stage – the overall assessment is used to design and develop new products tailored to reduce the environmental load. In addition, environmental monitoring based on ISO 14001 is being widely adopted by Japanese firms.[13] Thus firms use life cycle assessment and ISO 14001 to improve their environmental performance on a continuing basis. An increasing number of firms also publish corporate environmental reports, which often work as an image-enhancing mechanism.[14]

Another development is environmental accounting, upon which the Japanese Environment Agency published draft guidelines in March 1999. These guidelines divide the costs of environmental maintenance into the following items: (1) the direct cost of waste disposal and the removal of other sources of pollution; (2) the indirect cost of training employees in environmental management; (3) the cost of recycling products; and (4) the cost of associated research and development.

Fujitsu, Japan IBM, Kirin Beer, Matsushita, NEC and Sony have already begun to practice environmental accounting on a tentative basis, and have published the relevant figures in their corporate environmental reports.

The green procurement movement is spreading rapidly among large electrical equipment and car manufacturers, many of whom require their subcontractors and suppliers to be competent not only in the traditional areas such as price and quality but also in reducing pollutants, saving resources and energy, and monitoring environmental performance and management. For these reasons, small and medium-sized firms are now being prompted to obtain ISO 14001 certification.

In the public policy domain, emphasis is shifting towards the enhancement of public environmental consciousness and the promotion of voluntary responses to environmental issues on the part of industry through a proper governmental framework. It is likely that the government will promote the green labelling movement, expand the tax reduction programme for environmental R&D and implement new environmental taxes. Furthermore national policy will have to be coordinated with international requirements. There is a need for harmonized international environmental standards, regulations and environmental taxes. In the private sector it will become essential for industrial associations to formulate their own environmental code of behaviour and promote voluntary responses by firms to global environmental issues.

We should also note the following. First, dealing with global environmental issues requires step-by-step interactions between government and business. Second, the management of global environmental issues must shift from more adherence to the regulations to the prevention of pollution, and further to the implementation of environmental strategies. Accordingly, government policies must shift from direct regulations to market-based indirect incentives.

It is most important for firms to make voluntary choices in their response to global environmental issues and to implement those choices. Their responsibilities should not stop at merely obeying government regulations. Firms should be responsible, on behalf of the consumers of their products and the residents of the areas where they operate, for administering common property such as air, water and soil. This is the firms' stewardship obligation. Firms do not own all the resources they use; rather they have a community responsibility to manage these resources. We regard this as the social responsibility of contemporary firms.

It will be important as well for industrial associations to cooperate with and facilitate their members' environmental responses. The Japanese Chemical Industry Association (1990), the International Chamber of Commerce (1991) and the Japan Federation of Employers (Keidanren, 1991) are already promoting voluntary and active responses to global environmental issues among their member firms.

Our view is that, because of their complexity and global coverage, today's environmental problems cannot be tackled entirely by government regulations, as they were in the 1960s and 1970s. Proactive participation in the process by such corporate stakeholders as managers, employees, customers, consumers and local residents is essential.

For Japanese society fully to address global environmental issues it is necessary to have (1) well-articulated government policies that provide private firms with the incentive to align themselves with social environmental goals, and (2) a real change in attitude towards the environment on the part of corporate managers and consumers. As individual citizens begin more fully to understand the problem of the global environment and firms begin to accept their responsibility in this area, solutions to the problem will begin to emerge.

Notes

1. M. Nakamura's research was in part supported by the Social Science and Humanities Research Council of Canada and the Japan Foundation.
2. In 1974 a law was enacted to compensate individuals whose health was harmed by pollution. This law allowed the Japanese government to tax firms for emitting noxious substances such as SO_x. In 1979 a tax levy of 1300 yen per cubic meter of SO_x was implemented in areas where air pollution was particularly severe. The money collected from polluting firms under this law was used for the medical expenses and income maintenance of those who were certified to be suffering from environmental pollution-based diseases. This law may be viewed as a solution based on economic means. At the same time electric power companies, which were major polluters of the atmosphere, were required to remain within a set level of SO_x emissions. The power companies responded by installing SO_x-removal equipment. The cost to the companies of removing one cubic meter of SO_x ranged from 2100 to 3400 yen, which exceeded the tax levy on SO_x emissions discussed above by a large amount. This made the incentive plan less than fully effective. We conclude that in the 1970s direct government regulations were much more effective than indirect and economic regulations (see Horiuch, 1981).

3. A wide range of dioxin isomers are produced in low-temperature combustion processes using fuels that contain carbon and chlorine. Dioxins are, however, destroyed above a certain temperature (800 °C). People who live or work near municipal incinerators and coal-fired power plants are thought to be potentially at risk.

4. CFCs are stable, non-flammable, low in toxicity and inexpensive to produce. Hence they are widely used in refrigerants, solvents, foam-blowing agents and other applications. Other widely used chlorine-containing compounds include methyl chloroform (a solvent), carbon tetrachloride (an industrial chemical), halons (extremely effective fire extinguishing agents) and methyl bromide (an effective crop and soil fumigant). All of these compounds have atmospheric lifetimes that are long enough to allow them to be transported by wind into the stratosphere. Because they release chlorine or bromine when they break down, they damage the protective ozone layer.

5. After the original protocol was signed, new measurements showed more damage to the ozone layer than had been expected. In 1992, reacting to the latest scientific assessment of the ozone layer, the signatory parties decided to end the production of halons by the beginning of 1994 and CFCs by the beginning of 1996 in developed countries. For example Japan had ceased production of CFCs by the end of 1995. The use of CFCs as aerosol propellants had been voluntarily terminated by product manufacturers prior to December 1995, but the exact date of this is not known.

6. The Brundtland Commission made the concept of sustainable development a mainstream issue. Sustainable development is defined by the Brundtland Commission as 'development that meets the need of the present without compromising the ability of future generations to meet their own needs' (WCED, 1987).

7. See *Business Week*, May 3 1999.

8. The Japanese Car of the Year is a prestigious award given by an association of 27 popular Japanese magazines including 21 magazines specializing in motoring matters.

9. For example the Mitsubishi Motor Corporation (MMC) has successfully developed a low-pollution and energy-saving engine that emits substantially less hydrocarbon and NO_x than conventional engines. In November 1999 Honda began to sell a hybrid car, the Insight, which has the world's best fuel economy (35 km per litre of petrol). Car makers are facing keen competition in the development of such engines. Recently, cash-strapped MMC was reported as asking Daimler Chrysler to buy into 33.4 per cent of the company (*Nihon Keizai Shimbun*, 7 March 2000). MMC said that without such an outside equity injection it would not be able to invest adequately in environment-related projects and hence would not survive.

10. Toyota's hybrid car, the Prius, generates 50 per cent less CO_2 than conventional engines and emits less than one tenth of the maximum allowable emissions of carbon monoxide, hydrocarbons and NO_x.

11. Examples of the figures for some products are as follows:

Product	Target date	Goal
Air conditioners	2004	63 per cent improvement in energy efficiency over the 1997 level.
Television sets	2003	16 per cent improvement in electricity consumption over the 1997 level.
Petroleum-powered cars	2010	23 per cent improvement in mileage over the 1995 level.

12. This is also the case with some Canadian firms. It was reported that a consortium of Canadian companies (including power producers such as Atco Electric and BC Hydro) plans to buy credits for harmful emissions from a group of farmers in the US Midwest (*Globe and Mail*, 19 October 1999). The idea is that the consortium will pay farmers to till their fields less as tilling releases carbon dioxide into the soil, which in turn is believed to contribute to global warming.
13. According to *ISO World*, the number of ISO 14001 certifications as of October 1998 was 1320 for Japan, 950 for Germany and 1000 for Britain. If we include EMAS certifications, Germany's figure becomes 2757.
14. Japanese breweries are competing to achieve zero emissions by eliminating waste and recycling all materials. Kirin Brewery conducts an annual life-cycle analysis of the emission of CO_2, SO_x and NO_x in its production, transportation and consumption processes and publishes the results in its environment report.

References

Fruin, W. M. and M. Nakamura (1977) 'Top-Down Production Management: A Recent Trend in the Japanese Productivity-Enhancement Movement', *Managerial and Decision Economics*, vol. 18, pp. 131–139.
Grossman, G. and A. Krueger (1991) *Environmental Impacts of a North American Free Trade Agreement*, CEPR working paper 644 (London: CEPR).
Hayami, H., M. Nakamura, K. Asakura and K. Yoshioka (1999) 'The Emission of Global Warming Gases: Trade between Canada and Japan', Working Paper Series on *International Business, Trade and Finance* (Vancouver: Faculty of Commerce and Business Administration, University of British Columbia).
Hayami, H., M. Nakamura, M. Suga and K. Yoshioka (1997) 'Environmental management in Japan: Applications of input-output analysis to the emission of global warming gases', *Managerial and Decision Economics*, vol. 18, pp. 195–208.
Horiuchi, K. (1981) 'Policy for Investment in Anti-pollution Equipment', in Japan Development Bank (ed.), *Evaluation of Policy Implementation Loan* (Tokyo: Japan Development Bank).

Horiuchi, K. (1998a) *The Vision and Policy of the Japanese Economy: From Growth to Development* (in Japanese) (Tokyo: Tokyo Keizai).

Horiuchi, K. (ed.) (1998b) *Global Environmental Measures* (in Japanese) (Tokyo: Yuhikaku).

International Chamber of Commerce (1991) *Business Charter on Sustainable Development* (Tokyo: International Chamber of Commerce).

Japan Chemical Industry Association (1990) *JCIA Guidelines on Environment and Safety* (Tokyo: JCIA).

Japanese Environmental Agency (1995) *Environmentally Friendly Firm Behaviour* (Tokyo: JEA).

Japanese Environmental Agency (1998) *White Paper on the Environment* (Tokyo: JEA).

Japanese Environmental Agency (1999) *Guidelines on the Calculations and Disclosure of Environmental Maintenance Cost* (Tokyo: JEA).

Keidanren (Japanese Federation of Economic Organizations) (1991) *Keidanren Global Environmental Charter* (Tokyo: Keidaren).

Kirin Brewery (1999) *Environmental Report* (Tokyo: Kirin).

Mani, M., and D. Wheeler (1998) 'In search of pollution havens? Dirty industry in the world economy, 1960 to 1995', *Journal of Environment and Development*, vol. 7, pp. 215–47.

Nakamura, M., T. Takahashi and I. Vertinsky (forthcoming) 'Firms' Responses to Environmental Issues: Japanese Manufacturing Industries', *Journal of Environmental Economics and Management*.

Nishimura, H. (1995) 'The greening of Japanese industry', in M. D. Rogers (ed.), *Business and Environment* (New York: St.Martin's Press), pp. 21–38.

OECD (1994) *OECD Environmental Performance Review: Japan* (Paris: OECD).

Porter, M. E. and C. van der Linde (1995) 'Toward a new conception of the environment–competitiveness relationship', *Journal of Economic Perspectives*, vol. 9, pp. 97–118.

Selden, T. M. and D. Song (1992) *Environmental Quality and Development: Is There a Kuznez Curve for Air Pollution* (Syracuse, New York: Syracuse University).

Toyota Motors (1999) *Environmental Report* (Tokyo: Toyota).

United Nations (1995) *IPCC Second Assessment Report: Climate Change 1995*, report of the Intergovernmental Panel on Climate Change (New York: UN).

Uzawa, H. (1995) *Thinking Global Warming* (in Japanese) (Tokyo: Iwanami).

Uzawa, H. and M. Kuninori (eds) (1993) *Economic Analysis of Global Warming* (in Japanese) (Tokyo: Tokyo University Press).

World Business Council for Sustainable Development (1997) *Eco-efficiency* (Cambridge, Mass.: MIT Press).

World Commission on Environment and Development (WCED) (1987) *Brundtland Commission Report* (New York: United Nations).

Part VI
Conclusion

14 Conclusion

Masao Nakamura

The prolonged recession that followed the bursting of the financial bubble in 1990 has prompted many aspects of the Japanese business and economic system to change. What kinds of change are likely to contribute to Japan's long-term economic growth? The discussions presented in this book provide some thoughts on this. Here we shall consider the labour market, technology and corporate governance issues in turn. US–Japanese trade negotiations and government–business relations in Japan are intertwined with many of these issues, including the handling of intellectual property rights, both foreign and domestic; the handling of anticompetitive practices; and protection of the properly rights of US shareholders in Japanese firms. Japan's new initiatives could trigger substantial changes in current Japanese business and economic practices.

THE LABOUR MARKET

Many of the Japanese firms that faced excess capacity due to over-investment (or, more accurately, overinvestment in unpromising lines of business) during the bubble period had no choice but to lay off workers, despite the practice of long-term employment. Hollowing out due to Japan's continuing foreign direct investment also contributed to these lay-offs. The Japanese labour market, which used to match new graduates with potential employers who wanted to train their employees from scratch, has not been able to deal with such a large number of laid-off men and women seeking employment in their mid careers. On the employers' side, many Japanese firms are not ready to accept substantial numbers of mid-career workers who have been bumped out by other firms. Firms' personnel management practices are still predicated on the assumption that workers will remain attached to the firm until retirement, leaving little room for mid-career entrants from outside.

The Japanese labour market is entering the 21st century with structural problems, lacking both the facility to match experienced workers with appropriate jobs and the mechanisms for taking in laid-off workers, even if they have advantageous skills.

Another implication of the previously unthinkable massive lay-offs is the erosion of workers' trust in firms' long-term employment practices. Such a breach of the implicit labour contract may very well result in Japanese workers having less loyalty to their employers and erosion of the important productivity-enhancing benefits of the traditional Japanese industrial relations practices, including participatory employment practices.

On the positive side, more frequent job changes by primary workers may facilitate the development of mechanisms to place mid-career workers. There are many highly skilled mid-career job changers and female workers who return to the labour market after child rearing. Given the rapid aging of the workforce and the low birth rate, as well as large numbers of unemployed workers and the serious mismatches that exist between employed workers' skills and the skill requirements of their employers, the labour market can contribute to economic growth by providing an efficient matching mechanism. Unfortunately, because of government regulations that restrict third-party recruiting efforts in the private sector and the traditional policy of mainly hiring new graduates, new recruiting mechanisms for experienced workers have been very slow to develop.

TECHNOLOGY

Technology continues to play an important role in economic growth. Internet-related technologies and biotechnologies, for example, currently drive economic growth in North America, the EU and Japan. In the United States it is thought that many of the growing NASDAQ stocks represent internet and other newly emerging technologies. Japan is no exception. For example Fujitsu, which owns Japan's largest internet service provider, Nifty, has recently increased its market value significantly compared with other Japanese electronics product manufacturers. The types of manufacturing technologies and production management methods characterized by Toyota's just-in-time system will continue to be important in manufacturing, but these technologies have been transferred to many countries, often with significant success. At the same time, in the changing Japanese labour market, many Japanese manufacturers may not be able to train and maintain highly skilled workers in the long run. More significantly, a massive shift of value added from manufacturing operations to service and internet-related operations will no doubt force Japanese firms to invest more in high-growth non-manufacturing areas.

It is not clear how prepared Japan is to move towards an economy driven by new technologies such as the internet and intellectual property rights. Perhaps some historical lessons can be drawn upon in this respect. The internet could be likened to a new source of energy similar to petroleum and electricity in the late 19th century. Yet the internet, at least for global transactions, will continue to be dominated by the English language, a characteristic not shared by the technologies imported into Japan in the 19th century. Will this language requirement form a permanent technology gap between the United States and Japan? Given the relatively low level of English proficiency in Japan, despite the enormous expenditure on English education (Japan has one of the lowest TOEFL scores among the Asian countries), such a scenario is not totally unthinkable.

For Japan to encourage the development of intellectual-property-rights-based technologies it will be essential to introduce transparency into the legal environment in respect of antimonopoly (antitrust) laws, the protection of intellectual property and anticompetitive behaviour. The implementation of laws in these areas lacks transparency largely due to the Japanese corporate culture, business–government relations and governmental behaviour. Irrespective of whether or not this problem remains on the US–Japanese negotiation agenda, Japan needs to face the problem and make some real changes so that creative activities necessary for economic growth are fostered.

Internet technologies have made it possible for the workers of many firms to operate outside large cities or even outside their company offices. This is particularly true for non-manufacturing, high-value-added operations. In this sense the internet may provide a real opportunity for Japan to reorganize its cities, many of which are extremely congested. The internet also provides employment opportunities for previously unutilized but skilled workers at home, such as women and disabled people (there are many such people without employment in Japan). Exploiting such opportunities for gainful work will contribute to Japan's economic growth.

CORPORATE GOVERNANCE

The recent liberalization measures adopted in Japan's finance industry will no doubt change the role of Japanese banks in corporate governance. For example corporations now have greater access to standard unsecured corporate bond financing, which increases firms' financial choices. Furthermore banks now face more competition from other firms entering the banking industry. At the same time banks are now allowed to become more heavily involved in the securities business. This may change the banking industry in fundamental ways. For instance, it is possible that their involvement in stockbroking may change the attitude of banks towards the stocks of firms in which they are stable shareholders or cross-holding shareholders. But the nature of these changes is difficult to predict. For example, as shareholders, will they demand the maximization of share value rather than protection of their loans? Another interesting but unanswered question is whether Japanese firms will shift their financing methods from bank-based indirect financing to more direct capital-market-based financing such as bonds and equity.

If Japanese banks find it against their economic interest to hold equity in other firms, as US and Canadian banks have found, then Japan's bank-based corporate governance will permanently change. Despite many announced bank mergers, which often go across the horizontal *keiretsu* groups, it is by no means obvious that these banks are willing to give up their equity shareholder position as the main bank for the client firms in their *keiretsu*. To the extent that the shares banks hold are used to strengthen their rights as creditors, Japanese corporate governance will continue to have some of the characteristics that have plagued the Japanese economy during the bubble and post-bubble periods.

The prevailing Japanese business practices discussed above that are associated with the labour market, new technologies and corporate governance have formed over many decades as a consequence of collaborations between the private and government sectors. The societal practices, education system and human behaviour in Japan have also been compatible (or conditioned to be compatible) with many of the industrial goals. The role of government in terms of formal and informal regulations and the direct personnel connections provided, for example, by *Amakudari* (descent from heaven; bureaucrats landing jobs in the industries they used to regulate), has been overwhelming. It is inevitable that many Japanese firms try to influence government policies to the detriment of the national welfare. This firm behaviour is prevalent in but not limited to heavily regulated industries such as finance, communications, transportation, construction and education. Many of the options discussed above for economic growth will require both individuals and firms to rely much more on their own initiative and market signals. Government measures are also needed to make markets function in a non-regulated manner.

In the labour market, third-party recruiting, which is currently heavily restricted, needs to be deregulated. The government-run job-matching service is technically obsolete and has not been able to meet the needs of many of the workers who have been laid off or displaced. Use of the internet has not spread widely to individual households, probably because of the high telephone charges, which mostly reflects the monopoly power of the Nippon Telephone and Telegraph Corporation (NTT). Improving the legal enforcement of intellectual property rights within and outside the Japanese corporate environment will also have to be addressed if entrepreneurs are to create a new economy driven by internet businesses and biotechnologies. By the same token, if individual shareholders' rights are to be given due respect by implementing corporate policies to maximize the firm's market value, the corporate governance system must become less influenced by banks than is presently the case. Right now banks, as equity holders, act aggressively to protect their position as creditors.

Having to incorporate *keiretsu* relationships into their purchasing strategies has been very costly for many Japanese firms facing keen global competition, and many manufacturers have found it much cheaper to buy from suppliers outside their *keiretsu* groups. Nevertheless such a relationship can be effective when a firm faces high demands. This is probably why the *keiretsu* system has not been abandoned in a meaningful way. US carmakers have begun to use the internet for parts procurement, and such e-commerce practices may eliminate some of the advantages provided by Japanese vertical *keiretsu* groups. *Keiretsu*-based supplier relationships, on the other hand, may work positively for manufacturing assemblers in the car and electronics industries if these interfirm relationships can be used to facilitate development of e-commerce assembler–supplier transactions. The advantages of this may very well extend to their overseas operations.

Finally, the remarkable increase in the late 1990s of foreign takeovers of major Japanese firms in financial distress deserves some discussion. Such takeovers have almost always been friendly and have occurred only when troubled Japanese firms have exhausted their search for domestic solutions. Such firms in the finance industry include Yamaichi Securities, the Long Term Credit Bank and a number of life insurance firms. Many of these firms have since been restructured. The Japanese car industry, which was seen as the driving force of the economy, now faces an enormous cash requirement for projects such as the development of environmentally friendly vehicles. Given the poor prospect of financing such large-scale projects on their own, most carmakers have opted to transfer effective management control (at least 33.4 per cent of their equity, as required by Japanese law) to foreign competitors. Thus Nissan has been taken over by Renault, Mazda by Ford, Mitsubishi by Daimler Chrysler, Isuzu by GM and Suzuki by GM. Toyota and Honda are the only two remaining Japanese-run carmakers. The impact of the foreign takeover of major Japanese firms on Japanese corporate governance and other management practices is expected to be significant. For example, shortly after its takeover of Mazda, Ford proceeded to restructure Mazda's suppliers, while Ford promoted all those female workers who deserved to be promoted but had been denied promotion under the previous Mazda management. It seems possible that these large foreign-controlled firms will lead the way in the 21st century by introducing Western-style management methods to Japan.

Index

393